CORRECTIONS, MENTAL HEALTH, AND SOCIAL POLICY: INTERNATIONAL PERSPECTIVES

CORRECTIONS, MENTAL HEALTH, AND SOCIAL POLICY

International Perspectives

Edited by

ROBERT K. AX, Ph.D.

and

THOMAS J. FAGAN, Ph.D.

CHARLES C THOMAS • PUBLISHER, LTD.
Springfield • Illinois • U.S.A.

Published and Distributed Throughout the World by

CHARLES C THOMAS • PUBLISHER, LTD.
2600 South First Street
Springfield, Illinois 62704

©2007 by CHARLES C THOMAS • PUBLISHER, LTD.

ISBN 978-0-398-07756-3 (hard)
ISBN 978-0-398-07757-0 (pbk.)

Library of Congress Catalog Card Number: 2007013359

Printed in the United States of America
SR-R-3

Library of Congress Cataloging-in-Publication Data

Corrections, mental health, and social policy : international perspectives / edited by Robert
K. Ax and Thomas J. Fagan.
  p. ; cm.
  Includes bibliographical references and index.
  ISBN 978-0-398-07756-3 (hard) -- ISBN 978-0-398-07757-0 (pbk.)
  1. Prisoners--Mental health services. 2. Prisoners--Mental care. 3. Prisons--Government
policy. I. Ax, Robert Kirk, 1952- II. Fagan, Thomas J., 1949-
  [DNLM: 1. Mental Health Services--organization & administration. 2. Prisoners--
psychology. 3. Prisons--organization & administration. 4. Public Policy. WA 305 C8246
2007]

RC451.4.P68C67 2007
365'.66--dc22

2007013359

ABOUT THE EDITORS

Robert K. Ax, Ph.D., is a licensed clinical psychologist who received his Ph.D. in clinical psychology from Virginia Polytechnic Institute and State University. He retired in June, 2005, from the U.S. Federal Bureau of Prisons (BOP), after practicing in state and federal corrections for more than 20 years. He developed the predoctoral psychology internship model now used throughout the BOP, and was the training director at the Federal Correctional Institution, Petersburg, Virginia. He is a Fellow of the American Psychological Association (APA), a member of the Canadian Psychological Association and Amnesty International USA, and a former president of the APA Division of Psychologists in Public Service (18). He has twice been the recipient of Division 18's Distinguished Service Award. Dr. Ax is the co-editor, with Dr. Thomas J. Fagan, of the *Correctional Mental Health Handbook,* published by Sage in 2003. He has published many articles on mental health training and correctional issues, and currently serves on the editorial board of the journal *Criminal Justice and Behavior.*

Thomas J. Fagan, Ph.D., received his Ph.D. in clinical psychology from Virginia Polytechnic Institute and State University and is a licensed clinical psychologist. He is currently an associate professor of psychology at Nova Southeastern University and his professional interests are in the areas of psychology career development and correctional mental health. He worked for the BOP for 23 years, serving as the agency's coordinator of clinical training, where he developed and administered a range of training programs for the agency's psychologists. He served as the BOP's chief hostage negotiator, and has consulted with many federal and state agencies on hostage negotiation, critical incident stress debriefing, and other mental health issues. Dr. Fagan is a Fellow of APA, and is the past chair of the National Commission on Correctional Health Care. He is the author of *Negotiating Correctional Incidents: A Practical Guide* (American Correctional Association, 2003). He has published many articles in psychology and correctional journals, has written several book chapters, and has served as a reviewer for a number of professional journals. He has also been a regular presenter at national correctional and mental health conferences. Dr. Fagan was the recipient of the 2006 American Psychological Association Award for Distinguished Contributions to Practice in the Public Sector.

ABOUT THE AUTHORS

Jennifer L. Boothby, Ph.D., is an Associate Professor of Psychology and Associate Dean of the College of Arts and Sciences at Indiana State University. She received her Ph.D. in clinical psychology from the University of Alabama with a specialty in psychology-law. She completed a predoctoral internship at the Federal Medical Center in Butner, North Carolina, and the University of North Carolina at Chapel Hill. Dr. Boothby has worked in federal, state, and county-level corrections. Her research focuses on the mental and physical health of offenders, correctional mental health treatment, and professional issues for correctional psychologists.

Shelia M. Brandt, Psy.D., Dr. Brandt earned her doctorate in clinical psychology in 1998 from the Minnesota School of Professional Psychology. She completed her predoctoral internship at the Federal Correctional Institution in Petersburg, Virginia. She subsequently worked for the Virginia Department of Corrections as the director of a residential mental health unit. Dr. Brandt then served as a senior doctoral psychologist with the Wisconsin Resource Center, where she began her training in risk assessment with civilly committed sex offenders, and then at the Federal Correctional Institution in Waseca, Minnesota, where she provided drug treatment programming and forensic evaluation services. She joined the staff of State Operated Forensic Services as a forensic evaluator in 2005, becoming the director of psychology services in 2006. She is an adjunct professor at St. Mary's University and at Gustavus Adolphus College. Dr. Brandt has published several book chapters related to the provision of psychological services to individuals in jails and prisons and is an associate editor for *Psychological Services,* the journal of Division 18 (Psychologists in Public Service) of the American Psychological Association. Dr. Brandt's professional interests include sentencing alternatives for the seriously mentally ill; international perspectives on criminal justice systems; encouraging psychologists to use the science of psychology to inform public policy and legislation related to classification, sentencing, and treatment of criminal offenders; and prescriptive authority for psychologists.

R. Scott Chavez, Ph.D., M.P.A., received his Ph.D. in Health Services Administration from Walden University. He is Vice President of the National

Commission on Correctional Health Care (NCCHC), and is a nationally recognized correctional health services analyst. Since 1987, Dr. Chavez has advocated for responsive, quality, and cost effective health services in correctional institutions. He has assisted federal, state, and local government officials in improving their effectiveness, efficiency, and accountability for correctional health services. He has conducted health system reviews of over 500 prisons, jails, and juvenile detention/confinement centers in the United States and Puerto Rico. He coordinates national policy and clinical guideline development activities, is involved in technical assistance, standards writing, and educational services for NCCHC. He has written numerous journal articles and chapters on issues related to correctional health services administration and has made numerous presentations at state and national professional meetings.

Joyce K. Conley, Ph.D., is the Assistant Director of the Federal Bureau of Prisons' Correctional Programs Division in Washington, DC. In that capacity, she directs the security, intelligence, counter-terrorism, unit management, psychology, religious services, community corrections, and privatization management functions for federal correctional facilities nationwide. Dr. Conley has worked in correctional settings for 19 years, including positions as clinical psychologist at Los Angeles County Jail; chief psychologist at the Metropolitan Detention Center, Los Angeles; and Associate Warden at two federal facilities (Federal Correctional Institution, Butner, North Carolina, and United States Penitentiary, Terre Haute, Indiana). She then served as Warden at the Federal Correctional Institution in Beckley, West Virginia. She was appointed to the Federal Senior Executive Service in May 2000. In 2005, Dr. Conley was awarded the BOP's Norman A. Carlson Award for excellence in leadership

David A. Crighton, Ph.D., AFBPsS, is Deputy Chief Psychologist, National Offender Management Service based at the Ministry of Justice the Home Office in London. He holds a visiting Chair at London Metropolitan University. Previously he was deputy Head of Psychological Services for the Prison and Probation Services and a Consultant Psychologist in the National Health Service. He is a past Secretary and Treasurer of the Division of Forensic Psychology of the British Psychological Society (BPS). He is currently Chief Examiner for the BPS Board of Examiners in Forensic Psychology. Dr. Crighton has published extensively in the field of forensic mental health and is a former editor of the *British Journal of Forensic Practice*. Currently, he is on the editorial board of the *British Journal of Leadership in Public Services*.

Harry R. Dammer, Ph.D., is Professor and Chair of the Sociology and Criminal Justice Department at the University of Scranton. He is the author of *Religion in Corrections* (American Correctional Association, 1999), co-author (with

Erika Fairchild) of *Comparative Criminal Justice* (Wadsworth/Thompson Press, 2006), and co-author (with Todd R. Clear) of *The Offender in the Community* (Wadsworth/Thompson Press, 2003). He has also published or co-published numerous articles, manuals, and professional reports on a variety of criminal justice topics. In 1993–94 was awarded a Fulbright Scholarship to teach and conduct research in Germany.

Dr. Dammer has professional experience as a probation officer and served as a consultant for the National Institute of Justice, the National Institute of Corrections, the American Correctional Association, the National Conference of Christians and Jews, and private law firms. He has made numerous presentations at professional conferences in the United States and has lectured in Canada, South Korea, Hungary, Greece, Switzerland, Germany, England, Poland, and China. He is the former Chair of the International Section of the Academy of Criminal Justice Sciences (March 2003 to March 2004). He received his Ph.D. from The Rutgers University School of Criminal Justice (NJ).

Carol Gallo, M.S., was born in Hershey, Pennsylvania. She grew up in Baltimore and moved to New York for college, where she earned a Bachelor of Fine Arts in film from the School of Visual Arts in Manhattan. While there, she produced three documentaries about international affairs. She then went on to earn her Master of Science in global affairs and international human rights from New York University, where she graduated in 2006. She tutors a nine-year-old refugee from Sierra Leone on Sundays, a volunteer job facilitated by the International Rescue Committee, and she also interns part time in the media department of the International Center for Transitional Justice. For about a year she worked at Amnesty International USA part time as Research Assistant in the Executive Office. In September 2007, she will be attending Yale University's Graduate School of Arts and Sciences where she will earn a degree in African Studies and plans to pursue a Ph.D. in that field. She can be reached at carol.gallo@yale.edu.

Paul Gendreau, Ph.D., began working at Kingston Penitentiary in 1961 and later received his M.A. from the University of Ottawa and Ph.D. from Queen's University. After receiving his doctorate in 1968 he joined the faculty at Trent University. In 1972, he was appointed Regional Chief Psychologist with the Eastern Region of the Ontario Ministry of Correctional Services, where he was also initially affiliated with Carleton University and then became adjunct Clinical Full Professor with the University of Ottawa. In addition, he was seconded to the offices of the Deputy Prime Ministers of Prime Ministers Manley and Lange governments in Jamaica and New Zealand respectively to work on correctional issues in the 70s and 80s. In 1986, he retired from the Ontario Government and subsequently was appointed University Research Professor of Psychology at UNB, Saint John. He also worked in Australia as a Visiting Research Fellow at Edith Cowan University and Visiting Professor at Griffith University.

He retired in 2006 from the University of New Brunswick. Presently, he is Professor Emeritus at UNB and Visiting Scholar, Division of Criminal Justice, University of Cincinnati.

Dr. Gendreau is a former President of the Canadian Psychological Association having served on the Board of Directors of CPA from 1983–1991. He has received awards from CPA for Distinguished Contributions to Applied Psychology and the Career Contribution award from the CPA Section on Criminal Justice. He has also been recognized by the APA's Division 18 for his contributions to Public Service Psychology and was the recipient of the Margaret Mead Award for "contributions to social justice" from the International Community & Corrections Association.

In 2007, he was appointed an Officer of the Order of Canada "for achievement and merit of a high degree, especially service to Canada or to humanity at large."

He has published extensively on "what works" in the assessment and treatment of offenders, the effects of prison life, and has recently written about the use of statistics for the purposes of knowledge cumulation.

Claire Goggin, M.A., is a lecturer in the Department of Criminology and Criminal Justice, St. Thomas University, Fredericton, New Brunswick, Canada and is currently completing a Ph.D. in psychology at the University of New Brunswick at Fredericton. She is a member of a research team that has contributed a number of reports and articles on applied quantitative research methods and statistics in criminal justice, offender risk assessment and risk prediction, and correctional program effectiveness evaluation. Among her recent publications are chapters (with Drs. Paul Gendreau, Paula Smith, and Sheila French) in *The Handbook of Forensic Psychology* (3rd Edition), and (with Dr. Gendreau) in *Offending Behaviour Programmes: Applications and Controversies,* both published by John Wiley and Sons in 2006.

Annie Kensey, Ph.D., is responsible for research and statistics for the French Prison Administration. She specializes in prison demography. She is the author of *Les À-coups,* étude statistique des agressions contre le personnel de surveillance, (DAP) 1998, *Prisonniers du passé,* CNRS/DAP, 2003, *Arithmétique de l'exécution des peines* with Pierre Tournier, CESDIP/DAP, 2002. She has also published or co-authored numerous articles and professional reports on a variety of criminal justice topics. She was a member of the Scientific Council of the National Institute of Demographic Research (INED) from 2000 to 2005.

Dr. Kensey has consulted as an expert on correctional and criminal justice matters for the Council of Europe and the United Nations. She has made numerous presentations at professional and academic conferences in France and lectured in the United States (American Society of Criminology), Canada, South Korea, Mexico, Switzerland, Germany, England, Romania, and Turkey. She received her Ph.D. from the University Paris I- Panthéon-Sorbonne. Dr. Kensey's new book, *Prison and Recidivism* (Armand Colin Edition), will be published in 2007.

Andrea L. Kleiver, M.S., is currently a fourth-year clinical psychology graduate student at Nova Southeastern University (NSU). During her tenure as a graduate student, she has co-authored two articles and has been the recipient of a Certificate of Merit award from the American Psychological Association's Public Service Division (Division 18). She served as the campus representative with the American Psychological Association's Graduate Students-Advocacy Coordinating Team (APAGS-ACT), was a two-term president of NSU's Student Organization for the Advocacy of Psychology (SOAP), and is currently serving as chair for the Ad Hoc Committee for Student Involvement in Criminal Justice as part of the Criminal Justice Section of APA's Division 18. Currently, Ms. Kleiver is working full-time providing psychological services for the State of Michigan's Department of Corrections and is planning to begin her internship training in the fall of 2007.

Duyen Luong, BSc, is currently completing her M.A. in Applied Social Psychology (Forensic Concentration) at the University of Saskatchewan in Saskatoon, Canada, under the supervision of Dr. Stephen Wormith. She completed her Honours BSc at the University of Toronto, Ontario, Canada. Her current research interests include risk assessment, sexual offender treatment, psychopathy, mental health, and program evaluation. She has correctional research and/or evaluation experience at the federal level (under the direction of Dr. Calvin Langton at the Centre for Addiction and Mental Health in Toronto) and provincial level (Ontario Ministry of Community Safety and Corrections Services and Saskatchewan Department of Corrections and Public Safety). She recently completed an "evaluability assessment" and "preliminary process evaluation" of the Break and Enter Comprehensive Action Program (BECAP), a multiagency, municipal crime prevention initiative in Saskatoon, SK. She has also worked under contract with the Community Living Division of the Saskatchewan Department of Community Resources and was part of a team that completed an environment scan on risk assessment of aboriginal offenders with mental health problems for the National Parole Board of Canada. She has been active with numerous conference presentations including the Canadian Psychological Association and the Canadian

Evaluation Society. She was the 2006 recipient of the Student Award at the 11th Biennial Symposium on Violence and Aggression held in Saskatoon for her poster entitled "The effectiveness of psychological sex offender treatment: A meta-analysis." Ms Luong will be pursuing her Ph.D. in Forensic Psychology at Carleton University in Ottawa, Ontario, Canada, under the direction of Dr. Ralph Serin.

Jon T. Mandracchia, M.A., is a graduate student in the Counseling Psychology program at Texas Tech University. He currently conducts correctional and forensic psychology research focusing on criminal dysfunctional thinking and attitudes toward criminal justice issues. The Counseling Psychology Division at Texas Tech University awarded Mr. Mandracchia the Graduate Research Award for 2005–2006.

Crista McDaniel, Psy.D., received her doctorate from the University of Northern Colorado. She is a licensed clinical psychologist in the State of Delaware and in New Zealand. She is currently employed as a Senior Psychologist for the New Zealand Department of Corrections at Rotorua, where she is involved in a pilot programme for offenders with high psychopathy scores, in addition to her assessment and treatment work with the department. Previously, Dr. McDaniel worked as a psychologist for the U.S. Federal Bureau of Prisons, the Delaware Psychiatric Center, and the U.S. Indian Health Service. She also developed a chronic pain and biofeedback program for combat veterans through the Department of Veterans Affairs.

Alix M. McLearen, Ph.D. Dr. McLearen received her Ph.D. in clinical psychology and the law from the University of Alabama. She has worked in a variety of psycholegal settings, including state and federal prisons, a state forensic hospital, and a county jail. After completing an internship at the United States Medical Center for Federal Prisoners in Springfield, Missouri, she continued employment with the Federal Bureau of Prisons. Currently, she is the administrator of a unique residential treatment program for male inmates experiencing cognitive and adaptive deficits resulting from traumatic brain injury, psychosis, or congenital defects. Dr. McLearen is also the coordinator of Inmate Skills Development and Reentry for the Federal Bureau of Prisons' largest correctional complex. In this capacity, she is responsible for implementing workforce development initiatives and creating programs to prepare inmates for release to the community. Dr. McLearen has presented at conferences on topics relating to malingering, correctional mental health treatment, and law enforcement policy and procedure. She has published several book chapters and scientific articles, and is a co-author of the book *Detection of Deception* (Professional Resource Press, 2006).

Robert D. Morgan, Ph.D., is Associate Professor and Director of the Counseling Psychology Program at Texas Tech University. He is also the Associate Clinical and Forensic Director with Lubbock Regional Mental Health and Mental Retardation services. He was the recipient of the 2006 Outstanding Contribution to Science Award from the Texas Psychological Association and the 2003 Early Career Achievement Award from Division 18 of the American Psychological Association. He publishes in the areas of correctional mental health, forensic psychology, and professional development and training. He has co-authored/co-edited two books: *Life After Graduate School in Psychology: Insider's Advice from New Psychologists* (Psychology Press), and *Careers in Psychology: Opportunities in a Changing World* (2nd Ed.) (Wadsworth).

Llewelyn A. Richards-Ward, Ph.D., DipClinPsych, MNZCCP, holds a doctorate and a Post-Graduate Diploma in Clinical Psychology from Massey University. He is a registered clinical psychologist with the New Zealand Psychologists' Board and is a member of the New Zealand College of Clinical Psychologists. He was Principal Psychologist for the New Zealand Department of Corrections, Rotorua, from 2003–2007. That role involved clinical work, management and project work nationally. The most recent project involved developing a supervision framework for providers of group work to medium-risk prisoners that would enhance treatment integrity, and training psychologists to deliver this supervision. Currently, Dr. Richards-Ward is a partner in The Psychology Suite, specializing in the provision of education and training to forensic and clinical psychologists nationally and internationally, in addition to providing clinical services. Dr. Richards-Ward lectures on the psychology of criminal conduct and clinical psychotherapy. He also practices in the family court arena, specializing in care, protection and custody evaluations where clinical and criminal issues were extant.

Aven Senter, Ph.D., received his doctorate in counseling psychology from Texas Tech University. He completed his predoctoral internship with the Federal Bureau of Prisons at the Federal Medical Center, Carswell, Texas. He is currently a Postdoctoral Resident at the Federal Prison Camp, Alderson, West Virginia, specializing in residential drug treatment. His research interests include correctional mental health, psychologist burnout, and working with underserved populations.

Paula Smith, Ph.D., is the Associate Director of the Corrections Institute and an Assistant Professor in the Division of Criminal Justice at the University of Cincinnati. She was previously a Research Associate with the Center for Criminal Justice Studies at the University of New Brunswick in Saint John, New Brunswick, Canada. Her research interests include meta-analysis, the assessment of offender treatment and deterrence programs, the development of actuarial assessments for clinicians and managers in prisons and community corrections, the effects of prison life, and the transfer of knowledge to practitioners and policymakers. She has published numerous articles, and book chapters, and given many conference presentations on the above topics. Dr. Smith has also been involved in the development and delivery of treatment programs to federal parolees with the Correctional Service of Canada. At the present time, she provides workshops, training, and technical assistance to correctional agencies throughout the United States.

Graham J. Towl, M.Sc., AFBPsS, is Chief Psychologist, National Offender Management Service, based at the Ministry of Justice in London. He holds visiting Chairs at the Universities of Birmingham and Portsmouth. Previously, he was Head of Psychological Services for the Prison and Probation Services, where he led a strategic approach to the organization and delivery of psychological services over a five-year period. He was the recipient of the British Psychological Society (BPS) award for distinguished contribution to professional psychology in 2003. He is a past Chair and Treasurer of the BPS Division of Forensic Psychology and Chair of the Board of Examiners in Forensic Psychology. Prof. Towl has published extensively in the forensic mental health field and is editor of *Evidence Based Mental Health*. He is the founding editor of the *International Journal of Leadership in Public Services* and is an external examiner in Criminology at the University of Cambridge.

Michael von Tangen Page, Ph.D., is a graduate of the Universities of Ulster, St.Andrews and Bradford. He is currently employed by the United Nations Development Programme as the Security Development Advisor to the Kosovo Internal Security Sector Review. Prior to this he was a Senior Advisor for the London-based conflict transformation organization International Alert and a MacArthur Post-Doctoral Research Associate with the Department of War Studies at King's College, London University. He has published widely on the topic of conflict transformation and counterterrorism especially regarding penal policy. In 1998, he published the book *Prisons, Peace and Terrorism* (Macmillan/St. Martin's Press).

J. Stephen Wormith, Ph.D., is Chair of Forensic Psychology in the Psychology Department, University of Saskatchewan. Currently, he also provides forensic clinical consultation services to the Regional Psychiatric Centre (Prairies), the Correctional Service of Canada, the Saskatchewan Department of Corrections and Public Safety, the Ontario Ministry of Community Safety and Correctional Services, the National Parole Board, the Saskatoon Police Services Commission and various courts throughout Saskatchewan. Formerly, he was Psychologist-in-Chief for the Ontario Ministry of Community Safety (1989 to 1999) and Correctional Services and Deputy Superintendent (Treatment) at Rideau Correctional and Treatment Centre (1987 to 1989). He has also worked as a correctional psychologist and researcher with the Correctional Service of Canada, both in institutions and in the community. He is active in the voluntary sector as Chairperson of Crime Prevention Saskatchewan, Vice-president of the Canadian Training Institute, and a Board Member of The International Institute on Special Needs Offenders and Policy Research (Canada). He is Past Chair of the Criminal Justice Psychology Section of the Canadian Psychological Association (CPA). He is also CPA's representative on the National Associations Active in Criminal Justice (NAACJ). Dr. Wormith's research activities have concentrated on the assessment, treatment and therapeutic processes of offenders, including various special offender groups, such as young offenders, sexual offenders and mentally disordered offenders. He is co-author of the *Level of Service/Case Management Inventory* and is on the Editorial Board of *Psychological Services.*

Patricia A. Zapf, Ph.D., is an Associate Professor in the Department of Psychology at John Jay College of Criminal Justice, The City University of New York. She is originally from Canada and received her Ph.D. in clinical forensic psychology in 1999 from Simon Fraser University. She completed her clinical internship at the Florida Mental Health Institute, University of South Florida, and was an assistant professor in the clinical psychology and law doctoral program at the University of Alabama from 1999–2002. She is currently an Associate Editor for *Law and Human Behavior* and was appointed Fellow of the American Psychological Association in 2006 for outstanding contributions to the field of law and psychology. Her research and publications in the field of forensic psychology involve the assessment and conceptualization of various types of competencies and the utility of various methods of competency assessment as well as various aspects of forensic assessment (risk assessment, malingering, and insanity) and the development and validation of forensic assessment instruments. In addition to her research, she serves as a consultant to various criminal justice and policy organizations.

Dawn Zobel is employed as a Correctional Program Specialist for the BOP with an emphasis on Female Offender programs and services. She is currently stationed at the BOP's headquarters in Washington, D.C. She has worked for the BOP for 16 years, serving in varying capacities. During her tenure in the BOP's headquarters, she has been afforded collateral opportunities to work with staff in the Intelligence Division, formulating strategies for managing offenders that have been sentenced for their involvement or support of terrorist related activity. She assisted with site selection and activation of the

Counter Terrorism Management Unit and taken a lead role in the development of management practices and agency policies pertaining to foreign language translation proficiency standards and provision of uniformed foreign language translation services for timely monitoring of inmate communications, particularly those posing significant risk concerns. Her correctional background includes expertise in sentence computation principles, admission/release processes, and custodial regulations. Throughout her career with the BOP she has developed numerous programs and services which have served to enhance the correctional operations or provided cost-effective alternatives.

This book is dedicated to our mothers:

Laura MacCorkle Ax (1912-1967)
and
Frances M. Fagan (1927 -   )

PREFACE

In Section One, U.S. correctional mental health care is illuminated in its historical and international context, providing a framework from which its past and present can be understood and a more desirable future can be planned. The current state of affairs in U.S. prison systems is then described. The final chapter in this section views correctional mental health care from a public health perspective.

Section Two shifts the focus to mental health systems and services provided to those under the care, custody, and control of foreign governments. Our choices in this section represent Western democracies with whom we share much of our cultural, intellectual and institutional heritage. Authors emphasize innovative and data-based policies and interventions, discussing them in terms of the politics and policies of their respective countries.

In Section Three, the contributors consider special topics with national and international implications and consequences. Topics in this section include the benefit of empirical data in treating mentally disordered offenders, the death penalty, mental health care in nonwestern prison systems, prison gangs, imprisoned terrorists, and roles for non-governmental organizations. It is perhaps here that conventional concepts of *prison, treatment, crime,* and *inmate* will be disturbed and ultimately transformed for many readers.

Section Four consists of a final chapter which summarizes the lessons that have been learned, and those that still need to be, integrates and synthesizes the central ideas and concepts of the previous contributions, and offers an optimistic proposal for the international future of U.S. correctional mental health care and policy.

To care genuinely about the well-being and recovery of persons with serious mental illness is to be concerned about correctional mental health care. As we hope the reader will see, the history of corrections is replete with instances of failed policy and retrenchment. It is hoped that the pooling of ideas in this book will promote fresh thinking and new, effective treatment strategies. Those who work directly or otherwise concern themselves with incarcerated persons in the United States confront great obstacles associated with improving the lot of a devalued population in times when resources for the poor and marginalized are already scarce. That they should continue to do so is vital if we are to call ours a compassionate society.

Robert K. Ax

Thomas J. Fagan

REFERENCES

Ditton, P. (1999, July). *Mental health and treatment of inmates and probationers.* (Bureau of Justice Statistics Special Report, NCJ 174463). Washington, DC: National Criminal Justice Reference Service.

Fagan, T.J., and Ax, R.K. (2003). *Correctional mental health handbook.* Thousand Oaks, CA: Sage.

Glaze, L.E., & Pella, S. (2005, November). *Probation and parole in the United States, 2004.* (Bureau of Justice Statistics Bulletin NCJ 210676). Washington, D.C.: National Criminal Justice Reference Service.

James, D.J., & Glaze, L.E. (2006, September). *Mental health problems of prison and jail inmates.* (Bureau of Justice Statistics Special Report NCJ 213600). Washington, D.C.: National Criminal Justice Reference Service.

Harrison, P.M., & Beck, A.J. (2006, May). *Prison and jail inmates at midyear 2005.* (Bureau of Justice Statistics Bulletin NCJ 213133). Washington, D.C.: National Criminal Justice Reference Service.

Mauer, M. (2003, June 20). *Comparative international rates of incarceration: An examination of causes and trends.* Retrieved July 13, 2003, from http://www.sentencingproject.org/Admin/Documents/publications/inc_comparative_intl.pdf

INTRODUCTION

The justification for this book rests on three facts and one prediction. Here are the facts. First, the United States incarcerated more than 2,100,000 persons in its various prisons and jails in 2005 (Harrison & Beck, 2006) with more than an additional 5 million individuals under criminal justice supervision (Glaze & Pella, 2005). Second, at the time this project was getting underway, the U.S. incarceration rate was 6 times that of Canada, 5 times that of England and Wales, and 8 times that of France (Mauer, 2003). Third, more than 16% percent of the U.S. prison population is considered seriously mentally ill (Ditton, 1999) and according to some researchers, this may be an underestimate (James & Glaze, 2006).

Now for the prediction: current domestic and foreign policies, including those predicated on the necessity of confronting terrorism in the post 9/11 era, virtually guarantee that the United States will attain greater and greater oversight in the coming years for an ever increasing number of foreign-born prisoners. This process has already begun and includes many individuals who committed their crimes outside the United States, particularly those held as unlawful combatants or prisoners of war in Iraq, at the U.S. Naval Station in Guantanamo, Cuba, in secret CIA prisons in Europe, and in domestic facilities. The coming decade could see the United States become the world's jailer.

Given these circumstances, the task of providing adequate mental health care to the burgeoning U.S. prison population, including those thousands with serious mental illnesses who have defaulted from the nation's disjointed mental health systems, increasingly compels a consideration of approaches and ideas beyond those generated in the domestic academic-practitioner community. Beyond this, the government of the U.S. is increasingly confronted with mental health concerns that transcend borders and national sovereignty. In this category are the treatment and management of terrorists, immigrants, political prisoners, transnational gang members and drug traffickers, and those who have been victimized by imprisonment. These are matters which mental health professionals have chosen or been forced to confront for many years. Certainly, as the United States faces the social and political consequences of globalization, its correctional mental health professionals can benefit from the experiences of their foreign colleagues.

An earlier effort of ours (Fagan & Ax, 2003) was a survey of contemporary mental health theory, research, and practice in the United States. It was a guide to best practices, but also the delineation of an ultimately orthodox body of knowledge, written by U.S. academic and correctional mental health professionals. Accordingly, this book is intended as a complement to the *Correctional Mental Health Handbook*. It purposely takes a heterodox approach intended to challenge intellectual complacency, to leave readers with fresh perspectives regarding previously familiar concepts, and to propose new ideas and goals for correctional practice, research, teaching, advocacy, and social policy development.

Toward this end, we have invited several distinguished authors, many of them foreign mental health professionals or academics with a specialty in correctional mental health research and practice, to contribute to this volume, knowing that we will not agree with everything they say–and perhaps disagree vehemently in some instances–and that some of their comments may challenge the ways in which we approach correctional mental health issues. However, we have done so in the belief that their comments and insights can better inform and guide our own work here in "the States" as theorists, scientists, practitioners, and advocates.

CONTENTS

CORRECTIONS, MENTAL HEALTH, AND SOCIAL POLICY: INTERNATIONAL PERSPECTIVES

PART I

CORRECTIONS AND MENTAL
HEALTH IN THE UNITED STATES

Chapter 1

AN INTERNATIONAL HISTORY OF AMERICAN CORRECTIONAL MENTAL HEALTH: THE ENLIGHTENMENT TO 1976*

ROBERT K. AX

INTRODUCTION

This first chapter outlines the influence of several nations on the development of contemporary correctional mental health theory and practice in the United States, as well as the reciprocal impact of America on other Western democracies. Here, seemingly disparate themes and issues, several to be discussed in greater detail in subsequent chapters, are identified and integrated in order to show their impact on contemporary prison systems within and across these countries. The final product is a broader, more protean conceptualization of mental health in correctional systems, perhaps one that is at variance with the notions held by many readers. It necessarily involves considering all parties involved: citizen activists, governments, nongovernmental organizations (NGOs), health care providers, and particularly the individuals under the custody and control of their criminal justice systems, as active agents in shaping mental health missions and practice. With this shared heritage, it would seem reasonable that American policymakers and practitioners should look to these other countries' correctional systems and policies as they consider the ideas that will define domestic correctional mental health practice in the coming decades.

---

* Author's Note: For the general concepts on which the chapter is based, the author is particularly indebted to the work of Roy Porter and David Rothman.

THE NEW PRISON

The Penitentiary and the Rehabilitation Ideal

The modern prison has its origins in the eighteenth century. During this era, France and England were mainly and even collaboratively responsible for producing the Enlightenment, a fulmination of ideas and scientific knowledge which rapidly drew several prominent American colonials into its vortex. It inaugurated an intercontinental process of intellectual and political cross-fertilization which has since regularly influenced the terms of the debate over the constitution of a just and humane society. Enlightenment principles of liberty and equality framed Western liberal democracy, although class distinctions on both sides of the Atlantic endured.

Prior to this era, criminal matters in Europe were largely disposed of by secular and religious authorities through punishments ranging from milder forms: fines, admonitions and public shaming, to the harshest measures, torture and execution (Spierenburg, 1998). From the early eighteenth to the early nineteenth centuries, English common law provided the death penalty for over 200 hundred offenses, which came to be known collectively as the *Bloody Code* (Potter, 1965). Simultaneously, however, a countervailing force began gaining momentum—a sentiment that increasingly eschewed corporal and capital punishment in favor of confinement and rehabilitation. Houses of correction, the early antecedents of the penitentiary, originated in England in the sixteenth century. They had a rehabilitative mission and found their way to the American colonies in the late seventeenth century (Walker, 1998). With the dawn of the Enlightenment, a new sense of the power of environments to shape behavior prevailed, and social philosophers like Antoine-Nicolas de Condorcet (1795/1979) asserted that even the most flawed individuals could be improved by modern scientific methods. The eventual results were the penitentiary and the asylum (Rothman, 1971).

First, however, came the Philadelphia Jail, opened in 1790, which was the first to experiment with isolating prisoners as a means of rehabilitating them. The influence of the city's Quakers was considerable in establishing its mission and the form it took (Walker, 1998). It was only one of many instances of their involvement in various prison initiatives over the course of 300 years.

Isolation was central to the concept of the penitentiary that soon followed. Penitentiaries were of two distinct types. The Auburn, New York, facility employed the congregate system, in which inmates worked together during the day, but were separated at night. Penitentiaries in Pittsburgh and later in Philadelphia originated the silent system, enforcing solitary confinement at all times. Silence was also the rule under the Auburn system, even during work

(Rothman, 1971). In such conditions, it was believed, prisoners would contemplate the error of their ways and so turn toward virtue (Walker, 1998). These facilities constituted the dominant penological innovation of the century and in short order drew investigators from other countries. A committee from Ontario visited the new Auburn prison and subsequently used it and its congregate system as the basis for their prison at Kingston, Ontario. It was the first penitentiary in Canada, opening in 1835 (Hennessy, 1999). Alexis de Tocqueville, subsequently the author of *Democracy in America,* toured many of the prisons in the Eastern United States and returned to France enthusiastic about the potential of the American penitentiary there (Beaumont & Tocqueville, 1833/1979). William Crawford (1835/1969) performed similar services on behalf of the British government, and left one of the most detailed reports of the period on the status of American prisons. Pentonville, the first penitentiary in England, was based on the state prison Crawford visited in Trenton, New Jersey, which in turn served as the basis for many other European prisons (Johnston, 1969).

Cycles of Reform and New Problems

However, the desire to reform under humane conditions was coupled with the felt need for order in a young, growing nation: "The almshouse and the orphan asylum, the penitentiary, the reformatory, and the insane asylum all represented an effort to insure the cohesion of the community in new and changing circumstances" (Rothman, 1971, p. xviii). The new American penitentiaries, many opening in the Northeastern States during the first half of the nineteenth century, were facilities which served not only the rehabilitation mission, but, especially as prison sentences got longer, to remove the unwanted. So did the new mental asylums, which also proliferated during the era, and whose course was joined with the prison from the start.

By mid-century, the penitentiary experiment was in trouble. Aside from the expense of keeping all inmates in solitary confinement, the potentially iatrogenic effects of prison had been known from the start. In his report to the British government, Crawford (1835/1969) acknowledged the impossibility of keeping inmates from communicating and, consequently, from corrupting each other. "The shades of difference in the manners and corrupting influence of the ordinary felon and misdemeanant are often slight, and there exists in each class so great a variety of character as to defy every attempt to prevent contamination by the separation of classes" (p. 40). By the end of the Civil War, overcrowding, corruption, and regressive prison discipline undermined the reform ideal in American prisons (Rotman, 1995). Similarly, the Kingston, Ontario, penitentiary was troubled almost from the start by corruption and a sadistic warden, who permitted the brutalization of the prisoners, some of whom were juveniles (Hennessy, 1999). Nearly 20 years later, two American visitors characterized the place as "a wretched affair, and wholly unfit for the purposes of such an institution" (Wines & Dwight, 1867, pp. 81–82).

Prison observers continued to press for improvements in prisons, rather than to abandon them (Rotman, 1995). While reforming prisoners remained a desirable goal, at mid-century a greater priority was acknowledged. In their report to the Prison Association of New York, Wines and Dwight (1867) reaffirmed their support of the penitentiary's rehabilitation mission, but noted, "The one supreme aim of all public punishment is the protection of society by the prevention of crime" (p. 61). By the time the Kingston penitentiary opened, disillusionment with the rehabilitation experiment had already developed in Canada as well (Oliver, 1998). A similar situation occurred in British prisons. The report of a Select Committee of the House of Lords, subsequently incorporated into the Prisons Act of 1865, essentially foreclosed rehabilitation as a goal of the prison system and legitimized custodial care as a priority (Howard, 1960).

Yet the rehabilitation ideal was not dead, albeit the belief in the capacity of mere incarceration to reform was in disrepute. The penitentiaries endured. The latter half of the nineteenth century saw the increased use of probation, parole, and the indeterminate sentence in the United States (Walker, 1998). The humane intent of these innovative practices was undeniable. There was, for example, James G. Moylan in Canada, a committed reform advocate who held the post of Inspector of Penitentiaries from 1875 to 1895. Among other things, he prioritized the use of solitary confinement over corporal punishment, based on the advice of European prison administrators, who considered it more successful in reducing recidivism rates (Goff, 1999). In the United States, the attempts of Zebulon Brockway to create a model reform system at the new Elmira, New York prison, which opened in 1876, attracted interest around the world. This state of affairs presaged the Progressive movement of the early twentieth century, one which saw the rehabilitation mission re-ascendant and increasingly professionalized, with psychiatrists and psychologists brought into American prisons (Rotman, 1995).

The predominant trends in American criminal justice during the twentieth century were those of increased federal oversight and control and increased incarceration rates. The Federal Bureau of Prisons (created in 1930) and the Federal Bureau of Investigation (created in 1909) constituted the foundation of a national criminal justice and prison system that announced itself in Prohibition and the first wave of federal drug laws during the 1920s, and then in fighting political radicals during the 1930s. As criminal conspiracies, drug crimes, and other matters increasingly transcended the authority of single jurisdictions, the states ceded more authority to the federal courts and prisons. Prosecuting drug users resulted in an increasing presence of women and minorities in prisons. The passage of federal alcohol and drug laws led to the first federal women's prison, at Alderson, West Virginia, which opened in 1924, and the first federal treatment program for drug addicts in 1929, established at Leavenworth Federal Penitentiary (Cummings & McFarland, 1937).

Indeed, the early years of the twentieth century saw a reinvigoration of the rehabilitation effort, marked by the introduction of specialized correctional health professionals. Sanford Bates (1937), the first director of the Federal Bureau of Prisons, noted, "The psychologists and the psychiatrists are becoming a valuable addition to the staff of every up-to-date penal institution" (p. 121). Prison officials continued to seek out innovations in other countries' systems. For example, the report of the British Prison System Enquiry Committee (1922) noted the placement of the parole department at the New Jersey women's reformatory under the supervision of a psychologist. Bates (1937) himself was familiar with the prison systems of Europe.

Dating to early prison investigators' concerns about the spread of infectious disease through the prisons (Howard, 1792/1973) and the malign psychological influence of the prison milieu (Crawford 1835/1969), the potentially iatrogenic effects of incarceration had been documented. With larger prison systems, the twentieth century saw the advent of more systemic effects, such as that of "contagious" prison disturbances. In the first two decades of the twentieth century, disturbances and riots began to cluster. Adams (1992) associated this with Prohibition, which resulted in an increase in federal prosecution of crimes and prison crowding. Undesirable conditions eventually led to a "wave" of prison riots in 1929. These began at two New York state prisons and spread across the country, continuing until 1930. Subsequent events involving prisons in different states and, at times, Canadian prisons, continued to occur for the next several decades (Adams, 1992; Hennessy, 1999). The 1960s ushered in a type of politically informed prison event, as a chain of riots occurred over several years and reflected increased political awareness and cohesiveness among prisoners, particularly Blacks (Adams, 1992). The most notorious of these incidents occurred in September, 1971, in the state prison at Attica, New York. It was triggered by the killing of George Jackson, a nationally known prison inmate and prisoners' rights advocate in California (Wicker, 1975). The 1960s and 1970s were a similarly discordant time for prisons in other democracies, as Canada (Jackson, 2002), Great Britain (Adams, 1992), and France (Gallo, 1995) experienced clusters of prison disturbances.

Rehabilitation efforts never entirely lapsed, recurring in cycles and in different forms. As Rothman (1980) noted, "reform is the designation that each generation gives to its favorite programs" (p. 4). Patterns not only of reform, but later, resistance occurred in several Western democracies, transforming the nature and function of their prison systems. Despite these similarities, capital punishment laws marked a departure of United States criminal justice philosophy from that of other Western democracies in the late twentieth century. Although abolished in 1972 (*Furman v. Georgia*), the death penalty was reinstated only four years later by the United States Supreme Court in a series of decisions (*Gregg v. Georgia, Jurek v. Texas*, and *Proffitt v. Florida*) all handed down on July 2, 1976.

SOCIAL CONTROL AND COUNTERFORCE

Marginalizing People and Criminalizing Behavior

An understanding of the penitentiary as a mechanism of reform is inseparable from the experience of those the laws targeted most persistently. The context in which it came to exist included the privileged few, and many—women (particularly those who were married) and minorities: Blacks, indigenous peoples, and immigrants—with few or no rights. Accordingly, it will also be helpful to keep in mind that the eighteenth and nineteenth centuries constituted an era in which other forms of exclusion and containment originated or flourished. First, there was the removal of unwanted persons, starting with the transportation of criminals from France (Forster, 1996) and England (Hughes, 1988) to the New World; and the forced relocation of indigenous peoples to reserves and native schools in Canada (Milloy, 1999), the United States (Wilson, 1998), and Australia (Broome, 1995). The late nineteenth century saw the mass evacuation of destitute children from London to Canada (Kohli, 2003) and from New York City to the American West (Trattner, 1999). Large state mental asylums contained other unwanted persons beginning in the mid-nineteenth century (Rothman, 1971). Later, repressive laws and customs targeted racial minorities. After the Civil War, freed American slaves encountered discrimination in both the United States (Dray, 2003) and Canada (Winks, 1997), while in the late nineteenth and early twentieth centuries, growing hostility toward Asian immigrants was reflected in the passage of alien exclusion laws in the United States (Sung, 1967) and Canada (Bangarth, 2003). Of all these instruments of social control, the penitentiary proved to be the most durable. However, in the partitioning of society along class, racial and gender lines can be seen the constituent origins of the rights and reform groups that flourished during the twentieth century. Among these was the prisoner rights initiative.

Certain forms of unruly, albeit consensual, behavior constituted another threat to the social order. The most sweeping attempts at controlling these offenses by criminalizing them occurred in the emerging democracies of

North America. Over time, the sex trade, insofar as it involved adults, received the least attention. The legal status of prostitution was ambivalent in Great Britain and France during the eighteenth and nineteenth centuries. What laws existed were capriciously enforced and usually targeted streetwalkers, the most visible and vulnerable members of the trade (Harsin, 1985; Henderson, 1999; Henriques, 1963). Enlightenment scientific thinking considered them victims of societal forces, a sentiment that led to the establishment in 1758 of the first Magdalene Hospital in London, where these women could be retrained for gainful employment (Porter, 2001). Walker (1998) noted a similarly ambivalent attitude toward sex among American colonials, which was reflected in contemporary law and a general reluctance to prosecute consensual sex outside marriage. In Canada, as in France and England, prostitution laws targeted the more visible practitioners of the trade, and those whose services were concealed through middle- and upper-class patronage (e.g., mistresses) were more effectively shielded (Lowman, 1993).

This state of affairs continued in the twentieth century. Some called for prostitution's legalization and regulation; enforcement has been lax in other quarters. The Prison System Inquiry Committee of Great Britain (1922) report noted the hopelessness of trying to control prostitution through incarceration: "The treatment of such offences is the outstanding problem of women's prisons. There is a remarkable unanimity amongst those qualified to judge, that the present plan is completely useless" (p. 338). The report further noted that criminalizing prostitution lent itself to the corruption of the police force. The one clear benefit was that periods of incarceration offered the opportunity to impose medical treatment for the venereal diseases that were a predictable occupational hazard, "partly perhaps, for the sufferer's own sake, but chiefly in the interests of public health" (p. 339). Through the twentieth century, attempts at the moral reform of prostitution met with indifferent results in Canada (Lowman, 1993) and the United Kingdom (Edwards, 1993), where the targets, again, were typically street prostitutes, and the laws varied and practically unenforceable. As of 1976 prostitution was legal in the United States only in Nevada, but effectively ceased to be a focus of reformation via incarceration. Few had any expectation that the relatively brief periods of time that prostitutes served in jail did more than incapacitate.

The legal course of alcohol and other drugs was much different, although originally these substances were both tolerated. Heavy alcohol consumption was common in early eighteenth century London, the era of the so-called gin craze (Porter, 1991). France also held liberal views with respect to alcohol use (Brennan, 1988). Less a concern in more stable, well-established societies, heavy alcohol consumption threatened nation-building efforts across the Atlantic, where it was nonetheless common. The deleterious influences of rum on the First Peoples of Canada, who were naïve to alcohol's effects, were noted by the French settlers. Their behavior so concerned the Catholic clergy that they declared rum trading with the Indians a mortal sin (Eccles, 1998). Rum was also a problem among Whites during the founding of Halifax, Nova Scotia, in 1749. Drinking houses arose almost immediately after the work began, with many of the rum purveyors coming from New England (Raddall, 1993). Heavy alcohol use was common in colonial America and an integral part of everyday life (Peele,1984). Opium had been known in the ancient world and was dispensed liberally and cheaply for medicinal purposes in England through the nineteenth century (Courtright, 2001; Berridge & Edwards, 1981). Crèvecoeur (1782/1981) noted the prevalence of opium use, particularly among women, in colonial Nantucket: "They have adopted these many years the Asiatic habit of taking a dose of opium every morning . . ." (p. 160). Hemp was evidently introduced to the North American continent by the French in 1606 in Nova Francia (later Nova Scotia), and shortly thereafter the pilgrims began planting it in New England to make cloth. Its recreational use appears to have been quite limited among the White population of North America prior to the twentieth century (Commission of Inquiry into the Non-Medical Use of Drugs, 1972).

With the nineteenth century came new and more powerful forms of narcotics. Morphine was introduced in 1820, cocaine in the 1850s, and in 1898, the German company Bayer introduced heroin as a cough medication. Leveraging the power of these drugs was the hypodermic syringe, developed in 1843 (Hickman, 2004). Widely used by physicians to treat a variety of ailments, morphine was soon recognized as having a high potential for abuse, addiction and death. A regulatory act was passed in Britain in 1868, followed by an imperial decree in Germany a few years later in attempts to curb the problem. Opiate addiction spread in the United States during the latter half of the nineteenth century largely as an iatrogenic effect of medical treatment. It was generally White, affluent, middle-aged individuals—those who could afford to consult physicians—rather than poor Black men and women, who became morphine or opium addicts (Davenport-Hines, 2002). These drugs remained legal and readily available in America through the end of the century.

Temperance movements began in both the United States and eastern Canada during the first half of the nineteenth century (Noel, 1995), as did one in Britain (Harrison, 1971). Temperance, however, never captured the popular imagination in France. In 1846, the movement became truly international when the World's Temperance Convention took place in London. Among the American representatives were the abolitionists Frederick Douglass and William Lloyd Garrison. In the same year, Maine became the first state to pass a prohibition law. Several other states followed, although many of these laws were held unconstitutional, amended, or repealed, such that the prohibition movement was essentially quiescent in the United States by 1860 (Tyler, 1944/1962). It continued with varying success in Britain throughout the century (Harrison, 1971).

A revived anti-alcohol movement led to the passage of the Eighteenth Amendment (the Volstead Act), which made it a federal crime to make, possess, or distribute alcohol anywhere in the United States between 1920 and 1933. Popular opposition to the law, the practical impossibility of enforcing it, and a recognition of its counterproductive effects (e.g., an increase in crime and promotion of organized racketeering), soon led to its repeal (Walker, 1998). Subsequently, the United States adopted the regulatory approach it has since maintained with regard to both alcohol and tobacco. Several Canadian provinces voted to prohibit alcohol in the early decades of the twentieth century, though all except Prince Edward Island repealed these measures by 1930 (Cook, 1996).

Criminal laws against opium use in the United States became increasingly strict in the early twentieth century as the typical addict, formerly an older White woman, had become poor and Black (Courtwright, 2001). Concerns about the impact of drugs on the poor, and continuing fears of the poor and minorities helped promote the passage of drug laws in the United States well into the twentieth century (Schroeder, 1975). As Courtwright (2001) noted, "What we think about addiction very much depends on who is addicted" (p. 4). The early twentieth century saw a move away from the largely noninterventionist approach that Western governments had previously taken regarding psychoactive substances and toward regulatory and prohibitionist models. With the passage of the Pure Food and Drug Act in 1906, the United States federal government began to assume a significant measure of control over the manufacture and distribution of a range of medicines, including psychoactive substances. Among other things, the Act required that preparations containing opiates in significant quantities be labeled. The Harrison Act of 1914 criminalized the possession of cocaine and opium, unless prescribed (Davenport-Hines, 2002). During the next few years, attempts were made to establish opium maintenance programs, and some flourished for a brief period, but these ultimately failed in the face of the federal government's adamant opposition. By 1921, they were almost completely shuttered (Courtwright, 2001).

American influence on world opium policy was considerable during the twentieth century. Beginning with laws banning importation and sale of opium in the newly annexed Philippine Islands in 1908, it continued with the convening of the Opium Commission in 1909 in Shanghai, which focused on suppressing the opium trade in the Far East. The International Opium Convention, held at the Hague in 1912, and also convened by the United States, was focused on controlling opium in Europe and North America, and included sanctions on cocaine and morphine. Commencing with the Nixon "War on Drugs" in the 1960s, the United States' influence on European drug policy, largely through American drug enforcement agents, was to encourage the use of more aggressive investigative approaches, such as informants and undercover surveillance (Davenport-Hines, 2002).

By the 1960s, entire new classes of synthetic drugs, which could be manufactured domestically and outside the control of pharmaceutical houses, had begun to appear in the United States. LSD was synthesized by street chemists like Owsley Stanley. With the "Baby Boom" generation coming of age, there was an increased demand for these and other psychoactive drugs. The so-called Rockefeller Drug Laws, enacted in New York State in 1973, called for severe penalties even for relatively minor drug offenses, marking a legislative shift away from criminal reform in the United States (Mauer, 1999). At the same time, federal oversight of illegal drugs increased further with new layers of bureaucratic infrastructure. Notably, administrative responsibility was shifted from the Food and Drug Administration to the Department of Justice in 1968 (Renshaw & Powers, 1992). More drugs, more laws, and more regulatory authority meant more prisoners. The incarceration rate, which had fallen to 93 per 100,000 in 1972, began to climb the following year, reaching a rate of 120 by 1976, continuing thereafter to unprecedented levels (Minor-Harper, 1986).

Whereas the United States was promoting absolute prohibition of both alcohol and non-medicinal opium during the 1920s, the English did neither. Pursuant to the recommendations of the Rolleston Committee of 1924, Great Britain adopted a regulatory model, under which addicts could be given maintenance doses of opiates by physicians. This led to a decrease in the number of addicts, and nobody went to prison merely for possession of heroin or morphine. Americans visiting England were impressed with the medical approach, but their proposals for similar narcotics dispensing systems in the United States were soundly rejected. The British approach was maintained in principle, although in the 1960s, the system was modified to move treatment from the control of individual physicians to specialized clinics (Brecher and the Editors of Consumer Reports, 1972).

As Canada had experimented with alcohol prohibition, it also followed U.S. anti-narcotics policy, passing stricter laws over the years, leading eventually to mandatory minimum sentences for drug offenders similar to those in the United States (Brecher and the Editors of Consumer Reports, 1972). In doing so, they achieved similar results. Morton (1996) noted that drug convictions rose from 354 in 1957 to 30,845 by 1974. Notably, Canada's attitude toward marijuana, at least, began moderating by the 1970s when the Le Dain Commission published a report on cannabis use. In separate opinions, the members recommended decriminalization for personal use, or punishment

merely by fines even for second and subsequent offenses. None recommended maintaining imprisonment as a penalty for marijuana possession and use
(Commission of Inquiry into the Non-Medical Use of Drugs, 1972).

Although suffrage was the cause around which women initially organized in
the nineteenth century, their reproductive capacity also put them at risk
before the law. Abortion was first criminalized in the United States when 10
states passed laws between 1821 and 1841 (Tone, 2001). Yet with the contemporary ignorance of women's fertility cycles and the attendant lack of effective
means of contraception, abortion remained the most common method of han-
dling unwanted pregnancy through the mid-nineteenth century (Hymowitz &
Weissman, 1978). In 1873, the Comstock Act not only outlawed contraceptives, it made merely communicating information through the U.S. mails
about birth control or abortion illegal as well. Among the early opponents of
the law was Margaret Sanger, who, in an act of civil disobedience, challenged
it by opening a birth control clinic in New York City in 1916, and went to jail
as a result (Sanger, 1938/1999). In Canada, the laws regarding birth control
and abortion were similar to, and based on, those of the United States, and it
was illegal there to possess, mail, or otherwise provide information about birth
control. The situation in Toronto between 1900 and 1920 was much the same
as in American cities: women sought illegal procedures and sometimes died
from botched abortions. Physicians performed them in secret and were sometimes arrested and charged. Birth control devices were distributed secretly
(McLaren, 1978/1981). For nearly a century, despite a series of legal battles,
the Comstock Act significantly restricted the dissemination of information
about birth control in the United States. Finally, the *Griswold v. Connecticut*
Supreme Court decision of 1965 marked the end of its influence (Tone, 2001).
The abortion rights battle was fought state-by-state in the United States, until
the *Roe v. Wade* decision in 1973, which effectively invalidated all existing state
abortion laws. The United Kingdom legalized abortion in 1967 (Brookes,
1988), followed by Canada in 1969 (Pelrine, 1972), and France in 1975 (Price,
1993).

Prison Reform and Prisoners' Rights

The prison reform movement originated with the work of several intrepid
individuals motivated by religious convictions. It was perhaps in this regard
that European thinking had its most enduring impact on the early American
prison system. Over the course of 150 years, it evolved into an international
and secular network of institutionalized advocacy and professional organizations. Foucault (1975/1995) observed, "Prison 'reform' is virtually contemporary with the prison itself: it constitutes, as it were, its programme" (p. 234).

The complicated relationship of which he spoke was personified in the Englishman George Fox, the founder of both the prison reform movement and Quakerism during the late seventeenth century, and who himself spent eight terms in prison. Fox's impact was enormous and international in scope. He traveled throughout Great Britain and the American Colonies, setting a pattern followed by many later reformers associated with the prison or mental health reform movements. Like many other reformers, Fox had embraced several causes. He preached on behalf of better treatment of the insane and Native Americans, meeting with the latter on several occasions during his visit to America, and opposed capital punishment. He met and influenced William Penn, founder of the colony of Pennsylvania, whose major city, Philadelphia, became the seat of the Quaker reform movements in the Colonies (Russell, 1942). Despite his own experiences, however, Fox remained an advocate of prisons as instruments of reform.

Women would constitute a sizeable portion of the ranks of various reform movements, from prisons and mental hospitals to suffrage, the abolition of slavery, and eugenics, during the next three centuries. One such feminist of the late seventeenth century was Margaret Fell Fox, the wife of George Fox, whose stance was grounded in Quaker doctrine. She, too, was imprisoned on several occasions for her religious beliefs and political activities (Ferguson, 1985). As both a woman and a Quaker, Fox was the forebear of Elizabeth Fry, who was active in the early nineteenth century. Starting in London, Fry made the welfare of women prisoners, including those awaiting transportation to the Australian penal colonies, her special concern. Her work eventually took her throughout the British Isles and then, on five occasions, to the European continent (Smillie, 1981).

During the late eighteenth century, the English sheriff John Howard undertook inspections of the prisons and jails of his own country and later those of Europe. His findings (Howard, 1791/1973, 1792/1973) constituted the first published survey of prisons and propelled the prison reform movement. Howard's concerns varied from inmates' living conditions and the manner in which they were treated, to their spiritual needs, and to institutional health matters, particularly the potential of cramped prisons to spread infectious disease.

Cesare Beccaria, an Italian nobleman, was the signal theoretician of prison reform of the early modern era. He published the first edition of his *Essay on Crimes and Punishments* in 1764. In this treatise, he advocated abolition of capital punishment and torture, and supported restraints on the power of the state with respect to interrogation and imposition of punishment (Beccaria, 1775/1992). Perhaps most profoundly, in a world still rigidly structured by social class, Beccaria advocated equality of punishment for aristocrats and commoners alike: "I assert that the punishment of a noble should in no wise differ from that of the lowest member of society" (p. 54). Among other American colonials, Beccaria's *Essay* was well-known to John Adams (McCullough, 2001), and was a particular influence on Thomas Jefferson, who used it as a guide in his proposed revisions of the laws of Virginia (Wills, 1978/2002).

The pivotal Colonial-era figure in both American psychiatry and prison reform was the Quaker-born Benjamin Rush. He studied medicine in Scotland, and met and was influenced by a number of Enlightenment thinkers during his European travels. Among Rush's accomplishments was co-founding the Philadelphia Society for Alleviating the Miseries of Public Prisons. He fought for improved care for the insane, founded a free medical clinic for the poor, and was an abolitionist, although he owned a slave (Hawke, 1971). Rush was also the chief motivating force on behalf of temperance in America during this era (Tyler, 1944/1962).

Among nineteenth century figures, William Wilberforce, best known for his long and ultimately successful campaign to abolish slavery throughout the British Empire, was also an advocate of medical care for the poor and for prison reform (Pollock, 1977). Dorothea Dix, the American reformer of the mid-nineteenth century, adopted prison and mental hospital oversight as related causes. She traveled extensively in Europe, visiting facilities there and making recommendations based on her findings there (Brown, 1998). In 1850, she proposed the construction of an insane asylum in Nova Scotia (Dowbiggin, 1997). One can see in Fox, Rush, Wilberforce, and Dix a general manifestation of the reforming impulse, a desire to improve the lot of humanity that extended beyond specific issues and national borders.

These reform initiatives were gradually institutionalized. The first Geneva Convention took place in 1864 under the auspices of the International Committee of the Red Cross. Fifteen European nations, including England and France, plus the United States, were in attendance. Signatories agreed to abide by a set of rules for the treatment of sick and injured soldiers in wartime (Gumpert, 1942). It was the first step in the establishment of international law and NGOs relevant to the treatment of prisoners. The "internationalization of [prison] reform" (O'Brien, 1995; p. 191) was considered to have taken place during the second half of the nineteenth century. In fact, internationalization was integral to prison reform from its inception, as reflected in the careers of the Foxes, Howard, Rush, Tocqueville, and Fry. What *was* new at this point was the movement's recasting in formal, often secular, organizations and the involvement, even dominance, of professionals: scientists, physicians, academics, the clergy, and bureaucrats. These meetings provided forums where new penal reforms, such as the suspended sentence, could be discussed (O'Brien, 1995). The first such congress met in 1846 in Frankfurt (O'Brien, 1982), and was followed by a proliferation of meetings of various penological and related associations in Europe and then America. The National Congress on Penitentiary and Reformatory Discipline, the forerunner of the American Correctional Association, was founded as an international organization and had its first meeting in Cincinnati, Ohio, in 1870. It was attended by representatives from the United States, Canada, and South America (Travisono, 1995).

The prisoners' rights movement evolved in a culture of empowerment that had matured among marginalized groups during the nineteenth and early twentieth centuries. Civil disobedience became an accepted means of seeking redress of grievances such as labor inequities and denial of suffrage. Admirable men and women such as Margaret Sanger, Mother Jones, and Mohandas Gandhi went to prison for their beliefs. Their tactics had engaged the attention of the media, and sometimes the support of the public for their causes. Other disenfranchised individuals began to understand this process as a roadmap to power. Just as important, they began to recognize the alternative identities and communities available to them. Eventually, these dynamics would play out in the criminal justice system, where, in more than one case, empowerment was to lead beyond litigation and civil disobedience to violence. When American Black leaders like Marcus Garvey and W.E.B. DuBois emerged during the first decades of the twentieth century, they brought a message based on the rejection of assimilationist goals: American Blacks must henceforth chart their own course (DuBois, 1968/1997; Essien-Udom, 1967). Garvey's influence was acknowledged by a separatist Black leader of a later generation, Malcolm X, whose father had been one of Garvey's disciples (X, 1964/1990).

The international ethos in which American prisoner rights law evolved after mid-century included the recent horrors of the Nazi concentration camps and then the Third Geneva Convention of 1949, which, among other things, outlawed the torture of prisoners (Diplomatic Conference for the Establishment of International Conventions for the Protection of Victims of War, 1949). Political forces, organized around resentments that had been coalescing over decades were catalyzed by "baby boomer" demographics in the 1960s, the civil rights movement, and the divisive Vietnam War. Berkman (1979) identified both the civil rights movement and a liberal Supreme Court as causative factors in the success of the prisoners' rights legal struggle. Central to the nature of the movement was the fact that prisoners themselves became litigants, no longer depending solely on sympathetic outsiders. Significant among early Supreme Court decisions in which inmates were plaintiffs was *Estelle v. Gamble* (1976), which affirmed inmates' constitutional rights to proper medical care.

The Black Muslims, as they came to be popularly known, provided an alternative to the more conciliatory civil rights initiatives sponsored by mainstream Black groups such as the National Association for the Advancement of Colored People (NAACP) and the Southern Christian Leadership Conference. The larger civil rights movement, as Berkman (1979) pointed out, originally had relatively little interest in prisoners' rights. Among others, the Black Muslims attracted young men such as Malcolm Little, later Malcolm X, who was converted while in the Massachusetts state prison system (X, 1964/1990). He proved to be a charismatic leader whose message of solidarity and empowerment resonated with disenfranchised Blacks and helped inaugurate a broader Black Power movement (Foner, 1998). Certainly, a large audience was available among the nation's prisoners and ex-offenders. By 1960, Black males comprised over a third of the nation's prisoners (Cahalan, 1986). As of 1974, Black males in the U.S. were six times as likely to have been in prison at some point in their lives as Whites, with incarcerations rates of 8.7 percent vs. 1.4 percent (Bonczar, 2004).

Berkman (1979) asserted that the Black Muslim movement's world view of Black subordination as class oppression offered a counterargument to the idea of individual pathology. By extension, it constituted a challenge to the traditional reform mission of the prison and to the medical model of individual deficits or flaws that needed to be cured through psychotherapy, or, in the prison setting, suppressed by institutional discipline. Reframed as a mechanism of class oppression, modern prisons were now ironically a further source of corruption of mind, body and spirit, rather than the means of their residents' redemption. This perspective was reflected in a letter the militant prison rights advocate, George Jackson, wrote from the Soledad, California state prison: "So most of these inmates are sick, my friend, but who created the monster in them? They all stand right now as products of their environment" (Jackson, 1970; p. 163).

American prisoners were also supported in their struggles by sympathizers including members of the academic community who helped them articulate and publicize their concerns. One such person was Angela Davis, a philosophy professor at the University of California at Los Angeles who supported George Jackson and other prisoners involved in the protests at Soledad Prison. She, herself, became a fugitive and was incarcerated after being accused–but ultimately acquitted–of aiding an escape attempt in which Jackson's brother Jonathan was killed (Major, 1973). Psychologists Stanley Brodsky, Raymond Fowler, Carl Clements, and Thomas Hilliard supported legal efforts on behalf of prison reform during the 1970s (Haney & Zimbardo, 1998).

Existing human rights groups, such as the American Civil Liberties Union (ACLU), the Red Cross, and the Quakers, provided aid and comfort to prisoners, and new groups were organized around legal and prisoner rights issues. For example, the ACLU and the more sympathetic NAACP filed amicus curiae briefs in *Furman v. Georgia*, the Supreme Court case that resulted in the temporary abolition of the death penalty in the United States (see below). The National Organization for the Reform of Marijuana Laws (NORML), was founded in 1970 for the purpose of decriminalizing marijuana possession (About NORML, n.d.).

Other nations experienced similar events among their prison populations and advocacy groups. In fact, the Irish nationalist movement and its impact on British-run prisons had preceded the American experience by several decades. After the failed uprising of 1916, Michael Collins and other imprisoned Irish Republican Army (IRA) members proved successful at maintaining discipline among their own ranks and even running operations outside the facilities in which the British incarcerated them. Collins and his confederates insisted on political prisoner status, resolutely resisting criminalized identities (Coogan, 1996). Renewed sectarian violence in the early 1970s led to attempts at suppression, including detention of both loyalist and republican activists, many of whom were detained without trial. The prisoners protested for political prisoner status by way of hunger and food strikes. This was finally granted in 1972, when the "Special Category" status was implemented by the prison system. This involved better treatment than they received on general population compounds and resulted in the ability of these groups to co-exist peaceably in the same facilities during the four years that the status pertained. It was ended in 1976 in favor of a criminalization policy, which immediately resulted in the resumption of protests, including hunger strikes, and an increase in funds sent by republican sympathizers in the United States (Crawford, 1999).

The French riots of May, 1968, which began with students and ultimately included the trade unions, mirrored American political protest in many ways. The leaders were young, well-educated people with leftist politics, who were angry over American involvement in Vietnam. These incidents energized a variety of liberal causes: women's and gay rights, and the environmental movement, as was the case in America (Jones, 1994). The prison disturbances of the early 1970s also occurred within the revolutionary cultural milieu fostered by France's intellectual standard bearers, like Jean Genet, the novelist, playwright, and former prison inmate, who wrote a sympathetic introduction for George Jackson's *Soledad Brother* (1970).[1] In 1974, 80 disturbances took place in just two months. During this time, some prison doctors and psychologists in the French system were radicalized and declared themselves autonomous from prison administrations (Gallo,1995).

In Canada, anti-Americanism fed on Vietnam War protests in the United States and energized Québécois nationalism. In 1970, growing unrest culminated in street riots in Montreal and the imposition of martial law (Morton,

---

1. In turn, Jackson's writings influenced Bobby Sands, who led the IRA prison hunger strike in 1981. He and nine other prisoners ultimately died to protest the British "criminalisation" policy (Beresford, 1997).

1996). Canada's prison riots of the early 1970s were related to those occurring in the United States, as noted previously, but Canadian prisoners there had their own grievances, supported by a growing sense of their rights. While no immediate legal changes resulted, these disturbances did call attention to the prisoners' concerns. Government inquiries followed and the late 1970s would see the first legal decision supporting prisoners' rights: one involving an allegation of improper procedure by a prison disciplinary board (Jackson, 2002). By this time, the prisoners' rights movement was well organized in Canada, with two organizations that reflected the enduring Quaker legacy of prison reform. The first John Howard Society was formed in Vancouver in 1931 to support prisoners and ex-offenders, and to advocate for humane prison conditions. It became a national organization with branches throughout Canada (John Howard Society History, n.d.). The first Elizabeth Fry Society, specifically for the support of women involved in the criminal justice system, was founded in the same city in 1939, and branches have since proliferated across Canada (History of the Elizabeth Fry Societies, n.d.).

Alternative Reform Models

By the mid-1970s, three reform models had been developed–the abolition, restorative justice, and community models–that seemed to offer viable alternatives to established correctional practices in Western countries. They had in common the fact that they transcended and challenged the criminal justice system and were advocated by system outsiders. Implicit in each was the idea of prisons and prisoners as existing within the larger society. All had the goal of reintegrating the offender into the community from which he or she had been estranged. Legislators and prison administrators, therefore, might see these as impositions coming from illegitimate, self-entitled interest groups whose purpose was to undermine their authority, and whose sympathy lay inordinately with criminals rather than with victims or society as a whole. Correctional mental health professionals operating according to these models might be seen as adversarial to the prevailing order. Their services, to the extent required, might be offered within a nontraditional framework, the location might be in the community rather than the jail, their authority would be proportionally reduced, and the criminal justice system would be accordingly minimized as a "client."

A call for prison abolition came from Scandinavia with the publication of Thomas Mathiesen's *The Politics of Abolition* (1974). In its extreme form, as articulated by Mathiesen, it meant entirely eliminating prisons, whereas more moderate forms suggested utilizing alternatives as much as possible. Knopp et al. (1976), from an American perspective and a Quaker affiliation, took a stance very similar to Mathiesen's. Prisoners' rights groups in Australia (Zdenkowski & Brown, 1982) and Sweden (Mathiesen, 1974) argued for prison abolition during this period. The American psychiatrist Karl Menninger advocated abolishing jails as particularly inhumane, places where one "might observe torture being administered to young men, boys, even children, almost any day" (Menninger, 1973, p. 60).

As a concept, restorative justice dates from antiquity. Modern programs reflect the tenets of major religions, particularly Christianity and Buddhism, but there is also a compatibility with those of indigenous persons, including Native Americans of the United States and First Peoples of Canada, and the Māori of New Zealand (Braithwaite, 2002). The parties involved in righting a wrong meet to discuss the problem and agree on a resolution, which involves restitution to the victim and reconciliation of the perpetrator with the community. The resurgence of the practice dates from the 1974 formation of a victim-perpetrator reconciliation program, the *Victim Offender Reconciliation Program* (VORP), in Kitchener, Ontario. This grew to hundreds of such programs in North America and Europe. Knopp et al. (1976), tellingly described VORP as ". . . in the system but not of the system" (p. 121), and further noted the involvement of a local Mennonite group in its formation. The concept had modern-era precedents, however. Eglash (1958), for example, described a "creative-restitution" plan, which involved victim-offender reconciliation, and provided several examples of how it could be adapted to prison settings. In contrast, Knopp and her colleagues (1976) clearly viewed restorative justice as an *alternative* to incarceration.

The community model was implicit in the work of community psychologists like Julian Rappaport (1977). It differed from the more traditional clinical perspective partly in that provision of direct services to incarcerated individuals was only one of many possible intervention points. Yet it maintained the value of the psychologist's professional expertise. It was a system concept, prevention-oriented, data-based, and one which cast the psychologist in the role of organizational change agent. The mental health professional-as-outsider could maintain different allegiances and would experience different pressures with regard to recommending interventions. Such an individual might even be what Brodsky (1973) called a "system challenger." "A system-challenger assumption is that negative, harmful activities are perpetrated by justice agencies. Thus the professional's role should be as system or agency skeptic for these settings that have poorly implemented but reasonable objectives and system saboteur in 'harmful' agencies" (Brodsky, 1973; p. 47). The mental health professional working outside the system, or perhaps *within but not of it* (as in the VORP model, above), could advocate seemingly radical changes he or she saw as ultimately beneficial to the best interests of the criminal justice system, offenders, and society at large.

MENTAL HEALTH AND CORRECTIONS

Asylums and Prisons

Until the late eighteenth century, the treatment of mental illness was primarily custodial where it existed at all. The England of the early eighteenth century confined fewer than five thousand persons in their public and private asylums (Shorter, 1997). There were institutional alternatives, including workhouses and private "madhouses," though most afflicted individuals were maintained in their homes, boarded out, or simply permitted to wander (Porter, 1987).

The French Company of the Holy Sacrament was a Counter-Reformation cabal whose members included laymen and women as well as the clergy, and who were partly responsible for the *hôpital generaux,* founded in the 1650s. These were catch-all institutions in which one percent of the population of Paris was confined at one point. In these facilities, both innocent paupers and criminals, and later the insane, gypsies, and the children of Huguenots (Protestantism having been outlawed in France in 1685) were placed as a means of reform and social control (Brockliss & Jones, 1997). Their function, however, was primarily custodial, not rehabilitative (Shorter, 1997). "Interned usually without any medical examination, the mad were invariably left to rot. If a physician or surgeon was paid to visit a town's *hôpital général,* it was not to treat insanity but to deal with the epidemic diseases that the inmates were invariably prone to" (Brockliss & Jones, 1997; p. 443).

The modern era of psychiatry is commonly held to have begun in the second half of the eighteenth century (Kolb, 1973; Lyons & Petrocelli, 1987; Shorter, 1997). Prior to this time, care of the insane, when they received it, would be at the hands of their families, quacks, the clergy, or, rarely, doctors with no specialized training. Philippe Pinel, who was popularly supposed to have loosened the chains of the mental patients at the asylum at La Salpêtrière (which also functioned as a prison [Schama, 1989]), made three contributions to modern psychiatry that are significant here. First was his use of the scientific method of classification. Second was his articulation and use of *moral treatment,* an approach involving transactions with the patient's emotions and intellect, rather than somatic treatments such as bleedings. Third, Pinel recognized the competence of certain non-psychiatrists, based on their experience and sound judgment, as healers of the insane (Goldstein, 2001).

Psychologists, nurse-practitioners, clinical social workers, and other non-physicians working with persons suffering from serious mental illness can, in some respects, trace their professional space back to the work of Pinel and his English counterparts. In this regard, it is notable that moral treatment (or therapy) developed independently in England (Millon, 2004; Porter, 1997), and was implemented at the York Asylum, founded by Quakers led by William Hack Tuke. After this parallel process was discovered, French and English healers began visiting each other's hospitals, another example of the international collaboration and knowledge-sharing that was occurring in the scientific arena by this time (Millon, 2004).

Institutional care for the mentally ill in North America evolved slowly, with a course that paralleled the development of the penitentiary. In colonial Canada as in colonial America, care for the insane was piecemeal. Francis (1977/1981) asserted that "the first Canadian mental institution was a building in Saint John, New Brunswick originally constructed as a cholera hospital, and converted in 1836 to accommodate "fourteen lunatics in its depths and as many sick paupers upstairs" (p. 93). Ultimately, it came to house *only* the mentally ill, and was in that sense Canada's first mental institution (Dowbiggin, 1997). However, French Canada had places of confinement for the insane and other disenfranchised or dependent persons a hundred years earlier. *Hôpitaux* in Quebec and Montreal, reminiscent of those in France, housed an aggregation of the elderly, chronically ill, and the insane, as well as sexually profligate young women who, it was hoped, would be reformed by their detention (Eccles, 1998). By and large, however, housing in local jails in Quebec was to be a common recourse into the mid-nineteenth century for mentally ill persons unable to stay with their families (Moran, 2000).

During the first half of the eighteenth century, houses of correction and workhouses began to proliferate in larger American cities. These were commonly places where criminals, the insane and other persons were housed together (Deutsch, 1937). In 1751, a petition drawn up by Benjamin Franklin advocated the establishment of what would become the first general hospital in America, the Pennsylvania Hospital in Philadelphia. It was modeled on similar establishments in Great Britain and took in mentally ill individuals, among others. However, the mentally ill were confined to the cellar and frequently chained. Their attendants' chief duty was preventing their escape. Though their treatment in fact differed little from those of the prisoners with whom they had previously been confined, in principle, the Pennsylvania Hospital was the first facility in America intended to treat, and perhaps occasionally cure, mentally ill persons, rather than merely confine them (Deutsch, 1937).

The first public hospital exclusively for the treatment of the mentally ill was Eastern State Hospital, opened in 1773, in Williamsburg, Virginia. Notably, its first patient was delivered from the local jail, where he had been held for the previous nine months. Preservation of community order against disruption from the insane was its fundamental purpose (Gardner, 1975), a portent of events occurring decades later. Just as reform failed in the penitentiaries by the mid-nineteenth century, so were the period's new large insane asylums found wanting in the cures that moral treatment had once promised. They, too, became increasingly custodial in nature. In America, financial considerations led local officials to send their most refractory, chronic cases to the state facilities, while keeping those thought to be more curable. In addition, asylums housed more and more of the unwanted poor and foreign-born, further reinforcing the rationale for their new custodial mission (Rothman, 1971).

The eclipse of environmental-Enlightenment theories of the cause and cure of criminality and insanity roughly coincided with the advent of theories of innate causation. For penologists and reformers, it was a propitious moment. France, for example, experienced a period of anti-psychiatry in the 1860s, as the public became disillusioned with asylums. A new theory, hereditarianism, quickly won adherents among French psychiatrists, who could blame factors beyond their control for their low cure rates. According to this school, some families were predestined to degenerate into madness or idiocy, and then sterility over the course of four generations. This theory cast a wide, and for the medical profession, useful social net, making asylum medical theory relevant both in the courts and to the diagnosis of a range of psychiatric disorders (Dowbiggin, 1991).[2]

Classification and the Health Care Professions

Prisoner classification *per se* was first a means of ordering and controlling inmates, later studying and reforming them, and when the health care professions became involved in the criminal justice system, classification and diagnosis was their core function. Howard (1791/1973) observed that in the galleys at Toulon, prisoners "were obliged always to wear a bonnet or cap, on which is fixed a tin plate with a number. Their caps were grey, green, and red, to distinguish, deserters [*sid*] smugglers, and thieves; these last were always branded before they leave the prison of the place where they were condemned" (p. 54). Basic classification of prison inmates involved age, gender, and the nature of the crime, reasonable enough since many of the early prisons mixed men, women and children together. Separating these groups, the predators from the vulnerable, was a basic goal of Quaker prison reformers like Howard (1791/1973; 1792/1973), and, later, Elizabeth Fry (Smillie, 1981).

A significant modification of psychiatrists' scope of practice occurred when they began offering their diagnostic expertise in legal cases. In the early nineteenth century, doctors were still rare in the English courts. The legal system

---

2. Other theories emerging during the nineteenth century that emphasized or implied the heritability of personality and behavioral characteristics, included phrenology (Combe, 1835), criminal anthropology (Horn, 2003) and eugenics (Kevles, 1995).

relied on the testimony of those who knew the defendant–friends, family, and acquaintances–to establish insanity (Porter, 1987). However, English prisons, as well as the asylums, gradually became the points at which psychiatrists initiated contacts with defendants and, increasingly, places where they studied mental illness (Eigen, 1995). In France by this time, the involvement of physicians in forensic cases had become common (Goldstein, 2001). The specifics of the case of the Frenchman Pierre Rivière bear striking similarities to those of modern insanity cases. He was arrested in 1835 for the senseless murder of several family members. A group of physicians, including the psychiatrist Esquirol, provided depositions concerning his mental status. Initially found guilty and sentenced to death, Rivière's sentence was commuted after the king was successfully petitioned on the grounds that the defendant had "killed his mother and sister in consequence of religious hallucinations" (Foucault, 1973/1975; p. 169). During his incarceration, he attempted suicide and was placed in an observation cell. A subsequent attempt by hanging, while he was isolated from other prisoners because of his bizarre behavior, was successful (Foucault, 1973/1975). His history of mental illness, method of choice, and location in isolation are now identified as high-risk factors for prison suicide. Rivière's case helped spur changes in French law, which became effective in 1838, allowing for the voluntary or involuntary commitment to asylums of persons thought to be insane (Castel, 1975).

An early hallmark in the development of modern forensic psychology was J. McKeen Cattell's analogue experiment in eyewitness testimony, conducted at Columbia University in 1893, which yielded high levels of observer inaccuracy. The study engaged the interest of researchers in Europe, including Alfred Binet, who replicated the experiment, and German psychologist William Stern, who conducted further work based on Cattell's experiment using a staged quarrel in front of law students. As early as 1896, German psychologists were serving as expert witnesses, testifying on matters of fact and opinion, in criminal cases. In the same year, Hugo Munsterberg, a student of Wilhelm Wundt, arrived in the United States and began proselytizing on behalf of psychology's involvement in a broad range of applied fields, including the courts (Bartol & Bartol, 1987). When psychologists found their way into the American prison system some 20 years later, it was as psychometricians whose primary mission was classification (Clear & Cole, 1997).

Mental Health and Corrections in the Twentieth Century

Theories of criminal thinking and behavior multiplied in the twentieth century. Among the most influential were the constitutional theories of the psychologist William Sheldon and the criminologists Sheldon and Eleanor

Glueck. These purported to recognize in body-type an outward manifestation of more or less fixed and enduring personality characteristics, in much the same way as Lombroso's criminal anthropology had in the previous century (Horn, 2003). William Sheldon undertook studies of youthful delinquents and young men during the 1930s and 1940s in an attempt to document a relationship between physique and temperament. He claimed to have found relationships between three major somatotypes—prototypically muscular mesomorphs, fat endomorphs, and thin ectomorphs—and personality, with mesomorphs most inclined to crime (Sheldon, 1942). The Gluecks (1956/1970) based their later theories on Sheldon's somatotype taxonomy, and arrived at similar conclusions, albeit their conceptualization allowed for more of an environmental impact than did Sheldon's.

Efforts at defining, quantifying, and predicting criminal behavior continued. In particular, the early twentieth century saw the emergence of the modern concept of psychopathy. Schulsinger (1977) traced it from Pinel in France (*mania sans délire,* or mania without delirium) to the Englishman Pritchard (moral insanity) early in the nineteenth century to Koch in Germany, who coined the term "psychopathy" late in the century. It was also in Germany in the 1930s that research began into the possible influence of heredity on psychopathy. It gained further currency as a diagnostic entity from its inclusion in the empirically-based Minnesota Multiphasic Personality Inventory (MMPI) (Hathaway & McKinley, 1940). Later work, e.g., by the Canadian psychologist Robert Hare and his colleagues, portrayed the psychopath as characterized by innate deficits in the capacity for empathy and delay of gratification (Hare, 1970; Hare & Schalling, 1978). The growing view of psychopathy's etiology as endogenous (e.g., Kleinmuntz, 1974) recalled hereditarian theories of the previous century.

Mental health specialists began their formal involvement in American prisons in 1917, when a psychiatric clinic was established in conjunction with a study of the prisoners at upstate New York's Sing Sing Prison (Deutsch, 1937). One of the earliest clinical psychology internships was established at Western State Prison in Pennsylvania in 1923 (Morrow, 1946). By mid-century, clinical psychology was becoming a presence in American prisons. Of the 78 correctional "psychologists" (only 21% had a doctorate) in Burton's (1949) sample, approximately 80 percent were employed in state correctional systems. The number of psychologists providing mental health services in American prisons increased appreciably between 1950 and 1976. Marking this trend was the formation of the American Association for Correctional Psychology in 1953 (Bartol & Freeman, 2005). The Federal Bureau of Prisons' annual report for 1969 documented the agency's core of 18 psychologists and 20 psychiatrists, who provided treatment to 20,000 inmates in 35 facilities (U.S. Bureau of Prisons, 1969; cited in Carter, Glaser, & Wilkins, 1972). According to the American Psychological Association's 1975 Manpower Survey, 349 psychologists identified the criminal justice system as their primary employment setting (American Psychological Association, 1978).

Watkins (1992) dates the emergence of correctional practice among Canadian psychologists as the early 1950s, impelled by the Archambault Commission report of 1938. This prioritized the reform of offenders, and, after World War II, led to the assignment of the first classification officer in the Canadian Penitentiary Service. Soon thereafter, such officials, usually bachelor's-level professionals, were assigned throughout the federal system. The 1960s was a period of growth, with more positions than recruits available, and turnover patterns for Canadian correctional psychologists in the 1960s were similar to those of their American counterparts (Watkins, 1992). This may have been due to the political turmoil in prisons and competition from other, more traditional employers. However, the late 1960s and early 1970s saw the inauguration of the research on correctional populations for which Canadian psychologists have justly been celebrated (Rice and Quinsey,1986).

It was also after 1950 that physician mental health providers became more of a presence in Canadian prisons. Guy Richmond was appointed the first full-time prison physician in British Columbia in 1952, and, based on his experiences there, took an interest in a broad range of issues relevant to correctional mental health such as substance abuse, psychopathy, sex offenders, and prevention approaches (Jack, 1981). By 1971, there were 23 psychiatrists and about 30 psychologists available to treat the approximately 7,500 inmates incarcerated in the Canadian Penitentiary Service (as the Correctional Service of Canada was then known) (Gosselin, 1982).

Under the Law of 1838, French prisoners who suffered from serious mental illness were sent to psychiatric hospitals. By the early 1970s, there were also two facilities for housing psychopathic prisoners, whose presence in general population would have been considered disruptive. In 1965, a one-year course was created to offer physicians a specialization in prison medicine, including such topics as "prison psychiatry" and "medico-legal psychiatry" (Fully, 1973).

In Britain as elsewhere, prison mental health services grew during this era. Social workers were first appointed to prison staffs in 1955 to assist prisoners with discharge plans. The first "visiting psychotherapist" was appointed to the Wormwood Scrubs prison in the 1930s (Gray, 1973), although as late as 1959 most prisons had no staff psychologists (Howard, 1960). By 1970, there were 66 psychologist posts authorized for the British prison system with a ratio of one psychologist for every 2,569 prisoner admissions. Their jobs consisted mainly in consultative duties, such as advising on personnel selection, and consulting with prison management. Some worked with prisoners, usually for assessment, occasionally for psychotherapy (Donald, 1970). At this point, there were also psychiatrists and art therapists, as well as 55 visiting psychotherapists providing mental health services to British prison inmates (Gray, 1973). A notable feature of the British prison system of this period was the Grendon Underwood psychiatric prison, opened in 1962, with a therapeutic community milieu, and a multidisciplinary approach utilizing psychiatrists, psychologists, a psychiatric social worker, and welfare officers. Rehabilitation was a priority and post-release hostel facilities were available for released homeless inmates (Gray, 1973).

Where asylums and prisons had grown in a similar pattern during the nineteenth and early twentieth centuries, the years after 1950 marked a profound divergence in their respective roles in the social network of Western democracies. There had been calls for "deinstitutionalization" of overcrowded mental hospitals in the United States as early as the 1930s (Grimes, 1934), but the movement gained momentum in the 1950s and 1960s. It was made possible because of advances in conceptualizing and treating serious mental illness. It was made *desirable* because of perceived violations of the rights of psychiatric inpatients and the putative economic advantages of community-based over hospital-based treatment (Lamb, 1984). The deinstitutionalization of the mentally ill began at roughly the same time in Canada (Sealy & Whitehead, 2004), Britain (Goodwin, 1989), and in Queensland, Australia (Doessel, Scheurer, Chant, & Whiteford, 2005).

Deinstitutionalization suggested that persons with troubled minds would gain a greater measure of freedom. So did science in the mid-twentieth century. There were new conceptualizations of mental illness: biological, psychoanalytic, and behavioral-environmental, which intensified the debate concerning its etiology, and new treatments, which held out a renewed promise of greater cure and relief rates. This state of flux also invigorated the allied mental health professions, and provided an entry into clinical work in psychiatric hospitals and community facilities for psychologists and social workers.

Unfortunately, the obverse of deinstitutionalization proved to be the criminalization of mental illness. By the early 1970s, persons released from American psychiatric hospitals were finding their way into the criminal justice system in increasing numbers (Abramson, 1972). Ultimately, deinstitutionalization and the prosecution of drug offenses contributed to the increased presence of the mentally ill and the addicted in the criminal justice system. From the 1960s on, as psychiatric inpatients were being released to community care, criminality evolved as a more parsimonious concept, the criminal mind less and less a consideration than the criminal act itself, as reflected in the prescient comments of Thomas Szasz, a psychiatrist and the era's foremost antipsychiatrist: "Even if we accept the argument that many criminals are mentally sick, it does not follow that they should be in mental hospitals rather than in prisons. Mental hospitalization of offenders should not be, and cannot be, a substitute for prison reform" (Szasz, 1968, p. 230).

CONCLUSIONS

In the Bicentennial year of 1976, the future of American correctional policy was uncertain. That year, prisoners were granted the right to health care but the death penalty was restored. Some were optimistic that a more benign approach to dealing with crime and criminals would emerge from the social and political turmoil of the period. The psychiatrist Karl Menninger (1973) believed that jails were closing and would become obsolete, that victimless crimes–personal drug use, gambling–might soon be decriminalized, and that sentencing policy was becoming more generally enlightened. Another observer (McGee, 1972) cautiously opined that the future of corrections would involve fewer offenders sentenced to long prison terms, greater emphasis on rehabilitation than security, and smaller prisons, of perhaps a hundred inmates or less. A new and enlightened vision of the correctional mission seemed possible throughout Western democracies.

However, the United States was about to embark on a course that would lead by the twenty-first century to incarceration rates more than five times those of other Western nations (Mauer, 2003). It would be further distinguished as virtually the only one of these to maintain the death penalty (Abolitionist and Retentionist Countries, n.d.). What also prevailed in America were political polarization and a pervasive disillusionment with correctional programs. The noted judge David Bazelon commented, "I think we have to ask whether these elaborate and costly programs for research and rehabilitation serve any function other than providing staff–including correctional psychologists–with jobs and income" (Bazelon, 1973, p. 153.), conclusions which Robert Martinson's infamous "nothing works" (1974) article was seen to echo. American prisons and jails, reminiscent of the *hôpital generaux,* again became places for accommodating the seriously mentally ill, the addicted, the foreign-born, and disproportionate numbers of minority inmates for lengthier sentences.

From its inception as a clinical specialty, correctional mental health care functioned within a rigid organizational hierarchy where treatment missions were necessarily subordinate to those of safety and security. Even as their numbers grew, professionals were confronted with the accumulating data suggesting–or being interpreted to suggest–that rehabilitation programs were ineffective (Martinson, 1974), or that prisons by their nature could damage both staff and inmates (Haney, Banks, & Zimbardo, 1973). Legal decisions increasingly compelled and constrained the operations of correctional settings, including the provision of health and mental health services. A divided public castigated the prison system's failures and lauded the enactment of harsher sentences, such as the Rockefeller drug laws in New York State. As the nation began its third century, mental health professionals practicing in the American prison system were faced with a difficult decision. They could continue in the face of what appeared to be the empirical negation and political suppression of the prison's rehabilitation mission, hoping for the inauguration of another reform cycle. Alternatively, they could leave the system and look for new ideas outside it, perhaps in academia. Finally, they could challenge it, for example, through advocacy efforts, such as those of Brodsky, Fowler, Clements, and Hilliard.

The lawyer and historian James Whitman (2003) has written of the United States' "harsh justice" in his study comparing the criminal justice and correctional practices of this country to those of France and Germany. These two nations, as he pointed out, both descend from traditions of authoritarian government, and yet, he asserted, their justice is more magnanimous than that of the U.S. Why? Partly, he proposed, because the United States is a more violent country. Beyond this, he suggested a more complex, sadly ironic, and certainly disturbing cause: American egalitarianism—a distaste for social hierarchy and an aversion to state authority that speaks to the core of our national identity. In essence, he suggested, America reduced the treatment of the "aristocrat" to that of the commoner, whereas France and Germany had done more the opposite. Whitman asserted that it is a fundamental *failure of mercy* in the American criminal justice and correctional systems that distinguishes ours from those of France and Germany. In light of the incarceration rates cited above, one might extend that argument to a comparison of the American system with those of other Western nations.

How did the United States reach this point, and what does it say about the place of mental health practice and policy in contemporary corrections? Is the United States a different kind of country now, with an ethos fundamentally opposed to the rehabilitation mission of prisons, and to which those working in correctional settings must accommodate? Is it perhaps in the vanguard in confronting challenges—poverty, terrorism, criminal organizations, and the easy availability of drugs and weapons—that all democracies must face in the twenty-first century? If so, it might be reasonable that our policies and practices should embrace an intellectual solipsism. At the same time, the latter perspective implies the need to accept further increases in prison populations, of which the weakest and most vulnerable will inevitably comprise a larger percentage. The intellectual and democratic traditions and the humanitarian ideals we share with other Western nations suggest other options are possible. The remaining chapters of this book are largely predicated on that belief.

REFERENCES

Abolitionist and Retentionist Countries (n.d.). Retrieved on October 11, 2006, from http://web.amnesty.org/pages/deathpenalty-countries-eng

About NORML (n.d.). Retrieved on July 30, 2005, from http://www.norml.org/index.cfm?Group_ID=5493

Abramson, M.F. (1972). The criminalization of mentally disordered behavior. Possible side-effect of a new mental health law. *Hospital and Community Psychiatry, 23,* 101–105.

Adams, R. (1992). *Prison riots in Britain and the USA.* New York: St. Martin's Press, Inc.

American Psychological Association (1978). Report of the task force on the role of psychology in the criminal justice system. *American Psychologist, 33,* 1099–1113.

Bangarth, S.D. (2003). 'We are not asking you to open wide the gates for Chinese immigration': The Committee for the Repeal of the Chinese Immigration Act and early human rights activism in Canada. *The Canadian Historical Review, 84,* 395–422.

Bartol, C.R., & Bartol, A.M. (1987). History of forensic psychology. In I.B. Weiner and A.K. Hess (Eds.), *Handbook of forensic psychology* (pp. 3–21). New York: John Wiley & Sons.

Bartol, C.R., & Freeman, N. (2005). History of the American Association for Correctional Psychology. *Criminal Justice and Behavior, 32,* 123–142.

Bates, S. (1937). *Prisons and beyond.* New York: The Macmillan Company.

Bazelon, D.L. (1973). Psychologists in corrections – Are they doing good for the offender or well for themselves? In. S.L. Brodsky (Ed.), *Psychologists in the criminal justice system* (pp. 149–154). Urbana, IL: University of Illinois Press.

Beaumont, G., & Tocqueville, A. (1979). *On the penitentiary system in the United States and its application in France.* Carbondale, IL: Southern Illinois University Press. (Original work published 1833).

Beccaria, C. (1992). *An essay on crimes and punishments* (4th ed.) (Anon. Trans.). Boston, MA: International Pocket Library, Inc. (Original work published 1775)

Beresford, G. (1997). *Ten men dead: The story of the 1981 Irish hunger strike.* New York: Atlantic Monthly Press.

Berkman, R. (1979). *Opening the gates: The rise of the prisoners' movement.* Lexington, MA: Lexington Books.

Berridge, V., & Edwards, G. (1981). *Opium and the people: Opiate use in nineteenth-century England.* London: Allen Lane/St. Martin's Press.

Bonczar, T.P. (2003, August). *Prevalence of imprisonment in the U.S. population, 1974–2001* (Bureau of Justice Statistics Special Report, NCJ 197976). National Criminal Justice Reference Service. Retrieved March 20, 2004, from http://www.ojp.usdoj.gov/bjs/pub/pdf/piusp01.pdf

Braithwaite, J. (2002). *Restorative justice and responsive regulation.* New York: Oxford University Press.

Brecher, E.M., & The Editors of Consumer Reports (1972). *Licit and illicit drugs.* Boston, MA: Little, Brown and Company.

Brennan, T. (1988). *Public drinking and popular culture in eighteenth-century Paris.* Princeton, NJ: Princeton University Press.

Brockliss, L., and Jones, C. (1997). *The medical world of early modern France.* Oxford, Great Britain: The Clarendon Press.

Brodsky, S.L. (1973). *Psychologists in the criminal justice system.* Urbana, IL: University of Illinois Press.

Brookes, B. (1988). *Abortion in England 1900–1967.* New York: Croom Helm Ltd.

Broome, R. (1995). Victoria. In A. McGrath (Ed), *Contested ground: Australian aborigines under the British crown* (pp . 121–167). St. Leonards, NSW: Allen & Unwin.

Brown, T.J. (1998). *Dorothea Dix: New England reformer.* Cambridge, MA: Harvard University Press.

Burton, A. (1949). The status of correctional psychology. *The Journal of Psychology, 28,* 215–222.

Cahalan, M.W. (1986, December). *Historical corrections statistics in the United States, 1850–1984.* (Bureau of Justice Statistics Special Report, NCJ 102529). Washington, DC: National Criminal Justice Reference Service.

Castel, R. (1975). The doctors and the judges. In M. Foucault (Ed.), *I, Pierre Rivière, having slaughtered my mother, my sister, and my brother . . . : A case of parricide in the 19th century* (F. Jellinek, Trans.) (pp. 250–269). New York: Random House. (Original work published 1973).

Clear, T.R., & Cole, G.F. (1997). *American Corrections* (4th ed.). Belmont, CA: Wadsworth Publishing Company.

Combe, G. (1835). *A system of phrenology.* (3rd American ed. from the 3rd Edinborough edition). Boston, MA: Marsh, Capen, and Lyon.

Commission of Inquiry into the Non-Medical Use of Drugs. (1972). *Cannabis: A Report of the Commission of Inquiry into the Non-Medical Use of Drugs.* Ottawa, Ontario: Information Canada.

Condorcet, A-N. (1979). *Sketch for a historical picture of the progress of the human mind* (J. Barraclough, Trans.). Westport, CT: Greenwood Press. (Original published in 1795)

Coogan, T.P. (1996). *Michael Collins: The man who made Ireland.* Boulder, CO: Roberts Rinehart Publishers.

Cook, R. (1996). The triumph and trials of materialism (1900–1945). In C. Brown (Ed.), *The illustrated history of Canada* (2nd rev. ed.) (pp. 375–466). Toronto, Ontario: Lester Publishing Limited.

Courtwright, D.T. (2001). *Dark paradise: Opiate addiction in America before 1940.* Cambridge, MA: Cambridge University Press.

Crawford, C. (1999). *Defenders or criminals? Loyalist prisoners and criminalisation.* Belfast, Northern Ireland: The Blackstaff Press Limited.

Crawford, W. (1969). *Report on the penitentiaries of the United States.* Montclair, NJ: Patterson Smith. (Original work published 1835).

Crèvecoeur, J.H.S. (1981). *Letters from an American farmer and sketches of 18th-century America.* New York: Penguin Books. (Original work published 1782).

Cummings, H., & McFarland, C. (1937). *Federal justice: Changes in the history of justice and the federal executive.* New York: The Macmillan Company.

Davenport-Hines, R. (2002). *The pursuit of oblivion.* New York: W.W. Norton.

Deutsch, A. (1937). *The mentally ill in America: A history of their care and treatment from colonial times.* Garden City, NY: Doubleday, Doran & Company, Inc.

Diplomatic Conference for the Establishment of International Conventions for the Protection of Victims of War. (1949, August 12). *Geneva convention relative to the treatment of prisoners of war.* Retrieved June 14, 2006, from http://www.unhchr.ch/html/menu3/b/91.htm

Doessel, D.P., Scheurer, R.W., Chant, D.C., & Whiteford, H.A. (2005). Australia's National Mental Health Strategy and deinstitutionalization: Some empirical results. *Australian and New Zealand Journal of Psychiatry, 39,* 989–994.

Donald, J. (1970). Psychologists in the prison service. *Occupational Psychology, 44,* 237–244.

Dowbiggin, I.R. (1991). *Inheriting madness: Professionalization and psychiatric knowledge in nineteenth century France.* Berkeley, CA: University of California Press.

Dowbiggin, I.R. (1997). *Keeping America sane: Psychiatry and eugenics in the United States and Canada, 1880–1940.* Ithaca, NY: Cornell University Press.

Dray, P. (2003). *At the hands of persons unknown: The lynching of Black America.* New York: The Modern Library.

DuBois, W.E.B. (1997). *The autobiography of W.E.B. DuBois.* New York: International Publishers. (Original published in 1968).

Eccles, W.J. (1998). *The French in North America, 1500–1783* (Revised edition). Markham, Ontario: Fitzhenry & Whiteside.

Edwards, S.S.M. (1993). England and Wales. In N.J. Davis (Ed.), *Prostitution: An international handbook on trends, problems, and policies* (pp. 108–128). Westport, CT: Greenwood Press.

Eglash, A. (1958). Creative restitution: Some suggestions for prison rehabilitation programs. *American Journal of Correction, 20,* 20–22, 34.

Eigen, J.P. (1995). *Witnessing insanity: Madness and mad-doctors in the English court.* New Haven, CT: Yale University Press.

Essien-Udom, E.U. (1967). An introduction to the second edition. In M. Garvey (1967). *Philosophy and opinions of Marcus Garvey, or Africa for the Africans* (pp. vii–xxvii). London: Frank Cass and Company Limited. (Originals published in two volumes, 1923 and 1925).

Estelle v. Gamble, 429 U.S. 97 (1976).

Ferguson, M. (1985). *First feminists: British women writers, 1578–1799.* Bloomington, IN: Indiana University Press/Old Westbury, NY: The Feminist Press.

Foner, E. (1998). *The story of American freedom.* New York: W.W. Norton & Co.

Forster, C. (1996). *France and Botany Bay: The lure of a prison colony.* Victoria, Australia: Melbourne University Press.

M. Foucault (Ed.) (1975). *I, Pierre Rivière, having slaughtered my mother, my sister, and my brother . . . : A case of parricide in the 19th century.* (F. Jellinek, Trans.). New York: Random House. (Original work published 1973)

Foucault, M. (1995). *Discipline and punish: The birth of the prison.* (A. Sheridan, Trans.). New York: Vintage Books. (Original work published 1975)

Francis, D. (1977). The development of the lunatic asylum in the Maritime Provinces. *Acadiensis, 6* (2), 23–38. (Reprinted in *Medicine in Canadian Society: Historical Per-*

spectives, pp. 93–114, by S.E.D. Shortt, Ed., 1981, Montreal & Kingston, Canada: McGill-Queens University Press).

Fully, G. (1973). Penitentiary medicine in France. In A. Storr (Chair). *Medical care of prisoners and detainees* (pp. 79–86). Amsterdam: Associated Scientific Publishers.

Furman v. Georgia, 408 U.S. 238 (1972).

Gallo, E. (1995). The penal system in France: From correctionalism to managerialism. In V. Ruggiero, M. Ryan & J. Sim (Eds.), *Western European penal systems* (pp. 71–92). London: Sage Publications Ltd.

Gardner, R.D. (1975). The bicentennial of Eastern State Hospital. In G. Kriegman, R.D. Gardner, & D.W. Abse (Eds.) *American psychiatry, past present, and future* (pp. 3–8). Charlottesville, VA: University Press of Virginia.

Glueck, S., & Glueck, E. (1970). *Physique and delinquency*. New York: Harper & Row. (Original work published 1956)

Goff, C. (1999). *Corrections in Canada*. Cincinnati, OH: Anderson Publishing Company.

Goldstein, J. (2001). *Console and classify: The French psychiatric profession in the nineteenth century*. Chicago: The University of Chicago Press.

Goodwin, S. (1989). Community care for the mentally ill in England and Wales: Myths, assumptions, and reality. *Journal of Social Policy, 18*, 27–52.

Gosselin, L. (1982). *Prisons in Canada*. Montreal, Quebec: Black Rose Books.

Gray, W.J. (1973). The English prison medical service: Its historical background and more recent developments. In Ciba Foundation Symposium 16. *Medical care of prisoners and detainees* (pp. 129–142). New York: Associated Scientific Publishers.

Gregg v. Georgia, 428 U.S. 155 (1976).

Grimes, J.M. (1934). *Institutional care of mental patients in the United States*. Chicago: Author.

Griswold v. Connecticut, 381 U.S. 479 (1965).

Gumpert, M. (1942). *Dunant: The story of the Red Cross*. Garden City, NY: Blue Ribbon Books.

Haney, C., Banks, W., & Zimbardo, P. (1973). Interpersonal dynamics in a simulated prison. *International Journal of Criminology and Penology, 1*, 69–97.

Haney, C., & Zimbardo, P. (1998). The past and future of U.S. prison policy: Twenty-five years after the Stanford prison experiment. *American Psychologist, 53*, 709–727.

Hare, R.D. (1970). *Psychopathy: Theory and research*. New York: John Wiley & Sons, Inc.

Hare, R.D., & Schalling, D. (1978). *Psychopathic behaviour: Approaches to research*. New York: John Wiley & Sons, Inc.

Harrison, B. (1971). *Drink and the Victorians: The temperance question in England 1815–1872*. Pittsburgh, PA: University of Pittsburgh Press.

Harsin, J. (1985). *Policing prostitution in nineteenth-century Paris*. Princeton, NJ: Princeton University Press.

Hathaway, S.R., & McKinley, J.C. (1940). A multiphasic personality schedule (Minnesota): I. Construction of the schedule. *Journal of Psychology, 10*, 249–254.

Hawke, D. (1971). *Benjamin Rush: Revolutionary gadfly*. New York: Bobbs-Merrill Company, Inc.

Henderson, T. (1999). *Disorderly women in eighteenth-century London: Prostitution and control in the metropolis 1730–1830*. New York: Pearson Education Limited.

Hennessy, P.H. (1999). *Canada's big house: The dark history of the Kingston Penitentiary.* Toronto, Ontario: The Dundurn Group.

Henriques, F. (1963). *Prostitution in London and the new world.* London: MacGibbon & Kee.

Hickman, T.A. (2004). "Mania Americana": Narcotic addiction and modernity in the United States, 1870–1920. *The Journal of American History, 90,* 1269–1294.

History of the Elizabeth Fry Societies. (n.d.). Retrieved on August 2, 2005, from http://www.elizabethfry.ca/ehistory.html

Horn, D.G. (2003). *The criminal body: The anatomy of deviance.* New York: Routledge.

Howard, D.L. (1960). *The English prisons: Their past and their future.* London: Methuen & Co. Ltd.

Howard, J. (1973). *Prisons and lazarettos. Volume one: The state of the prisons in England and Wales.* (4th ed.). Montclair, NJ: Patterson Smith. (Original work published 1792)

Howard, J. (1973). *Prisons and lazarettos. Volume two: An account of the principal lazarettos of Europe.* (2nd edition). Montclair, NJ: Patterson Smith. (Original work published 1791).

Hughes, R. (1988). *The fatal shore: The epic of Australia's founding.* New York: Vintage Books.

Hymowitz, C. & Weissman, M. (1978). *A history of women in America.* New York: Bantam Books.

Jack, D. (1981). *Rogues, rebels, and geniuses: The story of Canadian medicine.* Toronto, Ontario: Doubleday Canada Limited.

Jackson, G. (1970). *Soledad brother: The prison letters of George Jackson.* New York: Bantam Books.

Jackson, M. (2002). *Justice behind the walls: Human rights in Canadian prisons.* Vancouver, BC: Douglas & McIntyre.

John Howard Society History. (n.d.) Retrieved on August 2, 2005, from http://www.johnhoward.ca/jhsback.htm

Johnston, N. (1969). Introduction. In W. Crawford (1969). *Report on the penitentiaries of the United States* (pp. vii–xvii). Montclair, NJ: Patterson Smith. (Original work published 1835)

Jones, C. (1994). *France.* London: Cambridge University Press.

Jurek v. Texas, 428 U.S. 262 (1976).

Kevles, D.J. (1995). *In the name of eugenics: Genetics and the uses of human heredity.* Cambridge, MA: Harvard University Press.

Kleinmuntz, B. (1974). *Essentials of abnormal psychology.* New York: Harper & Row.

Knopp, F.H., Boward, B., Brach, M.J., Christianson, S., Largen, M.A., Lewin, J., Lugo, J., Morris, M., & Newton, W. (1976). *Instead of prisons: A handbook for abolitionists.* Syracuse, NY: Prison Research Education Action Project.

Kohli, M. (2003). *The golden bridge: Young immigrants to Canada, 1833–1939.* Toronto, Ontario: Natural Heritage Books.

Kolb, L. (1973). *Modern clinical psychiatry* (8th edition). Philadelphia: W.B. Saunders Company.

Lamb, H.R. (1984). Deinstitutionalization and the homeless mentally ill. *Hospital and Community Psychiatry, 35,* 899–907.

Lowman, J. (1993). Canada. In N.J. Davis (Ed.), *Prostitution: An international handbook on trends, problems, and policies* (pp. 56–86). Westport, CT: Greenwood Press.

Lyons, A.S., & Petrocelli, R.J. (1987). *Medicine: An illustrated history.* New York: Abradale Press.

Major, R. (1973). *Justice in the round: The trial of Angela Davis.* New York: The Third Press.

Martinson, R. (1974). What works?–Questions and answers about prison reform. *The Public Interest, 35,* 22–54.

Mathiesen, T. (1974). *The politics of abolition.* New York: Halsted Press.

Mauer, M . (1999). *Race to incarcerate.* New York: The New Press.

Mauer, M. (2003). *Comparative international rates of incarceration: An examination of causes and trends.* Retrieved July 13, 2003, from http://www.sentencingproject.org

McCullough, D. (2001). *John Adams.* New York: Simon & Schuster.

McGee, R.A. (1972). Preface. In. R.M. Carter, D. Glaser, L.T. Wilkins (Eds). *Correctional institutions* (pp. ix–xviii). Philadelphia: J.B. Lippincott Company.

McLaren, A. (1978). Birth control and abortion in Canada, 1870–1920. *Canadian Historical Review, 59,* 319–340. (Reprinted in *Medicine in Canadian Society: Historical Perspectives,* pp. 285–313, by S.E.D. Shortt (Ed.), 1981, Montreal & Kingston, Canada: McGill-Queens University Press).

Menninger, K. (1973.) *Whatever became of sin?* New York: Hawthorn Books, Inc.

Millon, T. (2004). *Masters of the mind: Exploring the story of mental illness from ancient times to the new millennium.* Hoboken, NJ: John Wiley & Sons, Inc.

Milloy, J.S. (1999). *A national crime: The Canadian government and the residential school system, 1879–1986.* Winnipeg, Manitoba: The University of Manitoba Press.

Minor-Harper, S. (October, 1986). *State and federal prisoners, 1925–1985* (NCJ-102494). Washington, DC: National Criminal Justice Reference Service.

Moran, J.E. (2000). *Committed to the state asylum: Insanity and society in nineteenth-century Quebec and Ontario.* Montreal, Quebec/Kingston, Ontario: McGill-Queen's University Press.

Morrow, W.R. (1946). The development of psychological internship training. *Journal of Consulting Psychology, 10,* 165–183.

Morton, D. (1996). Strains of affluence (1945–1996). In C. Brown (Ed.), *The illustrated history of Canada* (2nd rev. ed.) (pp. 467–562). Toronto, Ontario: Lester Publishing Limited.

Noel, J. (1995). *Canada dry: Temperance crusades before Confederation.* Toronto, Ontario: University of Toronto Press.

O'Brien, P. (1982). *The promise of punishment: Prisons in nineteenth-century France.* Princeton, NJ: Princeton University Press.

O'Brien, P. (1995). The prison on the continent: Europe, 1865–1965. In N. Morris and D.J. Rothman (Eds.), *The Oxford history of the prison: The practice of punishment in Western society* (pp. 178–201). New York: The Oxford University Press.

Oliver, P. (1998). *'Terror to evil-doers': Prisons and punishment in nineteenth century Ontario.* Toronto, Ontario: University of Toronto Press.

Peele, S. (1984). The cultural context of psychological approaches to alcoholism: Can we control the effects of alcohol? *American Psychologist, 39,* 1337–1351.

Pelrine, E.W. (1972). *Abortion in Canada.* Toronto, Ontario: New Press.

Pollock, J. (1977). *Wilberforce.* London: Constable and Company.

Porter, R. (1987). *Mind-forg'd manacles: A history of madness in England from the Restoration to the Regency.* Cambridge, MA: Harvard University Press.

Porter, R. (1991). *English society in the eighteenth century.* (Rev. ed.). New York: Penguin Putnam, Inc.

Porter, R. (1997). *The greatest benefit to mankind: A medical history of humanity.* New York: W.W. Norton & Company.

Porter, R. (2001). *The creation of the modern world: The untold story of the British Enlightenment.* New York: W.W. Norton & Company.

Potter, J.D. (1965). *The art of hanging.* New York: A.S. Barnes and Company.

Price, R. (1993). *A concise history of France.* Cambridge, England: Cambridge University Press.

Prison System Enquiry Committee. (1922). *English prisons today.* London: Longmans, Green and Co.

Proffitt v. Florida, 428 U.S. 242 (1976)

Raddall, T. H. (1993). *Halifax, warden of the North.* Halifax, Nova Scotia: Nimbus Publishing Limited.

Rappaport, J. (1977). *Community psychology: Values, research, and action.* New York: Holt, Rinehart and Winston.

Renshaw, B.H., & Powers, L.L. (December, 1992). *Drugs, crime, and the justice system: A national report* (NCJ-133652). Washington, DC: Bureau of Justice Statistics.

Rice, M.E., & Quinsey, V.L. (1986). Contributions of Canadian applied psychological research to correctional and psychiatric institutions. *Canadian Psychology, 27,* 1–21.

Rothman, D.J. (1971). *The discovery of the asylum: Social order and disorder in the new republic.* Boston: Little, Brown and Company.

Roe v. Wade, 410 U.S. 113 (1973).

Rothman, D.J. (1980). *Conscience and convenience: The asylum and its alternatives in Progressive America.* Boston: Little, Brown & Company.

Rotman, E. (1995). The failure of reform: United States, 1865-1965. In N. Morris and D.J. Rothman (Eds.) *The Oxford history of the prison: The practice of punishment in Western society* (pp. 151–177). New York: Oxford University Press.

Russell, E. (1942). *The history of Quakerism.* New York: The Macmillan Company.

Sanger, M. (1938/1999). *Margaret Sanger: An autobiography.* New York: Cooper Square Press. (Original work published in 1938)

Schama, S. (1989). *Citizens: A chronicle of the French Revolution.* New York: Alfred A. Knopf.

Schroeder, R. (1975). *The politics of drugs: Marijuana to mainlining.* Washington, DC: Congressional Quarterly, Inc.

Schulsinger, F. (1977). Psychopathy: Heredity and environment. In S. Mednick & K.C. Christansen (Eds.), *Biosocial bases of criminal behavior.* (pp. 109–125). New York: Gardner Press, Inc.

Sealy, P., & Whitehead, P.C. (2004). Forty years of deinstitutionalization of psychiatric services in Canada: An empirical assessment. *Canadian Journal of Psychiatry, 49,* 249–257.

Sheldon, W. (1942). *The varieties of temperament: A psychology of constitutional differences.* New York: Harper & Row.

Shorter, E. (1997). *A history of psychiatry: From the era of the asylum to the age of Prozac.* New York: John Wiley & Sons, Inc.

Smillie, E.M. (1981). *Elizabeth Fry.* Maple, Ontario: Belsten Publishing Ltd.

Spierenburg, P. (1998). The body and the state: Early modern Europe. In N. Morris & D.J. Rothman (Eds.) *The Oxford History of the Prison: The practice of punishment in Western society* (pp. 44–70). New York: Oxford University Press.

Sung, B.L. (1967). *Mountain of gold.* New York: The Macmillan Company.

Szasz, T. (1968). *Law, liberty, and psychiatry: An inquiry into the social uses of mental health practices.* New York: Collier Books.

Taylor, A. (2001). *American colonies: The settling of North America.* New York: Penguin Books.

Tone, A. (2001). *Devices and desires: A history of contraceptives in America.* New York: Hill and Wang.

Trattner, W.I. (1999). *From poor law to welfare state: A history of social welfare in America* (6th ed.). New York: The Free Press.

Travisono, A.P. (1995). *Building a voice: 125 years of history.* Lanham, MD: American Correctional Association.

Tyler, A.F. (1962). *Freedom's ferment: Phases of American history from the colonial period to the outbreak of the Civil War.* New York: Harper Torchbooks. (Original work published 1944).

U.S. Bureau of Prisons. (1969). U.S. Bureau of Prisons, annual report–1969. Washington, DC: U.S. Government Printing Office (excerpt, reprint). In R.M. Carter, D. Glaser, & L.T. Wilkins (Eds.) (1972). *Correctional institutions* (pp. 99–109). Philadelphia: J.B. Lippincott Company.

Walker, S. (1998). *Popular justice: A history of American criminal justice.* (2nd edition). New York: Oxford University Press.

Watkins, R.E. (1992, August). *An historical review of the role and practice of psychology in the field of corrections.* Retrieved July 4, 2004, from http://www.csc-scc.gc.ca/text/rsrch/reports/r28/r28e_3.shtml

Whitman, J.Q. (2003). *Harsh justice: Criminal punishment and the widening divide between America and Europe.* New York: Oxford University Press, Inc.

Wicker, T. (1975). *A time to die.* New York: Quadrangle/The New York Times Book Co.

Wills, G. (2002). *Inventing America: Jefferson's Declaration of Independence.* New York: Houghton Mifflin Company. (Original work published 1978)

Wilson, J. (1998). *The earth shall weep: A history of Native America.* New York: Grove Press.

Wines, E.C., & Dwight, T.W. (1867). *Report on the prisons and reformatories of the United States and Canada.* Albany: Van Benthuysen & Son's Steam Printing House.

Winks, R.W. (1997). *The Blacks in Canada: A history* (2nd ed.). Montreal, Quebec: McGill-Queens University Press.

X, M. (1990). *The autobiography of Malcolm X.* New York: Ballantine Books. (Original published 1964)

Zdenkowski, G., & Brown, D. (1982). *The prison struggle: Changing Australia's penal system.* Maryborough, Victoria: Penguin Books.

Chapter 2

CONTEMPORARY UNITED STATES CORRECTIONS, MENTAL HEALTH, AND SOCIAL POLICY

JENNIFER L. BOOTHBY

INTRODUCTION

Rates of violent and nonviolent crimes in the United States have steadily dropped for decades and only recently leveled out (Catalano, 2006). Despite this trend, fear of crime is pervasive and has, in part, accounted for criminal justice policies that are focused on punishment and retribution. Corrections has become a dumping ground for marginalized segments of society, such as drug users, illegal immigrants, and the mentally ill, and society now relies on correctional systems to provide social services and treatment programs to these populations. However, jails and prisons are beyond their capacities and unable to effectively provide the services and treatment that many offenders require. This chapter will provide an overall description of U.S. correctional systems and populations, primarily focusing on issues relevant to correctional mental health and on emerging challenges.

CORRECTIONAL SYSTEMS

Correctional facilities in the U.S. include jails, state and federal prisons, and private prisons. In 2000, there were 1,668 state, federal, or privately-operated prison facilities in the U.S. (Stephan & Karberg, 2003). This figure does not include military facilities or facilities operated by the Immigration and Naturalization Service. The boom in prison construction that began in the 1980s has largely continued, and between 1995 and 2000, the number of prison facilities increased by 14 percent. However, much of this increase was due to the proliferation of privately-operated prisons, which grew by 140 percent during this time period. Private facilities accommodate a relatively small proportion of the total inmate population, but this also appears to be increasing. For example, between 1995 and 2000, private facilities experienced a 459 percent growth in their prison population.

Prison construction has been big business in the U.S. for several decades. However, the number of new facilities does not seem to keep pace with the burgeoning prison population. Although 204 new prison facilities were built between 1995 and 2000 (Stephan & Karberg, 2003), many prisons are overcrowded. It seems the idea, "build them and they will come," holds true for American prisons. Recent data suggests that the federal system is 40 percent above its population capacity, state systems are from 1 percent below to 15 percent above their capacity, and jails are approximately 5 percent below their capacity (Harrison & Beck, 2006a).

The privatization of corrections is a controversial issue. Many individuals in the criminal justice field argue that private prisons primarily serve a function of reducing overcrowding and increasing efficiency, thus, reducing costs in state and federally-operated facilities (Price, 2006). Another potential cost-saving benefit of private prisons is that they foster competition among agencies vying to receive governmental contracts to run facilities. Competition between businesses lowers costs for consumers, in this case, for government. However, critics of privatization express concern that governments lose accountability when states hire private companies. Private companies were involved in the management of prisons in the late 1800s and early 1900s, and this practice ended due to "rampant prisoner abuse" in private facilities (Price, 2006, p. 5). Critics also argue that the primary focus of for-profit providers of prisons is to make money by maximizing prisoner populations (Schlosser, 1998). This predominant financial focus could lead companies to lobby for criminal justice policies that increase incarceration and lengthen sentences (Price, 2006). A separate issue is the privatization of specific prison services, such as health care or food services, but this practice seems to draw less criticism from anti-privatization proponents. Whether the U.S. continues to expand the use of private prisons is unclear, but with rates of recent construction for such facilities, it appears that privatization will be a continued issue for corrections.

THE CORRECTIONAL POPULATION

Over two million individuals are incarcerated in U.S. prisons and jails. This amounts to one of every 136 U.S. residents being incarcerated, two-thirds of them in state or federal prisons and the rest in jails (Harrison & Beck, 2006a). When these numbers are extended to include those on probation and parole, the rates are staggering. Almost seven million people in the U.S. are under some form of correctional supervision. In other words, at any given time, one of every 31 adults is either incarcerated or on probation or parole (Glaze & Palla, 2005). On average, the annual growth of the prison population has been approximately 3 percent. Thus, the numbers incarcerated in 1980 (501,886) and 1994 (1,483,410) pale in comparison to current figures (Gilliard & Beck, 1995).

The vast majority of U.S. inmates are male (93%). However, the female inmate population has been growing at a faster rate (4.7% annually) than the male population (3%) for over a decade (Harrison & Beck, 2006a). In terms of race, approximately 41 percent of inmates are Black, 34 percent are White, and 19 percent are of Hispanic origin. As compared to statistics from the general population, these figures represent an undue burden on Black and Hispanic communities. For example, 3.2 percent of all Black men and 1.2 percent of Hispanic men are incarcerated, as compared to 0.04 percent of White men. When looking at those age groups most significantly represented in prisons and jails (e.g., 25–34 years), over 8 percent of Black men, 2.5 percent of Hispanic men, and 1.2 percent of White men are incarcerated. Recent estimates suggest that approximately one in three Black men will be incarcerated at least once during their lifetime, a rate six times as high for White men (Bureau of Justice Statistics, 2003).

Overall, approximately 4 percent of the U.S. prison population is comprised of noncitizens (Harrison & Beck, 2006a). The percentage of noncitizens in the federal system is considerably higher, with 19 percent of all federal inmates being noncitizens. Although the rate of incarcerating noncitizens leveled off between 1994 and 1995, it has steadily risen since that time. Following passage of the Illegal Immigration Reform and Immigrant Responsibility Act of 1996, there was a large influx of noncitizens into the federal prison system (Scalia & Litras, 2002). For example, 1,593 noncitizens were incarcerated for immigration offenses in 1985, and this number rose to 13,676 by 2000.

Similar to the graying of the U.S. population as a whole, prison and jail populations are also experiencing an increase in the average age of inmates. Currently, the average age of male offenders is approximately 29 years, and the average age of female offenders is approximately 33 years (Harrison & Beck, 2006a). The number of offenders above the age of 55 was reportedly 33,499 in 1990 and had risen to 125,000 by 2002 (Aday, 2003). Although the number of older offenders represents a relatively small proportion of the total prison population, the number of older offenders is growing more quickly than other age groups. Continued increase of this population will bring new challenges to corrections, particularly in the areas of health care, mental health care and housing issues. In contrast to the growing older offender population, the number of juveniles housed in adult facilities has been steadily declining since 1995. At the end of 2005, the number of inmates under the age of 18 housed in adult, state prisons was 2,266 as compared to 5,309 in 1995 (Harrison & Beck, 2006a). As research shows that juvenile offenders housed in adult facilities have a significantly higher suicide risk (Daniel, 2006), these data are reassuring.

As of 2003, a majority (52%) of state prison inmates were convicted of violent crimes (Harrison & Beck, 2006b). This represents a 5 percent increase in the overall proportion of violent offenders from 1995. The violent crimes most represented include robbery (14% of all crimes), murder (12%), rape and other sexual assaults (12%), and assault (10%). Offenders convicted of property crimes account for 21 percent of all state inmates, and those convicted of drug offenses account for another 20 percent. Compared to 1995 data, the proportion of offenders convicted of property or drug offenses has slightly decreased. Approximately 7 percent of all state inmates were convicted of public-order offenses, such as drunken driving, weapon possession, and commercialized vice. By comparison, only 9 percent of those incarcerated in federal facilities were convicted of violent crimes in 2003, and 56 percent were convicted of drug crimes (Bureau of Justice Statistics, 2003).

The drug policies initiated in the 1980s and 1990s have substantially impacted prison population rates. For example, between 1985 and 1995, drug-related offenses accounted for 74 percent of the increase in prison populations (Mauer, 1999). U.S. drug policies are just one example of an increasing trend toward federalization of crime. In 1998, more than 40 percent of the federal criminal offenses on record had been enacted in the last 30 years, demonstrating increased federal involvement in criminal justice practices (Jackson & Anderson, 2004). If new federal laws focused on the reduction of violent offenses, such involvement might have been more helpful. However, the vast majority of federal crimes involve public welfare offenses, such as drug offenses and immigration violations. Moreover, federal statutes for these offenses tend to largely duplicate state laws, and federal sentences tend to be harsher than state sentences for the same offense, For example, Rudolph Giuliani developed an anti-drug policy called "Federal Day" while he was a U.S. Attorney for New York in the 1980s (Jackson & Anderson, 2004). One day each week was considered "Federal Day," and offenders arrested that day were prosecuted in federal court. Offenders arrested on other days of the week were prosecuted in state court. "Thus a crack cocaine offender arrested on Monday, say, would face a 10-year mandatory minimum sentence, while a crack offender arrested on Tuesday that same week would face perhaps 18 to 20 months of prison time under state law" (p. 5). Thus, in addition to being redundant, these practices can result in a grossly disparate application of penalties. Regardless of how drug offenders became incarcerated, they present a treatment challenge to an overburdened correctional system.

MENTAL HEALTH AND SUBSTANCE ABUSE ISSUES

Currently, there are three times as many mentally ill individuals living in correctional facilities as there are living in psychiatric facilities (Human Rights Watch, 2003). This is a longstanding problem, stemming back to the 1960s and the movement toward deinstitutionalization of the mentally ill. Due to a number of factors, including a reduction in the number of psychiatric hospitals and psychiatric beds, and a lack of funding for outpatient mental health treatment, many individuals with mental illness have become homeless or incarcerated (Teplin, 1984; Torrey, 2001). Prisons and jails are not well-equipped to provide psychiatric treatment, and thus, many mentally ill inmates do not receive adequate treatment.

Many studies have investigated the prevalence of mental illness in incarcerated populations and consistently find that rates of mental illness in prisons and jails are higher than that found in community samples. Prevalence estimates vary depending on the specific methodology employed in the research and the way that mental illness is defined. Linda Teplin and her colleagues have conducted several large-scale epidemiological studies in the Cook County Jail in Chicago, Illinois (Abram, Teplin, & McClelland, 2003; Teplin, 1994; Teplin, Abram, & McClelland, 1996). These studies employ a structured diagnostic interview and define severe psychiatric disorder as meeting the "severe or definite criteria of the Diagnostic Interview Schedule" for a major depressive episode, manic episode, schizophrenia, or substance use disorder (Teplin, 1994, p. 291). These studies report that approximately 31 percent of male jail detainees have a current severe psychiatric disorder and 62 percent meet the criteria for a lifetime diagnosis. Additionally, approximately 20 percent of female jail detainees are estimated to have severe psychiatric disorders (Teplin, Abram, & McClelland, 1996).

Prevalence studies by the Bureau of Justice Statistics define mental illness as "a recent history or symptoms of a mental health problem" (James & Glaze, 2006, p. 1). A history of mental health problems consisted of previous treatment by a mental health professional or a previous clinical diagnosis. The most recent study by the Bureau of Justice Statistics reported that 56 percent of state inmates, 45 percent of federal inmates, and 64 percent of jail inmates have either current symptoms or a history of mental health problems (James & Glaze, 2006). Those offenders with mental health problems were more likely to have been homeless prior to incarceration, have a history of physical or sexual abuse, and have a parent with an incarceration or substance abuse history as compared to offenders without a mental health problem. Although the rates of substance abuse are high for all offenders, inmates with mental health problems were more likely to report regular use of alcohol and drugs and to be using alcohol or drugs at the time of their offense. Additionally, those with mental health problems were more likely to have been injured in a fight during their period of incarceration and more likely to break prison rules as compared to those without mental health problems. Finally, research shows that mentally ill and mentally retarded offenders are more likely to serve their full sentences and less likely to receive parole as compared to other offenders (Couturier, Maue, & McVey, 2005).

Although overall rates of mental illness are high in prisons and jails, certain groups within correctional facilities appear to have particularly high rates of mental disorders. For example, a substantially higher percentage of female inmates (73%) have a mental health problem compared to male inmates (55%) in state prisons. Similarly, White offenders (62%) have higher rates of mental disorders than Black (55%) or Hispanic (46%) inmates, and younger offenders (63% of those under 24 years of age) have higher rates than older offenders (51% of those over the age of 45) (James & Glaze, 2006).

The types of mental health problems experienced by offenders run the full continuum of severity, from severe and chronic mental illness to milder difficulties adjusting to incarceration. It is concerning that so many inmates meet criteria for the more severe types of disorders. For example, between 43 percent and 54 percent of inmates meet criteria for mania, between 23 percent and 30 percent meet criteria for major depression, and between 15 percent and 24 percent meet criteria for a psychotic disorder (James & Glaze, 2006). These figures are substantially higher than the 11 percent prevalence estimates from community surveys for these disorders in 2001–2002. Moreover, it is common to find offenders with comorbid substance use and severe mental disorders. Approximately 76 percent of jail inmates, 74 percent of state inmates, and 64 percent of federal offenders have co-occurring mental health and substance abuse or dependence disorders (James & Glaze, 2006). Additionally, a substantial number of offenders have substance abuse or dependence problems in the absence of other mental health problems. All offenders are more likely to abuse or be dependent on drugs as opposed to alcohol.

MENTAL HEALTH AND SUBSTANCE ABUSE TREATMENT

Recent data suggests that a minority of offenders with mental health problems receive treatment while they are incarcerated. Among those with mental health problems, approximately 34 percent of state inmates, 24 percent of federal offenders, and 18 percent of jail inmates reported receiving mental health treatment since their incarceration (James & Glaze, 2006). Treatment most often consisted of psychotropic medication, but many also reported receiving either group or individual psychotherapy. Despite increased attention to issues regarding the mentally ill in jails and prisons, data suggests that the overall number of offenders receiving mental health services only slightly increased between 1997 and 2004 (from 17% to 19%). Clearly, more resources need to be directed toward increasing access to mental health services in jails and prisons.

Several studies have documented an actual increase in mental health services being provided in correctional facilities (Beck & Maruschak, 2001; Boothby & Clements, 2000; Manderscheid, Gravesande, & Goldstrom, 2004). However, the increase in services has not kept pace with the ever-growing offender population. For example, Manderscheid et al. (2004) noted that "mental health services were offered in significantly more facilities in 2000 than in 1988" (p. 871), and the number of offenders accessing services during this time period also increased substantially. However, during this same time period, there was a 114.5 percent increase in the overall number of offenders incarcerated in state prisons, an increase significantly larger than the percent increase in service delivery. Boothby and Clements (2000) reported that, on average, state and federal correctional facilities have one masters or doctoral-level psychologist on staff for every 750 inmates. Estimating that approximately one-fourth to one-third of offenders have a current, severe mental disorder, each clinician would be responsible for the treatment of 188–248 severely mentally ill offenders. This is likely a conservative estimate, as some studies report that up to almost 60 percent of offenders have current symptoms, or a significant history, of mental illness (James & Glaze, 2006). Thus, access to mental health services remains difficult in many institutions.

Mental health treatment is administered in a variety of modalities, and by an assortment of practitioners, within correctional settings. It is estimated that almost four percent of correctional employees in any given facility serve a mental health or counseling role, with many of these individuals being paraprofessional staff (Camp & Camp, 1999). Many paraprofessional staff have the title "correctional counselor," and these professionals largely serve a day-to-day unit management function. For example, correctional counselors manage daily problems, such as serving on disciplinary hearing boards, completing parole or transfer plans, and fielding offenders' complaints. Other paraprofessional staff might lead psychoeducational groups or provide substance abuse treatment. Because paraprofessionals and other mental health workers without graduate training make up a majority of the mental health treatment team in correctional settings, psychologists often spend much of their time in supervisory or administrative roles (Boothby & Clements, 2000).

Given the large number of mentally ill offenders in corrections and the comparatively sparse resources for mental health treatment in many facilities, it follows that group treatment would be a preferred method of treatment delivery. However, although group treatment is offered in many facilities, Boothby and Clements (2000) found that most treatment is provided on an individual basis. A survey of offenders also noted a preference for individual counseling over other modes of treatment (Morgan, Rozycki, & Wilson, 2004). Moreover, much treatment takes the form of acute crisis intervention, such as suicide prevention. Suicide is the second leading cause of death in U.S. jails and the third leading cause of death in prisons (Daniel, 2006).

With over half of all offenders reporting substance abuse problems (James & Glaze, 2006), it follows that substance abuse treatment should be an integral part of corrections. However, only 43 percent of jails reported offering substance abuse treatment programs in a 1998 survey (Wilson, 2000). The jails also reported that most of their programs consisted entirely of self-help programs, such as Alcoholics Anonymous (AA) or Narcotics Anonymous (NA). Only 12 percent of jails indicated that they provided a combination of treatment services, and an earlier study found that even fewer jails offer transition services to assist offenders with substance abuse problems in getting treatment upon release (Peters, May, & Kearns, 1992). For those offenders who do receive substance abuse treatment while incarcerated, research finds lower rates of rearrest and relapse (Peters & Matthews, 2003).

CONTINUITY OF CARE

The corrections community has an opportunity to prevent and treat mental and physical health problems among millions of individuals and to provide transitions into communities that sustain health. Although the public often chooses to ignore the needs of offenders, it is important to remember that "correctional facilities are part of our communities, not separate from them" (Hammett, Roberts, & Kennedy, 2001, p. 2). Approximately 635,000 individuals are released from federal and state prisons annually in the United States and an additional 12 million are released from jails (Lincoln & Miles, 2006). A startling number of these individuals have infectious diseases in addition to mental health problems. Data from 1997 found that approximately one-third of individuals living in the community with hepatitis C or tuberculosis and one-fourth of individuals living with HIV infection or AIDS spent time in a correctional facility that year (Hammett et al., 2001). Many offenders have dual and even triple diagnoses, including mental health, substance abuse, and chronic health problems. The public health implications of not providing adequate prevention and treatment services during incarceration are staggering. This is a real problem for prisons and the community alike, one calling for an interdisciplinary approach and the commitment of more resources (see Chavez, Chapter 3, for a more detailed discussion of public health issues).

The transition from prison to the community is difficult for many offenders. For example, a recent study on the prevalence of suicide among recently released offenders found that suicide rates were significantly higher in this population as compared to the general population (Pratt, Piper, Appleby, Webb, & Shaw, 2006). Within one year of release from prison, men were eight times more likely and women were 36 times more likely to commit suicide as compared to men and women in the general population. All offenders could benefit from discharge planning and programs that link them with community opportunities for housing, financial assistance, vocational training, and health care. Community reentry is currently being targeted by the federal government as a priority in reducing recidivism, and targeting reentry also has potential public health benefits. The Prisoner Reentry Initiative is a recent federal initiative that involves both institution-based and community-based programs targeted to prepare offenders for release and to sustain support and success following reentry (Office of Justice Programs, 2007). Mental health and addictions treatment are one aspect of this initiative.

Prior to the recent focus on reentry, discharge planning and continuity of care for offenders was rarely adequate. For example, approximately one-third of prisons with greater than 1,000 offenders provide a 14- or 30-day supply of medication, and only one-fourth provide prescriptions upon release (Lincoln & Miles, 2006). Continuity of medications is particularly important for offenders with serious mental illness and/or infectious diseases, such as active tuberculosis and HIV.

A promising development is the Centers for Disease Control and Prevention's recent partnership with seven state health departments to work with corrections and community agencies in enhancing services for offenders with or at risk for infectious diseases (Hammett et al., 2001). A primary focus of service improvement is in the areas of discharge planning and continuity of care. The Maryland Community Criminal Justice Treatment Program is another example of fostering effective reentry for mentally ill offenders (Hills, Siegfried, & Ickowitz, 2004). This program uses an advisory board made up of representatives from community agencies, and establishes agreements regarding the services each agency will provide offenders. Such a collaborative effort fosters continuity of care, even among community agencies. Another model of service delivery exists in Hampden County, Massachusetts. This program assigns offenders with serious medical and mental health needs to a team of

providers located in their zip code of residence. The health care team provides services to the offender while they are in jail and then in a community
mental health setting on release. Offenders who participated in the program
had lower recidivism rates than those who did not participate (Hammett et al.,
2001). Numerous other programs have been developed and are in various
stages of evaluation.

Lincoln and Miles (2006) describe several components of successful continuity of care programs. First, case management services are recommended.
Case management post-release has been shown to reduce recidivism and
increase access to drug treatment among substance-involved offenders
(Rhodes & Gross, 1997). However, intensive case management has been
shown in some studies to result in a greater number of rearrests for those with
mental illness (Solomon, Draine, & Marcus, 2002; Solomon, Draine, & Meyerson, 1994). One possible explanation for this finding is that the increased
monitoring associated with intensive case management makes it more likely
that offenders will be reincarcerated for technical violations.

Second, Lincoln and Miles (2006) suggest that it is important that health
care workers provide services both in the correctional institution and in the
community to which the offender will return. This allows for the development
of a personal connection between offender and treatment provider that can
continue upon release. Research shows that offenders who developed a personal connection with a treatment provider that continued post-release were
more likely to attend follow-up appointments (Conklin, Lincoln, & Flanigan,
1998) and less likely to recidivate (Sheu et al., 2002). The Hampden County,
Massachusetts program described above is a good example of this model
(Hammett et al., 2001). Clearly, this type of model can work well for city and
county jails where offenders are more likely to be incarcerated in their city or
county of residence. However, such a model is more difficult for correctional
systems like the Federal Bureau of Prisons where offenders might be incarcerated thousands of miles from home.

Third, appointments should be scheduled for follow-up care in the community. Veysey et al. (1997) found that although most mentally ill offenders in
their study were provided a referral for follow-up care post-release, only those
with actual scheduled appointments were likely to show up for services.
Fourth, it is recommended that a summary record of diagnoses, medications,
treatments, and other pertinent health information be compiled and shared
with community treatment providers. Such a document increases efficiency
and the likelihood of providing adequate treatment. Finally, Lincoln and
Miles (2006) discuss the importance of timely medical benefits post-release.
States manage benefit enrollments in various ways, with some states terminat-
ing benefits upon incarceration and other states merely suspending benefits
until the individual is released. Case managers can assist offenders in apply-

ing for benefits, if necessary, and can educate them about the steps they should take post-release to ensure prompt receipt of benefits.

MENTAL HEALTH AND DRUG COURTS

Although not developed to increase continuity of care, mental health courts serve to divert mentally ill offenders from jail/prison to community treatment. Thus, mental health courts keep this subset of offenders in our communities, allowing potentially for uninterrupted provision of services. To date almost 100 mental health courts exist in 34 states (Redlich, Steadman, Monahan, Robbins, & Petrila, 2006). The primary functions of these courts are to reduce "the detrimental cycle of revolving in and out of jail" (p. 349) and to mandate mental health treatment with sanctions for noncompliance. Similarly, treatment compliance is often rewarded with dropped or reduced charges.

Although innovative, mental health courts are not uniformly supported by correctional or mental health professionals. For example, some professionals believe that these courts are coercive, result in greater stigma for the offender, and lead to higher arrest rates for the mentally ill, as police arrest more people due to an increased awareness of treatment options for those with mental illness (Stefan & Winick, 2005). Other concerns are focused on presiding judges, with claims that judges use inappropriate discretionary power and make clinical decisions without concomitant training (Redlich et al., 2006). Despite such concerns, mental health courts and other specialty courts are increasing in number and impact thousands of mentally ill defendants each year.

Do mental health courts actually improve outcomes for mentally ill defendants, and do they decrease recidivism? Surprisingly, relatively little outcome research exists on the effectiveness of mental health courts, and the few studies that have been done offer mixed findings. Herinckx, Swart, Ama, Dolezal, and King (2005) evaluated rearrest rates for 368 mentally ill offenders involved in a mental health court. The authors found that those offenders who graduated from the program were 3.7 times less likely to reoffend as compared to nongraduates. Similarly, Trupin and Richards (2003) found mental health court participants to have lower rates of rearrest as compared to nonparticipants. In contrast, a separate study reported no significant differences in rearrest rates or time to rearrest between defendants enrolled in a mental health court and a comparison group (Christy, Poythress, Boothroyd, Petrila, & Mehra, 2005). Another study found no impact on symptom reduction for mental health court participants (Boothroyd, Mercado, Poythress, Christy, &

Petrila, 2005). Thus, the benefits of these specialty courts to mentally ill offenders and to the larger society are currently unclear.

Drug courts, by comparison, have been well-studied and offer some evidence for their effectiveness in reducing recidivism and decreasing costs (Belenko, 1998). However, evaluation research on drug courts has been fraught with methodological limitations and only recently achieved scientific standards for reliability and validity (Wolff & Pogorzelski, 2005). Continued evaluations are needed in order to determine whether drug courts are more effective than other interventions and to evaluate the components of drug courts that contribute to their effectiveness. Whether dual diagnosed (and multiply-diagnosed) offenders benefit from participation in specialized courts also merits empirical study. History has demonstrated that the number of offenders involved in the U.S. criminal justice system will continue to swell, and identifying alternatives to incarceration will continue to be of significant importance.

ELDERLY OFFENDERS

An emerging issue in U.S. prisons is that of the aging offender population. It has been estimated that between 2005 and 2020 the population of individuals in the U.S. over the age of 65 will grow by 50 percent. By comparison, the population of individuals under the age of 65 is expected to grow by 9 percent (Health Resources and Services Administration, n.d.). Although the proportion of older individuals in corrections is unlikely to increase at the same rate, recent data supports an increase in the overall numbers of older offenders (Aday, 2003), and estimates suggest that long-term offenders over the age of 50 will continue to climb (Chaneles, 1987). Older offenders tend to receive more lenient sentences and are less often incarcerated for similar crimes as compared to other age groups (Steffensmeier & Motivans, 2000). However, there is a sizable number of offenders with sentences of life without parole, 20 years or longer, and many on death row (Chaneles, 1987). Thus, the increase in the older offender population appears to be driven more by long prison terms as compared to a significant rise in offenders entering the system over the age of 50. Although the number of older offenders does not presently represent a crisis for corrections, the increase in this population poses a number of costly problems for the future.

Older offenders have unique medical, mental health, and institutional needs as compared to other offenders. For example, older offenders are believed to suffer from three chronic medical conditions on average (Aday, 1994), resulting in the more frequent use of medical services and potential increased need for prescription medications. They are likely to experience dementia, organic brain syndrome, and other cognitive disorders at higher rates than other offenders. They may experience problems with mobility that are exacerbated by the physical layout of the institution. Many older offenders will experience declines in auditory and visual abilities, as well as reduced physical capabilities, which can make them feel particularly vulnerable in a predatory correctional environment. For those offenders with significant health care problems and disabilities, 24-hour nursing care might be required. Thus, the cost of incarcerating an older person is potentially much greater than that of a younger offender. The needs of this population may be better served in health care settings, but community agencies are often not equipped for managing offenders.

Although correctional facilities will need to develop strategies to manage older offenders on an institution-by-institution basis, policies and programs will need to be created at the federal, state, and local levels to plan for a more comprehensive and long-term approach to solving the complex problems presented by this population. In an effort to describe current approaches for managing older offenders, Aday (1994) surveyed health services administrators for each of the state correctional systems. Approximately half of the states indicated that they house older offenders together and in separate units or facilities from the general population, and about 35 percent of states reported no special programs or housing for older inmates. Some states referred to having "geriatric facilities" for older offenders, but the degree of special programming or services that such facilities provide is unclear. When asked to describe the most pressing problem related to older offenders in their state, administrators overwhelmingly cited rising medical costs and chronic health care needs as the two primary problems. Aday's study is over a decade old, and relatively little has been written on this issue since that time. Research that examines the specific needs of older offenders, costs associated with specialized programs and facilities, and alternatives to incarceration for this population are clearly needed.

End-of-life care also presents challenges for correctional institutions, and many offenders describe the prospect of dying in prison as "the ultimate personal failure" (Dawes, 2002, p. 192). Some correctional systems offer hospice programs to assist with end-of-life care, and these programs are administered by a mixture of medical and mental health staff, community volunteers, and inmate volunteers. Many states have developed compassionate release policies which allow terminally ill offenders to apply for early parole in order to spend time with family and loved ones in the community. This is also referred to as medical parole, and the impetus for such policies appears to be a humanitarian concern for the dying (Boothby & Overduin, in press). In practice, very few offenders are ever released through compassionate release (Beck, 1999;

Kaplan, 2007). The application process must be initiated by a physician in most correctional systems, and the amount of time that passes between application and review can be quite lengthy. Because an offender must be declared terminally ill to apply for medical parole, they often do not have considerable time to live, and delays can result in offenders dying in prison. New York passed a medical parole law in 1992, and by 1997, 610 offenders has applied for early release under this policy. However, 67 percent of those offenders died while waiting for the review process to be completed (Kaplan, 2007). Not surprisingly, a recent study found that individuals living in the community have generally negative attitudes about compassionate release programs (Boothby & Overduin, in press). Thus, it is unlikely that changes in these policies to facilitate a more efficient process will be demanded (or even wanted) by the public.

SEXUAL VICTIMIZATION IN CORRECTIONAL INSTITUTIONS

Sexual violence in prisons is often sensationalized in popular film and media. Despite public knowledge, or at least speculation, about prison rape, relatively little public attention has been directed toward studying or preventing sexual victimization in corrections. By comparison, sexual violence in community settings has received significant public and professional attention, with hundreds of studies being conducted with female and child victims. To date, approximately 15 studies have been conducted on sexual victimization in prisons, and it is estimated that approximately 13 percent of adult offenders have been sexually assaulted during their period of incarceration (Gaes & Goldberg, 2004).

Being the victim of a sexual assault has substantial health and mental health implications. Many offenders experience significant physical injury during the course of an assault, and the risk for infectious disease is also increased. Although it is believed that most cases of HIV are not infected while incarcerated (Braithwaite, Hammett, & Mayberry, 1996), sexual contact substantially increases the risk of HIV and rates of other sexually transmitted diseases, such as gonorrhea and hepatitis. In terms of emotional consequences, inmates who have experienced sexual victimization report heightened depression, anxiety, distrust, and PTSD-like symptoms such as flashbacks (Struckman-Johnson, Struckman-Johnson, Rucker, Bumby, & Donaldson, 1996). Additionally, although most perpetrators of prison rape are other offenders, many cases are described in which correctional staff are the perpetrators. Struckman-Johnson et al. (1996) found that 18 percent of male sexual assault victims reported being victimized by one or more correctional staff. Finally, certain correctional populations seem to be at particular risk for sexual assault, including first-time offenders, mentally ill inmates, and older offenders (P.L. 108-79; Reimer, 2006).

National organizations, such as Human Rights Watch and Amnesty International have long voiced concerns regarding inmate abuse. Only recently, however, has the federal government become actively involved in demanding attention and resources be directed toward the issue of sexual victimization in prison. On September 4, 2003, the Prison Rape Elimination Act (PREA) was signed into law. This legislation describes ambitious goals of determining the incidence of prison rape, developing "standards for the detection, prevention, reduction, and punishment" of sexual assaults in prison, and establishing "a zero tolerance standard" for the occurrence of prison rape (P.L. 108-79, p. 3). PREA's agenda is far-reaching and hopefully results in a long-term commitment to reducing prison rape and developing resources for offender victims. Sexual assault is not an inevitable result of incarceration, and creating a climate of intolerance for such acts is an important goal.

CULTURAL CHALLENGES IN CORRECTIONS

Another emerging issue for corrections is the large influx of foreign-born offenders and non-English speaking offenders into U.S. prisons and jails. A majority of these offenders reside in federal prisons with convictions for illegal entry, illegal alien smuggling, or drug trafficking (Scalia & Litras, 2002). Most offenders incarcerated on immigration charges are from Mexico and have a history of previous convictions, with approximately half of those convictions for felony offenses. The Immigration and Naturalization Service also houses immigrants in detainment facilities, and similar to jails and prisons, these facilities are full. Research has found that individuals living in these facilities have high rates of depression and are subject to sexual assault (Mautino, 2001).

With over 90 nationalities represented in U.S. prisons, language barriers are a significant challenge (Richardson, 2003). Many facilities have correctional staff who are fluent in Spanish, but staff with other language capabilities are likely minimal. Language barriers present challenges for correctional officers in daily interactions with offenders, and health staff also experience difficulties in the assessment and treatment of non-English speaking offenders. For example, how is informed consent obtained and how is an accurate mental health or medical history collected? Although the specific mental health needs of this population are not thought to differ from those of other offenders, immigration offenders often have different medical needs (Richardson, 2003). For example, offenders may be lacking immunizations or may suffer from conditions rarely encountered in the U.S. Additionally, cultural beliefs about health care may impede access to services. Thus, correctional staff who work with foreign-born populations should receive special training in cultural issues relevant to the population they are serving.

Potential methods for addressing language barriers in corrections include the use of translators, phone translator systems, and other telecommunications, such as videoconferencing (Heilman & Lawson, 2000; Richardson, 2003). Videoconferencing allows offenders at one institution to be linked with a translator at a separate location. Behavioral telehealth utilizes similar technology to provide medical and mental health services to offenders, and research has found telehealth to be cost-efficient and largely well-received by offenders (Magaletta, Fagan, & Ax, 1998; Magaletta, Fagan, & Peyrot, 2000). Videoconferencing may have similar benefits for non-English speaking offenders and the larger institution.

THE FUTURE

This chapter has discussed a few of the pressing and emerging issues for U.S. corrections. Many of the challenges discussed stem from broader social problems, particularly the marginalization of certain populations in the U.S., resulting in increased incarceration rates for the mentally ill, substance abusers, and immigrants. Thus, although corrections must develop methods for addressing these issues, substantial change requires changes in public policies. Moreover, U.S. corrections should not have to "reinvent the wheel" in tackling these issues. Correctional administrators would benefit from exploring how correctional systems in other parts of the world address these problems. If not collaboration, certainly communication with international systems would be beneficial. A model of looking to international policy to address American legal issues has been used by some Supreme Court Justices (Toobin, 2005). Justice Anthony Kennedy, for example, has described the use of foreign law as "an inevitable effect of an increasingly interconnected world" (p. 47). Indeed, if American corrections hopes to alter its current path, borrowing policies and practices that have already been evaluated and found successful is an intelligent strategy.

REFERENCES

Abram, K. M., Teplin, L. A., & McClelland, G. M. (2003). Comorbidity of severe psychiatric disorders and substance use disorders among women in jail. *American Journal of Psychiatry, 160,* 1007–1010.

Aday, R. H. (1994). Golden years behind bars: Special programs and facilities for elderly inmates. *Federal Probation, 82,* 47–54.

Aday, R. H. (2003). *Aging prisoners: Crisis in American corrections.* Westport, CT: Praeger.

Beck, J. A. (1999). Compassionate release from New York State prisons: Why are so few getting out? *Journal of Law, Medicine, and Ethics, 27,* 216–233.

Beck, A. J., & Maruschak, L. M. (2001, July). *Mental health treatment in state prisons, 2000* (Bureau of Justice Statistics, NCJ 188215). Washington, DC: National Criminal Justice Reference Service.

Belenko, S. (1998). Research on drug courts: A critical review. *National Drug Court Institute Review, 1,* 1–42.

Boothby, J. L., & Clements, C. B. (2000). A national survey of correctional psychologists. *Criminal Justice and Behavior, 27,* 716–732.

Boothby, J. L., & Overduin, L. Y. (in press). Attitudes regarding the compassionate release of terminally ill offenders. *Prison Journal.*

Boothroyd, R. A., Mercado, C. C., Poythress, N. G., Christy, A., & Petrila, J. (2005). Clinical outcomes of defendants in mental health court. *Psychiatric Services, 56,* 829–834.

Braithwaite, R. L., Hammett, T. M., & Mayberry, R. M. (1996). *Prisons and AIDS: A public health challenge.* San Francisco: Jossey-Bass.

Bureau of Justice Statistics (2003). *Compendium of Federal Justice Statistics, 2003* (NCJ 210299). Washington, DC: National Criminal Justice Reference Service.

Camp, C. G., & Camp, G. M. (1999). *The corrections yearbook 1999: Adult corrections.* Middletown, CT: Criminal Justice Institute.

Catalano, S. M. (2006, September). *Criminal victimization, 2005* (Bureau of Justice Statistics, NJC 214644). Washington, DC: National Criminal Justice Reference Service.

Chaneles, S. (1987, October). Growing old behind bars. *Psychology Today,* pp. 46–51.

Christy, A., Poythress, N. G., Boothroyd, R. A., Petrila, J., & Mehra, S. (2005). Evaluating the efficiency and community safety goals of the Broward County Mental Health Court. *Behavioral Sciences and the Law, 23,* 227–243.

Conklin, T. J., Lincoln, T., & Flanigan, T. P. (1998). A public health model to connect correctional health care with communities. *American Journal of Public Health, 88,* 1249–1250.

Couturier, L., Maue, F., & McVey, C. (2005, April). Releasing inmates with mental illness and co-occurring disorders into the community. *Corrections Today, 67,* 82–85.

Daniel, A. E. (2006). Preventing suicide in prison: A collaborative responsibility of administrative, custodial, and clinical staff. *Journal of the American Academy of Psychiatry and Law, 34,* 165–175.

Dawes, J. (2002). Dying with dignity: Prisoners and terminal illness. *Illness, Crisis, and Loss, 10,* 188–203.

Gaes, G. G., & Goldberg, A. L. (2004). *Prison rape: A critical review of the literature.* Washington, DC: National Institute of Justice.

Gilliard, D. K., & Beck, A. J. (1995, December). *Prisoners at midyear 1995* (Bureau of Justice Statistics, NCJ 158021). Washington, DC: National Criminal Justice Reference Service.

Glaze, L. E., & Palla, S. (2005, November). *Probation and parole in the United States, 2004* (Bureau of Justice Statistics, NJC 210676). Washington, DC: National Criminal Justice Reference Service.

Hammett, T. M., Roberts, C., & Kennedy, S. (2001). Health-related issues in prisoner reentry. *Crime and Delinquency, 47,* 390–409.

Harrison, P. M., & Beck, A. J. (2006a, May). *Prison and jail inmates at midyear 2005* (Bureau of Justice Statistics, NJC 213133). Washington, DC: National Criminal Justice Reference Service.

Harrison, P. M., & Beck, A. J. (2006b, November). *Prisoners in 2005* (Bureau of Justice Statistics, NJC 215092). Washington, DC: National Criminal Justice Reference Service.

Health Resources and Services Administration. (n.d.). *Physician supply and demand: Projections to 2020.* Retrieved on January 17, 2007, from http://bhpr.hrsa.gov/healthworkforce/reports/physiciansupplydemand/growthandaging.htm

Heilman, K., & Lawson, K. M. (2000). Facilitating communication with limited- and non-English speaking offenders. *Corrections Today, 62,* 84–87.

Herinckx, H. A., Swart, S. C., Ama, S. M., Dolezal, C. D., & King, S. (2005). Rearrest and linkage to mental health services among clients of the Clark County Mental Health Court Program. *Psychiatric Services, 56,* 853–857.

Hills, H., Siegfried, C., & Ickowitz, A. (2004). Effective prison mental health services: Guidelines to expand and improve treatment. Washington, DC: U.S. Department of Justice.

Human Rights Watch. (2003). *Ill-equipped: U.S. prisons and offenders with mental illness.* New York: Human Rights Watch.

Jackson, C. E., & Anderson, W. (2004). Washington's biggest crime problem. *Reason online.* Retrieved January 18, 2007, from http://www.reason.com/news/printer/29099.html

James, D. J., & Glaze, L. E. (2006, September). *Mental health problems of prison and jail inmates* (Bureau of Justice Statistics, NJC 213600). Washington, DC: National Criminal Justice Reference Service.

Kaplan, S. (1999, July 12). *Terminally ill prisoners rarely freed under early parole laws.* Retrieved January 18, 2007, from http://www.stateline.org/live/ViewPage.action?siteNodeId=136&languageId=1&contentId=13735

Lincoln, T., & Miles, J. R. (2006). Correctional, public, and community health collaboration in the United States. In M. Puisis (Ed.), *Clinical practice in correctional medicine* (pp. 343–356). Philadelphia: Mosby Elsevier.

Magaletta, P. R., Fagan, T. J., & Ax, R. K. (1998). Advancing psychology services through telehealth in the Federal Bureau of Prisons. *Professional Psychology: Research and Practice, 29,* 543–548.

Magaletta, P. R., Fagan, T. J., & Peyrot, M. F. (2000). Telehealth in the Federal Bureau of Prisons: Inmates' perceptions. *Professional Psychology: Research and Practice, 31,* 497–502.

Manderscheid, R. W., Gravesande, A., & Goldstrom, I. D. (2004). Growth of mental health services in state adult correctional facilities, 1988–2000. *Psychiatric Services, 55,* 869–872.

Mauer, M. (1999). *Race to incarcerate.* New York: W.W. Norton and Company.

Mautino, K. S. (2001). Health issues among detained immigrants. *Journal of Immigrant Health, 3,* 115–117.

Morgan, R. D., Rozycki, A. T., & Wilson, S. (2004). Inmate perceptions of mental health services. *Professional Psychology: Research and Practice, 35,* 389–396.

Office of Justice Programs. (2007). *Reentry.* Retrieved January 12, 2007, from http://www.reentry.gov/

Peters, R. H., & Matthews, C. O. (2003). Substance abuse treatment programs in prisons and jails. In T. J. Fagan & R. K. Ax (Eds.), *Correctional mental health handbook* (pp. 73–99). Thousand Oaks, CA: Sage.

Peters, R. H., May, R. L., & Kearns, W. D. (1992). Drug treatment in jails: Results of a nation-wide survey. *Journal of Criminal Justice, 20,* 283–297.

Pratt, D., Piper, M., Appleby, L., Webb, R., & Shaw, J. (2006). Suicide in recently released prisoners: A population-based cohort study. *Lancet, 368,* 119–123.

Price, B. E. (2006). *Merchandizing prisoners: Who really pays for prison privatization?* Westport, CT: Praeger.

Prison Rape Elimination Act of 2003, P.L. 108-79, 117 Stat. §§ 972-87 (2003).

Redlich, A. D., Steadman, H. J., Monahan, J., Robbins, P. C., & Petrila, J. (2006). Patterns of practice in mental health courts: A national survey. *Law and Human Behavior, 30,* 347–362.

Reimer, G. (2006, October). *The graying of the incarcerated population.* Paper presented at the National Conference on Correctional Health Care, Atlanta, GA.

Rhodes, W., & Gross, M. (1997). *Case management reduces drug use and criminality among drug-involved arrestees: An experimental study of an HIV prevention intervention.* Washington, DC: U.S. Department of Justice.

Richardson, L. (2003). Other special offender populations. In T. J. Fagan & R. K. Ax (Eds.), *Correctional mental health handbook* (pp. 199–216). Thousand Oaks, CA: Sage.

Scalia, J., & Litras, M. F. X. (2002, August). *Immigration offenders in the federal criminal justice system, 2000* (Bureau of Justice Statistics Special Report, NCJ 191745). Washington, DC: National Criminal Justice Reference Service.

Schlosser, E. (1998). The prison-industrial complex. *The Atlantic Monthly, 282* (6), 51–77.

Sheu, M., Hogan, J., Allsworth, J., Stein, M., Vlahov, D., Schoenbaum, E. E., et al. (2002). Continuity of medical care and risk of incarceration in HIV-positive and high-risk HIV-negative women. *Journal of Women's Health, 11,* 743–750.

Solomon, P., Draine, J., & Marcus, S. C. (2002). Predicting incarceration of clients of a psychiatric probation and parole service. *Psychiatric Services, 53,* 50–56.

Solomon, P., Draine, J., & Meyerson, A. (1994). Jail recidivism and receipt of community mental health services. *Hospital and Community Psychiatry, 45,* 793–797.

Stefan, S., & Winick, B. J. (2005). A dialogue on mental health courts. *Psychology, Public Policy, and Law, 11,* 507–526.

Steffensmeier, D, & Motivans, M. (2000). Older men and older women in the arms of criminal law: Offending patterns and sentencing outcomes. *The Journals of Gerontology. Series B: Psychological Sciences and Social Sciences, 55,* 141–151.

Stephan, J. J., & Karberg, J. C. (2003, August). *Census of state and federal correctional facilities, 2000* (Bureau of Justice Statistics, NCJ 198272). Washington, DC: National Criminal Justice Reference Service.

Struckman-Johnson, C., Struckman-Johnson, D., Rucker, L., Bumby, K., & Donaldson, S. (1996). Sexual coercion reported by men and women in prison. *The Journal of Sex Research, 33,* 67–76.

Teplin, L. A. (1984). Criminalizing mental disorder: The comparative arrest rate of the mentally ill. *American Psychologist, 39,* 794–803.

Teplin, L. A. (1994). Psychiatric and substance abuse disorders among male urban jail detainees. *American Journal of Public Health, 84,* 290–293.

Teplin, L. A., Abram, K. M., & McClelland, G. M. (1996). Prevalence of psychiatric disorders among incarcerated women: Pretrial jail detainees. *Archives of General Psychiatry, 53,* 505–512.

Toobin, J. (2005, September 12). Swing shift. *New Yorker, 81,* 42–51.

Torrey, E. F. (2001). *Surviving schizophrenia: A manual for families, consumers, and providers.* New York: Harper Collins.

Trupin, E., & Richards, H. (2003). Seattle's mental health courts: Early indicators of effectiveness. *International Journal of Law and Psychiatry, 26,* 33–53.

Veysey, B. M., Steadman, H. J., Morrissey, J. P., & Johnson, M. (1997). In search of the missing linkages: Continuity of care in U.S. jails. *Behavioral Sciences and the Law, 15,* 383–397.

Wilson, D. J. (2000, May). *Drug use, testing, and treatment in jails* (Bureau of Justice Statistics Special Report, NCJ 179999). Washington, DC: National Criminal Justice Reference Service.

Wolff, N., & Pogorzelski, W. (2005). Measuring the effectiveness of mental health courts: Challenges and recommendations. *Psychology, Public Policy, and Law, 11,* 539–569.

Chapter 3

U.S. PRISONS: A PUBLIC HEALTH PERSPECTIVE

R. Scott Chavez

Our goal is to find that elusive balance between the "care" and "custodial" aspects of correctional health and to develop an integrated strategy of responding to the health care needs of inmates to protect them–and the many people they will encounter when they are released back into their communities.

> U.S. Surgeon General Richard H. Carmona,
> MD, MPH, CCHP (2003)

INTRODUCTION

Surgeon General Carmona succinctly described the objective of U.S. correctional health care, balancing the demands of public safety and public health while providing incarcerated men, women, and juveniles with constitutional levels of care. It is time for the American public, policymakers, and the judicial branch to seriously examine how to more efficiently manage prison health care. In 2000, the rate of active tuberculosis (TB) cases among incarcerated individuals was 10 to 20 times greater than that of the general U.S. population. Latent tuberculosis infection (LTBI), with its prevalence among prisoners estimated to be between 14 and 25 percent, was also a problem. The prevalence of hepatitis C virus (HCV) has been reported to be between 12 to 30 percent within inmate populations (Spaulding et al., 2006). In addition, it is well documented that the rate of human immunodeficiency virus (HIV) among prisoners is five times greater than that of the general U.S. population (National Commission on Correctional Health Care [NCCHC],

2002), while AIDS has been reported as six times greater in incarcerated populations (Dean-Gaitor & Fleming, 1999).

If this was not cause enough to examine how health care is delivered in prisons, prisons have become the "new asylums"–managing serious psychiatric illnesses such as psychoses, schizophrenia, and suicidal behaviors (James & Glaze, 2006). According to James and Glaze, 15 percent of state prisoners and 24 percent of jail inmates report symptoms that meet criteria for a psychotic disorder. Inmates with mental health problems are not necessarily associated with a more serious criminal history (Mateyoke-Scrivner, Webster, Hiller, Staton, & Leukefeld, 2003); however, they are associated with lifestyles such as homelessness, unemployment, and poor hygiene, which make them more susceptible to various infectious diseases.

The time to act is long overdue. Without action, the public's safety and health are put at risk in two major ways when offenders are released. First, releasing offenders expose the community to diseases they might be carrying and consequently may have an impact on the general health of the community. As a result, ". . . the massive movement of individuals into jails and then back to the community must become part of public health interventions to abort disease transmission of a number of important communicable diseases . . ." such as TB and HIV (Lincoln & Miles, 2006, p. 349). Second, there is an added burden to society in cost and health resource utilization to manage undiagnosed or untreated former offenders.

Glaser and Greifinger (1993) raised the issue that opportunities exist to improve the public's health by focusing on correctional health systems. Since that time, many other authorities have argued for improved screening and treatment of prisoners as a means of reducing the burden of disease and protecting the public's health (Institute of Medicine [IOM], 2000; NCCHC, 2002; Hammett, 1998; and National Institute of Corrections [NIC], 2003). What prevents this from happening is lack of a federal mandate, political will, public support, and sufficient resources. In addition, the public may fear criminals, especially those with mental illness, and prefer a simpler solution–that they simply stay behind bars for longer periods of time. The public's fear of the mentally ill and their desire to avoid them is well documented (Link, Phelan, Bresnahan, Stueve, & Pescosolido, 1999). In order to change these conditions, efforts will need to be made to raise the collective consciousness of the general public so they better understand the scope of the problem and the potential extent of public harm.

This chapter describes the key factors needed to improve correctional health services in the U.S. and their implications for improved public health. First, it describes the health disparities occurring in correctional health care systems. Second, it presents strategies necessary to sustain development of public health activity in correctional health care systems. Lastly, it concludes with solutions needed for stronger systems that will improve the delivery of inmate health care in correctional systems.

HEALTH DISPARITIES AMONG PRISONERS

Many health disparities in the U.S. are linked to inequalities in education, income, and race (House & Williams, 2000). With more than two million people confined in U.S. prisons and jails, the incarcerated population is currently 87.7 percent male, 38.6 percent African American, and 15.2 percent Hispanic (Harrison & Beck, 2005). This group is highly representative of the poor and undereducated, resulting in a wide range of disparate health conditions. This will require correctional facilities to assume a far greater burden and share of the public health responsibility in the U.S. than they currently do.

Globalization and immigration also impact U.S. correctional institutions. The prevalence of diseases such as TB, HCV, and HIV in U.S. correctional facilities is attributable in part to foreign born offenders. Estimates regarding the number of foreign born inmates in federal prisons range from 19 percent (Harrison & Beck, 2006) to 25 percent (Bick, 2002a) and it is reported that these offenders have higher incidence rates of diseases like TB (Bick, 2002a). In a study of one New Jersey jail, it was found that LTBI rates were more likely to be positive on a tuberculin skin test if the inmate was foreign born (Hayden, et al., 2005).

Another reason why there is such a wide range of disparate health conditions in U.S. correctional facilities is that incarcerated individuals have not been frequent seekers of health services prior to their incarceration. Research suggests that incarcerated individuals are typically undereducated, underinsured or uninsured; have risky lifestyles associated with drug usage and unprotected sex; and have inconsistent access to health care services. Inmates, then, are patients who generally present to correctional clinics either with undiagnosed diseases/disorders or who are late in the course of their diseases/disorders. Some studies have suggested that the need for prison health services can be predicted based on race, gender, age, education, self-maintenance and adherence to therapy, and access to health services prior to entering prison (Anno, 1997; Garrity, Hiller, Staton, Webster, & Leukefeld, 2002; Marquart, Merianos, Hebert & Carroll, 1997; Lindquist & Lindquist, 1999; Suls, Gaes, & Philo, 1991). It is suggested that poor health behaviors, lack of education, and inadequate access to health services likely determine levels of acuity, chronicity, and health care utilization during incarceration.

Correctional institutions are inadequately prepared to address serious and chronic disease within their populations. Since correctional health care has its roots in a military sick call system, the focus is generally on acute, episodic care (Kim, Shansky, & Schiff, 2006). As a result, specialty care in some areas is not a focus and in many institutions is not readily available. While some effort has been made by correctional systems to bring specialty care to correctional populations (such as through the use of teleradiology or telepsychiatry), these efforts are still not sufficient or widespread. The management of chronic disease, mental health, and communicable disease requires different systems from the management of acute and episodic health problems (Kim, et al., 2006). In fact, evidence has existed for some time now that many prisons and jails are not adequately addressing three infectious and highly communicable diseases in particular–HIV/AIDS, TB and HCV (Hammett, Harmon, & Maruschak, 1999; Macalino et al., 2004). What follows is a discussion regarding the management of these three communicable diseases in U.S. prisons.

HIV/AIDS

There are sharp racial disparities among HIV diagnoses in the U.S. (Centers for Disease Control and Prevention [CDC], 2005). Specifically, the rate of HIV infection among African American males is 103.4 per 100,000. Among African American females, the rate is 53 per 100,000. The rate among White males and females is 15.2 and 2.9 per 100,000, respectively. Additionally, the CDC (2006) reported that for 2003, HIV was the fifth, third, and first leading cause of death for Black males aged 25 to 29, 30 to 34, and 35 to 39 respectively. The rates of HIV diagnosis among Hispanic males (40.4 per 100,000) and females (10.9 per 100,000) are also disproportionately high when compared to their White counterparts. Prisons, which house a disproportionate share of minorities, report HIV rates five times higher than those found in the general population. Yet they do not routinely offer specialized HIV programming (Hammett, et al., 2002). As a result, incarcerated African Americans and Hispanics face a disproportionate increase in HIV risks and a general lack of service (Bernard, Sueker, Colton, Paris, & DeGroot, 2006; Lemelle, 2003; Davis & Pacchiana, 2004). Given this increased risk and lack of service in U.S. prisons, the problems faced by HIV-infected prisoners need to be more adequately addressed. Four particular barriers to effective care are discussed below: stigmatization, cost, continuity of care, and discharge planning.

Under the best of circumstances, being identified as an HIV-infected person can have serious consequences including stigmatization and isolation. These consequences are only magnified in prison. For example, maintaining confidentiality is a major concern and barrier in the care of the HIV-infected prisoner. The manner in which medications are distributed, specialists brought in, or clinics arranged can quickly telegraph to other patients and non-medical staff who has, or is suspected of having, an HIV infection. A few prisons have even segregated their HIV infected prisoners (Maruschak, 2002). Alabama's correctional system is one such system and there have been court actions to challenge this segregation policy. Alabama Rep. Laura Hall (D-Huntsville) who heads the Governor's HIV Commission for Children, Youth and Adults, has said that the segregation policy "deprives HIV-positive inmates of critical opportunities for rehabilitation afforded to the other inmates" (CDC, 2003, p. 1). Stigmatization of HIV infection is difficult to avoid and may be compounded by the way a prison manages this disease. As a matter of good public health and medical ethics, correctional institutions should take precautions to provide HIV care without fostering stigmatization of patients.

A second significant barrier to effective treatment is the cost of care. Although prices of HIV medications have decreased in the past few years, they are still quite expensive and are among the three costliest classes of drugs for prison systems. This is due to the higher prevalence of HIV-infected individuals found in prisons, and to the community standard which mandates aggressive treatment of HIV in order to reduce complications and hospitalizations. Thus, prisons must earmark a disproportionate outlay of their medical resources for the management and treatment of HIV, if these services are to be provided adequately and in conformance with community standards.

Maintaining continuity of care is another difficulty that HIV-infected inmates experience, especially in jails. This is because inmates are constantly either entering or leaving institutions. A regular routine, involving medication management and programming, is difficult to maintain since inmates do not have control over their day-to-day schedule or long-range plans. As a result, HIV case management requires correctional authorities to expend considerable effort on information exchange and coordination. System failures in communication and organization result in poor HIV care and patient outcomes.

As HIV-infected prisoners are being prepared for discharge to the community, significant prison resources must be spent. For example, supplying medications, making appointments for follow-up, and facilitating the acquisition of medical insurance coverage each require staff time to assure that such services are provided. Yet even with such assistance, there is no assurance that discharged prisoners will access community-based HIV clinics for continued treatment. In fact, upon their return to jail or prison, many HIV-infected prisoners are found to be sicker than when they were released from prison because of their failure to adhere to prescribed therapies (Bernard, et al., 2006). This last point may also speak to the need for correctional health care workers to provide inmates with better disease education prior to release and to encourage them to assume more active responsibility for their health care in the community—two additional time-consuming, yet vital services.

Tuberculosis

Although the "... threat of [multi-drug resistant] MDR TB is decreasing, and the transmission of MDR TB in health-care settings continues to decrease because of implementation of infection-control measures and reductions in community rates of TB...." (Jensen, Lambert, Iademarco, & Ridzon, 2005, p. 1), there is evidence that such reductions in TB case rates are not occurring in correctional institutions (MacNeil, Lobato, & Moore, 2005). Using data from the national TB surveillance system from 1993 through 2003, MacNeil, et al. (2005) note that:

> Federal and state prison case rates were 29.4 and 24.2 cases per 100,000 inmates, respectively, which were considerably higher than those in the non-inmate population (6.7 per 100,000 people). Inmates with TB were more likely to have at least 1 TB risk factor compared with non-inmates (60.1% vs. 42.0%, respectively) and to receive directly observed therapy (65.0% vs. 41.0%, respectively); however, they were less likely to complete treatment (76.8% vs. 89.4%, respectively). Among inmates, 58.9% completed treatment within 12 months compared with 73.2% of non-inmates. (p. 1800)

Inmates have a rate of TB that is 17 times higher than that found in the general population. Why do correctional settings harbor so many TB cases? First, TB rates remain high among people living in poverty, migrant workers, foreign-born individuals (especially those from less developed countries), racial and ethnic minorities, those who participate in high risk sexual and drug use activity, and those who fail to adhere to prescribed TB therapy. It is these cohorts that mostly comprise incarcerated populations. Second, the longer a prisoner is held, the more likely it is that he or she will have a positive TB skin test (Bick, 2002b), since the chances of exposure are greater in confined areas like prison and jail cells.

Screening for TB is common in prisons, but not jails. More than 90 percent of state and federal prisons, and about 50 percent of jails, routinely screen for latent TB infection and active TB disease during the initial intake screening process (Bick, 2002a). There is tremendous economic, public health, and social benefit to screening and treating TB in correctional institutions.

First, any realistic expectation to eliminate TB in the U.S. will have to include a commitment for TB eradication among prisoners and foreign born persons. Although most migrant workers and foreign-born nationals are not imprisoned, their generally poor physical and mental health has been documented and they are overrepresented in U.S. jails and prisons. For example, in one study 80 percent of the jailed TB positive inmates were foreign-born Hispanics (Tulsky, White, Dawson, Hoynes, Goldenson, & Schecter, 1998).

Second, TB treatment requires directly observed therapy and prisons can play a large role in that effort, in a cost-efficient manner. Third, success in TB elimination will require public education and the building of coalitions to "help design and implement intensified community TB prevention and control efforts" (CDC, 1992, p.1). Prisons and jails represent one critical point where intensive screening of at-risk populations for TB infection might generate a significant return on the publics' investment of health dollars (Taylor & Nguyen, 2002).

However, TB elimination requires the political will and commitment to ensure that correctional health care system infrastructures are sufficiently supported. To accomplish this, medical directors and staff at federal, state, county, and local public health agencies who advocate, plan, and work at controlling and preventing TB will need to place TB control in correctional institutions at the top of their priority list. Their collective redirection of resources towards jails and prisons can improve TB control in these institutions and ultimately improve the health and safety of the public. However, to accomplish this redirection of resources both community and correctional health care agencies will need to act proactively; define and work toward common goals; plan in multiyear, rather than one year budget cycles, so that initial program start-up costs and subsequent cost benefits can be considered as a whole; and provide appropriate oversight to insure that funds are being used for their intended purpose and desired outcomes are being met.

Hepatitis

Random seroprevalence studies of state correctional facilities in California, Virginia, Connecticut, Maryland, and Texas have found hepatitis C (HCV) infection rates ranging from 29 percent to 42 percent, compared to a 2 percent seropositive rate in the general U.S. population (Spaulding et al., 2006). According to Spaulding, et al. (2006), the prevalence of chronic hepatitis C virus infection in prisons ranges from 12 percent to 31 percent.

With nearly one million inmates infected with the HCV, prisons are currently absorbing the public burden of evaluating and treating this disease. HCV-infected individuals require expert care in hepatology and infectious disease, to which many correctional systems do not have easy access. As a result, the clinical care, prevention, and collaboration needed to provide HCV management to prisoners is extremely costly. Each HCV-infected prisoner's treatment cost is estimated at $14,000 per year (Spaulding et al., 2006). Correctional systems bear these high costs by reducing other nonessential services and finding effective ways for early release.

In describing this situation, Spaulding, et al. (2006) comment:

> There are generally accepted–albeit still evolving–guidelines for identification and treatment of hepatitis C in the community. However, there is less agreement

among health professionals caring for prisoners about best practices for identification, medical management, and treatment of hepatitis C. Inmates often lack
health care before incarceration. In prisons, infected persons could be identified
and the management of infection initiated; however, the high prevalence of
HCV infection among prisoners would impose a disproportionate cost for hepatitis C care on the correctional system. (p. 763)

They conclude by proposing that:

The optimal solution is for prison and public health systems in the United States
to jointly provide targeted HCV testing and standard-of-care hepatitis C medical management, treatment, and prevention programs to prison inmate populations. . . . (p. 765)

SPECIFIC SOLUTIONS FOR PUBLIC HEALTH

Since the solution to the health care problems found in prisons will require
a coordinated effort from both prison and community health officials, it is
important to examine what might be done from a bilateral perspective realiz-
ing that significant barriers must be overcome before a coordinated solution
can be effected. Among the barriers that prevent many public health and correctional systems from coordinating their activities are the lack of communication between agency administrators, separate budget authorizations, and
different governing authorities. These barriers will need to be addressed
before effective coordinated services are possible. However, there are some
prisons and jails that are working with their state and local public health
departments to improve services (Roberts, Kennedy, & Hammett, 2004). For
example, the New York City Department of Corrections at its Rikers Island
facility collaborated with the New York City Department of Health to institute
a voluntary rapid HIV screening program for incoming inmates. This collaboration provided staff training and educational videos and pamphlets for
inmates. In 2003 there were a total of 6,500 voluntary HIV tests performed;
by the end of 2005 there were 26,000 voluntary tests administered. As a result,
New York City was able to test a larger segment of its 60,000 to 65,000 admissions (unique individuals) to Rikers Island and found that while more people
received a positive test result, HIV positive inmates did not represent a higher proportion of all inmates–remaining at approximately two percent positive.
However, there were problems in administering the voluntary test. Either
health staff continued to screen and failed to offer the voluntary test or
dropped it entirely because of staff shortages and increased workload. This
case illustrates the need for consistent training and adequate staffing to implement public health measures in correctional settings.

So what should be done to eliminate these barriers? In 2002, the IOM proposed six action areas to reduce health disparities and improve public health in this country (see Text Box 3.1). Also in 2002, NCCHC concluded a three-year study on inmate health care and proposed numerous recommendations to Congress to improve correctional health care (see Text Box 3.2). Considering these two sets of recommendations may offer some valuable insights, since it will take a two-pronged approach involving public health officials and correctional administrators to effect improvement in correctional health care systems and thus relieve the burden on the U.S. public health system. What follows is a discussion of the IOM and NCCHC recommendations to improve the efficiencies of these two systems.

IOM Recommendations

1. Adopting a population health approach that considers the multiple determinants of health.

The IOM population-based approach focuses on efforts to reduce individual health disparities between and among groups. Research has shown that multiple factors influence the health of a population. Income, employment and working conditions, education, culture, and gender are among these factors (Backlund, Sorlic, & Johnson, 1996; Berkman & Lochner, 2002; Department of Health and Human Services, 2000; Epstein & Avanian, 2001). As a population, incarcerated individuals experience many health disparities and are ideal candidates for targeted health interventions.

TEXT BOX 3.1

Institute of Medicine's Six Action Areas for Public Health Reform (2002)

1. Adopting a population health approach that considers the multiple determinants of health;
2. Strengthening the governmental public health infrastructure, which forms the backbone of the public health system;
3. Building a new generation of intersectoral partnerships that also draw on the perspectives and resources of diverse communities and actively engage them in health action;
4. Developing systems of accountability to assure the quality and availability of public health services;
5. Making evidence the foundation of decision making and the measure of success; and

---

> 6. Enhancing and facilitating communication within the public health system (e.g., among all levels of the governmental public health infrastructure and between public health professionals and community members).

Source: Adapted from Institute of Medicine (U. S.). (2002). Committee on Assuring the Health of the Public in the 21st Century. *The Future of the Public's Health in the 21st Century*. Washington, DC, USA: National Academies Press.

Improvement of health literacy within this group is a population health-based approach that should take priority. The lack of awareness of issues such as sexually transmitted infections, alcohol and tobacco abuse, and violence prevention further detracts from achieving the U.S. Surgeon General's Healthy People 2010 goals (Department of Health and Human Services, 2000) and threatens overall public health. Since the jail setting may be the only access point to the health care system for incarcerated populations, jails and prisons may be the only places where efforts to improve health literacy can be successful with this population. Determinants of health are individually improved when health literacy is raised and individuals assume greater control over their health care outcomes.

A population-based approach also calls for a reduction in factors such as violence and substance abuse that are strongly correlated with criminal behavior. Exposure to violence and criminal behavior can have a direct impact on a person's health and incarcerated individuals are frequently defined by both their high-risk lifestyles and exposure to violence. A population-based approach to treatment, therefore, calls for serious efforts to ameliorate poverty and substance abuse, rather than just maintaining a focus on the treatment of traditional health markers. Without addressing factors such as poverty and addiction, personal change becomes more difficult (see Ax, Chapter 1, for a more detailed discussion of "community" interventions).

Improving health care access for all is important, since "adequate population health cannot be achieved without making comprehensive and affordable health care available to every person residing in the United States" (IOM, 2002, p. 12). Any gains achieved in correctional institutions would be lost if there is no parity in our communities. Society's approach should be inclusive so that health disparities in both incarcerated and nonincarcerated populations are addressed.

However, there are political barriers to reaching this population. Incarcerated men and women have no political cachet. They lack the power to influence decision-makers and legislative agendas. Thus, the impetus for political change will unlikely come from the population itself, but rather must come from advocates (e.g., nongovernmental organizations like Human Rights

Watch or Amnesty International) (see Gallo, Chapter 9, for a more detailed discussion of NGOs) who see solutions to bigger problems through more efficient management of specialized populations or from judicial mandates (e.g., *Estelle v. Gamble*, 1976). Without political vision, direction, and impetus to address this issue and without continued involvement from advocacy groups and/or judicial bodies, little change is likely in this area.

2. Strengthening the governmental public health infrastructure, which forms the backbone of the public health system.

The IOM suggests that all "governmental public health agencies develop strategies to ensure that public health workers who are involved in the provision of essential public health services demonstrate mastery of the core public health competencies appropriate to their jobs" (IOM, 2002, p. 5). Since correctional health systems are an important element in assuring good public health, any discussion involving the public health workforce should be extended to correctional health care workers as well. Credentialing, training, leadership, and support are necessary to strengthen health care delivery systems and assure that the quality of public health services remains consistently high in all venues. Such efforts can also be extended to prisons and jails.

Health promotion and disease prevention efforts improve when multidisciplinary treatment teams are involved. For example, when medical and mental health professionals work together to address behavioral health concerns, health care delivery systems are strengthened. When medical and mental health professionals confer on patients seen by both, efficiencies are created saving time for all staff and improving care to the patient. When security staff are available to efficiently escort patients to their medical or mental health appointments, more patients can be seen. Despite the intuitive appeal of these ideas, not all correctional systems function with such simplicity. Too often, health services operate in "silos" creating barriers to efficient medical and mental health communication.

There is much inefficiency in government, including a lack of coordination between various departments and agencies. With competing goals, service redundancies, shrinking budgets, and a lack of communication between and within governmental agencies, greater cooperation is needed in order to effect change and improve operational efficiencies. Strengthening government, then, also means strengthening the criminal justice system. The creation and use of drug and mental health courts are promising strategies to reduce the involvement of people with substance abuse and mental illness in the criminal justice system. Although the generation of empirical research to determine the effectiveness of drug and mental health courts is still in its infancy, some preliminary data has shown that drug courts appear to create opportunities for defendants to participate in court-supervised treatment, benefiting both individuals and communities by reducing the number of days spent in jail by 75 percent and by reducing crime (Boothroyd, Poythress, McGaha, & Petrila, 2003). More emphasis on strategies such as opioid replacement therapy, mental health courts, jail diversion programs, and community corrections would resolve a number of problems such as jail overcrowding and recidivism.

3. Building a new generation of intersectoral partnerships that also draw on the perspectives and resources of diverse communities and actively engage them in health action.

This IOM recommendation calls for the building of partnerships in order to improve healthy populations and communities. Both public and private agencies face economic realities to do more with less. Public-private and public-public partnerships promote high quality services in a cost-effective manner. As a result, by working together, public and private agencies can create synergisms whereby operational and cost efficiencies are gained within both sectors.

Correctional institutions are constitutionally required to provide adequate health care to inmates for their serious medical needs (*Estelle v. Gamble*, 1976). To meet the demanding medical requirements of the inmate population, a health care delivery system is needed that has sufficient physicians, nurses, mental health specialists, counselors, and dentists. Because of the rising costs of care and personnel, many prison systems find themselves overstretched and unable to provide appropriate health services. One solution has been to rely on outsourcing health care to private companies. By partnering with outside agencies, lawmakers and prison officials have created a competitive environment where health care services can potentially be delivered in a more efficient, cost-effective way without compromising quality. When these partnerships are synergistic, inmate patients and the tax paying public both benefit. However, when government bureaucracy and the profit motive collide, neither society nor inmates benefit.

The public-private partnership is not without controversy. There are those who argue that quality of care is not the ultimate goal of either corrections or the private vendors (Gondles, 2003). However, correctional systems do gain from the technological, economic, managerial, and financial resources of the private vendors and this ultimately results in improved service quality for inmates. In addition, the private sector is more accountable to the public when it participates in private-public partnerships, because of governmental controls over the project.

Public entities can also link together to improve governmental services. For example, prison systems have awarded contracts to state medical schools to provide medical care for their prison populations, thus sharing state resources. This strategy has been shown to have advantages such as "improved quality of care, exposure of students and residents to an important high-risk population, and the linkage of the academic community to underserved" and disparate populations (American College of Physicians–American Society of Internal Medicine, 2000, p. 4).

4. Developing systems of accountability to assure the quality and availability of public health services.

Accountability for services is missing in both the correctional and non-correctional environments. Both claim that it is the other's responsibility to ensure adequate public health services. In many locales, authorities from public health departments and corrections departments do not even engage in a dialog about these issues (Robillard, Garner, Laufer, Ramadan, Barker, Devore et al., 2003).

Correctional authorities often argue that they are being expected to fund a public health mandate without the necessary funds or legal mandate to do so (Gondles, 2003). Ownership of the problem, and its solution, is the first step toward change and expanding public health services. By definition then, health disparity reduction requires an expansion of health care access. To accomplish this, sufficient public health infrastructures are needed in order to improve the quality and availability of public health services in and out of prisons.

What will it take to reduce health disparities? Should corrections and public health departments be mandated to share information, budgets, and staff? Should one super health care agency be created that addresses public health in and out of prison? Should an all out "war" on health disparity be declared to capture public support or should incremental changes in policy be made? Will broad national health care reforms be necessary to ensure access to health services for the disadvantaged and disenfranchised? While there are no clear or easy solutions, at a minimum, the definition of public health should be expanded to include correctional health in order to ensure that correctional health care remains on the public's radar as these issues are debated and solutions proposed.

5. Making evidence the foundation of decision making and the measure of success.

The IOM (2002) recommendation to base and evaluate decisions for change on evidence is both laudatory and correct. Evidenced-based decision making promotes system efficiencies by building consensus among the many stakeholders and by building upon known success. Stakeholders include the public, health professionals, correctional administrators, and courts. However, this begs the question, is there sufficient evidence on what works, especially within correctional health care systems? Most U.S. correctional health care specialists agree that there is a lack of evidence-based studies on incarcerated populations and that one of the first ways of understanding health care needs in prisons is to increase surveillance of chronic and communicable disease.

6. Enhancing and facilitating communication within the public health system (e.g., among all levels of the governmental public health infrastructure and between public health professionals and community members).

The IOM call to enhance communication at all levels of the public health infrastructure should be extended to the criminal justice system. For example, judges often have a faulty understanding of public health issues, arguments, and data (Kerr, 2006). And while correctional administrators may view health services as a necessary support service, they often do not possess a clear understanding of how or what is important in the delivery of these services. Improving the linkages between public health and criminal justice leaders is a major first step toward creating solutions.

SPECIFIC SOLUTIONS FOR CORRECTIONAL HEALTH

One organization that is working toward improving the public health and criminal justice dialogue is the NCCHC, a not-for-profit organization comprised of representatives from 39 public health, medical, legal, and criminal justice organizations. NCCHC's mission is to improve the quality of health care provided in correctional institutions and to extend the continuum of care in a seamless manner from the criminal justice system to the public domain. Just as the IOM's 2002 recommendations sought to improve the public health infrastructure, the NCCHC, also in 2002, issued the *Health Status of Soon-To-Be-Released Inmates* report proposing a series of recommendations to Congress on what is necessary to improve health services provided in U.S. correctional institutions (see Text Box 3.2). The nation's leading correctional health care professionals and researchers, the National Institute of Justice and the CDC, were also involved in this project from the outset and helped in the design and implementation of the study as well as in writing the final report. What follows is a brief synopsis of NCCHC's recommendations.

TEXT BOX 3.2

NCCHC's Summary of Policy Recommendations (2002)

1. Promote surveillance of selected communicable diseases, chronic diseases, and mental illnesses among inmates in all correctional jurisdictions.
2. Promote the use of nationally accepted evidence-based clinical guidelines for prisons and jails to assure appropriate use of resources for pre-

---

venting, diagnosing, and treating selected communicable diseases, common chronic diseases, and mental illnesses that are prevalent among inmates.

3. Establish a federally funded national vaccine program for inmates to protect them and the public from selected vaccine-preventable communicable diseases.

4. Develop and maintain a national literature database for correctional health care professionals, including a compendium of policies, standards, guidelines, and peer-reviewed literature.

5. Establish a national advisory panel on ethical decision making by correctional and health authorities to help them address ethical dilemmas encountered in correctional health care.

6. Identify and eliminate barriers to successful implementation of public health policy.

7. Support research in correctional health care to identify and address problems unique to correctional settings.

8. Improve the delivery of inmate health care in correctional systems.

9. Provide prerelease planning of health care and related services for all soon-to-be-released inmates.

Source: Adapted from National Commission on Correctional Health Care (2002).

Ernest Drucker (2005) observed that the consequences of incarceration affect our communities in multiple ways:

> The impact of incarceration extends well beyond the massive populations in prisons. It has profound consequences for the families and communities who are its principal targets–the Black and Hispanic urban communities, which account for more than 80% of all inmates in the United States. Over 2.5 million school-aged children currently have an incarcerated parent. This has important adverse effects on the mental health of these children and families, both when the family member is put behind bars and after release. Over 600,000 prisoners in the United States reenter the community each year, with powerful consequences for urban community life due to their social, political, and economic disenfranchisement. (p. 164)

Why should the general public care about this issue? Aside from the moral argument that everyone lives under "one tent" and what affects one affects everyone (Jackson, 2000), there are a number of economic, social, ecological, and legislative reasons why the general public should care about incarcerated populations (NCCHC, 2002; Szreter, 1997). Billions of dollars are being spent each year on an industry that is not efficient. From a taxpayer standpoint, it is reasonable to demand that economies be achieved in the way prisons are managed and in how treatment and care is provided to prisoners. In that sense everyone should care.

Additionally, the U.S. has the highest incarceration rate in the world. For some, incarceration has become a way of life—proceeding from one generation to the next. To date, the U.S. response to this issue has been to build and staff more prisons. However, dollars spent on prisons are dollars not spent on education, elder care, road construction, and other projects that benefit the greater good. At what point will taxpayers be unwilling to continue funding new prisons? Also, how a society manages its disenfranchised populations speaks to the kind of society it is. To be a more compassionate, humane society and to break the ever escalating incarceration rates, alternatives to incarceration need to be sought.

It is essential, then, that legislators, correctional administrators, and correctional health care staff begin to alter the way correctional health systems are managed. *The Health Status of Soon-to-be-Released Inmates* report (NCCHC, 2002) provides a reasoned basis for understanding that health care behind bars has a profound effect on the health of our communities. As NCCHC points out, the criminal justice system has a unique opportunity to protect communities by supporting and working with the public health system. NCCHC also argues that public investment in improved correctional health care can result in cost savings to the public. For example, it has been shown that although syphilis screening programs would require initial start-up costs, "the savings in downstream medical costs of syphilis should more than pay for the program" (Kraut, Haddix, Carande-Kulis, & Greifinger, 2002, p. 89).

NCCHC RECOMMENDATIONS

To accomplish greater collaboration between public and correctional health care, NCCHC makes nine key recommendations.

1. Promote surveillance of selected communicable diseases, chronic diseases, and mental illnesses among inmates in all correctional jurisdictions.

The evidence is clear that communicable, chronic diseases and mental illness are disproportionately high among incarcerated individuals. Yet, individual correctional systems really do not have a clear picture of the extent or cost of such diseases/disorders within their systems. Since individual correctional systems can only understand the problem through the use of basic epidemiological techniques, it is imperative that federal/state governments organize integrated surveillance programs to monitor disease and mental illness in U.S. correctional facilities. The collection of health/mental health data and its evaluation assists correctional health officials in characterizing the prevalence and outcomes of disease in their inmate population. This information is critical to plan, implement, and evaluate inmate health/mental health needs. Improved surveillance can lead to a better understanding of the scope of the problem. However, surveillance must be organized and funded (to avoid an unfunded mandate) at the national level, mandating all correctional institutions to screen for and report on specified physical and mental disorders. Without this mandate, there is little incentive for state or local authorities to fund screening and surveillance practices.

2. Promote the use of nationally accepted evidence-based clinical guidelines for prisons and jails to assure appropriate use of resources for preventing, diagnosing, and treating selected communicable diseases, common chronic diseases, and mental illnesses that are prevalent among inmates.

The NCCHC found that few prison systems were systematically using clinical guidelines in the diagnosis and treatment of communicable and chronic disease. Mental disorders were not managed with evidence-based guidelines. Clinical guidelines support clinical decision making "in areas where scientific evidence of the value of selected interventions exists to improve survival and clinical outcomes and to reduce morbidity and the cost of care" (NCCHC, 2002, p. 60). As a result, since its 2002 study, NCCHC has been working with its partner organizations such as the Society of Correctional Physicians and the American Diabetes Association to develop clinical guidelines for the treatment of various adult disorders. These guidelines, posted on the NCCHC website (www.ncchc.org.guidelines) identify key barriers and solutions to the provision of care for common clinical problems such as HIV, hypertension, diabetes, seizure control, high blood lipids, asthma, and schizophrenia. Guidelines for the management of adolescent clinical problems in correctional institutions have also been developed. NCCHC ensures that its clinical guidelines are consistent with nationally accepted disease definitions and evidence-based guidelines used for the general population. NCCHC updates its clinical guidelines as often as necessary.

3. Establish a federally funded national vaccine program for inmates to protect them and the public from selected vaccine-preventable communicable diseases.

NCCHC's study found that correctional institutions do not provide immunizations on a regular basis. The use of immunizations is an important public health strategy that prevents the development of a variety of communicable diseases in individuals. Immunizations have been found to be cost-saving and highly cost-effective. Hepatitis B, poliomyelitis, measles, mumps, and rubella immunizations prevent the transmission of disease to susceptible individuals in confined environments and are promoted by the CDC. Hepatitis A vaccines and advances in vaccine-mediated prevention and immunotherapy of human papilloma viruses (HPV) induced cervical cancer, has promise for eliminating long-term medical/hospital costs associated with the treatment of these diseases (Cohen, 2005). As a result, NCCHC recommends that Congress establish and fund a national vaccine program for the protection of inmates and the general public.

4. Develop and maintain a national literature database for correctional health care professionals, including a compendium of policies, standards, guidelines, and peer-reviewed literature.

Key decision makers and health care clinicians need access to the medical literature in order to make evidence-based decisions. As NCCHC's (2002) study pointed out, correctional health administrators do not have a clear understanding of what does and does not work in correctional health care and existing resources do not provide a literature base with this specificity. A national correctional health care literature database is needed so that key stakeholders in the public health, criminal justice, and legal domains can make informed decisions especially as they relate to correctional health care issues. Where solid empirical literature is absent or deficient, research agendas should be generated and funded.

5. Establish a national advisory panel on ethical decision-making by correctional and health authorities to help them address ethical dilemmas encountered in correctional health care.

Delivery of health care in a criminal justice environment is unique and can sometimes result in conflict and tension between medical and administrative authorities over issues of policy, budgets, priorities, and staffing. Limited opportunity for peer review of medical policies creates an even greater potential for health clinicians to acquiesce to custody policies and minimize health services— thus affecting health of the incarcerated and non-incarcerated populations.

This analysis may also be viewed through the lens of an ethicist. The ethical paradigm to ensure equality of health services in and out of correctional settings demands that systems are operating at full ethical capacity. Thus, a national forum is needed to discuss issues such as confidentiality, informed consent, and management decisions. NCCHC recommended that a national advisory panel on ethical decision-making among correctional and health authorities be created to assist decision-makers in addressing ethical dilemmas encountered in correctional health care.

6. Identify and eliminate barriers to successful implementation of public health policy.

Mirroring the IOM, NCCHC argues that originators of public policy at all government levels should reduce obstructions to effective public health programs both in correctional facilities and the community. One such barrier to good public health policy is the removal of Medicaid benefits for eligible inmates throughout their incarceration. Many states as well as the federal government remove individuals from Medicaid enrollment once they become incarcerated. Upon release, it often takes six to eight weeks for inmates to reenroll in the Medicaid program, which may be too late for many who need medication and follow up care immediately following release. It is NCCHC's recommendation that good public health policy would maintain continuity of ex-offender health care by mandating immediate Medicaid eligibility for those previously covered as soon as they release from a correctional institution. This is merely a step on the road to creating a "seamless" U.S. health care system.

7. Support research in correctional health care to identify and address problems unique to correctional settings.

Since little is known about the epidemiology of disease in correctional populations and the effectiveness of programs implemented to improve inmate health, there is a need to conduct correctional health care research. As such, federal funding is needed for research that identifies barriers to prudent medical/mental health care and good public health practices in correctional institutions.

8. Improve the delivery of inmate health care in correctional systems.

NCCHC's study identified variations in policy and resources (e.g., staffing, funding, and programming) both within and across correctional systems that create inequities in the delivery of health care. Without clearly defined policies and adequate resources, mortality, morbidity, costs, and system operations are affected. As such, congress and appropriate federal agencies should promote improvements to the delivery of inmate health care by "requiring federal, state, and local correctional systems to adhere to nationally recognized standards for the delivery of health care services in corrections" (NCCHC, 2002, p. 62). Change will be forthcoming when correctional systems are given sufficient resources to adhere to national standards and when such funding is linked to performance and adherence to national standards for health care delivery.

9. Provide prerelease planning of health care and related services for all soon-to-be-released inmates.

Finally, NCCHC recommended that federal, state, and local correctional facilities examine the needs of soon-to-be released inmates through extensive prerelease planning. Correctional systems should address the post-release housing, medical, and mental health needs of inmates. Correctional authorities need to take the lead in coordinating discharge planning efforts between correctional, parole, mental health, substance abuse, and public health agencies. Success in prerelease planning and post-release coordination can result in decreased disease transmission and improved public health. In addition, effective discharge planning helps to reduce the community's health care costs for untreated and undertreated illness.

CONCLUSION

Solving the problems of health care disparities is no easy task. Those interested in correctional health care need to "study the problem production system, and find structural interventions that begin to disrupt it" (Burris, 2003, p.151). Correctional health care is a perfect locus to begin change since it impacts health care and social problems on many different levels. The need to increase funding and staffing and to implement changes to the current system is vital to the goal of improving the long-term health of both incarcerated individuals and the general public. The need to develop a public health model in correctional institutions is vital to achieving this goal. Additionally, the public's understanding that correctional institutions are an important part of the larger public health care system and need to be incorporated into community planning and development decisions, is also vital to the long-term success of improved public health.

REFERENCES

American College of Physicians–American Society of Internal Medicine (2000). *Correctional medicine: A public policy paper of the American College of Physicians–American Society of Internal Medicine.* Retrieved August 11, 2006, from www.acponline.org/hpp/pospaper/correct_med.pdf

Anno, J. (1997). Health behavior in prisons and correctional facilities. In D. S. Gochman (Ed.), *Handbook of health behavior research: Vol. 3. Demography, development, and diversity* (pp. 289–303). New York: Plenum.

Backlund, E., Sorlic, P. D., & Johnson, N. J. (1996). The shape of the relationship between income and mortality in the United States: Evidence from the National Longitudinal Mortality Study. *Annals of Epidemiology, 6,* 12–20.

Berkman, L. F., & Lochner, K. A. (2002). Social determinants of health: Meeting at the crossroads. *Health Affairs, 21,* 291–293.

Bernard, K., Sueker, J. J., Colton, E., Paris, J., & DeGroot, A. S. (2006). Provider perspectives about the standard of HIV care in correctional settings and comparison to the community standard of care: How do we measure up? *Infectious Disease in Corrections Report, 9*(3), 1–6.

Bick, J. A. (2002a). Tuberculosis in corrections: 2002 Update. *HIV & Hepatitis Education Prison Project, 5,* 1–2, 4–8.

Bick, J. A. (2002b). Managing pain and end-of-life care for inmate patients: The California Medical Facility experience. *Journal of Correctional Health Care, 9,* 131–147.

Boothroyd, R., Poythress, N., McGaha, A., & Petrila, J. (2003). The Broward mental health court: Process, outcomes and service utilization. *International Journal of Law and Psychiatry, 26,* 55–71.

Burris, S. (2003). Foreword: Envisioning health disparities. *American Journal of Law & Medicine, 29*(2 & 3), 151–158.

Carmona, R. H. (2003, October). *Public Health and Corrections.* Keynote Address, National Commission on Correctional Health Care Conference, Austin, Tx.

Centers for Disease Control and Prevention (1992). Prevention and control of tuberculosis in U.S. communities with at-risk minority populations. Recommendations of the Advisory Council for the Elimination of Tuberculosis. *MMWR Recommendations and Reports, 41*(RR-5), 1–11.

Centers for Disease Control and Prevention (2003, May 1). Alabama: Study says segregating HIV and AIDS prisoners costly. *The CDC HIV, STD, TB Prevention News Update.* Retrieved, January 23, 2007, from http://www.thebody.com/cdc/news_updates_archive/2003/may1_03/aids_prisoners.html

Centers for Disease Control and Prevention (2005). *HIV/AIDS Surveillance Report. Cases of HIV infection and AIDS in the United States and dependent areas, 2005.* Vol 17. Retrieved January 23, 2007, from http://www.cdc.gov/hiv/topics/surveillance/resources/reports/2005report/pdf/2005SurveillanceReport.pdf

Centers for Disease Control and Prevention (2006). *Deaths, percent of total deaths, and death rates for the 15 leading causes of death in 5-year age groups, by race and sex: United States, 2003.* Retrieved January 23, 2007, from http://www.cdc.gov/nchs/data/dvs/lcwk4_2003.pdf

Cohen, J (2005). High hopes and dilemmas for a cervical cancer vaccine. *Science 308,* 618–621.

Davis, L. M. & Pacchiana, S. (2004). Health profile of the state prison population and returning offenders: Public health challenges. *Journal of Correctional Health Care, 10,* 303–331.

Dean-Gaitor, H. D., & Fleming, P. L. (1999). Epidemiology of AIDS in incarcerated persons in the United States, 1994-1996. *AIDS, 13,* 2429–2435.

Department of Health and Human Services (2000). *Healthy people 2010. A systematic approach to health improvement: 1, Vol. 1.* Retrieved September 25, 2006, from: http://www.healthypeople.gov/Document/pdf/uih/2010uih.pdf

Drucker, E. M. (2005). Incarcerated people. In B. S. Levy (Ed.), *Social injustice and public health* (pp. 161–175). Cary, NC: Oxford University Press, Inc.

Epstein, A. M., & Avanian, Z. (2001). Racial disparities in medical care. *New England Journal of Medicine, 344,* 1471–1473.

Estelle v. Gamble, 429 U.S. 97 (1976).

Garrity, T. F., Hiller, M. L., Staton, M., Webster, J. M., & Leukefeld, C. G. (2002). Factors predicting illness and health services use among male Kentucky prisoners with a history of drug abuse. *The Prison Journal, 82,* 295–313.

Glaser, J., & Greifinger, R. B. (1993). Correctional health care: A public health opportunity. *Annals of Internal Medicine, 118,* 139–145.

Gondles, J. (2003, January 25). *Welcoming remarks.* Address presented at Management of Hepatitis C in Prisons Conference, San Antonio, Texas.

Hammett, T. M. (1998, July). *Public health/corrections collaborations: Prevention and treatment of HIV/AIDS, STDs, and TB.* Washington, DC: National Institute of Justice/Centers for Disease Control and Prevention, Office of Justice Programs, U.S. Department of Justice.

Hammett, T. M., Harmon, P. & Maruschak, L. M. (1999). *1996–1997 Update: HIV/AIDS, STDs, and TB in correctional facilities, issues and practices* (National Institute of Justice Report, NCJ 176344). Washington, DC: U.S. Department of Justice.

Hammett, T. M., Harmon, M. P., & Rhodes, W., (2002). The burden of infectious disease among inmates of and releasees from U.S. correctional facilities. *American Journal of Public Health, 92,* 1789–1794.

Harrison, P. M., & Beck, A. J. (2006, May). *Prison and jail inmates at midyear 2005* (Bureau of Justice Statistics Special Report, NCJ 213133). Washington, DC: National Criminal Justice Reference Service.

Hayden, C. H., Mangura, B. T., Channer, I., Patterson, G. E., Passannante, M. R., & Reichman, L. B. (2005). Tuberculin testing and treatment of latent TB infection among long–term jail inmates. *Journal of Correctional Health Care, 11,* 99–117.

House, J. S., & Williams, D. R. (2000). Understanding and reducing socioeconomic and racial/ethnic disparities in health. In B. D. Smedley & S. L. Syme, (Eds.), *Promoting health: Intervention strategies from social and behavioral research.* (pp. 81–124). National Academy Press: Washington, DC.

Institute of Medicine (U. S.). (2002). *The Future of the Public's Health in the 21st Century.* (A report prepared by the Committee on Assuring the Health of the Public in the 21st Century).Washington, DC: National Academies Press.

Jackson, J. (2000, September). *Opening session presentation.* Address presented at the 24th National Conference on Correctional Health Care, St. Louis, MO.

James, D. J. & Glaze, L. E. (2006, September). *Mental health problems of prison and jail inmates* (Bureau of Justice Statistics, Special Report, NCJ 213600). Washington, DC: National Criminal Justice Reference Service.

Jensen, P. A., Lambert, L. A., Lademarco, M. F., & Ridzon, R. (2005). Guidelines for preventing the transmission of Mycobacterium tuberculosis in health-care settings. *MMWR Recommendations and Reports, 54* (RR17), 1–141.

Kerr, T. (2006, August 15). Reconsidering the public health failings of the criminal justice system: A reflection on the case of Scott Ortiz. *Harm Reduction Journal, 3* (1), 25.

Kim, S., Shansky, R., & Schiff, G. D. (2006). Using performance improvement measurement to improve chronic disease management in prisons. In M. Puisis (Ed.), *Clinical practice in correctional medicine* (2nd ed., pp. 503-509). Philadelphia: Mosby Elsevier.

Kraut, J. R., Haddix, A. C., Carande-Kulis, V., & Greifinger, R. B. (2002). Cost-effectiveness of routine screening for sexually transmitted diseases among inmates in United States prisons and jails. In National Commission on Correctional Health Care, *Health Status of the Soon to be Released Inmate: Vol. 2* (pp. 81–108). Chicago: Author. Retrieved August 2, 2006 from http://www.ncchc .org/stbr/Volume2/Report5_Kraut.pdf.

Lemelle, A. J., Jr. (2003). Linking the structure of African American criminalization to the spread of HIV/AIDS. *Journal of Contemporary Criminal Justice, 19,* 270–292.

Lincoln, T. & Miles, J. (2006). Correctional, public, and community health collaboration in the United States. In M. Puisis (Ed.), *Clinical practice in correctional medicine* (2nd ed., pp. 343–356). Philadelphia: Mosby Elsevier.

Lindquist, C. H., & Lindquist, C. A. (1999). Health behind bars: Utilization and evaluation of medical care among jail inmates. *Journal of Community Health, 24,* 285–303.

Link, B. G., Phelan, J. C., Bresnahan, M., Stueve, A., & Pescosolido, B. A. (1999). Public conceptions of mental illness: Labels, causes, dangerousness, and social distance. *American Journal of Public Health, 89,* 1328–1333.

Macalino, G. E., Vlahov, D., Sanford-Colby, S., Patel, S., Sabin, K., Salas, C., et al. (2004). Prevalence and incidence of HIV, hepatitis B virus, and hepatitis C virus infections among males in Rhode Island prisons. *American Journal of Public Health, 94,* 1218–1223.

MacNeil, J. R., Lobato, M. N., & Moore, M. (2005). An unanswered health disparity: tuberculosis among correctional inmates, 1993 through 2003. *American Journal of Public Health, 95,* 1800–1805.

Marquart, J.W., Merianos, D. E., Hebert, J. L., & Carroll, L. (1997). Health conditions and prisoners: A review of research and emerging areas of inquiry. *The Prison Journal, 77,* 184–208.

Maruschak, L. (2002, October). *HIV in prisons, 2000* (Bureau of Justice Statistics, Special Report, NCJ 196023). Washington, DC: National Criminal Justice Reference Service.

Mateyoke-Scrivner, A., Webster, J. M., Hiller, M. L., Staton, M. & Leukefeld, C. (2003). Criminal history, physical and mental health, substance abuse, and services use among incarcerated substance abusers. *Journal of Contemporary Criminal Justice, 19,* 82–97.

National Commission on Correctional Health Care. (2002). *The health status of soon-to-be-released inmates: Vols. I and II.* Retrieved October 12, 2006, from http://www .ncchc.org/pubs/pubs_stbr.html

National Institute of Corrections (2003). *Special Issues in Corrections: Corrections agency collaborations with public health.* U.S. Department of Justice, Washington, DC. Retrieved January 23, 2007, from http://www.nicic.org/Downloads/pdf/2003/ 019101.pdf

Roberts, C., Kennedy, S. & Hammett, T. M. (2004). Linkages between in-prison and community-based health services. *Journal of Correctional Health Care, 10,* 333–368.

Robillard, A. G., Garner, J. E., Laufer, F. N., Ramadan, A., Barker, T. A., Devore, B. S., et al. (2003). CDC/HRSA HIV/AIDS intervention, prevention, and continuity of care demonstration project for incarcerated individuals within correctional settings and the community: Part I, a description of corrections demonstration project activities. *Journal of Correctional Health Care, 9,* 453–486.

Spaulding, A. C., Weinbaum, C. M., Lau, D. T., Sterling, R., Seeff, L. B., Margolis, H. S. et al. (2006). A framework for management of hepatitis C in prisons. *Annals of Internal Medicine, 144,* 762–769.

Suls, J., Gaes, G., & Philo, V. (1991). Stress and illness behavior in prison: Effects of life events, self-care attitudes, and race. *Journal of Prison & Jail Health, 10,* 117–132.

Szreter, S. (1997). Economic growth, disruption, deprivation, disease, and death: On the importance of the politics of public health for development. *Population and Development Review, 23,* 693. Retrieved August 2, 2006, from Questia database: http://www.questia.com/PM.qst?a=o&d=5000586895

Taylor, Z. & Nguyen, C. (2002). Cost-effectiveness of preventing tuberculosis in prison populations. In National Commission on Correctional Health Care (Ed.), *Health status of the soon to be released inmate: Vol. II* (pp. 109–124). Retrieved October 12, 2006, from http://www.ncchc.org/stbr/Volume2/Report6_Taylor.pdf

Tulsky, J. P., White, M. C., Dawson, C., Hoynes, T. M., Goldenson, J., & Schecter, G. (1998). Screening for tuberculosis in jail and clinic follow-up after release. *American Journal of Public Health, 88,* 223–226.

PART II

CORRECTIONS AND MENTAL HEALTH IN THE WESTERN EUROPEAN TRADITION

Chapter 4

PSYCHOLOGICAL SERVICES IN ENGLISH AND WELSH PRISONS

Graham Towl and David Crighton

INTRODUCTION

Correctional Services in the United Kingdom (UK) are divided into three separate national systems. Scotland and Northern Ireland have separate and largely autonomous systems. England and Wales is by far the largest correctional system and is the focus of this chapter.

England and Wales is, in terms of land mass, slightly smaller than Oregon but has a population of just over 50 million people (Office of National Statistics, 2006). There is thus a relatively high population density, with the majority of people living in highly urbanised areas. It is also a multicultural society with a broad mix of ethnic backgrounds found. This is not a new phenomenon with immigration to England being evident from the time of the Roman Empire and before. It has, though, accelerated in recent years driven, largely, by immigration from parts of the old British Empire. At the turn of the twentieth century there were large influxes of Irish immigrants, the 1930s and 1940s saw fresh influxes of primarily Jewish European immigrants, the 1950s and 1960s saw immigration primarily from former British Empire nations and in particular the Caribbean, India and Pakistan. Today, the majority of immigrants are from Eastern Europe.

Historically, England and Wales was a major industrial country but has experienced a period of relative decline of its traditional heavy industries such as shipbuilding, coal mining and manufacturing, with a growth in service sectors. Unemployment across the UK is running at around one million, representing a slightly higher proportion of the working age population than in the USA but somewhat lower than most other European countries. All the UK countries are part of the European Union (EU) and European Economic Area

(EEA) and are subject to European laws which are increasingly influencing English law. As in the USA the legal system is based on Common Law.

Accountability for corrections in England and Wales rests with the Ministry of Justice, the Government department which also has responsibility for areas such as the Courts, Policing and Immigration. Correctional services are organised within the recently established National Offender Management Service (NOMS) which brings custodial (prisons) and community (probation) services more closely together. Although prisons and probation remain, at present, separate services they are being required to work more closely together, to ensure effective continuity in work with offenders (Carter, 2003; Home Office, 2003; 2004; Towl & Crighton, 2005).

Prison services are delivered through a mix of state and private providers. The vast majority of prisons are managed by the state agency Public Sector Prisons. A small number of prisons are managed by private companies on the basis of service level agreements with NOMS. Correctional services such as prisoner transportation between the courts and prisons are currently delivered by private sector companies under contract.

Health care is provided from a form of state insurance via the National Health Service (NHS). This means that residents of the UK can access most types of necessary health care free at the point of service delivery, but it is paid for by taxation. In recent years responsibility for health care with prisoners has also passed to the NHS. It had previously been the responsibility of an in-house Prison Health Service.

It is clear that correctional settings hold large numbers of people with very significant needs. The vast majority of these could, in the broad sense, be conceptualised as psychological. However, within this chapter the focus is very much on those key areas where psychological interventions have had the greatest input to date.

Having outlined the needs presented within correctional settings, recent approaches to addressing these are considered. There has been a significant growth in the use of psychological interventions across mental health, substance misuse and offence focused psychological therapies and these three areas are the focus for the discussion.

THE PRISON POPULATION

In September 2006, the prison population stood at 79,355 with projections showing continued growth in numbers (National Offender Management Service, 2006). There has been almost continuous growth in the proportion of people sent to prison since the 1950s with, in recent years, a marked acceleration in the rate of growth. The rate of imprisonment in England and Wales in 2006 was approximately 145 per 100,000 of population. This gives England and Wales one of the highest rates of imprisonment in Europe, well above the rates for comparable Western European nations such as Germany, at 95 per 100,000, and France, at 88 per 100,000.[1] Rates of imprisonment, though, remain well below the rates seen in the United States: 738 per 100,000, and also the rates seen in Russia and some former Eastern European countries (International Centre for Prison Studies, 2006).

The prison population in England and Wales share many characteristics seen internationally. As a group they show high concentrations of people with physical health, mental health, and what might broadly be termed socio-economic disadvantages. The action and interaction of such difficulties and the relationship of these to criminal behaviour remains poorly understood (Crighton, 2004; McNeil, Batchelor, Burnett, & Knox, 2005; Towl, 2005a; 2006).

Coherent models for what might broadly be termed the public health needs of prisoners are largely lacking, although recent efforts have been made in this area (Towl & Crighton, in press). This model recognises that prisoners may have a broad range of difficulties. Such needs might productively be seen as hierarchical with basic needs such as food and shelter, underpinning more complex needs (Maslow, 1970).

Figure 4.1 Hierarchy of Needs.

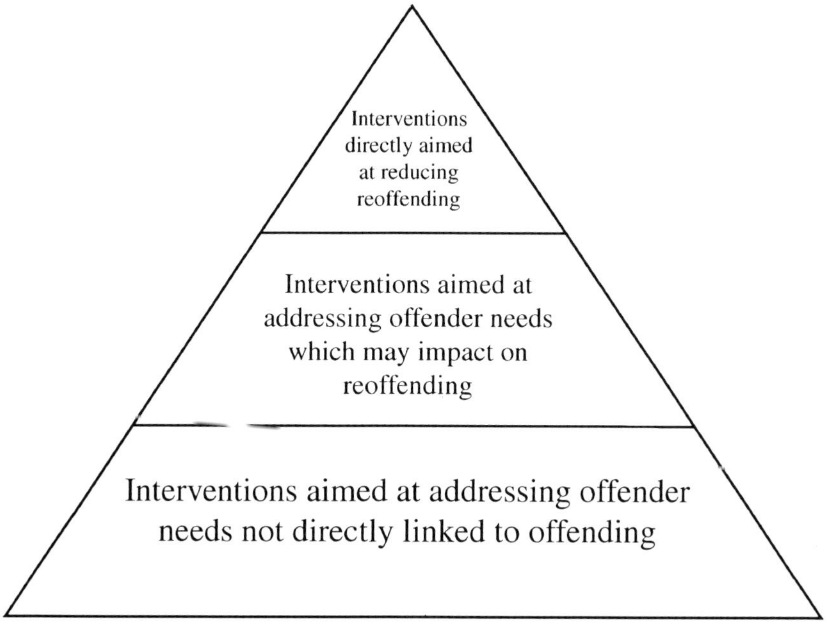

In 2002, the UK Government's Social Exclusion Unit, based in the then Office of the Deputy Prime Minister, published a highly influential report entitled "Reducing Re-offending by Ex-prisoners" (Social Exclusion Unit, 2002). The report provided a wide-ranging summary of the factors linked to reoffending amongst prisoners. The report drew on a broad evidence base in drawing conclusions about the most promising approaches to tackling reoffending.

The report outlined the considerable challenges involved in work with prisoners and ex-prisoners. It noted the finding that amongst 18–20-year-old prisoners in England and Wales, 72 percent went on to be reconvicted within two years of release from prison and nearly half (47%) were back in custody. The cost of recorded crime by ex-prisoners was estimated at eleven billion pounds per year. The cost of keeping a person in prison averaged £37,500 per year (Social Exclusion Unit, 2002). At the rate of exchange that applied in November 2006 this equates to around $71,000.

Recorded crime in turn was estimated to account for between a quarter and a tenth of crime actually occurring in England and Wales. This suggests that the financial cost of the crimes of ex-prisoners might be multiplied by a factor of between 4 and 10. This is setting aside the emotional and social costs of crime, which cannot convincingly be assessed in financial terms. The report concluded that there are very good economic and social reasons to intervene to improve the outlook of prisoners on release.

The Social Exclusion Unit (SEU) report went on to highlight nine major factors that linked to the causes of crime—education, employment, drug and alcohol misuse, mental and physical health, attitudes and self-control, institutionalisation and life skills, housing, financial support and debt and finally family networks. Each of these problem areas was relatively more common amongst prisoners. Employment and accommodation provide strong illustrative examples. A high proportion of prisoners are without regular employment prior to imprisonment and many are unemployed on discharge from prison. Yet by being in employment the level of risk of reoffending is reduced by between a third and a half. Likewise, those in stable accommodation have a reduced level of risk by about one-fifth but a high proportion of prisoners were found to have no stable accommodation on discharge from prison (Social Exclusion Unit, 2002).

In terms of background experiences, prisoners often present with a range of adverse experiences. They are 13 times more likely than the general population to have been placed in the care of social services as a child and to be unemployed. Educational skills are typically poor, with low levels of literacy and numeracy, in turn making it harder to gain employment. Imprisonment itself may act to increase the risk of reoffending by removing some potential protective factors. Of those prisoners who have been in employment immediately prior to their imprisonment two-thirds lost their job, around a third lose their accommodation whilst in prison.

Public Health Needs

Mental health has been widely recognised as a significant issue within the prison population and the mental health of prisoners has been subject to extensive study. Such studies present a number of significant methodological challenges, many of which are common across the mental health field.

The most detailed study of the prevalence of mental disorder amongst prisoners in England and Wales was undertaken in 1997. Baseline data on the mental health of male and female prisoners across age groups was collected (Singleton, Meltzer, & Gatward, 1998). The study focussed on mental disorder rather than broader mental health issues. The research involved a large sample size (n = 3,563) with 88 percent of these (3142) being interviewed by research staff. The study used sample fractions; 1 in 34 for sentenced men, one in eight for remanded men and one in three for women prisoners.

Diagnostic and Statistical Manual IV (DSM IV) (American Psychiatric Association, 1994) categories of mental disorders were used. It was found that 78 percent of male remand prisoners, 64 percent of male sentenced prisoners and 31 percent of female prisoners met the criteria for "personality disorders," anti-social personality disorder being the most common reported category. Prisoners categorised as having personality disorders tended to be young, unmarried, White and charged with acquisitive offences.

The rates of those meeting the criteria for psychotic disorders across all those studied ranged between 4 percent and 21 percent with the rates for sentenced prisoners being around 4 percent. The rates for psychotic disorders amongst women on remand were higher than those for men. These figures, though, included psychotic experiences for up to a year before the interviews took place. This suggests that some of the psychotic experiences may have happened prior to imprisonment and some of those assessed as being within this group would not have shown current psychotic symptoms.

Levels of administration of prescription drugs were relatively high. About half of the women prisoners studied were prescribed drugs and about a fifth of men. Prisoners were commonly prescribed hypnotics, anxiolytics and antipsychotic drugs.

Victims and perpetrators of crimes are by no means located within mutually exclusive categories, with prisoners as a group showing high levels of victimisation. One in three women prisoners reported that they have been victims of sexual abuse. The figure for men was lower but still very high at one in ten men. This is a striking finding and given the well documented high levels of underreporting of sexual crimes this may underestimate the actual levels of sexual abuse. Women prisoners in particular also reported high levels of having been the victims of family violence (Singleton et al., 1998).

The combination of high levels of being victims of crime and the manifestation of behaviours associated with mental disorders combine to result in a group of people with potentially very high levels of mental health needs. This problem is exacerbated by what appears often to be a professional reluctance to work with this group of people notwithstanding these levels of need.

Broadly defined notions of "self-harm" including suicidal ideation, suicide and intentional self-injury and poisoning were considered within this study. It was reported that two percent of men on remand reported attempting suicide in the previous week. Overall remand prisoners reported slightly higher levels of suicidal ideation and attempts. In general there appears to have been higher rates of "self-harm" as broadly defined for White prisoners than Black prisoners. This is consistent with the UK large scale record based studies into prisoner suicides (Crighton & Towl, 1997; Towl & Crighton, 1998; Crighton, 2002; Crighton & Towl, 2002). Prisoners have been assessed as presenting a much higher risk of suicide than those in the general community, particularly during the early stages in custody. However, it is unclear the extent to which this is due to the nature of the prison environment and the extent to which it is due to the increased social and economic disadvantages of those coming into prison custody (Crighton & Towl, 2002; Towl & Crighton, 1998).

Drug and alcohol abuse were both found to be common problems for prisoners in England and Wales. Alcohol was the most commonly misused drug, with 63 percent of men and 39 percent of women prisoners reporting a history of excessive alcohol use. The rates of misuse for White prisoners were just under double the rate reported for Black and Asian prisoners. White prisoners were also more likely to report misuse of opiates and/or stimulants. Women prisoners held on remand had the highest reported levels of injecting drug use, with 28 percent reporting that they had injected drugs in the month before their imprisonment and 40 percent having injected drugs at some time. Overall just under half of prisoners were reported to have a measure of dependence on drugs in the year before their imprisonment. There are some marked age related differences in reported drug misuse with a strong inverse association between dependence on drugs in the year prior to imprisonment and age. Drug use in prisons, as in the community, was most prevalent in the young. Married individuals were also less likely to report drug misuse.

As in the United States, prisons in England and Wales also contain relatively high proportions of those with serious physical health problems, such as HIV, Hepatitis B, tuberculosis (including drug resistant varieties) and a range of other physical health problems. In the early 1990s government policy set a focus on five aspects of health related behaviours; smoking, drinking, drug use, physical activity levels and diet. In seeking to take this policy forward health care services in prisons commissioned a national survey of the physical health of male prisoners (Bridgwood & Malbon, 1995).

The survey of prisoners aimed at working with a representative sample (n= 992) of sentenced male prisoners. The study revealed a great deal about the health status of prisoners and is a key source document in this important area. The sample covered 32 of 139 prisons, with 85 percent of prisoners who were approached agreeing to take part. The study found a prison population on average markedly younger than the general population. However, the age-based differences did suggest the need for caution in comparisons with any global notions of "the general population."

Smoking was reported as commonplace in prisons, with prisoners aged 18–49 being more than twice as likely to be smokers compared to the general population. There was a slight increase in the percentages reporting smoking amongst younger age groups (16–24 year olds when compared with the overall figure for prisoners which was 81%).

Amongst prisoners under age 21 years, 82 percent reported heavy alcohol use compared with 25 percent amongst those prisoners in the 45 and over age band. Heavy alcohol use is implicated in much of the violent crime in England and Wales. It is also something of a health time bomb with increasing rates of physical health problems due to excessive alcohol consumption amongst many in younger age groups.

In other areas of physical health prisoners, especially younger prisoners, fare somewhat better. This was reflected in some of the physical measures studied. Prisoners tended to have lower Body Mass Index (BMI) scores than the general population, suggesting lower levels of obesity. Such comparisons, as noted above, do however depend on careful matching of prison and general population groups and it is possible that this may, at least in part, account for such findings. The reasons for such apparent differences are unclear but may be linked to increased access to and use of sports facilities in prison. It may also be linked to prisoner's access to a better balanced diet in prison compared to eating habits outside and reported eating less sweets, biscuits and cakes. In this area prisoners were healthier than their general population peers with rates of obesity measured at 6 percent of the prisoner population compared with 12 percent of the general population. Problems associated with obesity were also less common in prisoners, with systolic blood pressure being lower than the general population.

WORK WITH PRISONERS

Health Interventions

In 2001, the Department of Health for England and Wales (Department of Health, 2001) published a document which introduced policy in relation to mental health care for prisoners. In relation to prisons this document stressed the need for mental health work to be more effectively integrated between prisons and the community and better linked to interventions to address drug misuse. It set targets for improving the work of community based mental health teams in prisons, with funding for dedicated staff for this role.

A major objective of the changes brought about was to ensure that prisoners identified as mentally ill or mentally handicapped could be treated in hospitals rather than prisons, as far as possible. In addition, standards for mental health care in prisons were to be brought into line with those available to the general population (Cinamon & Bradshaw, 2005; Lane-Morton, 2005). This approach has a number of additional benefits since prisons tend to hold large numbers of people with mental health problems who would be difficult to reach when in the community. For example, those with mental illness and drug use problems, sometimes termed "dual diagnosis" frequently enter prisons. It should be noted, though, that levels and patterns of health care delivered to the UK population by the NHS can vary markedly by geographical area. So in this sense the notion of baselining care against that for the general population can be problematic.

In achieving notions of parity the underlying approach has stressed broad equivalence of services, partnership working across relevant agencies and the transfer of services and commissioning for services to the NHS (Cinamon & Bradshaw, 2005). In practical terms this has involved the development of primary health care services along the lines of general practice in the community, with greater use of multidisciplinary teams to address a broader range of health needs. A greater stress on the prevention of illness has also been central, alongside improved health education services and access to specialist health care services (Department of Health, 2002).

Policy for the development of mental health services was set out in a publication called "Changing the Outlook" (Department of Health, 2001). In relation to prisons this has involved improving the provision of multidisciplinary mental health teams providing visiting services (often termed 'in-reach'). By 2004, an extra 320 specialist mental health staff had been employed in such roles. The National Institute of Mental Health, working in collaboration with the Prison Service's Safer Custody Unit had also developed eight regional forums, to help implement best practice in reducing levels of suicide and self-injury in prisons (Cinamon & Bradshaw, 2005; Sedenu, 2005).

Historically, interventions in more public health-related areas has have been patchy but with some notably positive efforts (Curran, McHugh and Nooney, 1989). Significant investment has recently been made into the improved prevention and management of infectious diseases, by implementing effective public health models in prisons. Examples here include the provision of hepatitis B vaccination and improved provision of sexual health services in prisons (Cinamon & Bradshaw, 2005; Lee & George, 2005).

Provision of condoms in prisons for the prevention of HIV and other sexually transmitted infections has been a matter of debate in the UK and internationally from the 1980s. Progress in this area in England and Wales has been relatively slow but in 1991 prisons began to introduce schemes for prisoners being released from custody (permanently or temporarily) giving them access to condoms. A review by the AIDS Advisory Committee in 1995 recommended on public health grounds that all prisons should introduce such schemes for male prisoners while serving their sentences. This Committee similarly called for dental dams to be made available to women prisoners (MacDonald & Berto, 2002). All the recommendations made were accepted except for the suggestion that condoms should be made available to male prisoners during sentence. There is therefore no national scheme for general availability of condoms, although senior managers are not prevented from distributing condoms within their prisons. Given the lack of general availability of condoms, there were concerns about the potential legal liability of prison health care staff if a prisoner contracted HIV or other infection sexually while in prison. For this reason the then Director of Health Care issued guidance which encouraged doctors in prisons to prescribe condoms and lubricants to individual prisoners, when there was judged to be a risk of HIV infection through sexual behaviour (British Medical Association Foundation for AIDS, 1997).

In theory this means that prisoners can access condoms but the reality of this compromise situation has been subject to criticism. It has been noted that condoms are not easily available in most prisons (British Medical Association Foundation for AIDS, 1997). It has also been argued that in practice it is normally difficult for prisoners to obtain condoms and to do so in a confidential way, which acts against prisoners taking up this service (MacDonald & Berto, 2002).

The question of needle exchange has, if anything, been more problematic. Current policy in England and Wales involves provision of advice about harm minimisation. In a number of prisons equipment to sterilize needles may be made available, for example where there has been an outbreak of blood-borne infections. However, the issuing of clean needles has not been taken forward (HM Prison Service, 1999). In this respect practice in England and Wales is somewhat behind that seen in other European countries, where needle exchange within prisons has been implemented on a similar basis to that that available in community settings (Dolan, Rutter & Wodak, 2003).

Drug Use Interventions

Estimating the prevalence of problem drug use is not straightforward and estimates vary significantly in this area. It has been estimated that there are at least 250,000 problem drug users in England and Wales and a relatively high proportion of this group will, at one time or another, be located in prisons. A comprehensive drug strategy was introduced to prisons in 1998 and updated in 2002 (Lee & George, 2005). This strategy has since been amalgamated with the NOMS strategy for addressing drug use and has three main themes:

1. Reducing demand through effective treatment interventions
2. Reducing supply in prisons
3. Building and maintaining effective thoroughcare

Drugs are probably less available in prisons than in the community and this provides an ideal chance for prisoners to address their drug use. A variety of clinical services have been put in place to assist with this.

A key part of the work undertaken with prisoners has been the development of clinical services in line with those available in the community. This has involved the implementation of effective clinical assessment and intervention work with those entering custody. Such prisoners often experience marked withdrawal on entering custody. The response to this varies depending on the individual's health history and the drugs they have been using. It will generally, though, involve pharmacological and psychological interventions to reduce symptoms of withdrawal.

Broad based intervention work is available under the "CARATS" scheme, which stands for Counselling, Assessment, Referral and Throughcare scheme. This scheme provides prisoners with access to initial counselling on drug use and an assessment of their needs. The scheme is also concerned with accessing prisoners to mainstream health and voluntary services to address their treatment needs. It has been described as a low-level intervention but includes a range of interventions including group-based work, individual counselling, advice on harm minimisation and relapse prevention (Lee & George, 2005).

A wide range of interventions have been implemented across prisons. In 1997 nine systematic interventions were being delivered in prisons. By 2005 this had increased to 120 running in 103 prisons (Lee & George, 2005). The approaches used can be characterised as being within one of three main traditions of what may be broadly termed psychological therapies: cognitive-behavioural interventions, 12-step approaches similar to that used by Alcoholics Anonymous, and therapeutic communities.

Supply reduction and the testing of prisoners for drug use has also been a key part of the strategy put in place. Concerted efforts have been made to reduce the smuggling of drugs into prisons, although such efforts need to be balanced against maintaining a humane regime and the unacceptably high costs of trying to end all drug supply. Mandatory Drug Testing (MDT) of a random sample of prisoners each month has also been introduced. This serves to monitor levels of drug use in prisons and may also act to deter use. Those failing mandatory drug tests face disciplinary sanctions including having days added to their sentence. Additional efforts to control supply within prisons includes the systematic use of intelligence to target those thought to be supplying and misusing drugs, involving joint work with police services. Controls in prison visits areas have also been increased with the use of Closed Circuit Television (CCTV) surveillance. Visits areas have also been redesigned to make it more difficult to pass drugs undetected.

It is currently possible for prisoners to agree to voluntary contracts for drug testing and become liable to a minimum of 18 drug tests per year. This provides a means of helping prisoners to remain free from drug use. Such prisoners also become eligible for additional benefits within prison and are likely to be viewed more favourably when considered for parole. Other prisoners may be subject to mandatory drug tests with disciplinary sanctions being applied when results are positive.

Central Government policy is that interventions to help to address drug misuse will become available to all those who may need them. Prison staff have a central role to play in meeting this objective because a high proportion of those who misuse drugs will pass through prisons, often for relatively short sentences. This has led to increased efforts to focus interventions on short term prisoners, who in the past have often had poor access to services. The scale of the task is significant and in 2006–2007 prisons in England and Wales will aim to deliver 50,000 entrants to detoxification, 55,000 CARATS assessments, and 7000 entrants to drug rehabilitation. In addition, 40 percent of prisoners signed up for voluntary drug testing (Lee & George, 2005; Towl, 2006).

Intervention work has been developed for illicit drugs and alcohol. Initial health screening on entry to prisons is used to try to identify those with the most marked problem levels of use. Such prisoners would then be assessed more thoroughly to identify those at immediate need for the management of symptoms of withdrawal and detoxification. This can then be followed up by structured counselling, addressing issues of motivation to change, social and inter personal skills, behavioural self-control training, systemic therapy and relapse prevention. Where appropriate, prisoners may also be referred to special residential interventions (National Offender Management Service, 2005). Where prisoners are thought likely to benefit, they may be referred to self-help interventions such as Alcoholics Anonymous. Those assessed as requiring specialised treatment for physical health problems associated with drug or alcohol abuse are referred to the local specialist health services (National Offender Management Service, 2005).

The broad range of services available to prisoners falls under the CARATS scheme outlined above. Initial assessment of the need of prisoners is undertaken by prison staff in order to develop systematic care plans. As part of this they may refer prisoners to short-term counselling or group work interventions within prison. Prisoners may be referred to a short duration or an intensive drug rehabilitation intervention dependent on needs. At this point they may also be offered systematic advice on harm-minimisation. Efforts will also be made to ensure that prisoners are effectively linked into mainstream community addiction services, to try to ensure continuity of effective care on release.

Offence Focused Interventions

Since the mid 1990s in England and Wales there has been a large scale investment in what may broadly be termed psychological therapies with prisoners aimed at addressing offending directly. This work can be seen as focused primarily on the apex of Figure 4.1 above, with a stress on addressing attitudes to offending and some areas of social and interpersonal skills. The approach drew heavily on approaches developed in Canada (Hanson & Bussière, 1996; Robinson, 1995) and gave rise to a series of highly structured group work-based interventions produced in manual form, for delivery by a range of staff in prisons. This manualised approach was based on an assessment of a narrow part of the evidence base in relation to criminal behaviours.

This approach has been subject to high quality evaluation by the Home Office, with disappointing results (Falshaw, Friendship, Travers & Nugent, 2004). Reactions to these results have ranged from denial through to a focus on why such negative results have followed investment in such highly structured and manual-based approaches. It has been argued that there are a number of reasons why this approach may be largely (or completely) ineffective. These include the view that the act of structuring and manualising the approach serves to "dumb down" the therapeutic process and, in doing so, take away much of what is known to be effective in such approaches (Towl, 2003, 2004, 2006; Thomas-Peter, 2006). It has also been suggested that work on areas such as attitudes to offending is unlikely to be effective in the absence of work at more fundamental levels such as ensuring that prisoners have a basic education, somewhere to live, money to live on, work and social supports (Crighton, 2004; McNeil et al., 2005; Towl, 2006).

The evidence base on psychological therapies more generally is instructive here and suggests that effective interventions need to be broadly conceived, grounded in the broad evidence base and have sufficient flexibility to allow those working with prisoners to meet the needs they present with (Crighton, 2004, 2006; McNeil et al., 2005; Towl, 2003, 2004, 2006; Towl & Crighton, in press). This represents something of a challenge to earlier rather limited approaches, which stressed an exclusive focus on factors that show a moderate statistical correlation with the development of criminal offending. This approach was based on a narrow part of the evidence base, which has in more recent years been increasingly called into question. Such approaches have perhaps made the error of conflating the distinctive issues of development and maintenance of criminal behaviours. Indeed taking the parallel of tobacco smoking as an example, young people may start to smoke as a result of peer pressure and a desire to rebel against authority. The processes of helping individuals to successfully stop smoking, though, are unlikely to require teaching older smokers to resist adolescent peer pressures and encouraging them to conform to authority.

More broad based conceptions of intervention have recently gained significant ground. These break with "one size fits all" approaches and suggest the need for tailored programmes of interventions addressing a broad range of needs (Crighton, 2004; McNeil et al., 2005; Towl, 2003). These approaches seem likely to address the differing needs that prisoners have, addressing these at differing stages. The managerial system for ensuring this is being termed "offender management." This is essentially a system of planning and supporting assessment and intervention work with offenders. The system is designed to work in prisons and the community, creating a common approach across correctional services. The overall aim is to "resettle" prisoners into the community, helping them to lead law abiding lives. The notion of resettlement for prisoners has been persuasively criticised as something of a misnomer, given that many offenders could not accurately be described as "settled" in the first place. In reality it is often settlement that needs to be achieved rather than an imagined process of "resettlement" (Social Exclusion Unit, 2002; Towl, 2006).

Offender management in England and Wales will involve correctional staff in addressing a range of the needs of prisoners. This will involve correctional staff in helping prisoners to achieve the basics such as the resources to secure food and shelter. It has also involved significant investment in efforts to get prisoners into constructive employment. It seems likely that promising work in these areas will develop further in the coming years.

Offence focussed interventions have benefited from very high levels of investment in recent years. They fall into two broad groups, general cognitive and social skills interventions which aim to address a wide range of offending and similar approaches which are targeted specifically at sexual offenders.

Until recently a majority of funding went into a small number of group based interventions, based largely on cognitive-behavioural approaches developed in Canada (Hanson & Bussière, 1996; Robinson, 1995). Delivery of these was achieved by "manualisation" with the nature of the intervention being to a high degree centrally specified. This allowed for a rapid roll out of such interventions and their delivery by a broad range of staff with limited experience of psychological therapies. These have run with large numbers of prisoners for a number of years and have been subject to high quality evaluations (Falshaw et al., 2004). To date the UK-wide evidence for the efficacy of these approaches have been very disappointing, with little evidence of positive impact on reoffending amongst prisoners.

A similar approach has been taken to work with sex offenders with manual based group interventions being implemented. This has similar strengths and weaknesses to those seen for more generic "offending behaviour" interventions. Again this approach has been subject to high quality evaluation and the results have been similarly disappointing (Falshaw et al., 2003a, 2003b, 2004; Kenworthy, Adams, Bilby, Brooks-Gordon & Fenton, 2003; Crighton, 2006a). This has led to a number of concerns about the approach taken to this broad group of serious offenders (Thomas-Peter, 2006).

Bringing It All Together: An Evidence-Based Approach to Reducing Offending

Within prisons in England and Wales there is a degree of inconsistency in the use of the term programme, which is used in different and sometimes misleading ways. This is more than a semantic point since it has influenced policy and practice. In relation to offence focused interventions the term programme has often been applied to specific group based interventions. In the context of work in the field of mental health and drugs the term has generally been used to describe a coordinated set of interventions addressing a range of needs.

The latter view of the term programme is more in keeping with usage in the international literature and is, it can be argued, more logically coherent in terms of the evidence base. Of the range of potentially available interventions, some are evidently more promising than others but all are, to varying degrees "experimental." In developing effective and evidence-based work with prisoners, this needs to be explicitly recognised and, hard as it may be, unpromising approaches will need to be discarded.[2] What seems clear is that effective approaches will need to be multimodal, addressing a range of needs.

The emerging evidence in the UK has suggested that effective interventions to reduce criminal behaviour need to be based on a fuller understanding of the motivations that are associated with engaging in crime, as well as those which maintain offending. There is also a need for better understanding and application of the psychological processes of change (Crighton, 2004, 2006b, 2006c; McNeil et al., 2005; Towl, 2003, 2006).

In some respects this may lead to factors that appear directly related to criminal behaviour but in others may not. For example, areas such as basic education (literacy and numeracy) may appear less directly linked to offending than attitudes, yet they may provide a more effective way to reduce criminal behaviour. There is some clear learning here from public health models (Rothman & Greenland; 1998; Crighton, 2004, 2006b, 2006c). By way of analogy no competent public health practitioner would argue that the most effective way to address an infectious disease would be intensive intervention to address the symptoms of the disease, only in those who are ill and once the illness was well advanced. Instead they would advocate a broad-based approach concerned with preventing the causes of disease, breaking the causal chain of the disease at the most easily broken points. Such an approach makes far more logical sense with regard to addressing offending behaviour too.

In delivering this, a diverse mix of psychological knowledge, skills, approaches and employers is likely to yield a number of significant advantages in working in prisons. This has been recognised in the recent development of policies on the use of "Psychological Therapies" in England and Wales which have set the direction for future development (Department of Health, 2004). Government policy in this area is to broaden the development of the evidence base for the use of such interventions and develop greater multidisciplinary competence in the use of such approaches. Clearly such changes have significant implications for work in correctional settings which contain high proportions of prisoners who may clearly benefit from such input.

CONCLUSIONS

Debates in the UK in the last decade have tended to adopt somewhat parochial and superficially plausible notions such as the so-called "what works?" debate. Such an analysis has proven inadequate and has shown a marked over reliance on meta-analyses of nonrandomised studies, addressing a narrow part of the evidence base on psychological interventions, along with an undue emphasis on two and five-year reconviction rates (Towl, 2005a, 2006). This is inadequate on a number of levels. Firstly, such measures are very crude and do little to measure the true incidence of crime, focusing rather on detection. Secondly, they do little to address qualitative changes in offending, where individuals move, for example, from violent crimes to nonviolent crimes.

There has been a significant financial and professional investment in a range of experimental approaches and these have yielded variable results. Interventions to address basic education in prisoners have been delivered effectively but the impact on reoffending remains unclear. Improved employment opportunities show promise but have not been adequately evidenced

(Towl, 2005b, 2006). In contrast manualised cognitive-behavioural approaches targeting what have been characterised as "thinking skills" appear from the UK evidence largely unpromising, in their current form, whether for offenders in general or for sexual offenders.

A number of key lessons are emerging from relatively good quality data in England and Wales.[3] One of these is the need to bring together interventions in a more coordinated way into what might properly be termed programmes of assessment and intervention. Single interventions, misleadingly labelled as "programmes," in isolation, seem to have been largely ineffectual and, given what is already known about the complexity of determinants of human behaviour, this is perhaps unsurprising. Flexibility within interventions allowing therapists to respond effectively to emerging needs also seems to be a central characteristic of those interventions that have been effective. Approaches which have largely eliminated this have been largely ineffective (Crighton, 2004, 2005; Towl & Crighton, in press).

A further lesson here is the need to use more appropriate measures when researching the impacts of interventions and programmes of intervention. Recently this area has been dominated by short-term reconviction rates, often as short as two years. This is a largely unconvincing approach on a number of methodological levels. It is too short a time scale to convincingly measure the impacts of psychological therapies, whether positive or negative. Indeed one systematic trial looking at sexual offenders reported no clear effects from intervention at 10-year follow-up, with the possibility of a negative impact (Romero & Williams, 1983; Kenworthy et al., 2003). Given relatively low detection and conviction rates for crime it seems likely that, however inconvenient, much longer term research follow up will be necessary.

Short term reconviction can also be criticised as a very crude measure of the impact of interventions, whether at the level of the individual prisoner or in terms of social impacts. It fails to take account of issues such as the true levels of criminal behaviour, the latency to re-offending and the nature and severity of further offences. More detailed research measures will be necessary if we are to be able to relate the effects of interventions to the public experience of crime. Developments in England and Wales provide an opportunity for testing some of these difficult questions.

ENDNOTES

1. The use of rates of imprisonment by population has been subject to criticism and it has been suggested that rates of imprisonment by rates of recorded crime is more appropriate. By this measure rates of imprisonment in England and Wales are relative-

ly lower than some other Western European countries. Such measures are, however, subject to differences in the recording of crime.

2. In this respect the development of psychological therapies is similar to the development of pharmacological therapies where large sums are often spent developing promising drug interventions, which may ultimately have no efficacy or indeed may cause illness.

3. The data gathered in England and Wales has been of a good methodological standard and has involved large numbers of prisoners. It has not, though, taken the form of randomised control trials (RCT's). It has been convincingly argued that there are clear advantages in future research taking the form of RCT's (Crighton, 2004; Farrington, Hancock, Livingston, Painter & Towl, 2000).

REFERENCES

AIDS Advisory Committee. (1995). *The review of HIV and AIDS in prison.* London: HM Prison Service.

American Psychiatric Association. (1994). *Diagnostic and statistical manual of mental disorders* (4th ed.). Washington, DC: Author.

BMA Foundation for AIDS (1997). *Prescribing of Condoms in Prisons: Survey Report.* London: BMA Foundation for AIDS.

Bridgwood, A., & Malbon, G. (1995). *Survey of the Physical Health of Prisoners 1994, A survey of sentenced male prisoners in England and Wales, carried out by the Social Survey Division of OPCS on behalf of the Prison Service Health Care Directorate.* London: HMSO.

Carter, P. (2003). *Managing Offenders, Reducing Crime Correctional Services Review (The Carter Report).* London: Home Office.

Cinamon, H., & Bradshaw, R. (2005). Prison health in England. *British Journal of Forensic Practice, 7*(4), 8–13.

Crighton, D. A. (2006a). Psychological research into sexual offenders. In G. J. Towl (Ed.) *Psychological Research in Prisons.* Oxford, UK : Blackwell.

Crighton, D. A. (2006b). Methodological issues in psychological research in prisons. In G. J. Towl (Ed.) *Psychological Research in Prisons.* Oxford, UK: Blackwell.

Crighton, D. A. (2006c) Psychological research into reducing suicides. In G. J. Towl (Ed.) *Psychological Research in Prisons.* Oxford, UK: Blackwell.

Crighton, D. A. (2005). Applied Psychological Services. *British Journal of Forensic Practice, 7* (4), 49–55.

Crighton, D. A. (2004). Risk assessment. In A. Needs & G. Towl (Eds.), *Applying psychology to forensic practice* (pp. 64–81). Oxford, UK: Blackwell.

Crighton, D. A. (2002). Suicide in prisons: A critique of UK research. In G. J. Towl, L. Snow & M. J. McHugh (Eds.) *Suicide in Prisons.* Oxford, UK: Blackwell.

Crighton, D. A., & Towl, G. J. (2002). Intentional self-injury. In G. J. Towl, L. Snow & M. J. McHugh (Eds.) *Suicide in Prisons.* Oxford, UK: Blackwell.

Crighton, D. A. & Towl, G. J. (1997). Self-inflicted deaths in prisons in England and Wales: Analyses of 1988–90 and 1994–5. In G. J. Towl (Ed). *Suicide in prisons: research directions in the 1990s.* Leicester, UK: British Psychological Society.

Curran, L., McHugh, M. J. and Nooney, K. (1989). *AIDS Care, 1* (1), 11–25.

Department of Health (2004). *Organising and Delivering Psychological Therapies.* London: Department of Health.

Department of Health (2002). *Developing and Modernising Primary Care in Prisons.* London: Department of Health.

Department of Health, (2001). *Changing the outlook: A strategy for developing and modernising mental health services in prisons.* London: Department of Health.

Dolan, K., Rutter, S., & Wodak, A. (2003). Prison-based syringe exchange programs: A review of international research and development. *Addictions, 98,* 153–158.

Falshaw, L., Friendship, C., Travers, R. & Nugent, F. (2004). Searching for "What Works": HM Prison Service accredited cognitive skills programmes. *The British Journal of Forensic Practice, 6* (2), 3–13.

Farrington, D. P., Hancock, G., Livingston, M., Painter, K. A. & Towl, G. (2000). *Evaluation of Intensive Regimes for Young Offenders (Home Office Research Findings No. 121.)*. London: Home Office.

Hanson, R.K., & Bussière, M.T. (1996). Predicting relapse: A meta-analysis of sexual offender recidivism studies. *Journal of Consulting and Clinical Psychology, 63,* 802–809.

HM Prison Service (1999). Blood Borne and Related Communicable Diseases Prison Service Order Number 3845. London: HM Prison Service. Retrieved November 28, 2006, from http://pso.hmprisonservice.gov.uk/PSO_3845_ blood_borne_ related_communicable_diseases.doc.

Home Office (2004). *Reducing Crime–Changing Lives*. London: Home Office.

Home Office (2003). *Driving Delivery: A Strategic Framework for Psychological Services in Prisons and Probation*. London: HM Prison and National Probation Services.

International Centre for Prison Studies (2006). *World Prison Brief.* Retrieved August 19, 2006, from http://www.kcl.ac.uk/depsta/rel/icps/worldbrief/world_brief.html.

Kenworthy, T., Adams, C.E., Bilby, C., Brooks-Gordon, B. & Fenton M (2003). Psychological interventions for those who have sexually offended or are at risk of offending. *Cochrane Database of Systematic Reviews 2006* Issue 3 10.1002/14651858.CD004858 first published online: 20 October 2003 in Issue 4, 2003.

Lane-Morton, T. (2005). What health partnerships should seek to provide for offenders. *British Journal of Forensic Practice, 7*(4), 3–7.

Lee, M. & George, S. (2005). Drug strategy unit. *British Journal of Forensic Practice, 7*(4), 39–48.

MacDonald, M. and Berto, D. (2002). Harm Reduction in Italian and UK Prisons: The Gap Between Policy and Implementation for HIV and Drugs. Paper presented at The 13th International Conference on the Reduction of Drug Related Harm, Ljubljana, Slovenia, 3–7 March 2002. Retrieved November 28, 2006, from http://www.uce.ac.uk/crq/publications/morag/sloveniagap.pdf

Maslow, A.H. (1970). *Motivation and personality* (2nd edition). New York: Harper & Row.

McNeil, F., Batchelor, S., Burnett, R. & Knox, J. (2005). *Reducing re-offending: Key practice skills*. Edinburgh, UK; Scottish Executive.

National Offender Management Service (2005). *Strategy for the Management and Treatment of Problematic Drug Users within the Correctional Services*. London: Home Office.

National Offender Management Service (2006). *Population in Custody MONTHLY TABLES September 2006 England and Wales*. London: Home Office. Office of National Statistics (2006). Online reference www.statistics.gov.uk/CCI/ nugget.asp?ID=6

Robinson, D. (1995). *The impact of the Cognitive Skills Training on post-release recidivism on Canadian federal offenders*. Research Report R-41. Ottawa, Ontario: Correctional Service of Canada.

Romero, J. J. & Williams, L. M. (1983). Group psychotherapy and intensive probation supervision with sex offenders. *Federal Probation, 47,* 36–42.

Rothman, K. J., & Greenland, S. (1998). *Modern epidemiology.* Philadelphia: Lippincott Williams & Wilkins.

Sedenu, A. (2005). Safer custody group. *British Journal of Forensic Practice, 7* (4), 14–20.

Singleton, N., Meltzer, H. & Gatward, R. (1998). *Psychiatric Morbidity Among Prisoners in England and Wales.* London: Office for National Statistics.

Social Exclusion Unit (2002). *Reducing re-offending by ex-prisoners.* London: The Stationary Office.

Thomas-Peter, B. A. (2006). The Modern Context of Psychology in Corrections: Influences, Limitations and Values of "What Works." In G. J. Towl (Ed.) *Psychological research in prisons.* Oxford, UK: Blackwell.

Towl, G. J. (2006). Drug misuse intervention work. In G. J. Towl (Ed.) *Psychological research in prisons.* Oxford, UK: Blackwell.

Towl, G. J. (2005a). Risk assessment in evidence based mental health. *Evidence Based Mental Health, 8,* 91–93.

Towl, G. J. (2005b). National Offender Management Services: Implications for applied psychologists in probation and prisons. *Forensic Update, 81,* 22–26.

Towl, G. J. (2004). Applied Psychological Services in HM Prison Service and the National Probation Service. In A. P. C. Needs & G. J. Towl (Eds.). *Applying psychology to forensic practice.* Oxford, UK: Blackwell.

Towl, G. J. (2003). Psychological Services in HM Prison Service. In G. J. Towl (Ed.) *Psychological research in prisons.* Oxford, UK: Blackwell.

Towl, G. J. and Crighton, D. A. (in press). Psychologists in Prisons. In J. Burnett, B. Crewe & A. Wahidin (Eds). *Prison staff.* Cullompton, UK: Willan Publishers.

Towl, G. J. & Crighton, D. A. (2005). Applied Psychological Services in the National Probation Service for England and Wales. In D. A. Crighton & G. J. Towl (Eds.) *Psychology in Probation Services.* Oxford, UK: Blackwell.

Towl, G. J. & Crighton, D. A. (1998). Suicide in prisons in England and Wales from 1988 to 1995. *Criminal Behaviour and Mental Health, 8,* 184–192.

Chapter 5

CORRECTIONS IN FRANCE: CURRENT ISSUES AND FUTURE CHALLENGES

ANNIE KENSEY[1] AND HARRY R. DAMMER

INTRODUCTION

The French Republic, with a population of 63 million persons, is divided into 26 administrative regions, 22 of which are on the mainland (Metropolitan France). France is a unitary State that has always prized a highly centralized form of government, in which all major decisions are made through a national bureaucracy located in Paris. France also maintains a strongly republican style of government, of which a president is the head. The main power remains in the hands of citizens: they vote for representatives, who in turn are responsible to the electorate. France's 22 administrative regions are further divided into 96 provinces that are in contact with the central government. A prefect, the person named by the government to enforce the laws of the Nation, administers each province (World Factbook, 2007).

CRIME, CORRECTIONS, AND THE MENTAL HEALTH SYSTEM

As of January 2004, there were 189 prison institutions in France, with varying degrees of security, which are administratively allocated to 10 regions. Of these correctional facilities, 65 are prisons for offenders sentenced to more than one year, 116 are remand prisons that house unconvicted offenders, inmates with less than a one-year sentence, or convicted offenders seeking

---

1. The opinions expressed here are those of the authors only and do not necessarily reflect the official views of the French Prison Administration, Ministry of Justice.

appeal. In some cases, separate institutional arrangements exist for women, juveniles, the mentally ill, and the elderly. Remand prisons in France are often much smaller than U.S. jails, housing fewer than 50 inmates in many cases. The prisons are either high-security facilities or detention centers that allow for more freedom and individual responsibility (ICPS, 2004; Terrill, 2003).

There are also 13 facilities for semi-liberty that can be compared to halfway houses, and various community-based facilities in the United States. Semi-liberty (semi-liberté), like day leave, and "placement outside" *(placement à l'extérieur)* are individualized measures that allow convicted prisoners to work, get training outside the prison, participate in a treatment program, or participate in family life. Much like probation or parole in the United States, these measures allow for the community supervision of a convicted offender by the Penitentiary Service of Rehabilitation and Probation (SPIP).

As of January 2006, 58,344 individuals were detained in the French prison system, including both metropolitan France and overseas regions. An additional 871 were under electronic monitoring and 307 were placed in some other form of community corrections (semi-liberty). The incarceration rate for France on January 1, 2006 was 92 per 100,000. The rate of incarceration in France has increased steadily since the early 1980s, despite a drop in 1982. After reaching an all-time high of 95 per 100,000 in 2004, the incarceration rate has remained relatively stable. Amnesty laws and the frequent use of collective pardons often lower the number of prisoners. Since 1991, collective pardons have occurred each year on "Bastille Day"[2] and such pardons have apparently helped to slow down the rate of increase in the prison population. Table 5.1 and Figure 5.1 below graphically present information relative to incarceration trends in France from 1980 to the present (Kensey, 2006).

The socio-demographic data of convicted prisoners in France reflect some predictable results. In general, the typical prisoner in France is a male, between the ages of 25 and 40, and more likely to be listed as "foreigner" than a few years ago. Recent research on offenders' family history and incarceration also shows that many of these men are social outcasts (Kensey, Cassan, & Toulemon, 2000). Below is a general summary of the data relative to gender, age, and nationality, with a graphic illustration depicted in Table 5.2.

Women in French prisons comprised 3.7 percent of the total number of detainees on January 1, 2006. This number has remained relatively stable over the last 10 years. Forty-four percent (44%) of inmates in French prisons are between 25 and 40 years old. However, the average age of inmates has

---

2. Usually, an amnesty law occurs after a presidential election. An amnesty deletes the conviction on the criminal file and the type of amnestied conviction is different each time. Collective pardons are different: by decree, the president of the Republic grants an exceptional reduction of sentence for convicted persons. Usually, it occurs for the 14th of July - Bastille Day.

TABLE 5.1
PRISON POPULATION (1996–2006)

Area covered: metropolitan France and overseas departments

At 1 January	Detainees	% Annual increase *	Rate of detention per 100000 inhabitants **	Observations
1996	55,043	-1.0%	91.7	Collective pardon in July
1997	54,496	-1.2%	90.3	Collective pardon in July
1998	53,844	-1.5%	88.9	Collective pardon in July
1999	53,055	-2.2%	86.5	Collective pardon in July and December
2000	51,903	-7.8%	81.8	Collective pardon in July
2001	47,837	1.6%	78.9	Collective pardon in July
2002	48,594	14.0%	84.5	Collective pardon in July, law of amnesty
2003	55,407	6.9%	92.6	Collective pardon in July
2004	59,246	-0.1%	95.0	Collective pardon in July
2005	59,197	0.5%	94.7	Collective pardon in July
2006	59,522			

Source: Kensey (2006).

* % annual increase: prison population declined by 1.0% between January 1 2006 and January 1 2007.

** Rate of detention: ratio between the number of inmates and the number of inhabitants at January 1 of each year.

increased from 29.8 in 1996 to 32.2 years old in 2006. The number of senior inmates (over 60 years old) has almost tripled over the last 10 years. Although the overall French population is getting older, the rate of aging of the prison population has been twice as fast as that of the general population. This increase is due to several factors including the fact that more and more offenders are being sentenced later in life and are also receiving longer sentences. Additionally, the number of offenders over 50 who are sentenced for sexual assault has increased considerably. They represented 21 percent of all those sentenced for this crime in 1990 versus 49 percent in 2000.

From 1974 to 1994, the number of inmates referred to as "foreigners" doubled, increasing from 15 percent to 30 percent. In the last 10 years, however, that number dropped to 20 percent. This evolution is due to the rise in, and then recent crackdown on, illegal immigration.

A review of the types and percentages of principal crimes committed by offenders incarcerated in France reflects two typical results and one disturbing trend. The two crimes for which inmates are most likely to be serving time in France are assault and drug related crimes. Together, they account for almost one-third (32.6%) of all those incarcerated. Throughout the world, it is not

Figure 5.1
Prison Population in France (1980–2006)

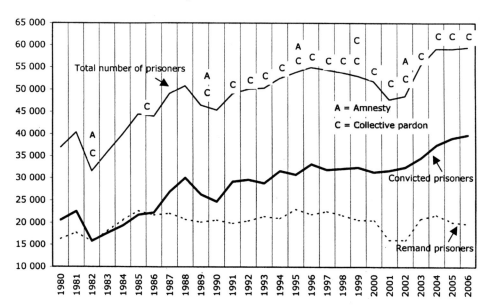

uncommon for both assault and related crimes against persons, and drug related offenses to account for a large percentage of those incarcerated. A less
common and more disturbing finding, however, is the number of sexual
offenders in prison. Rape and related sexual offenses account for 21.1 percent
of those incarcerated. The reasons for the increase in incarceration for sexually related crimes are unclear, but it is possible that the viewed seriousness of
these crimes by both the general public and government officials has led to a
call for increased punitiveness and harsher sentences. The increase in the convictions of these offenses is shown in Table 5.4.

There have been some considerable changes in the convicted population
by type of offense. As of January 1, 2006 the number of persons convicted for
simple theft represented 7.5% of the prison population vs. 20% 10 years earlier (and down from 50% in 1976). Those convicted for "rape and sexual
assault" currently come in first (21%) though their number has decreased since
2001 (24%). They represented 4% of convicted offenders in 1976. Those convicted for drug related crimes represent 14% in 2006, down from 21% in 1996.
Assault represents another jump from 6% in 1996 to 18% in 2006 (See Table
5.3 and 5.4).

Inmates sentenced to less than a year represent about one third of those
convicted for any crime in France on January 1, 2006, up 22 percent in 1996.
Those serving five years or longer make up 36 percent of the total convicted

TABLE 5.2
GENDER, AGE, AND NATIONALITY (1996–2006)

Area covered: Metropolitan France

	As of January 1996		As of January 2006	
	Number	%	Number	%
All prisoners	52,658	100.0	55,633	100.0
Male	50,525	95.9	53,566	96.3
Female	2,133	4.1	2,067	3.7
Under 18 years of age	514	1.0	659	1.2
18 to under 21	4,062	7.7	4,434	8.0
21 to under 25	9,373	17.8	9,477	17.0
25 to under 30	11,770	22.4	10,153	18.2
30 to under 40	15,342	29.1	14,395	25.9
40 to under 50	7,967	15.1	9,432	17.0
50 to under 60	2,762	5.2	4,968	8.9
60 years and up	868	1.6	2,115	3.8
Median age	29.8		32.2	
French	37,358	70.9	44,277	79.6
Foreigners	15,300	29.1	11,356	20.4

Source: Kensey (2006).

TABLE 5.3
CONVICTED PRISONERS: STRUCTURE ACCORDING TO TYPE OF
PRINCIPLE OFFENSE AS OF JANUARY 1, 2006

Area covered: Metropolitan France

	Number	%
All convicted prisoners	37,033	100.0
Intentional killing	2,999	8.1
Intentional killing of minor less than 15	262	0.7
Rape and sexual offenses	7,831	21.1
Non-intentional injuries or killing	2,075	5.6
Assault	6,757	18.2
Drug-related crimes	5,347	14.4
Simple theft	2,771	7.5
Aggravated theft	3,565	9.6
Procuring (promoting prostitution)	110	0.3
Breaches of military regulations	30	0.1
Fraud	2,356	6.4
Handling (fencing stolen goods)	94	0.3
False pretenses	173	0.5
Breaches of immigration legislation	498	1.3
Writing bad checks	25	0.1
Others	2,140	5.8

Source: Kensey (2006).

TABLE 5.4
CONVICTED PRISONERS: DIFFERENTIAL ANALYSIS
ACCORDING TO TYPE OF PRINCIPLE OFFENSE

Area covered: Metropolitan France

	% As of January 1		
	1996	2001	2006
All convicted prisoners	100.0	100.0	100.0
Intentional killing	9.6	10.7	8.8
Rape and sexual offenses	14.0	24.2	21.2
Drug related crimes	20.8	13.9	14.4
Assault	6.0	10.8	18.2
Simple theft	20.1	11.0	7.5
Aggravated theft	9.3	11.7	9.6
Handling and fraud	4.2	3.9	6.6
Breaches of immigration legislation	4.6	2.5	1.3
Others	11.0	11.3	12.4

Source: Kensey (2006)

populations, slightly more than in 1996 (34%). Over the last ten years, those serving 20 to 30 years are responsible for the largest change in growth, as their numbers have been multiplied by 3.5 (see Table 5.5).

The correctional system in France is currently under the supervision of the Minister of Justice. The Prison Service takes on a dual role: (1) it supervises individuals sentenced by the courts and (2) it prepares them for return to the community (Minister of Justice, 1998). Two distinguishing features of the French penal system are the office of corrections judge and the proportion of pretrial detainees. Recent figures reflect that at least one-third of inmates in French prisons are pretrial (called remand) inmates (Dammer, Fairchild, & Albanese, 2006; Kensey, 2006). These figures dropped from the mid-1980s, when the remand prisoners comprised 50 percent of those incarcerated. "Civil Law" nations typically have long pretrial detention, during which the case is thoroughly examined, but France is notorious for excessiveness in this area. Some detainees are kept in jail for several years while the examining magistrates are investigating their cases. Because of prison and jail overcrowding, efforts have been made in the past few years to cut down on these pretrial populations. Several proposals have been made, such as pretrial diversion programs or setting maximum pretrial detention periods–for adults, one year in less serious cases (those that would result in a sentence of less than five years) and one month for juveniles in these cases.

The office of correction judges *(juges de l'application des peines)* was instituted in 1958 and strengthened in 1970 and 1972 as a reform of the penal process. Correction judges are appointed by the State to perform several functions,

TABLE 5.5
CONVICTED PRISONERS: DIFFERENTIAL ANALYSIS
ACCORDING TO SENTENCE LENGTH

Area covered: Metropolitan France

	As of January 1996		As of January 2006		1996–2006
	Numbers	%	Numbers	%	Evolution (%)
All convicted prisoners	31,509	100.0	37,038	100.0	17.5
Sentenced for under 1 year	9,477	30.1	11,571	31.2	22.1
1 year to under 3 years	7,247	23.0	8,086	21.8	11.6
3 years to under 5 years	3,987	12.7	4,058	11.0	1.8
5 years to under 10 years	5,615	17.8	5,867	15.8	4.5
10 years to under 20 years	4,290	13.6	5,608	15.1	30.7
20 years to under 30 years	383	1.2	1,340	3.6	249.9
Life	510	1.6	508	1.4	-0.4

Source: Kensey (2006)

including setting the actual length of time that a particular prisoner remains in prison or is released on parole. Most interesting, however, is the function of overseeing prison conditions and prison disciplinary procedures. Correction judges are responsible for visiting the prison or prisons in their jurisdictions at least once a month, hearing individual inmate complaints, and keeping informed about prison programs, physical plants, and general living conditions. Although this program has met a good deal of opposition, especially from prison administrators, and can hardly be considered an unqualified success, it represents an effort to make the dark world of French prisons somewhat more open to outside scrutiny and thereby more accountable to the government and the public. In this sense, the office of correction judge performs some of the same functions as the Boards of Visitors have served in England for almost a century. At the same time, these officials have a major influence on the actual sentences served by particular inmates.

A law in January 1994 placed the health care of incarcerated people under the control of the National Health Care Service and the National Insurance System. As a result, inmates now benefit from the same physical, mental, preventive, and aftercare services as the general population. Health care is provided by an agreement with a local health unit in a nearby hospital. The local health units each form special outpatient departments called Consultation and Health Care Units (UCSAs) for each prison, which provide check-ups and deliver medication. In accordance with the National Hospital Admissions scheme (SNH) of 2003, short term and emergency hospital care are also delivered from the local units in the local hospitals. For longer, programmed hospitalizations, there are eight Interregional Safety Hospital Units (UHSI's) located in regional university hospitals (CHUs). For the Paris region, the interregional secure unit is the National Public Health Institution at Fresnes, in conjunction with the Pitié-Salpêtrière Hospital. Before this system was in place, prisoners were admitted to the local hospital or the nearest hospital which had the technical competence to deal with the particular case if the local hospital was unable to admit the patient.

For inmate psychiatric treatment a supplementary agreement is provided by the local health unit. General psychiatric care is provided through a supplemental agreement within the prisons by the outpatient department of the local health unit. There are 93 of these psychiatric sectors or "inter-sectors" which treat prisoners who don't need to be hospitalized and are also responsible for the hospitalization of those prisoners who require more extensive treatment as a result of a hospital order. When hospitalization is required, then 26 regional medical-psychiatric services, called regional medical-psychological services (SMPRs), provide intensive care and voluntary hospitalizations. Article 48 of a law implemented on September 9, 2002 calls for the creation of special hospital units (UHSA's) that allow mentally ill prisoners who are not fit for life in prison to receive psychiatric care.

CORRECTIONAL MODEL, PHILOSOPHY, AND SOCIAL POLICY

In the post-World War II years, France moved from an emphasis on prison reform and rehabilitation to a generally harsher philosophy of punishment. In the early 1970s, a series of prison riots that ended in a number of hostage deaths led to some reform efforts. These were aborted because of the large increase in the crime rate in the following years, which contributed to a repressive mood from both the general public and the government. Prison leaves and suspended sentences were limited, and harsher sentences were imposed. The Socialist government that came to power in 1981 proposed sweeping reforms of the criminal justice system, including abolition of capital punishment and protections against unwarranted pretrial imprisonment. It also expressed greater concern for prisoners' rights. However, once again, public concern over murders and terrorist bombings soon took precedence over this reformist sweep, and the generally hard-line mood intensified. The result has been a steady increase in the prison population, as described earlier.

The sentencing policy currently used in France can be described as a combination of determinate and indeterminate sentencing. As a result of a new Penal Code that was implemented in 1994, there have been some changes in the way offenders are sentenced in France. The changes call for fewer maximum or fixed sentences for all offenses and more judicial discretion. At the same time the new code aims to punish some special kinds of offenders more harshly, such as organized crime figures and terrorists (Terrill, 2003).

The French have lagged behind the rest of Europe in developing and implementing a range of alternatives to incarceration. Alternative sentences have increased considerably over the past 20 years. Probation started in 1958, but the actual mechanism of alternative sentences was introduced in 1975 by a law that included the suspension of the driving license and various fines or punishments. In 1988, day fine and community service were added as sentence alternatives. Recently, efforts have been made to increase their usage. There are primarily four noncustodial sanctions in France: fines, suspended sentence, community service, and probation. As of January 1999, over 150,000 offenders were serving their sentences in the community (Hill, 2002).

Capital punishment was abolished by parliamentary vote in France in 1981. The last execution in France took place in 1974. Protocol Number 13 of the European Convention of Human Rights, signed by France, as a member of the Council of Europe, prohibits the death penalty under any circumstances, both during peace time and war. Interestingly, at the time of abolition, the majority of citizens in France were still in support of the death penalty. According to public opinion polls (TNS SOFRES) a high of 65 percent of the French population supported the death penalty in 1985. In 2006, twenty-five years after abolition, 42 percent of the French still would support the reestablishment of the death penalty in France. Figure 5.2 depicts the views of French citizens relative to the death penalty over the last 28 years.

RELATIONSHIPS BETWEEN COURTS, CORRECTIONS, AND COMMUNITY ORGANIZATIONS

The accused, the victim, and the Public Minister serving as representative for the State can express their opinions at sentencing. Expert witnesses, such as psychiatrists and psychologists, also have a considerable influence on sentencing decisions. The court generally abides by the conclusions of expert witnesses. There is a psychologist or psychiatrist present in most prisons. They are more numerous and have a stronger presence in prisons where there is a regional medical-psychological hospital unit (SMPR). Other prisons depend on local resources for hiring and compensation of psychologists. All new arrivals to prison go through a psychological exam. Psychologists are generally under the control of the head of the prison. For long-term prisoners and juveniles, the main functions for psychologists are to conduct mental health assessments and to provide therapy and other mental health services to help offenders cope with their criminal sentences.

FIGURE 5.2
FRENCH CITIZEN ATTITUDES TOWARD DEATH PENALTY (1978-2006)

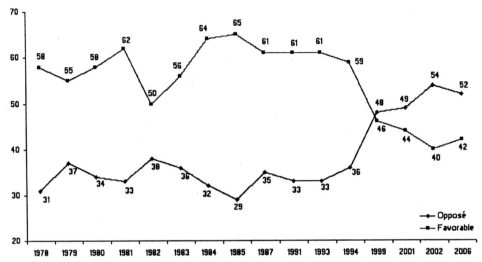

Source: TNS SOFRES: Taylor Nelson Sofres, Société Française d'études par sondage, French Society Research Polls (2006).

The French Prison system and the Ministry of Justice are generally in favor of allowing community organizations into the prisons to provide assistance in the rehabilitation of prison inmates. Educators, social workers, volunteer visitors, and clergy from a variety of religions are among those who regularly enter French Prisons. A list of some of the major organizations that enter, as well at their major goals, follows here.

- ANVP (Association Nationale des Visiteurs de Prison) is a national organization consisting of volunteers who meet with inmates, in particular those who have no family support, in order to bring them support and assist in plans for life after confinement. Prison social workers choose those inmates who receive this kind of support.

- The FARAPEJ (Fédération des Associations Réflexion Action Prison Et Justice) is a consortium of several community service groups. It provides several in-prison activities for inmates and their families, and provides assistance for those leaving prison. The organization also supports various alternative sanction initiatives.

- FNARS (Fédération nationale des associations d'accueil et de réinsertion sociale) offers a community service that provides freed inmates with housing, and teaches them basic skills like reading, writing, job searching, and how to manage a budget.

- FREP (Fédération des relais Parent enfants) and UFRAMA (Union des Fédérations Régionales des Associations de Maison d'Accueil de familles et proches de personnes incarcérées). Both are associations that try to maintain links between incarcerated parents and their children The UFRAMA also helps provide housing assistance for families while inmates are serving their sentence.
- French Red Cross has set up a hot-line inside the jails and they provide assistance for inmates with long term sentences and those without families or social networks.
- GENEPI (Groupement Etudiant National d'Enseignement aux Personnes Incarcérées) is a group of students who teach inmates such skills as reading literacy, math, computer science, language, or provide cultural opportunities like theater productions.

One of the social policy issues facing the French is the condition of the prison system. In the past several years, credible nongovernmental organizations (NGOs) have reported overcrowding and unacceptable hygiene conditions in French prisons. Although in 2002 it was reported that prison conditions generally met international standards, public debate is ongoing regarding this subject. The French Parliament has moved to address the issue of poor and overcrowded prison conditions by the recent approval of a prison reform bill that includes a plan to replace old prisons and to build 30 new prisons that will add 13,200 new prison beds.

Another public policy issue of concern related to prison conditions is the high number of inmate suicides. The Ministry of Justice (2006) reported 235 deaths of persons in custody in 2001, of which 104 were suicides. The number of suicides reported in 2002 was 122. With an estimated 52,000 persons in custody the suicide rate is at least seven times greater in prison than in the general population. Survey data has shown that suicide is correlated with anxiety in more than 90 percent of cases, impulsivity in 63 percent of cases, and addiction in 55 percent of cases. Suicide risk appears to increase with aging. Contrary to the general population, having a family, a companion or children constituted an increased suicide risk factor. Remand (jail) inmates that are violent offenders or sex offenders constitute more than two-thirds of people who committed suicide (Guillonneau & Kensey, 1997).

In recent years, because of several well-publicized cases of freed inmates returning to crime, French officials have become quite concerned with the recidivism rates of violent and mentally ill offenders. In 2005, a committee chaired by Jean-François Burgelin sent a report to the Ministers of Justice and Health (Ministry of Justice, 2005) with measures to reduce recidivism of particularly dangerous or mentally ill offenders. Proposals in the report include the extension of suspended sentences with supervision from the current five years to ten years. Another is the supervision after incarceration for all individuals that seem likely to be repeat offenders, not just for sexual offenders. For former inmates deemed dangerous and mentally irresponsible, the proposal calls for additional safety measures after incarceration including closed centers for protecting society, which would be similar to the practice of intensive supervision for paroled offenders in halfway houses.

SUBSTANCE ABUSE AND MENTAL HEALTH LAWS

Since the formation and implementation of a law passed in 1970, the French now have a legal policy for their fight against drug sale and addiction. The law sets the path for three main strategies: strict control of drug trafficking, prohibition of usage and offer of a therapeutic alternative to repression of abuse, and free anonymous treatment for all users.

Insofar as drug trafficking is concerned, the Law of 1970 has been modified on several occasions, both creating new offenses such as selling or supplying drugs for personal use (January 17, 1986) or drug-related money laundering (December 31, 1987), and enacting new procedures such as the confiscation of drug trafficking profits (November 14, 1990). Currently, trafficking offenses include selling or supplying drugs for personal use with a penalty of up to five years and a fine of up to 75,000 euros (French Penal Code [FPC]: Article 222-39) and a more serious offense for transportation, possession, supply, sale and illicit purchase of narcotics with a penalty of up to 10 years and a fine up to 7.5 million euros (FPC: Article 222-37). Encouraging a minor to use narcotics can entail five years of imprisonment and a fine of 100,000 euros, and if the minor is under the age of 15 or if the offense is committed in or around an educational establishment, the penalty increases to seven years in prison and a fine of 150,000 euros (FPC: Article 227-18). Finally, heading or organizing a group engaged in the production, manufacturing, import and export, transportation, possession, supply, sale, purchase or use of narcotics can lead to a life sentence and a fine of 7.5 million euros (FPC: Article 222-34). All of these provisions that reinforce repression against drug trafficking have contributed widely to prison population inflation by lengthening the duration of incarceration.

The Ministry of Justice—in a directive dated June 1999—asked prosecutors to prioritize treatment over incarceration for small-time offenders and problematic drug users. Today, the use of therapeutic alternatives for simple users is common practice. Most cases of simple drug use typically receive a warning with a request to contact a social or health service. When legal proceedings are undertaken, the magistrate may also force the accused to undertake a detoxification program, but then, judicial authorities rather than health authorities take the case in hand. In these cases, if the user completes the treatment, no penalties may be imposed on the individual, but the use of such diversionary measures is extremely rare. Detoxification treatment may also be a requirement to a conditional prison sentence, parole or judicial supervision.

The Code of Public Health also provides for the monitoring of drug users by health authorities (CPH: Article L3411-1). Prosecutors may not undertake legal action against an offender if that person can provide medical certification that he or she has undertaken some form of therapy or has submitted himself or herself to medical supervision since the commission of the infraction. However, if the offender does not supply a medical certificate to that effect, prosecutors may request that an individual who has made use of illicit drugs follow a drug addiction treatment program or be placed under medical monitoring (CPH: Article L3423-1). Involvement in a court-ordered treatment program suspends legal proceedings and these are not to be pursued if the individual completes the detoxification program. It is not uncommon for a repeat offender to be subjected to more than one court-ordered treatment program as more repressive measures are rarely used for simple drug use, particularly the use of cannabis.

The judicial authority in France usually follows the advice of psychiatric experts in order to determine if someone who has committed a crime (or misdemeanor) is culpable for his or her acts. The French penal code distinguishes between two cases for individuals who suffer from mental disorders at the time of a crime. The first is whether individuals can judge or control their acts totally and second whether they can judge or control their acts partially (modification of discernment) due to psychiatric or neuropsychiatric problems (FPC: Article 122-1). In the first case, when the person is not considered culpable, the examining judge can pronounce a dismissal of charge, an acquittal, or a discharge. If the person is deemed dangerous for society, he or she can be automatically committed to an institution simply by administrative decision. In the second case the person is viewed as fully culpable and may be sentenced to specific sanctions in order to prevent reoffending. These sanctions may include a series of medical and/or psychological visits, a suspended prison sentence with supervision, or more serious compulsory treatment. Since a law enacted in 2004, some offenders with serious mental health issues can be required to receive treatment for an unspecified length of time.

SUBSTANCE ABUSE AND MENTAL HEALTH ISSUES

Recent studies of French inmates at the time of admission to prison and after serving some time in prison clearly indicate that substance abuse and mental health issues are a problem for many inmates. Research conducted in 2003 by health practitioners inside the Health Care Units (UCSAs) for each prison stated that one-third (33%) of persons entering prison declared they had drinking problems, another third (33%) used drugs on a regular basis during the last 12 months prior to incarceration, 7 percent had injected drugs at least once in their lifetime, and at least 3 percent injected drugs in the last 12 months prior to incarceration. In addition, one person out of three used at least 2 risk consumptions (drugs, alcohol, tobacco) on a regular basis (Mouquet, 2005). A 2001 survey of inmates living in medical and psychiatric units (SMPRs) showed that among those with mental disorders, addiction was a problem for almost one-third (27%) of those entering prison and one-half of those inmates were considered seriously addicted. Further, certain psychiatric disorders have been found to be closely related to addictive behavior. More specifically, addictive disorders were found to be present in 48 percent of those with anti-social behavior, 46 percent of those with anxiety, 21 percent of psychotic inmates, and 20 percent of those who enter with depressions (Coldefy, Faure, & Prieto, 2002).

An epidemiological study carried out in 2003–2004 evaluated the prevalence of mental disorders in French penitentiaries. Two clinicians, a psychiatrist and a clinical psychologist, conducted interviews with 800 randomly selected inmates. First, the psychologist gave each a structured interview and then the psychiatrist followed with an unstructured interview. After these interviews, the clinicians interpreted the results and independently gave one (or multiple) diagnosis. Then the entire team met to collectively decide on a diagnosis and to assess the severity of the pathology. The results showed that 3.8 percent of inmates suffered from schizophrenia and required immediate treatment. This percentage is about four times as high as in the general population. Almost 18 percent (17.9%) were suffering from major depression, which is four to five times more than the general population. Twelve percent (12%) suffered from general anxiety. From these results it cannot be ascertained whether the disorders existed before incarceration, as a result of incarceration, or a combination of both. Other results from the study indicated that 9.4 percent were addicted to alcohol and 10.8 percent were addicted to other drugs. Those addictions often lead to incarceration and an increase in the risk of other psychological and medical problems such as dementia, cirrhosis, and HIV infection (Falissard, 2005).

As mentioned earlier, the public health service has been in charge of the organization of psychiatric treatments for inmates since 1986, with the creation of psychiatric units in prisons and regional centers (SMPRs) as early as 1977. Since the Law of 1994, each prison has signed an agreement with a local health unit for provision of psychiatric treatment. Patients in the local (SMPR) units are consenting inmates only. When people are sent to a hospital without giving their consent, they are automatically confined to a mental institution. These institutions for difficult mental patients, called *Unitè pour malades difficiles,* or UMDs, specialize in the treatment of very dangerous mentally ill patients. However, the UMDs are not just for correctional inmates. In fact, they mostly (over 75%) serve patients who are not correctional inmates but those who are involuntarily committed. There are four of these and they are located in Cadillac, Monfalet, Sarreguemines, and Villejuif. The hospitals admit three types of patients:

1. Inmate patients (as defined under article D398 of the penal procedure code). These patients are registered inmates, held legally responsible for their crimes but they have been found to be incurable by the local medical and psychiatric units (SMPRs) so they are transferred from the prison to the UMD.
2. Inmate patients under a judicial decision of direct involuntary commitment (in French "hospitalisation d'office" [HO]). They are also declared responsible for their crimes according to the FPC Article 122-1 or to FPC Article 64 that requires required compulsory treatment in prison. They may or may not be curable but they are sent directly to the UMD without first going to SMPRs.
3. Patients that are not held responsible for their crimes and are under a "classic" order of involuntary commitment (HO) according to PHC Article L 3213-1 through 3213-2.

Patients in each of these prisons are reexamined every six months by a medical commission (called the CSM). Statistics available from two of these UMDs (at Cadillac and Sarreguemines) indicated that as of January 2006 they were operating at 95 percent capacity and contained 11.3 percent of inmates from the first type, 13.4 percent of inmates from the second type, and 75.3 percent of inmates from the third type of inmates mention above (Tournier, 2007).

After being sentenced to serve time in a correctional facility in France, offenders are interviewed and tested at reception to determine if they have medical issues or if they are candidates for mental health or substance abuse treatment. If mental illness is an issue, a psychiatrist examines inmates during the first days of incarceration. During that examination the extent of the psychiatric disorder(s) is determined to ensure proper treatment. Also, the interview serves to inform the inmates and persons acting in their interest about psychiatric services inside the prison. Soon thereafter, prison personnel and the local health units are informed about the inmates and their mental health challenges. These interviews are especially important for inmates who have been designated by the investigating judge as in need of an emergency examination. Soon after the examination, psychiatric care is provided by the local care units within and outside the prison as discussed previously. During incarceration, efforts are also made by correctional personnel from within the institution and outside (e.g., probation, local mental health professionals) to provide services such as cultural activities, training, education or work aimed to help prevent mental illness and assist in rehabilitation.

Substance abuse is also seen as an essential function of correctional treatment. Efforts are made to tie in the sanitary needs of inmates and issues related to substance abuse (Ministère de la Justice, 2004 septembre[b]). When inmates are identified as addicts or at risk (tobacco included) health services personnel within the prison provide evaluation and treatment, including a prescription for substitution if needed, medical treatment for weaning the person off the addiction, and specialized education about the problem of addiction.

Soon after being incarcerated inmates are informed by the sentencing judge that they should continue treatment while in prison, inform the court of progress every six months, and that refusal of treatment is considered a lack of effort towards rehabilitation, which the judge may take into account when considering reduction of sentence (FPC: Article. 721-1). Correctional personnel, specifically parole authorities, are required to induce inmates to begin and complete programs that will assist in their rehabilitation.

As discussed previously, the French have tried various strategies to divert offenders with substance abuse and mental health issues. Treatment has been emphasized over incarceration for small-time offenders and problematic drug users. In some cases of simple drug use, particularly the use of cannabis, offenders receive a warning with a request to contact a social or health service. When legal proceedings are undertaken, judges often prescribe a detoxification program as a requirement connected with conditional release, and/or judicial supervision, such as probation or parole. Prosecutors in France are often limited relative to legal action if the person can demonstrate that he or she has been under medical supervision since the commission of a crime. If the offender is not under medical supervision, he or she may be ordered to follow a drug addiction treatment program or be placed under medical monitoring (CBH: Article L3423-1). For offenders with mental health issues the diversion alternative called *injonction thérapeutique* calls for treatment in the community rather than incarceration.

The psychiatrists and psychologists are the primary persons responsible for providing treatment to offenders with mental health and substance abuse issues. Most of these are under the control of the French health system. Additional psychologists, under the control of the head of the prison, are sometimes employed for special programs developed for inmates with special needs and for juveniles. Social workers and other health care professionals, such as substance abuse counselors, are also under the supervision of the specific prison administration even if they are volunteers from community-based agencies. To work with inmates in prison, personnel need to be certified by the Ministry of Justice and are required to undergo an orientation to become informed of security and functioning procedures. The issue of confidentiality between offenders and their doctors and other professionals is important in prison just like in civil society. However, confidentiality is sometimes secondary to the necessary collaboration between the judges and prison authorities especially when the issue is related to security.

An issue of growing concern for those who work in the French corrections system is the increasing number of convicted sex offenders entering the system. Their number has risen consistently for 20 years and as of 2006 they represent a quarter of all convicted inmates. Equally troubling is that among those convicted of sex offenses, there is a growing number of violent criminals. Because there is limited knowledge about the motives of sex offenders and how best to treat them, only a few professionals have the experience necessary to work in this area. Those who work with sex offenders must be wary of the complicated psychological issues of sex offenders and their unique abilities to deny responsibility for their crimes and/or manipulate mental health professionals. It is hoped that over time the development of professionals with expertise in the area will improve through information exchanges, training, and research. The challenges posed by sex offenders make it especially important for all correctional personnel, as well as judges and those who work with offenders outside prison, to be coordinated in their efforts when working with these inmates. Another issue of concern, especially for the inmates who admit to being sex offenders, is the threat of violence against them by other offenders. Similar to living in U.S. prisons, sex offenders usually rank among the bottom when it comes to gaining the respect of other inmates. Because inmates who are sex offenders are seen as the "lowest of the low" they are often susceptible to exploitation and violence from other inmates.

CURRENT TRENDS IN THE CRIMINAL JUSTICE SYSTEM

Over the past 20 years, the French have made efforts to address important criminal justice issues, especially in the areas of prevention, judicial alternatives to incarceration, and the treatment of those involved with the criminal justice system. Relative to the area of prevention and substance abuse, the French formed the Interministerial Mission for the Fight against Drugs and Drug Addiction (Mission interministérielle de lutte contre la drogue et la toxicomanie – MILDT) in 1982. This body, which has operated under various names since its creation, coordinates government action in the fields of prevention, health and social care, law enforcement, training, communication, research, and international cooperation. The MILDT prepares the government's plans in its fight against drugs and monitors their application. Since June 1999, its mandate includes not only illicit substances, but also abuse of alcohol, tobacco and psychotropic substances. This change is particularly important in understanding the direction of French public policy, as addressing alcohol abuse has become a main priority of the French government in recent years. The MILDT also oversees the activities of 17 ministries involved in the fight against drugs and the prevention of addiction and supports the work of other state and private partners. The funding for MILDT is derived from a consortium of government agencies and is responsible for funding public interest groups such as the French Monitoring Centre for Drugs and Drug Addiction (OFDT–Observatoire Français des Drogues et des Toxicomanies), which is an organization responsible for collecting available data on drugs and dependencies.

A second current trend in French criminal justice is the development of judicial alternatives and/or ways of diverting cases away from formal criminal sanctioning. Since the early 1980s new judicial responses to crime have been developed under the terminology coined the "third way." The goal of this movement is to develop options other than the two previously existing alternatives of formal processing of cases or closing cases without any formal legal action. In the latter case, prosecutors would often choose to close cases "without pursuit" due to their workload or the relative insignificance of specific cases. The alternative measures that have been developed include *penal mediation* (used in 12% of diversion cases), *remind of the law* (similar to verbal reprimand in USA and used in 50% of diversion cases), *reparation of the injury* (similar to financial restitution and used in 14% of cases). Some lesser employed strategies include referral to a professional organization for training, court ordered treatment, and a 1999 law called *procédure de composition pénale*. In this program prosecutors may utilize measures such as revocation of a person's driver's license and community service for certain misdemeanors and violations.

Finally, there are several initiatives that have taken place in France relative to how criminal justice personnel treat offenders and those in contact with police. A group called the League of Human Rights and of the Citizen (LDH) is concerned with the rights and treatment of those detained by police and in the correctional system. They denounce police abuse and the profiling of racial minorities. LDH also supports the view that prisons, as well as the police, must be under constant observation through the formation of citizen review boards. Another citizen group called the *Association loi de 1901* aims to provide the public with information about the problems of imprisonment and rehabilitation of prisoners. It is composed of former prisoners, journalists, academics, artists, other like-minded organizations, and individual citizens. The Association provides a communication network and web page access for those with similar interests.

CONCLUSIONS

Although it appears that there has been a concerted effort by the French Government to address the health needs of those incarcerated, it is equally clear that their work is far from completed. In fact, two major inspections have resulted in reports that have clearly documented the need for additional changes in the way health care is conducted in French prisons.

In 2001, a report by the French Inspector General stated that there has been an overall improvement in meeting the health care needs of inmates in the French correctional system. The 1994 law placing health care of incarcerated people under the control of the National Health Care Service and the National Insurance System was the main catalyst for change in this direction. However, there remain major concerns about the system. Probably the biggest concerns are the previously underestimated health care costs and the aging prison population. As mentioned earlier in this chapter, the French prison population, like that of the United States, is getting considerably older. This comes from the recent push to get tough on crime and to incarcerate serious offenders for longer periods of time. The report also pointed out a number of other challenges that must be addressed if the system is to be in compliance with current health standards and international norms. These challenges include the following:

• the need to improve cooperation between prisoners and health care professionals
• the need to improve safety related to the transfer of inmates to local hospitals and medical services
• the need to improve cooperation between social, medical and correctional services related to the treatment of drug addiction
• the need to address concerns about hygiene in health care and correctional facilities
• the need to address the increasing difficulty of taking care of inmates with mental challenges in prison. Prisons have seen a rise in the number of psychotic inmates, an increase in attacks on staff by inmates, and increase in inmate suicides (Inspection Generale, 2001).

More generally, there appears to be an increase in the demand for medical responses to deviant behavior, in particular for people who have committed sex-related offenses. However, formidable problems remain for the judiciary who must assess mental competence, the correctional system who deal with rehabilitation for those incarcerated, and the community health care system who deals with offenders upon release.

A second report published in January 2006 by the National Consultative Commission of Human Rights (CNCDH) described the current status of health care for correctional inmates. The results stressed the fact that the objective to provide the prison population with a health care service of the same quality and continuity as that provided for the rest of the French population was far from being realized. The major issue of concern in the CNCDH Report was prison crowding and its concomitant problems. The total number of persons incarcerated in France is above 51,000. More troubling, however, are the occupancy rates of prisons in France. As of January 2006 the ratio of the number of inmates to the number of prison beds was over 100 percent in more than half of the correctional facilities in France. And, in over one-third of the facilities the occupancy rate was above 150 percent. The crowding problem has led to a dearth of health provisions such as quality hygiene and health care coverage (Ministry of Justice, 2004). In some prisons there is no health care professional on duty in the evenings or weekends. Long waits to see a health care professional and the lack of escorts to and from hospital units in the community are commonplace (CNCDH, 2006). In addition to the problems endemic to the system, the inmates also complicate the problem of health care delivery. In some cases inmates with drug addictions and mental health issue refuse the compulsory care offered (Association Française de criminologie, 2002). This lack of cooperation can create conflicts with medical staff, prison officials, prison guards, and even the judiciary whose job it is to oversee legal rulings that serve society and benefit of the inmate.

The Ministry of Health and the Ministry of Justice are acutely aware of the problems of health care in French correctional institutions. Efforts to eradicate the crowding problem have included the planning of eight secure hospital units (UHSIs) that would house the growing number of inmates with mental health issues. Three are completed and presently functional. Even when institutions do provide adequate services, they struggle with the balance of providing sufficient health care while maintaining security. When inmates are released to community agencies and they return to crime, prison officials are open to criticism by the media for being too lenient on offenders. If an inmate dies while in the custody of the prison, officials are criticized for lack of control and supervision. Cries often follow to harden penal policies. Politics then come into play when elections result in the philosophical changes in policies. In France, the shift from a more liberal view of dealing with offenders to tougher policies has moved the discussion away from the reduction of incarceration and better prison conditions to more punitive incarceration policies. In spite of the challenges that are currently present, hope remains that prisons in France will continue to work to improve health and rehabilitation-related conditions for inmates while trying to address concerns about public safety.

REFERENCES

Association Française de criminologie (2002). Les soins obligés ou l'utopie de la triple entente. Editions DALLOZ.

CPH: French Code of Public Health. *Code de Santé Publique, lutte contre la toxicomanie, Livre IV, article L3411-1 à L3424-5.* French Code of Public Health, fight against addiction, Section 4, Article L3411-1 through L3424-5 and 3213-1 through 3213-2.

Coldefy, M., Faure, P. & Prieto, N. (2002). La santé mentale et le suivi psychiatrique des détenus accueillis par les services médico-psychologiques régionaux, Etudes et résultats, DREES, n° 181.

CNCDH (2006): Commission nationale consultative des droits de l'homme, propositions, adoptée par l'Assemblée Plénière le 19 janvier 2006).

Dammer, H., Fairchild, E. & Albanese, J. S. (2006). *Comparative criminal justice systems* (3rd ed.). Belmont, CA: Thomson Wadsworth Press.

Falissard, B. (2005). Etude épidémiologique sur la santé mentale des personnes détenues en 2003–2004, Ministère de la santé et ministère de la justice, en cours de publication.

FPC: French Penal Code. *Code Pénal, partie legislative, section 4, Du traffic de stupéfiants, article 222-34 à 222-43.* French Penal Code, legislative part, Section 4, Drug trafficking, article 222-34 through 222-43, 227-18, 122-1, 721-1 and 64.

Guillonneau, M., & Kensey, A. (1997). La santé en milieu carcéral, Eléments d'analyse démographique, *Revue française des affaires sociales, La santé en prison: un enjeu de santé publique, 1,* 41–59.

Hill, G. (2002). The French Prison Service steadily improves. *Corrections Compendium, 27,* 12–13.

ICPS–International Centre for Prison Studies. (2004). Retrieved July 24, 2004, from www.kcl.ac.uk/depsta/rel/icps/home.html

Inspection générale des affaires sociale (IGAS) / Inspection générale des services judiciaires (IGS) (2001) *'organisation de soins aux détenus: rapport d'évaluation,* La Documentation français.

Kensey, A. (2006, juin). Les détenus de 1996 à 2006, Quelques données comparatives, *Cahiers de démographie pénitentiaire*n°19. Paris: Ministère de la justice.

Kensey, A., Cassan, F., & Toulemon, L. (2000). La prison: Un risque plus fort pour les classes populaires, *Cahier de démographie pénitentiaire* n° 9, Paris : Ministère de la justice, DAP.

Ministry of Justice. (1998). *The prison service in France.* Paris: Central Headquarters of the Prison Service.

Ministère de la Justice (2004, septembre). *Guide méthodologique relatif à la prise en charge sanitaire des personnes détenues.* Paris: Ministère de la Santé et de la protection sociale, Ministère de la Justice.

Ministère de la Justice. (2005). *Rapport de la Commission santé-justice présidée par Monsieur Jean-François Burgelin.* Paris: Ministère de la justice; Ministère de la santé et des solidarités.

Ministère de la Justice (2006, janvier). *Les Chiffres clés de l'administration pénitentiaire . au 1er janvier 2006.* Paris: Ministère de la Justice.

Mouquet, M. C. (2005). La santé des personnes entrées en prison en 2003, *Etudes et résultats,* Direction de la recherche, des études, de l'évaluation et des statistiques (DREES) n° 386, mars 2005.

Terrill, R. J. (2003). *World criminal justice systems: A survey* (4th ed.). Cincinnati, OH: Anderson.

TNS SOFRES: Taylor Nelson Sofres, *Société Française d'études par sondage* (French Society research polls) (2006).

Tournier, P. V. (2007). *Des outils pour arpenter le champ pénal. Dictionnaire de démographie pénale,* ouvrage à paraître en 2007.

World Factbook (2007). *CIA world factbook: France.* Retrieved January 10, 2007, from https://www.cia.gov/cia/publications/factbook/geos/fr.html#Gov

Chapter 6

LEGAL AND PSYCHOLOGICAL CONTRIBUTIONS TO THE DEVELOPMENT OF CORRECTIONS IN CANADA

J. Stephen Wormith and Duyen Luong

INTRODUCTION: THE GEOPOLITICAL CONTEXT OF CANADIAN CORRECTIONS

Correctional agencies in Canada must span a huge land mass. As the world's second largest county, Canada covers almost 10 million square kilometers (Natural Resources Canada, 2001). Its population of approximately 32.6 million people (see Table 6.1; Statistics Canada, 2006) is concentrated in the southern extremity of the country in a one-hundred-mile ribbon that runs adjacent to the American border. This leaves vast expanses of thinly populated areas and substantial distances between major population centers.

Canada's cultural composition is unique, with two official languages (English and French) and a substantial Aboriginal population. Collectively, the First Nations, Métis and Inuit, along with their numerous subcultural groups constitute approximately 3 percent of the national population (Statistics Canada, 2001). The country has experienced a substantial transnational migration through the latter half of the twentieth century accepting approximately nine million people between 1950 and 2001 (Statistics Canada, 2005) such that international migration now accounts for about two-thirds of Canada's annual population growth (Statistics Canada, 2006). The process of assimilation of new Canadians has been referred to as a "vertical mosaic" in which a variety of ethnic groups are able to coexist while maintaining their cultural identities, a practice that differs somewhat from the historical "melting pot" of its southern neighbor, the United States of America (Porter, 1965, 1975). These geo-

TABLE 6.1
NATIONAL, PROVINCIAL, AND TERRITORIAL POPULATION
ESTIMATES AND CRIME RATES

Region	Population estimate[a]	Crime rate (per 100,000)
Canada	32,623,490	7,761[b]
Provinces		
Ontario	12,686,952	5,780[b]
Quebec	7,651,531	6,032[b]
British Columbia	4,310,452	11,947[b]
Alberta	3,375,763	10,023[b]
Manitoba	1,177,765	11,743[b]
Saskatchewan	985,386	14,320[b]
Nova Scotia	934,405	8,345[b]
New Brunswick	749,168	6,756[b]
Newfoundland and Labrador	509,677	6,089[b]
Prince Edward Island	138,519	7,985[b]
Territories		
Northwest Territories	41,861	42,126[c]
Yukon	31,229	23,125[c]
Nunavut	30,782	36,685[c]

Note. a. Adapted from: Statistics Canada, September 2006, Annual demographic estimates: Canada, Provinces and Territories, 2005–2006, Cat no. 91-215-XIE, 2006, p. 15. Adapted with permission of the author.
b. Adapted from: Statistics Canada, 2006, Crime Statistics in Canada, 2005, Cat no. 85-002-XIE, Vol 26, no. 4, 2005, p. 4 (Beattie, 2006). Adapted with permission of the author.
c. Adapted from Public Safety and Emergency Preparedness Portfolio Corrections Statistics Committee, 2005, Corrections and conditional release statistical overview, Catalogue no. PS1-3/2005E, pp 3–4.

graphic, ethnic and cultural dimensions have had important implications for the development and delivery of correctional services in Canada.

Crime and Corrections in Canada

Politically, Canada is a parliamentary democracy consisting of ten provinces and three territories, each of which, along with the federal government, has its own correctional agency. Since the passing of the *Constitution Act,* which declared Canada an independent country from Great Britain in 1867, corrections has been a joint responsibility of both the federal and provincial governments. Although there is one criminal code for the entire country, *The Criminal Code of Canada* (the *Code*; Criminal Code, 1985), the federal government is only responsible for offenders who are sentenced to periods of incarceration from two years to life imprisonment. Federal corrections consists of two federal agencies, the Correctional Service of Canada (CSC), which is responsible for the custody and care of all "federal offenders" and for their supervision in the community, and the National Parole Board (NPB), which is responsible for the release (parole) and revocation decisions pertaining to all federal offenders. Offenders who are sentenced to any other kind of sanction, including community service, fines, probation and periods of incarceration up to "two years less a day," are the responsibility of the provincial correctional agency in the province where the offense is committed.

Under the *Code,* all offenders sentenced to custody are eligible for statutory remission, which amounts to one third of their sentence length and may be released accordingly. However, inmates may be released even earlier, before their statutory release date, on parole (day or full parole). They may also lose some or all of their statutory remission for misbehavior. Moreover, offenders may be "detained" beyond their statutory release date (two-thirds of their sentence) until the complete expiration of their sentence if it has been determined that they are likely to commit a serious violent offense prior to the end of their sentence (their "warrant expiry"). While federal offenders who receive statutory release are supervised in the community until their warrant expiry, provincial offenders are not. However, provincial offenders' sentences may include a term of probation following their custodial sentence. Although aggregate national data are not available, Ontario (2006) reports that 30.5 percent of provincial custodial sentences in 2005/06 included a period of probation (up to three years) to follow the custodial portion of the sentence. Provincial inmates may also apply for parole, in which case the application is referred to the NPB in all but the two largest provinces (Ontario and Quebec), which have their own provincial parole boards. Provincial correctional agencies are also responsible for all remanded offenders and related activities such as conducting presentence reports for court. Although some provincial jurisdictions delegated some of their responsibilities to county jails in the past, counties no longer play any role in corrections in Canada. Consequently, with only two levels of government and 13 provinces and territories involved in the delivery of correctional services, it is a relatively simple correctional system in comparison to the U.S., but more complex than some European countries with their single justice and correctional systems.

In 2005, the national crime rate, based on crime reported to police, was 7,761 per 100,000 of the general population (Beattie, 2006). However, there is considerable variability in the provincial and territorial crime rates across the country (Table 6.1). The incarceration rate (including remanded prisoners) over the last five years has been quite stable, ranging from 134 per 100,000 adults in 2000/01 to 129 per 100,000 in 2004/05 (Beattie, 2006). Consequently Canada remains in the mid-range of incarcerating countries (Walmsley, 2003), along with Oceanic countries (110) and the United Kingdom (139), but considerably higher than southern European (69) and Scandinavian countries (59) and considerably lower than eastern European (213) and central Asian (416) countries and the United States (737; Harrison & Beck, 2006).

Although the federal correctional system receives prominent political, professional and public attention because of the seriousness of the crimes committed by its clientele, only 3.7 percent of all adult custodial sentences in 2002/03 were for federal terms (two years or more), while the majority (55.6%) were for less than one month (Public Safety and Emergency Preparedness Canada, 2004). In fact, less that 30 percent of the estimated 310,000 convictions in adult court during 2002/03 resulted in custodial sentences (27% in a provincial sentence and 1.4% in a federal sentence).

CSC consists of 54 penitentiaries, 17 community correctional centers, and 21 parole offices (Correctional Service Canada, 2005a). In 2005, 21,702 offenders, including 368 women, were under federal jurisdiction. Fully 70 percent of the CSC population was serving a sentence for a violent offence such as murder and sexual offences. Most federal offenders (58.2%) were incarcerated (Table 6.2), while almost a third of them (30.7%) were actively being supervised in the community (e.g., day parole, full parole, and statutory release). The majority of male and female inmates are classified as medium level security (Table 6.3; Correctional Service Canada). Approximately 70 percent of federally incarcerated offenders are Caucasian (Public Safety and Emergency Preparedness Canada, 2005). Although Aboriginal peoples represent 3 percent of the general population, 16 percent of the federally incarcerated population is Aboriginal (Correctional Service Canada). The average daily cost of housing a federal inmate was $259.05CDN in 2004/05 (Beattie, 2006).

In 2003/04, almost 20,000 offenders were provincially or territorially incarcerated (Beattie, 2006). For the first time, the proportion of remanded and sentenced inmates was the same (Table 6.2). This represents a dramatic change since 1996/97 when 72 percent of the provincial and territorial offender population consisted of sentenced inmates. This steady change in the provincial and territorial prison population has raised a number of concerns, including questions about why this trend has occurred and how a correctional agency can best serve its remanded prisoners. Current speculation is that a "two-for-one" sentencing policy is at least partially responsible for the increase in remanded prisoners as it may have created a disincentive for defense council to proceed in a timely fashion with court proceedings. In 2000, a Supreme Court of Canada's decision, *R. v. Wust*, declared that prisoners are to be granted two days off of their official sentence for every one day spent on remand on the assumption that "remand" time is considerably more onerous than sentenced time. As discussed below, the introduction of conditional sentences may also have affected the ratio of remanded-to-sentenced inmates in provin-

TABLE 6.2
DISTRIBUTION OF OFFENDERS UNDER FEDERAL, PROVINCIAL, AND
TERRITORIAL JURISDICTION

Disposition	n (%)
Federal sentence (total)[a]	21,702
Incarcerated[a]	12,624 (58.2%)
Active supervision[a]	6,656 (30.7%)
Temporarily detained[a]	1,142 (5.3%)
Unlawfully at large (UAL)[a]	646 (3.0%)
Deported[a]	420 (1.9%)
Escaped[a]	146 (0.7%)
Bail[a]	68 (0.3%)
Provincial and territorial sentence (total)[b]	133,362
Custodial[b]	19,816
Sentenced[b]	9,830 (49.6%)
Remand[b]	9,640 (48.6%)
Other (e.g., temporary detention)[b]	346 (1.7%)
Community supervision[b]	113,546
Probation[b]	98,805 (87.0%)
Conditional sentence[b]	13,931 (12.3%)
Parole[b]	810 (0.7%)

Note. a. Data adapted from Corrections and conditional release statistical overview, by Public Safety and Emergency Preparedness Portfolio Corrections Statistics Committee, 2005, Ottawa, ON: Public Works and Government Services Canada.
b. Data adapted from: Statistics Canada, 2006, Adult Correctional Services in Canada, 2004/2005, Cat no. 85-002-XIE, vol. 26 no. 5, 2004/2005, p. 5 (Beattie, 2006). Adapted with permission from author.

cial and territorial corrections. The average daily cost of incarcerating a provincial or territorial offender was $141.78CDN in 2004/05 (Beattie, 2006).

LEGAL AND HEALTH-RELATED PUBLIC POLICY

Sentencing in Canada

The sentencing practices described above represent an important difference between the justice system in Canada and the U.S. This is particularly apparent in the incarceration rate for adults in the two countries. In 2003/04, there was an average of 152,600 adults under correctional supervision in Canada (less than 1% of the population; Beattie, 2006) while in the United States, in 2005 at year-end, there were approximately 7.0 million adults (approximately 3% of the population) under correctional supervision (Harri-

TABLE 6.3
DISTRIBUTION OF FEDERALLY INCARCERATED OFFENDERS ACCORDING
TO ETHNICITY, SECURITY LEVEL, AND GENDER

	n (%)	
Ethnicity[a]		
Caucasian	15,266 (70.3%)	
Aboriginal	3,498 (16.1%)	
Black	1,344 (6.2%)	
Asian	860 (4.0%)	
Other/Unknown	596 (2.7%)	
Hispanic	138 (0.6%)	
	Male	Female
Security level[b]		
Maximum	1,737 (14%)	36 (9%)
Medium	7,359 (61%)	170 (45%)
Minimum	2,226 (18%	140 (37%)
Not yet classified	712 (6%)	33 (9%)
Total	12,034 (100%)	379 (100%)
Age group[c]		
Less than 18	5 (0.04%)	
18–19	125 (1%)	6 (2%)
20–29	3,354 (28%)	125 (33%)
30–39	3,889 (32%)	138 (36%)
40–49	2,950 (25%)	73 (19%)
50 and older	1,711 (14%)	37 (10%)

Note. a. Adapted from "Corrections and conditional release statistical overview," by Public Safety and Emergency Preparedness Portfolio Corrections Statistics Committee, 2005, p. 52, Ottawa, ON: Public Works and Government Services Canada.
b, c. Data adapted from "Basic facts about the Correctional Service of Canada," by Correctional Service Canada, 2005, pp. 11 b–12 c, Ottawa, ON: Public Works and Government Services Canada.

son & Beck, 2006; Glaze & Bonczar, 2006). The rate of incarceration in Canada has hovered around 150 prisoners per 100,000 people for a number of decades while in the United States, it has continued to creep upwards from around 150 prisoners per 100,000 people in 1980 to 491 sentenced prisoners per 100,000 U.S. residents in 2005 (Statistics Canada, 1997; Harrison & Beck, 2006). Moreover, the Canadian parliament abolished the death penalty in 1977 and in fact has not executed a prisoner since 1962 (Department of Justice, 2005). Although calls continue from various political and ideological circles for more "American style justice" including a return to capital punishment and the introduction of a "three strikes" law for violent and sexual offenders, such lobbying has not yet resulted in any substantial change in Canadian sentencing policy or practice.

These patterns of sentencing in Canada are rooted in the *Criminal Code of Canada,* which speaks to the fundamental principles of sentencing for the judiciary to apply throughout the country[1] (see Appendix A). Specifically, the *Code* speaks to proportionality[2] of the sentence and lists a number of aggravating and mitigating factors that must be considered.[3] Alternative measures and conditional sentences are also featured prominently. If the accused acknowledges the offense for which he or she has been charged, and agrees to participate in a program of alternative measures sanctioned by the Attorney General of the province and agreed upon by the victim, the court will dismiss the charge upon being convinced that the terms of the alternative measures as set out in the particular case have been met.[4]

Conditional sentences, which were introduced as a sentencing option in 1996, have also had a significant impact on the incarceration rate in Canada because of the breadth of cases to which they may be applied. For offences that carry a sentence of less than two years and which do not carry a minimum custody requirement, the court may order that the sentence be served in the community provided that the safety of the community is not compromised and is consistent with the aforementioned principles of sentencing.[5] The conditions of all conditional sentences are to keep the peace, appear before court, report to a supervisor, notify the court about a change of address and stay within the jurisdiction. Additional conditions tailored to the specifics of the case may include abstinence from the use of alcohol or drugs, abstinence from owning or possessing a firearm, provision of supportive care for dependents, performance of community service, and attendance at treatment programs. In the first four years of operation approximately 43,000 conditional sentences were issued (Roberts & LaPrairie, 2000), substantially reducing provincial prison populations of sentenced offenders. A more recent review of the use of conditional sentencing in Canada (Roberts & Gabor, 2004) indicated that the use of the conditional sentence appears to have been responsible for an actual *decline* in the overall number of incarcerated adults in Canada. Only the province of Prince Edward Island was exempt from this trend, with every other province showing a reduction in custodial sentences.

Important case law has also shaped sentencing practices in Canada with a number of decisions from the Supreme Court of Canada. For example, from *R v. Proulx,* the sentencing process must include principles of rehabilitation and restorative justice in addition to its punitive objectives. The Supreme

---

1. R.S., 1985, c. C-46, s. 718; R.S., 1985, c. 27 (1st Supp.), s. 155; 1995, c. 22, s. 6.
2. R.S., 1985, c. 27 (1st Supp.), s. 156; 1995, c. 22, s. 6.
3. 1995, c. 22, s. 6; 1997, c. 23, s. 17; 2000, c. 12, s. 95; 2001, c. 32, s. 44(F), c. 41, s. 20; 2005, c. 32, s. 25.
4. R.S., 1985, c. C-46, s. 717; 1995, c. 22, s. 6.
5. 1992, c. 11, s. 16; 1995, c. 19, s. 38, c. 22, s. 6; 1997, c. 18, s. 107.1.

Court also declared in *R. v. Gladue* that the sentencing of Aboriginal offenders must consider the social conditions that the Aboriginal community has endured for generations as a mitigating factor in sentencing. Elsewhere, it was determined by the Supreme Court of Canada in *R. v. Johnson*, that the principle of "least restrictive alternative" must be applied, not only to minor offenses, but in considering the most severe mode of punishment, an indefinite sentence, for offenders who are to be declared "Dangerous Offenders."

Health Care in Canada

Another important difference that distinguishes Canada from the U.S. is the means by which health care is delivered to its residents. It is not the intention of this chapter to conduct a review of the ongoing, heated debate about public versus private health care, but rather to describe the Canadian health care system in order to understand its implications for corrections in Canada. The concept of universal health care delivered by a public health care system was enshrined by the government of Canada in 1957, although the most recent version, the *Canada Health Act* was adopted in 1984. Although the delivery of health care services is the responsibility of each province, large transfer payments from the federal government to the provinces are contingent upon the provinces adhering to these fundamental principles of universal health care, and although there has been an increasing number of exceptions allowed for private health care in Canada, the availability of public health care services for all residents is considered a basic right within Canadian society (Department of Justice Canada, 1985). That having been said, however, services for mentally disordered individuals are often limited, particularly in rural and remote areas of the country (Sealy & Whitehead, 2004).

In spite of these legal, health, and social policy differences between the two countries, numerous similarities remain, some of which may be due to international trends and the consequence of geographic and economic ties such as the *North American Free Trade Agreement Implementation Act of 1993*. The deinstitutionalization movement, which began to empty traditional psychiatric hospitals throughout the Western world in the 1960s, remains a public health policy in Canada. Yet 40 years later, it continues to put a strain on community mental health resources across the country (Sealy & Whitehead, 2004). The incidence of mentally disordered offenders in correctional facilities is an important concern among mental health and correctional officials. This includes both the sentenced and remanded inmate population. Although some accused persons who have been remanded to custody with an apparent mental disorder may be transferred to a psychiatric setting for evaluation, this is often a time limited event (up to two months). However, many others are not, particularly if they have been charged with a relatively minor offense. Some seriously disordered offenders are convicted and then sentenced to a traditional term of incarceration in either the provincial or federal correctional system, rather than be found "not criminally responsible" on account of mental disorder and detained indefinitely under Canada's version of M'Naghten (1843).

Correctional Law, Policy, and Scrutiny

The *Canadian Charter of Rights and Freedoms,* which is now in *the Constitution Act* (1982), introduced a number of fundamental legal rights into Canada's constitution (see Appendix B). However, correctional services in Canada have not been without their difficulties. Prison disturbances and riots, staff and inmate deaths, allegations of abuse and neglect, complaints about health care and violation of fundamental rights, and the presence of contraband, including drugs and weapons, have occurred all too frequently in both federal and provincial correctional systems (e.g., Arbour, 1996; Hennessy, 1999). These events, however, have been taken very seriously at the political and administrative level of Canada's justice system, with a litany of commissions and other kinds of investigatory review following many of the most serious events that have occurred in Canadian prisons. These include the Ouimet Report (1969), the McGuigan Report (1977), the Carson Report (1984), the Vantour Reports (1975; 1984), the Daubney Report (1988), and the Arbour Report (1996) on the incarceration of women offenders. These investigations and reviews focused primarily, some exclusively, on the federal correctional system, originally known as the Canadian Penitentiary Service, but which amalgamated with the National Parole Service in 1977 to form the Correctional Service of Canada (Canada, 1977). These reports and inspired leadership of Ole Ingstrup (Jackson, 2002) led to a clearly delineated "mission" for CSC that formalized a respect for both offender and staff.

Another important activity in the 1980s was an examination of *The Criminal Law in Canadian Society* (CLCS; Canada, 1982). A component of CLCS was the Correctional Law Review, which included a systematic review of law pertaining to Canadian corrections and wide ranging consultations about the purpose and function of the Canadian correctional system. Inspired in part by the work of the Correctional Service of Canada, but proposed for correctional agencies throughout Canada, its statement of purpose and principles was as follows:

> The purpose of corrections is to contribute to the maintenance of a just, peaceful and safe society by:
>
> 1. carrying out the sentence of the court having regard to the stated reasons of the sentencing judge, as well as all relevant material presented during the trial and

    sentencing of offenders, and by providing the judiciary with clear information about correctional operations and resources;

2. providing the degree of custody or control necessary to contain the risk presented by the offender;

3. encouraging offenders to adopt acceptable behaviour patterns and to participate in education, training, social development and work experiences designed to assist them to become law-abiding citizens;

4. encouraging offenders to prepare for eventual release and successful reintegration in the society through the provision of a wide range of program opportunities responsive to their individual needs;

5. providing a safe and healthful environment to incarcerated offenders, which is conducive to their personal reformation, and by assisting offenders in the community to obtain or provide for themselves the basic services of all members of society. (Solicitor General Canada, 1986, p. 29)

    Other key guideposts for corrections in Canada over the last 20 years have been the *Canadian Charter of Rights and Freedoms* (1982) and the *Corrections and Conditional Release Act* (CCRA; 1992). The former enshrines the principle of cruel and unusual punishment in the Canadian constitution. The latter bill solidified the Office of the Correctional Investigator (OCI), which had been established in 1972, but now acts as an official and independent "watch dog" over correctional services in Canada and reports directly to the Minister of Public Safety and Emergency Preparedness. As an ombudsperson for federal offenders, the function of the Correctional Investigator is "to conduct investigations into the problems of offenders related to decisions, recommendations, acts or omissions of the Commissioner (of Corrections) or any person under the control and management of, or performing services for, or on behalf of, the Commissioner, that affect offenders individually or as a group" (CCRA, s. 167. (1). Inquiries may be initiated on the basis of a complaint or at the initiative of the Correctional Investigator. Investigators are given significant authority including the conducting of hearings under oath. The OCI may issue recommendations to the Commissioner. If the OCI determines that appropriate action is not taken within a reasonable period of time, he or she may report such conclusions to the Minister and include them in an annual report to the Parliament of Canada. In the last couple of years, the Annual Report of the OCI directed much of its attention to marginalized offender groups, in particular, to mentally disordered, Aboriginal, women, and elderly offenders (Sapers, 2006).

    Correctional case law has also played an important role in shaping Canadian corrections. For example, *Marineau v. Matsqui Institutional Disciplinary Board* held that rules put in place by a correctional agency (e.g., called Commissioner's Directives in CSC) are not the same as statutes and regulations in that they are internally developed, are not legally binding but administrative in nature and, in the end, amount to directions to staff as to how to carry out their jobs. As such, directives must be of an operational policy nature and are not about the rights of the offender, any limitation of which must be prescribed by law.

However, mission statements and declarations of purpose and value are not sufficient to maintain a fair, effective, and balanced correctional system. Two very important activities that followed were the Daubney Report (1988) and the Arbour Report (1996). In its most comprehensive review of sentencing and correctional practices, Daubney went a long way to extend the scope of sentencing practices to the myriad of alternatives that were either available previously but not used to their fullest extent (e.g., victim-offender reconciliation, mediation, restitution community service orders, and enhanced probation services), or emerged through subsequent legislation, such as the creation of "conditional sentences" in 1996.

Women and Aboriginal Offenders

Arbour (1996), supported by other initiatives, was instrumental in changing the manner in which women have been perceived and treated in federal corrections. Guided by the *Canadian Charter of Rights and Freedoms,* the CCRA (1992), the Task Force of Federally Sentenced Women (Ashton & Hawthorn, 1990), and the work of the Correctional Investigator, a national infrastructure of federal correctional facilities (CSC) was constructed for women across the country. This ended a centralist practice that had been in place since the construction of a single federal Prison for Women in 1934. Although CSC has conducted internal reviews of its services for female offenders, it has recently established an independent, expert panel to assess these reports and further examine the progress that the organization has made vis-à-vis women offenders in the ten years since the Arbour Report (Correctional Service of Canada, 2006).

Aboriginal offenders represent another offender group that warrants special consideration as they have been dramatically overrepresented in Canadian corrections for decades. This issue did not begin to receive serious and consistent attention until the late 1980s (Daubney, 1988; Hamilton & Sinclair, 1991; Ross, 1992). Since then, the treatment and processing of Aboriginal offenders by Canada's justice system has commanded considerable attention in government sponsored investigations, some of which have generated recommendations for massive systemic change, and in scholarly works.

A Manitoba Commission of Inquiry in 1991 led to the establishment of a permanent provincial Aboriginal Justice Implementation Commission (Chartrand, Whitecloud, McKay & Young, 2001) that has recommended the development of an Aboriginal employment strategy, more support for Aboriginal policing, employing more Aboriginal workers in corrections and probation, and greater use of alternative measures for Aboriginal youth. In Saskatchewan, a Commission on First Nations and Métis Peoples and Justice Reform (Littlechild, 2004) examined the "criminogenic social conditions" that lie behind Aboriginal offending. The Commission recommended widespread changes for police, court and correctional services, including a call for more therapeutic resources and sentencing alternatives with an Aboriginal focus. Academic scholars such as Waldram (1997; 2004) have investigated the collision between Aboriginal traditional culture and modern Western clinical practices in addressing the health care needs of Aboriginal offenders.

These efforts have generated a greater perspective of cultural awareness and acceptance by correctional officials to the extent that all federal facilities and many provincial ones, particularly those in the Prairie Provinces where there is a high local indigenous population, have culturally specific programs for Aboriginal offenders. They include programs that are uniquely Aboriginal (e.g., healing centers and sweat lodges) and the practice of other Aboriginal activities (e.g., Aboriginal art), as well as more generic programs that are specifically tailored to Aboriginal offenders, such as Aboriginal substance abuse or sexual offending (Ellerby, Bedard, & Chartrand, 2000; Williams, Vallee, & Staubi, 1997). However, the systematic evaluation of these types of programming is just beginning and it is premature to comment on their efficacy in terms of client outcome. Although not without difficulty, as one would expect when different world views and treatment paradigms are combined under one roof (Mason, 2001), these efforts attempt to combine "the best of both worlds." By melding the cognitive-behavioral modality with a spiritual healing modality, they represent an effort to simultaneously incorporate general and specific responsivity (Andrews, Bonta, & Hoge, 1990; Ellerby & Stonechild, 1998).

MENTAL HEALTH AND SUBSTANCE ABUSE ISSUES

A brief overview of the Canadian health care system as it relates to mental health is necessary to provide a context for later discussion on mental health and substance abuse issues in Canadian corrections. The *Canada Health Act* (1984), passed unanimously by the House of Commons and Senate in 1984, is the federal legislation on health insurance (Health Canada, 2002) guaranteeing universal health care services to all residents of Canada. Although provinces and territories are responsible for the delivery of health services as outlined by the *Canada Health Act,* the federal government is responsible for the health care of federally incarcerated offenders under the *Corrections and Conditional Release Act* (CCRA, 1992).

In 2001, Roy Romanow was appointed Commissioner of the Commission on the Future of Health Care in Canada to review the Canadian health care system and make recommendations on its long term sustainability. In the final report (completed in 2002 and known as the Romanow Report), mental health was described as the "orphan child" of the health care system (p. 178) and was identified as one of the three areas that should be addressed in the recommendation related to home care services. Specifically, "home mental health care management and intervention services should immediately be included in the scope of medically necessary services covered under the *Canada Health Act*" (p. 252). According to the Romanow report, with the movement towards deinstitutionalization, treatment of persons with mental disorders necessitates home care. However, persons with mental disorders are often not eligible for home care as these services are usually reserved for those who have a physical disability or require assistance with activities of daily living. Moreover, the closure of psychiatric hospitals during the deinstitutionalization movement was not met with a commensurate increase in psychiatric services in the community (e.g., Hartford et al., 2004) or appropriate housing for persons with mental disorders (Ormston, 2003). In addition to other factors, it is no surprise that persons with mental disorders often have difficulty accessing mental health services and the barriers to accessing these services are even greater for individuals who come into contact with the law or have criminal histories. However, it is necessary to understand the magnitude of the problem to appreciate the challenges that are presented.

Prevalence of Mental Disorders and Substance Abuse in Corrections

In examining the prevalence rates of mental disorders in the offender population, and particularly when comparing rates across studies, it is important to remember that differences in rates may reflect differences in methodology (e.g., diagnostic interviews, intake assessments, self-report) and diagnostic criteria (i.e., changes in diagnostic criteria in subsequent versions of the Diagnostic and Statistical Manual of Mental Disorders [DSM] may result in difference in prevalence rates) rather than actual differences in the rates of mental disorders. In addition, comparison of the prevalence of mental disorders across regions in Canada may be influenced by differential availability of mental health services as well as variations in recording practices (Canadian Public Health Association, 2004).

One of the earlier studies on the prevalence of mental health issues among federally incarcerated male offenders was conducted by Motiuk and Porporino (1991) using a combination of stratified (by region) and systematic random sampling for institutions that housed general population inmates, and the complete population of five specialized facilities (i.e., entire population of the two High Maximum Security Treatment Units, two Regional Psychiatric Centers, and one Regional Treatment Centre). A total of 2,185 interviews with the Diagnostic Interview Schedule (DIS), 260 of which were from the five specialized facilities, were completed to assess the presence of 8 categories of disorders from the *Diagnostic and Statistical Manual of Mental Disorders, Third Edition* (DSM-III; American Psychiatric Association, 1980). In addition, they used "wide" and "stringent" diagnostic criteria to establish the upper and lower bounds of the prevalence rates. The wide criteria ignore the issue of disorder severity and include disorders that may have resulted from other mental health problems whereas the stringent criteria require the presence of all the identifying behaviors and exclude disorders that may be due to other mental health problems.

The order of the lifetime prevalence rates for the eight categories of disorders were the same for both sets of criteria with antisocial (i.e., antisocial personality disorder), alcohol-related problems, and anxiety as the most frequently occurring categories of disorders. The prevalence rate for antisocial personality disorder was present in 56.9 percent to 74.9 percent (for stringent and wide criteria, respectively); alcohol-related problems were found in 47.2 percent to 69.8 percent of the sample; and anxiety disorders were reported in 44.1 percent to 55.6 percent of the sample. Substance-related and depressive problems were ranked as the fourth and fifth, respectively at 40.9 percent to 52.9 percent and 21.5 percent to 29.8 percent. Psychosexual, psychotic, and organic disorders were the least prevalent categories at 21.1 percent to 24.5 percent, 7.7 percent to 10.4 percent, and 0.1 percent to 4.3 percent, respectively. Moreover, they found that the prevalence rates across the five regions were comparable and differences may have been due to methodological artifacts (Motiuk & Porporino, 1991).

More recently, a large scale study of the health care needs of male and female offenders incarcerated in federal institutions was reported in a special issue of the *Canadian Journal of Public Health* (Canadian Public Health Association, 2004). Data from CSC's Offender Management System were gathered on the mental health needs of offenders admitted to institutions across the agency's five regions for a three-year period beginning in 1999. Mental health needs were identified in 11.9 percent and 20.5 percent of male and female admissions, respectively. The distribution of selected Axis I and Axis II disorders in each region is presented in Table 6.4. There appears to be substantial variation in proportion of disorders in each region. However, these differences may reflect differential availability of specialized services in the regions as well as reporting practices. For example, the institutions in the Pacific and Ontario regions record only the primary diagnosis (whether it be an Axis I or

TABLE 6.4
DISTRIBUTION OF SELECTED AXIS I AND AXIS II DISORDERS
AMONG PSYCHIATRIC IN-PATIENTS BY CORRECTIONAL
SERVICES OF CANADA REGION

Disorder	Percentage of the psychiatric in-patient sample within each region				
	Pacific	Prairie	Ontario	Quebec	Atlantic
Axis I disorders	N=190	N=281	N=221	N=134	N=69
Schizophrenia and other psychotic disorders	22	16	35	50	20
Substance-related disorders	6	57	6	23	27
Mood disorders	12	12	13	12	37
Sexual and gender identity disorders	20	6	28	0	0
Anxiety disorders	0	3	3	0	15
Axis II					
Antisocial personality disorder	65.4	82.0	36.7	39	39
Borderline disorder	7.7	6.2	0	35	22
Other	21.8	7.5	60	10	35

Note. Adapted from "A health care needs assessment of federal inmates in Canada," by Canadian Public Health Association, *Canadian Journal of Public Health, 95* (1), p. S42. Copyright 2004 by Canadian Public Health Association. Adapted with permission from assistant editor.

Axis II disorder), whereas other regions record both Axis I and Axis II disorders (Canadian Public Health Association, 2004).

Systematically collected prevalence information for provincial offenders is not as readily available. Wormith and McKeague (1996) found that 13.2 percent of their sample of Ontario provincial offenders supervised in the community had a psychiatric diagnosis and 6.4 percent had at least one admission to a psychiatric hospital. Nine percent of the sample scored below 51 on Global Assessment of Functioning (GAF), indicative of significant impairment due to mental health. Of the 328 offenders who had at least one psychiatric diagnosis, 98 had a second diagnosis. The most frequent category of disorders was alcohol and drug-related disorders (27.1%), followed by depression/bipolar disorders (15.5%), and sexual/personality disorders (14.2%). Anxiety/adjustment disorders and schizophrenia/psychotic disorders followed closely at 9.7 percent and 8.9 percent, respectively, of the sample with a psychiatric diagnosis.

Elsewhere, a survey was conducted to determine the prevalence of mental health issues among incarcerated women in British Columbia (Nicholls, Lee, Corrado, & Ogloff, 2004). Over half of the sample (58.8%) was on remand, while 29.9 percent were serving provincial custodial sentences. At the time of admission, 39.9 percent of the sample reported current or past use of medications to treat mental health issues, 28.9 percent had a history of receiving mental health treatment in the community, and 43.3 percent had a current problem with alcohol or drugs.

Although rates may vary from study to study and across the country, it is clear that a substantial proportion of offenders with serious mental health needs find themselves incarcerated in federal, provincial, and territorial correctional systems in spite of the various provisions that are available. Clearly, more services and options are required. This need is no longer apparent only to clinicians and researchers, but also to politicians. In a major and highly publicized review of mental health care in Canada, the needs of offenders with mental disorders, particularly those who are being jailed for nuisance behaviour, has been brought to the attention of the Canadian Senate for action (Kirby, 2006).

Mental Health and Diversion

Mental health diversion refers to the process by which individuals with mental illness who have come into contact with the law are diverted from the criminal justice system into the mental health system (Hartford et al., 2004). Diversion programs can generally be divided into "prebooking" and "postbooking" programs. Prebooking programs tend to be police-based. Rather than arresting and jailing a mentally ill individual who has committed a relatively minor offence, police may direct the individual to treatment services, such as a community crisis clinic. Post-booking programs may entail court-based diversion (which are employed before the individual is arraigned and may involve a stay of charges if the individual participates in treatment) or mental health courts, which are specialized courts that require the collaboration between agents from the criminal justice system, the courts, and treatment providers (Hartford et al., 2004). A sample of Canada's mental health diversion programs and services is presented below, followed by a brief discussion on the use of drug courts in Canada.

Calgary Diversion Project, Alberta

In 2001, the Alberta Mental Health Board (AMHB) sponsored the development and implementation of the Calgary Diversion Project (Alberta's Provincial Diversion Framework Working Committee, 2001). The original proposal for the project was presented to the Provincial Mental Health Advisory Board (PMHAB) by the Calgary Salvation Army in 1996 and involved the collaboration of the ministries of Justice, Solicitor General, Human Resources and Employment, and Health and Wellness.

The Calgary Diversion Project is a three-year pilot project that began accepting clients in January, 2002. Individuals who have committed a relatively minor offence, one which is judged to be due to a mental illness, may have his or her charge adjourned for three months. During this period, a more comprehensive assessment is completed and the project team will initiate linkages to community resources and ensure that the linkages are maintained by following up with the individual and the agencies to which he or she has been referred (Calgary Health Region, 2002). In addition, clients may access the Community Linkages and Social Support (CLASS) service which provide individually tailored services to address the needs and goals of the client. Prior to the end of the three-month period, the project team reports to the Crown Prosecutor's office detailing the individual's status and makes a recommendation with respect to withdrawal of charges (Calgary Health Region, 2005a).

During the pilot phase, 179 individuals had their charges adjourned for three months and 75 percent of this group had their charges withdrawn following successful progress in their diversion plan (Alberta Mental Health Board, 2004). At follow-up, 65 percent of the participants had established and maintained linkages with community services. In comparison to the nine-month period before diversion, the nine months after diversion saw reductions in the number of police complaints and charges (60% decrease), visits to the emergency room (20% decrease), days spent in the hospital (45% reduction), and number of court appearances (74% reduction; Calgary Health Region, 2005b). Furthermore, there was a 65 percent reduction in the number of admissions to inpatient hospital services among the clients who had their charges withdrawn (Alberta Mental Health Board). Finally, there was a saving of $1,721 per client in costs of acute care in the nine months following diversion compared to the preceding nine months (Calgary Health Region). The lessons learned from the Calgary Diversion Project have been applied to the development of similar initiatives in other areas of Alberta (Calgary Health Region). The program continues to operate through the support of the Alberta Mental Health Board and Calgary Health Region (Calgary Health Region, 2004).

The Ontario Experience

Court support services for people with serious mental illness who have come into contact with the criminal justice system are now available in all five of the Toronto area courthouses (Macfarlane et al., 2002). However, considerable effort was required to achieve the current status. In 1997, a Mental Health Court Support Network was established to facilitate the exchange of knowledge between the five courthouses. However, the operation of this network was short-lived and in 1998 a dedicated mental health court was established at one central location. A subsequent evaluation (Macfarlane et al., 2002) concluded that the development of services was unsystematic and largely independent of one another and therefore recommended the implementation of an "integrated court-based mental health Program" (p. 37). Since then a Mental Health Court Support Consortium has been created to establish "a formal network of organizations which provide mental health court support services to the five courthouses within the City of Toronto" (Mental Health Court Support Consortium, 2005, p. 4).

Four of the five courts have psychiatrists on-site to conduct fitness assessments. In addition, psychiatric assessments and court support services are provided by psychiatrists from a variety of sources including the Mount Sinai Hospital through the Assertive Community Treatment Team and in partnership with the Hong Fook Mental Health Association (Yang et al., 2005; Mental Health Court Support Consortium, 2005). Toronto is the capital of Ontario and is one of the most culturally-diverse cities in the world (City of Toronto, 2006). The Assertive Community Treatment Team from Mount Sinai is staffed by bilingual, bicultural staff from a number of ethno-cultural backgrounds and provides psychiatric outreach services to patients of severe and persistent mental illness of East or Southeast Asian, African, Caribbean, and Native descent (Yang et al., 2005).

Each of the five courthouses in Toronto also has staff to screen and identify individuals who may be eligible for pretrial mental health diversion. The diversion program is a voluntary program for individuals with serious mental illness who have been charged with a relatively minor offence. Participants must not have entered a guilty plea. Successful participants may have their charges stayed or withdrawn or be issued a peace bond, none of which will result in a criminal record (Mental Health Court Support Consortium, 2005).

In Northern Ontario, the city of Sudbury has a Mental Health Court Outreach program through which fitness and competency assessments, suicide risk, and screening for diversion or community treatment plans are completed (Stewart, 2005). The mental health court worker coordinates services in the community (e.g., housing, addictions services, and psychiatric services) so that the individuals can be managed in the community. Two justice case managers are responsible for supporting diverted individuals in the community by providing supervision, advocacy, and referrals to mental health services. In addition, the justice programs also offer release planning services for inmates with mental health issues who require assistance in accessing mental health services in the community (Canadian Mental Health Association–Sudbury Branch, 2005).

The evaluation literature on Canadian diversion programs is limited. The first published evaluation of a Canadian mental health pretrial diversion program was conducted in London, Ontario, and the surrounding area by

Swaminth, Mendonca, Vidal, and Chapman (2002). In this program, a formal application may be prepared by the defense attorney, treatment providers, police, or residents. The Crown Attorney reviews the applications and determines which applicants will be assessed for the diversion program. These assessments are conducted by psychiatric nurses who interview the applicants, review police and clinical files, establish linkages to community-based supports and services, and provide a report with recommendations to the Crown Attorney. The Crown Attorney then reviews the files and decides whether to proceed through the normal adversarial court system or recommend that the charges be stayed by the court. If the charges are stayed, the Crown Attorney and successful diversion applicant enter a diversion agreement which involves mandated supervision for one year, during which time the applicant receives previously determined treatment services. One year after commencing the diversion program, the recidivism rates were between two to three percent. However, it is unclear how these rates compare to the recidivism rates of unsuccessful applicants (Swaminath et al., 2002).

Saint John Mental Health Court, New Brunswick

The Saint John Mental Health Court (MHC), which began as a three-year pilot project in 2000, has been operating as a permanent program of the Provincial Court of New Brunswick since November, 2003 (Brien, 2004). The MHC utilizes a multidisciplinary team that consists of a dedicated judge, Crown and defense attorneys, psychiatrist, psychologist, psychiatric nurse, probation officer, and a community representative (Mental Health Court Canada, 2003). MHC consists of two main phases, admission and program. In the admission phase, individuals appear in the MHC and are made aware of the program, offered legal advice, and may undergo an assessment to determine fitness to stand trial or criminal responsibility. The Court decides whether the individual is eligible for the program, assesses whether the individual is willing to comply with the conditions of the program, and either accepts or rejects the individual. If accepted, the individual moves into the program phase during which he or she is required to abide by a specifically designed program and any other conditions that the court has imposed (e.g., curfews and residency). When the individual successfully completes the program phase, he or she may be given a noncustodial sentence or have the charges withdrawn (Mental Health Court Canada, 2003).

The Saint John MHC was recently evaluated against a regular court on psychiatric services utilization and recidivism for a one-year period (Joshi, 2005). MHC participants spend less time in jail and hospitals and received significantly more mental health services in the community than individuals who went through a regular court. Moreover, 78 percent of the participants who were accepted into the program phase graduated successfully and 82 percent of the MHC graduates had not committed a new offence.

Mental health courts are now appearing across the country. For example, one is being piloted in St. John's, Newfoundland (M. McNutt, personal communication, June 21, 2006) and plans are underway to implement them in Saskatchewan (K. Thompson, personal communication, August 24, 2006). Most of these courts target offenders who are 18 years or older who have been charged with a relatively minor offence. An exception is the Mental Health Court in Toronto which targets persons 16 years or older (Mental Health Court Support Consortium, 2005). Although the popularity of mental health courts continues to grow, their effectiveness in Canada has yet to be evaluated. The exceptions are the above-noted Calgary Diversion Project (Calgary Health Region, 2005b) and the Mental Health Court in New Brunswick, both of which have produced preliminary, but positive results (Joshi, 2005). It is also encouraging that most, if not all, of mental health court programs include an evaluation framework so that questions about their effectiveness can be evaluated when they have reached an appropriate level of maturity and stability.

Drug Courts

Canada's first drug court was established in Toronto in 1998. The basic objective of the court is to divert persons with drug addictions who have come into contact with the law into treatment. However, an interesting feature of this court is its differential processing of these offenders. Track I (preplea alternative) is reserved for clients who have been charged with simple possession and whose offence does not carry a sentence longer than three months. Offenders who have already been diverted or have previous conviction or discharge may be ineligible for this track. Charges may be stayed or withdrawn with successful completion of the mandated treatment. Track II (post-plea alternative) is for offences that carry custodial sentences of nine month or less. To be eligible for this track, offenders must plead guilty to the offence. Upon successful completion of treatment, offenders will be given a non-custodial sentence. Unsuccessful completion of the treatment under either track will result in the case being returned to a regular court for processing. In the case of offenders in Track II, their guilty plea will be struck. Offenders are excluded from diversion if the drug offence was committed for commercial gain, involved an individual under 18 years of age, was committed in an area that is frequented by persons under 18 years of age, or if the offence involved consumption while operating a motor vehicle. The core teams involved in this court are the court team (e.g., judge, attorneys, probation officers, police/court liaison, clerk), treatment team (i.e., service manager, therapist/case manager, program assistant, community court liaison, and nurse practitioner), and the community liaison team (i.e., community coordinator, department secretary, and medical review officer) (Toronto Drug Treatment Court, n.d.).

Similar to the mental health courts, drug courts are now appearing across the country. In 2001 a second drug court was opened in Vancouver and in 2004 the federal government issued a call for proposals to initiate more drug treatment courts in Canada. Proposals were reviewed by a cross-ministerial committee comprised of representatives from Health Canada, the Department of Justice Canada, and the Canadian Centre for Substance Abuse as well as experts in the treatment of addictions. Proposals have now been approved for the establishment of drug treatment courts in Edmonton, Regina, Winnipeg, and Ottawa (Department of Justice Canada, 2005b).

Mental Health and Corrections

The notion of the criminalization of the mentally ill is not new (e.g., Abramson, 1972; Lamb, Weinberger, & Gross, 2004; Teplin, 1983, 1984; Borzecki & Wormith, 1985). Weisman, Lamberti and Price (2004) suggested that jails and prisons may be the only route to psychiatric treatment for persons with severe mental illness as community-based treatment services are sorely lacking. In Ontario, Honourable Mr. Justice E. F. Ormston (2003) echoed this sentiment: "Jails were the only public institution left open to the homeless mentally disordered 24 hours a day" (p. 24). This is compounded by the tendency of police officers to consider an arrest to be a more efficient and reliable method of removing persons with mental illness from the community and directing them to assessment and treatment (e.g., Teplin, 1984). It also creates a vicious cycle whereby the difficulty in accessing community treatment services makes it more likely that persons with mental illness are arrested. However, one's history of arrest and incarceration presents a barrier to future access to community services (Weisman et al., 2004). Furthermore, Porporino and Motiuk (1995) found that offenders with a mental disorder were more likely to be suspended for violations of their conditions while being supervised in the community than a matched group of offenders without mental disorder, although they were less likely to commit a new offence. One interpretation of these findings is that correctional staff members were being particularly cautious in the supervision of offenders with mental disorders as the mental health services needed to address these offenders' needs were not available (Porporino & Motiuk, 1995). Clearly, the increased presence of persons with mental illness in correctional settings is an issue of great importance not only to the persons with mental illness, but to the police, court, treatment providers, and social policymakers.

The Canadian correctional landscape includes, within CSC, a specialized type of facility that is often considered the flagship of correctional mental health treatment in Canada. Unlike the Special Hospitals in the UK or major medical centers within large U.S. facilities, five regional treatment centers (i.e., one in each of the Pacific, Prairie, Ontario, Quebec, and Atlantic regions) were designed to provide mental health and related correctional treatment for federal offenders with mental disorders in CSC. These facilities were the brainchild of forensic psychiatrist Rhodes Chalke who was appointed the chair of a committee of psychiatric consultants commissioned to examine the mental health services provided to federally-incarcerated offenders. Some of the major issues challenged by the Chalke Report (1973) included housing offenders with mental illness with those without and the associated administrative problems, inadequate services to address the needs of offenders with mental disorders, and the lack of control over the admission of patients into psychiatric treatment facilities.

In his report to the then Canadian Penitentiary Service, Chalke (1973) set the course for mental health services in federal corrections for decades to come. The central idea was that separate, moderately sized (100 to 200 beds), stand-alone facilities that were modular in design and eligible for hospital accreditation, but owned and operated by the correctional agency, would best meet the mental health and correctional needs of sentenced offenders suffering from mental disorder. Although varied in their physical design, these facilities now provide specialized care and afford staff an opportunity to develop innovative treatment programs (e.g., the Aggressive Behavioural Control Program, the Intensive Healing Program for Women and the Intensive Treatment Program for Sexual Offenders; for a brief review, see Canadian Public Health Association, 2004). These facilities have also developed into important centers for correctional research and training (e.g., Beyko & Wong, 2005; Looman, Abracen, & Nickolaichuk, 2000; Maden, Williams, Wong, & Leis, 2004). The Ontario Correctional Institute is a similarly designed facility that offers equally intensive services for provincial offenders in Ontario. It received the Exemplary Offender Program award from the American Correctional Association in 1997 (American Correctional Association, 2006).

As mandated by the CCRA (1992), a sub-committee of the Standing Committee on Justice and Human Rights made numerous recommendations to the Parliament of Canada in its final report, *A Work in Progress: The Corrections and Conditional Release Act* (2000). In response to a recommendation regarding mental health services provided to offenders, CSC has implemented a strategy to coordinate a continuum of services for mentally ill offenders from admission to release into the community (Department of Justice Canada, 2005c). The Canadian government has allotted 29.5 million dollars over 5 years to enhance services (e.g., early release planning, employing mental health staff in parole offices, and mental health training for parole staff) to facilitate the transition of mentally ill offenders from the institution to the community (Correctional Service of Canada, 2005b). However, the Correctional Investigator (2005) noted that funds have yet to be secured to improve mental health services within the institutions (such as improvements to intake assessment, existing treatment centres, and mental health units in the institutions).

At the provincial and territorial level, mental health services within the smaller correctional systems are delivered by regional health authorities. For example, in New Brunswick, mental health professionals attend the institutions either on a scheduled or as requested basis. Alternatively, arrangements have been made to have community-based services available to inmates (J. Carter, personal communication, May 30, 2006). In Nova Scotia, the Correctional Services Division and Capital District Health Authority, represented by the East Coast Forensic Psychiatric Hospital (ECFPH) have a shared service agreement. The ECFPH provides health service, which includes psychiatric services, assessment and treatment, to the five adult correctional facilities in Nova Scotia (Shared Service Agreement, 2005). In Manitoba, forensic services are provided by the McDermott Group of Forensic Psychiatrists. They conduct forensic assessments and if time permits, assessment and treatment services. The Winnipeg Remand Centre has a psychologist on staff and the Portage Correctional Centre (facility for women) is attended by a part-time psychologist and a community psychiatrist. Five of the nine centers in Manitoba have mental health nurses on staff to provide services to inmates with mental health needs (M. Sloane, personal communication, May 29, 2006).

Forensic mental health services in the province of British Columbia are provided by the BC Forensic Psychiatric Services Commission (FPS), one of six health authorities in the province (BC Mental Health and Addiction Services, 2006a). While the other five health authorities provide health services within specific regions, FPS is responsible for the delivery of mental health services across the province. Secure, inpatient services are provided at the Forensic Psychiatric Hospital in Port Coquitlam, British Columbia. This 190-bed facility provides assessment, treatment, and clinical case management to adult forensic clients. Outpatient services are provided by six community clinics located throughout the province, with a higher concentration of clinics in the southern region and Vancouver Island. BC Mental Health and Addiction Services (2006b) has also been developing services for clients with concurrent substance use and psychiatric issues and implementation of the Concurrent Disorders Initiative is projected to begin soon.

Ontario forensic mental health services is subsumed more generally under the Ontario mental health system (Ministry of Health and Long-Term Care, 2006; for a review of the development of the forensic mental health system in Ontario, refer to Forensic Mental Health Services Expert Advisory Panel,

2002). Relative to most other provinces, Ontario has a large number of facilities that provide forensic mental health services including the Centre for Addiction and Mental Health (CAMH) and the Royal Ottawa Health Care Group.[6]

CAMH in Toronto, Ontario, was formed by the amalgamation of the Clarke Institute of Psychiatry, Addiction Research Foundation, and the Donwood Institute and Queen Street Mental Health Centre in 1998. The Law and Mental Health Program at CAMH provides assessment, treatment, and risk management services to clients who have either been referred for services by the court or the Ontario Review Board. CAMH provides inpatient (e.g., two 20-bed medium security units at the Queen Street site) and community-based services (e.g., Outpatient Service) as well as court support services to the Mental Health Court in Toronto (Centre for Addiction and Mental Health, 2006). The Integrated Forensic Program operated by the Royal Ottawa Health Care Group (2006) and on contract with the Ontario Ministry of Community Safety and Correctional Services provides forensic mental health services out of the Royal Ottawa Mental Health Centre and the Brockville Mental Health Centre. Services include assessment, treatment, discharge planning, and mental health diversion and are provided to clients who have been found unfit to stand trial or not criminally responsible as well as offenders serving provincial sentences.

Mental health services in the institutions and community are also provided by nongovernment organizations such as the Canadian Association of Elizabeth Fry Societies. A telephone survey was conducted to assess the mental health services provided to women by the local societies of the Elizabeth Fry Societies across Canada in 2002 (Pollack, n.d.). Twenty-one societies reported having provided services to women with psychiatric diagnoses, most commonly bipolar disorder, anxiety disorders, post-traumatic stress disorder, schizophrenia, and personality disorders such as borderline personality disorder. Institutional services were provided by 20 of the societies. These services include offender advocacy, release planning, individual support, and group programming for specific needs (such as substance abuse, addictions, sexual abuse, and Aboriginal healing circles). Twelve of the societies surveyed report having residential facilities for women who have been released to the community. Some of the beds at these facilities are provided to women who are either at risk of coming into contact with the criminal justice system or have mental health needs. The societies also reported having provided services to women who have a history of childhood abuse, suicide, addictions, or being victims to

---

6. For a listing of other service providers in Ontario and other provinces, refer to the directory by Provincial Health Services Authority (2006).

violence. Citing the importance of continuity of care from institution to community, the report concluded:

> . . . many institutions for women are not equipped to deal with women who require a supportive and therapeutic environment. Some women, whose coping strategies, such as anger, self-injury and dissociation are results of years of extreme abuse, are framed by correctional authorities as "difficult to manage" and/or classified as high risk. The correctional system's lack of expertise in dealing with mental health issues such as those resulting from child abuse and other types of trauma results in this group of women being over classified and subjected to increased security measures. . . . (p. 6)

A number of the issues identified in the Pollack (n.d.) survey were echoed in CSC's *Mental Health Strategy for Women Offenders* (Laishes, 2002). The strategy highlighted the need to incorporate the principles of wellness (e.g., holistic approach, collaboration with mental health professionals as well as family and community resources to develop treatment plans), access, women-centered (i.e., gender-specific and gender-appropriate), client participation, and least restrictive measures. The strategy also identified the importance of a physical and administrative environment that is conducive to promotion of wellness including the provision of training and education to staff to better equip them to respond to the mental health needs of female inmates, incorporating an interdisciplinary approach to case management, and providing continuity of care by developing linkages to service providers in the community prior to the offender's release.

Clearly, substance abuse is a critical criminogenic need for many offenders and mental health problems can be criminogenic, particularly for certain disorders. Therefore, it is important to consider mental health and substance abuse issues for the effective management, supervision, and treatment of offenders. This chapter now turns to the research base in Canadian corrections that drives much of clinical practice with disordered and nondisordered offenders.

THE IMPACT OF HOMEGROWN EXPERTISE ON CANADIAN CORRECTIONS

The Canadian justice system, and in particular the corrections component, has been in the enviable position whereby key pockets of corrections research have provided important theoretical and empirically based guidance for the delivery of correctional services. At the risk of overlooking some of the significant contributions made by particular individuals, historically, it would appear that there have been three loosely-aligned collections of researchers who have had a tremendous impact on Canada's correctional agencies and the psychologists who practice in them. Beginning in the early 1970s, these groups were led by inspirational and tireless leaders, each of whom brought his own perspective to correctional and forensic psychology. What seems to characterize all of these clusters is a strong affiliation between the researchers and the agencies within which they conducted their research, whether they were academics, employees of the agency or a combination of both. Secondly, over the last 25 years, key participants and former students from these centers have migrated to other parts of the country to new universities and correctional or forensic agencies—each taking with them the expertise and knowledge they had acquired and using it to build new pockets of correctional research excellence.

The west coast group was originally inspired by Robert Hare, Peter Suedfeld and John Yuille at the University of British Columbia, but also included a cadre of students, some of whom have migrated elsewhere, and a loosely affiliated group at Simon Fraser University, beginning with Ron Rush and Jim Ogloff, with input from Chris Webster (Webster, Eaves, Douglas, & Wintrop, 1995). Much of their energy has concentrated on psychopathy and related theory and measurement (Hare, 1990), on social psychological aspects of the correctional environment (Suedfeld, Ramirez, Deaton, & Baker-Brown, 1982), and on a host of law and psychology issues (Ogloff, 1990), including fitness and criminal responsibility (Viljoen, Roesch, Ogloff, & Zapf, 2003) and court-related interests (Yuille, 1989).

The group has also brought a stronger mental health focus to clinicians' work with offenders. Their impact has been particularly felt in the forensic mental health field (e.g., Roesch, 1995). But, as much of their original research was conducted first in federal and then provincial correctional facilities, they have had an important influence on the conceptualization, assessment, and now treatment, of the offender population, both nationally and internationally. Although perhaps best known for their work on the assessment of psychopathy, their research has created a heightened awareness amongst correctional clinicians, program developers and administrators about an array of associated issues including the etiology of psychopathy, psychopathy and violence (Douglas, James, Ogloff, & Hart, 2003), psychopathy and sexual offending (Porter et al., 2000), psychopathy and youth (Forth, Hart, & Hare, 1990) and treatment and programming for the psychopathic offender (Wong & Hare, 2005).

A second axis of researchers, led by Vernon Quinsey, at the Mental Health Centre in Penetanguishene, Ontario, and Queen's University has focused on risk assessment, sexual offenders, and various treatment modalities, particularly in the forensic mental health system, but its influence on corrections has been widespread. With colleagues, Grant Harris and Marnie Rice at Penetanguishene (Quinsey, Rice, Harris, & Cormier, 2005; Rice, Quinsey, & Harris, 1991) and then Edward Zamble, Bill Marshall and Howard Barbaree at Queen's University (Zamble & Quinsey, 1997; Quinsey & Marshall, 1983; Barbaree & Marshall, 1988), their loyalty to the scientific method and the empirical evidence has been their persistent message to administrators and clinicians for three decades. Although the consequences of such a strategy are not always popular, the Penetang-Queens group with its extension to the CAMH and the University of Toronto (Barbaree, Seto, Langton, & Peacock, 2001; Seto, Harris, Rice, & Barbaree, 2004; Seto & Lalumiere, 2001), is most respected for its loyalty to their first principle. This includes a watchful eye and healthy dose of skepticism about the impact of treatment on certain offender groups, including sexual offenders and psychopaths, as well as advocacy for high quality intervention (Marshall, Anderson, & Fernandez, 1999) and the creation of a risk assessment instrument that, although empirically validated, raises eyebrows in many circles (Rice, Harris & Cormier, 1992; Quinsey et al., 2005).

A third important nucleus of corrections research grew out of the work of Don Andrews and Paul Gendreau, at Carleton University and Rideau Correctional Centre, respectively. Their impact, along with that of colleague Bob Ross from the University of Ottawa and early students, Jim Bonta and Steve Wormith, on what we now know about offenders, their assessment, prediction and treatment, is profound (Andrews & Bonta, 2003; Andrews, Zinger et al., 1990; Gendreau & Andrews, 1990; Gendreau & Ross, 1987). Assisted by strong support from local and corporate level administrators, Andrews and Gendreau developed an excellent working relationship between academia and correctional agencies (Wormith, 2004). Perhaps the best glimpse of how they worked and why they have had such an impact of correctional practice may be found in a description of their consultation practices with various correctional agencies (Gendreau & Andrews, 1979). This chapter was a candid review of the successes and failures that they had experienced to that time. It also listed a number of principles that they had gleaned from their consultation experience and foreshadowed the development of the *Correctional Program Assessment Inventory* (CPAI), a scale that emerged 15 years later and was augmented by their many additional experiences in correctional consultation (Gendreau & Andrews, 2001).

This group has made important inroads into correctional agencies nationally and internationally with the fundamental principles of risk, need, and responsivity, and their implications for clinical practice including risk/need assessment and human service for offenders (Andrews, 2001; Andrews, Bonta & Hoge, 1990; Andrews, Bonta & Wormith, 2004; 2006). It has expanded its scope of influence, not only by means of its many important publications, but also by moving both academically, to the University of New Brunswick and

University of Saskatchewan, and bureaucratically, to the federal government's department of Public Safety and Emergency Preparedness (formerly Solicitor General, Canada).

What is particularly interesting about the impact of these three axes of corrections research is the means by which they have spread their influence across the Canadian correctional landscape. Most impressively, they have spawned at least three successive generations of young corrections researchers who are now establishing themselves both academically and with correctional operations in Canada and beyond. Loosely, these waves would include, but are not limited to, Guy Bourgon and Barbara Armstrong (2005), Franca Cortoni (Cortoni & Marshall, 2001), Christopher Earls (1988), Adele Forth and Steve Hart (Forth et al., 1990), Brian Grant (Gendreau, Grant, & Leipciger 1979), Jim Hempill (Hempill & Hare, 2004), Zoe Hilton (Hilton, Harris, & Rice, 2006), Wagdy Loza (Loza & Green, 2003), Jeremy Mills and Daryl Kroner (2006), Larry Motiuk and Ralph Serin (2001), Mike Seto and Martin Lalumière (2001), Dave Simourd (Simourd & Wormith, 1995), Pamela Yates (2005) and Ivan Zinger (Zinger, Wichman, & Andrews, 2001). More recently they have been joined, in what appears to be exponential growth, by Kelly Blanchette and Shelly Brown (2006), Rosalind Catchpole and Heather Gretton (2003), Kevin Douglas (Douglas, Ogloff & Hart, 2003), Craig Dowden (Dowden & Andrews, 1999), Sheila French (French & Gendreau, 2006), Claire Goggin and Paula Smith (Gendreau, Goggin & Smith, 2002), Andrew Harris (Hanson & Harris, 2002), Moira Law (Bonta, Law, & Hanson, 1998), and Steve Porter (Porter et al., 2000). Collectively, much of this work has focused on offender risk assessment and in particular for violent reoffending, but it has also brought a strong message to practitioners about the importance of treatment interventions adhering to sound theory and principles of integrity and service delivery amidst the "correctional quackery" that continues to rain down on correctional agencies (Gendreau, Goggin, French, & Smith, 2006). A great deal of the sound clinical work now being done in Canadian corrections can be traced to these three axes of research.

Associated legal scholars on correctional law have also been instrumental in the quest to maintain a balanced correctional system. In particular, Ron Price (1970, 1974) and Michael Jackson (1983, 2002) have a long history representing the legal concerns of Canadian offenders and challenging correctional practices, including those used and researched by psychologists. Additionally, Allan Manson (1999), Kent Roach (2000), and Tim Quigley (1999) maintain a close eye on sentencing patterns, conditional sentences, and restorative justice, particularly for the over-represented Aboriginal offender. Their influence has contributed, not only to the fairness, but to the quality of clinical practice in Canadian corrections.

Finally, the federal government has also been a key player in the development of corrections research in Canada in a couple of ways. CSC has made huge strides both in terms of its original research and technology transfer, whereby its research is turned into correctional practice. Its research department was initiated in 1990 by Ole Ingstrup, a visionary commissioner of CSC, who foresaw the potential benefit of a vibrant research department that was devoted to conducting research for the betterment of the agency. CSC now boasts a research capacity that includes a centralized corporate focus, a regional research capacity based in designated treatment facilities and a specialized research unit dedicated to substance abuse research. Its journal, *Forum on Corrections Research,* and important editions (e.g., Leis, Motiuk, & Ogloff, 1995; Motiuk & Serin, 2001) were designed particularly for the frontline scientist-practitioner and the enlightened bureaucrat to use in their daily correctional practice. Another important duty of CSCs researchers is the approval of research proposals submitted by the external research community, typically faculty and students. This has been a long and successful practice, to wit the aforementioned researchers, and will be an important mechanism for future corrections research in Canada. In an organization that is constantly shuffling its senior bureaucratic staff, it is interesting to note that CSC research has been headed by only two persons, Frank Porporino and Larry Motiuk, in its 16-year history.

Secondly, Emergency Preparedness Canada, of which CSC is a part, has had its own research capacity, including a strong corrections research component, since the late 1970s. In particular, Jim Bonta and Karl Hanson have been prolific in their research on offender risk assessment and treatment both generally and with special populations, such as mentally disordered offenders and sexual offenders (Bonta et al., 1998; Hanson & Bussiere, 1998; Hanson & Harris, 2002). Moreover, they have been tireless in their efforts to turn research into practice, working both with correctional agencies at the systems level and with individuals at the case-by-case, clinical level.

Other jurisdictions, such as the Province of Ontario, have also played an important role in the early days of developing a corrections research base in Canada (Gendreau, Gibson, Surridge & Hug, 1973; Gendreau et al., 1979), but are less active now due to fiscal cutbacks on the corrections research front. Elsewhere, the Forensic Psychiatric Services Commission of British Columbia has begun to emerge as an active forensic-corrections research center (e.g., Nicholls, Brink, Desmarais, Webster, & Martin, 2006).

Each of these groups has generated various spin off subgroups which have also contributed tremendously to the proliferation of Canadian correctional and forensic research with a very applied and practical focus, which has been of tremendous assistance to practitioners in the field and has done wonders for the reputation of correctional research in Canada. Much of the training in correctional psychology has been in the field, with only a smattering of academic programs affiliated with the pockets of researchers described above (Ogloff, 1999; Simourd & Wormith, 1995; Watkins, 1992). With some of the university psychology departments with forensic expertise now directing their attention away from forensic and correctional psychology, correctional agencies, clinicians and students are seriously concerned about the prospects for maintaining this rich history in correctional psychology.

Another product of the correctional treatment research base in Canada has been the strong collegial environment that it has spawned. Although there are some rather clearly identified theoretical differences in the perspectives of leading correctional researchers in Canada, the overall milieu is one of cooperation and collaboration. The objective has always been finding and delivering the best assessment, management, and treatment services for the offender client and, in so doing, contributing to the public safety of Canadians. This milieu is largely unencumbered by the adversarial tradition of the court room, where much of American forensic psychology is found. With the exception of the occasional debate between psychologists about the potential dangerousness of an offender who awaits sentencing by the court, or about what measure is most appropriate to measure this potential (e.g., Gendreau et al., 2002; Hempill & Hare, 2004), most clinical correctional psychologists, be they private practitioners or public employees work in consort with each other, advocating for their clients and working together to deliver appropriate services. In large part, this is because most clinical correctional psychologists in Canada share a common ideological perspective about their role in the justice system and a common clinical perspective about their clients' needs, both of which are derived from the principles of risk, needs and responsivity (Andrews, Bonta, & Hoge, 1990; Andrews & Bonta, 2003; Andrews, Bonta, & Wormith, 2006).

CONCLUSIONS

This long and rich tradition of correctional research by psychologists in Canada, with its specific focus on the effectiveness of correctional intervention, has caught the attention of correctional administrators. This in turn has afforded instant credibility for practicing psychologists in the field. It has opened doors for them to bring the lessons from their research colleagues to the agencies in which they work. Consequently, the problems of technology transfer that typically accompany the implementation of empirically based practices at the agency level are minimized. It has also generated a move toward accredited programs and services by large correctional agencies such as CSC. Although often criticized for their "overmanualized" interventions and "one size fits all" approach, accreditation, in particular, by panels of internationally renowned experts offers a means of maintaining program integrity and standards of service delivery over time and across setting. This is one kind of offender program review that would seem to have its place in the larger effort to maximize the positive impact that can be realized from what we know about "what works" in corrections (Clements et al., in press).

Appendix A

PRINCIPLES OF SENTENCING IN CANADA

718. The fundamental purpose of sentencing is to contribute, along with crime prevention initiatives, to respect for the law and the maintenance of a just, peaceful and safe society by imposing just sanctions that have one or more of the following objectives:
    (a) to denounce unlawful conduct;
    (b) to deter the offender and other persons from committing offences;
    (c) to separate offenders from society, where necessary;
    (d) to assist in rehabilitating offenders;
    (e) to provide reparations for harm done to victims or to the community;
    (f) to promote a sense of responsibility in offenders, and acknowledgment of the harm done to victims and to the community.

Moreover, the Code speaks to proportionality[7] of the sentence and lists a number of aggravating and mitigating factors[8] that must be considered.

718.1 A sentence must be proportionate to the gravity of the offence and the degree of responsibility of the offender.

718.2 A court that imposes a sentence shall also take into consideration the following principles:
    (a) a sentence should be increased or reduced to account for any relevant aggravating or mitigating circumstances relating to the offence or the offender, and, without limiting the generality of the foregoing,
    (i) evidence that the offence was motivated by bias, prejudice or hate based on race, national or ethnic origin, language, colour, religion, sex, age, mental or physical disability, sexual orientation, or any other similar factor,
    (ii) evidence that the offender, in committing the offence, abused the offender's spouse or common-law partner,
    (ii.1) evidence that the offender, in committing the offence, abused a person under the age of eighteen years,
    (iii) evidence that the offender, in committing the offence, abused a position of trust or authority in relation to the victim,
    (iv) evidence that the offence was committed for the benefit of, at the direction of or in association with a criminal organization, or
    (v) evidence that the offence was a terrorism offence
    shall be deemed to be aggravating circumstances;
    (b) a sentence should be similar to sentences imposed on similar offenders for similar offences committed in similar circumstances;
    (c) where consecutive sentences are imposed, the combined sentence should not be unduly long or harsh;

7. R.S., 1985, c. 27 (1st Supp.), s. 156; 1995, c. 22, s. 6.
8. 1995, c. 22, s. 6; 1997, c. 23, s. 17; 2000, c. 12, s. 95; 2001, c. 32, s. 44(F), c. 41, s. 20; 2005, c. 32, s. 25.

(d) an offender should not be deprived of liberty, if less restrictive sanctions may be appropriate in the circumstances; and

(e) all available sanctions other than imprisonment that are reasonable in the circumstances should be considered for all offenders, with particular attention to the circumstances of Aboriginal offenders.

Appendix B

CANADIAN LEGAL RIGHTS AS ESTABLISHED IN THE
CONSTITUTION ACT, 1982

7.[9] Everyone has the right to life, liberty and security of the person and the right not to be deprived thereof except in accordance with the principles of fundamental justice.

8. Everyone has the right to be secure against unreasonable search or seizure.

9. Everyone has the right not to be arbitrarily detained or imprisoned.

10. Everyone has the right on arrest or detention

a) to be informed promptly of the reasons therefor;

b) to retain and instruct counsel without delay and to be informed of that right; and

c) to have the validity of the detention determined by way of *habeas corpus* and to be released if the detention is not lawful.

11. Any person charged with an offence has the right

a) to be informed without unreasonable delay of the specific offence;

b) to be tried within a reasonable time;

c) not to be compelled to be a witness in proceedings against that person in respect of the offence;

d) to be presumed innocent until proven guilty according to law in a fair and public hearing by an independent and impartial tribunal;

e) not to be denied reasonable bail without just cause;

f) except in the case of an offence under military law tried before a military tribunal, to the benefit of trial by jury where the maximum punishment for the offence is imprisonment for five years or a more severe punishment;

g) not to be found guilty on account of any act or omission unless, at the time of the act or omission, it constituted an offence under Canadian or international law or was criminal according to the general principles of law recognized by the community of nations;

h) if finally acquitted of the offence, not to be tried for it again and, if finally found guilty and punished for the offence, not to be tried or punished for it again; and

i) if found guilty of the offence and if the punishment for the offence has been varied between the time of commission and the time of sentencing, to the benefit of the lesser punishment.

12. Everyone has the right not to be subjected to any cruel and unusual treatment or punishment.

13. A witness who testifies in any proceedings has the right not to have any incriminating evidence so given used to incriminate that witness in any other proceedings, except in a prosecution for perjury or for the giving of contradictory evidence.

14. A party or witness in any proceeding who does not understand or speak the language in which the proceedings are conducted or who is deaf has the right to the assistance of an interpreter.

---

9. Numbers correspond to the clause numbers in the *Constitution Act, 1982*; Part 1, Canadian Charter of Rights and Freedoms.

REFERENCES

Abramson, M. F. (1972). The criminalization of mentally disordered behaviour: Possible side-effects of a new mental health law. *Hospital and Community Psychiatry, 23*(4), 101–105.

Adelberg, C., & Currie, C. (1987). *Too few to count: Canadian women in conflict with the Law.* Vancouver, BC: The Press Gang.

Alberta Mental Health Board. (2004, November). Calgary Diversion Project: Success a product of committed partnerships. *Open Minds.* Retrieved June 22, 2006, from http://www.amhb.ab.ca/news/pdfs/OpenMindsNov2004.pdf

Alberta's Provincial Diversion Framework Working Committee. (2001). Alberta's Provincial Diversion Framework: Reducing the Criminalization of Individuals with Mental Illness. Alberta: Provincial Forensic Psychiatry Program (AMHB). Retrieved May 29, 2006, from http://www.amhb.ab.ca/publications/pdfs/ABProvDiv-ReducingCrime.pdf

American Correctional Association (2006). Exemplary Offender Program Award. Retrieved December 11, 2006, from www.aca.org/pastpresentfuture/pdf/ExemplaryOffender_2008.pdf

American Psychiatric Association. (1980). *Diagnostic and Statistical Manual of Mental Disorders (Third Edition).* Washington, DC: American Psychiatric Association

Andrews, D. A. (2001). Principles of effective correctional programs. In L. L. Motiuk & R. C. Serin (Eds.), *Compendium 2000 on effective correctional programming* (pp. 9–17). Ottawa: Correctional Service of Canada.

Andrews, D. A., & Bonta, J. (2003). *The psychology of criminal conduct.* (3rd ed.). Cincinnati, OH: Anderson Publishing Co.

Andrews, D. A., Bonta, J., & Hoge, R. D. (1990). Classification for effective rehabilitation: Rediscovering psychology. *Criminal Justice and Behavior, 17,* 19–52.

Andrews, D. A., Bonta, J., & Wormith, S. J. (2004). *The Level of Service/Case Management Inventory (LS/CMI).* Toronto: Multi-Health Systems.

Andrews, D.A., Bonta, J., & Wormith, J.S. (2004). *LS/CMI Level of Service/Case Management Inventor (LS/CMI): An offender assessment system: User's manual.* Toronto, Ontario: Multi Health Systems Inc.

Andrews, D. A., Bonta, J., & Wormith, J. S. (2006). The recent past and near future of risk and/or need assessment. *Crime & Delinquency, 52,* 7–27.

Andrews, D.A., Zinger, I., Hoge, R.D., Bonta, J., Gendreau, P., & Cullen, F.T. (1990). Does correctional treatment work? A clinically relevant and psychologically informed meta-analysis. *Criminology, 28,* 369–404.

Arbour, L. (1995). Commission of Inquiry into Certain Events at the Prison for Women in Kingston. Ottawa, Ontario: Public Works and Government Service Canada.

Ashton, J., & Hawthorn, F. (Co-chairs) (1990). Creating Choices. The Report of the Task Force on Federally Sentenced Women. Ottawa, Ontario: Correctional Service of Canada.

BC Mental Health and Addiction Services. (2006a). *Forensic Psychiatric Services Commission: 2005–2006 annual report.* BC: Author. Retrieved December 16, 2006, from

http://www.bcmhas.ca/NR/rdonlyres/6372BD93-8EAF-4B43-87C9-F6A362B7
2A74/19772/FPS_AReport_06Web_Version.pdf

BC Mental Health and Addiction Services. (2006b). *Forensic psychiatric services.* Retrieved December 16, 2006, from http://www.bcmhas.ca/ForensicService/default.htm

Barbaree, H. E., & Marshall, W. L. (1988). Deviant sexual arousal, offense history, and demographic variables as predictors of reoffense among child molesters. *Behavioral Sciences and the Law, 6,* 267–280.

Barbaree, H. E., Seto, M. C., Langton, C. M., & Peacock, E. J. (2001). Evaluating the predictive accuracy of six risk assessment instruments for adult sex offenders. *Criminal Justice and Behavior, 28,* 490–521.

Beattie, K. (2006) Adult correctional services in Canada, 2004/2005. *Juristat, 26*(5), 1–33 (85-002-XIE).

Beyko, M. J., & Wong, S. C. (2005). Predictors and treatment attrition as indicators of program improvement not offender shortcomings: A study of sex offender treatment attrition. *Sexual Abuse: A Journal of Research and Treatment, 17*(4), 375–389.

Blanchette, K., & Brown, S. L. (2006). *The assessment and treatment of women offenders: An integrative perspective.* Chichester, England: John Wiley & Sons.

Bonta, J., Law, M., & Hanson, R. K. (1998). The prediction of criminal and violent recidivism among mentally disordered offenders: A meta-analysis. *Psychological Bulletin, 123,* 123–142.

Borzecki, M., & Wormith, J. S. (1985). The criminalization of psychiatrically ill people: A review with a Canadian perspective. *Psychiatric Journal of the University of Ottawa, 10,* 241–247.

Bourgon, G., & Armstrong, B. (2005). Transferring the principles of effective treatment into a "Real World" prison setting. *Criminal Justice and Behavior, 32,* 3–25.

Brien, A. H. (2004). *Saint John Mental Health Court: Annual Report for period ending November 19, 2004.* Retrieved May 15, 2006, from www.mentalhealthcourt-sj.com/annualreport1.html

Calgary Health Region. (2002). *Adult mental health and psychiatric primary and community care program: Mental Health & Psychiatric Services 2001-2002 Year-End report.* Retrieved May 11, 2006, from http://www.calgaryhealthregion.ca/mh/Primary-Community.pdf

Calgary Health Region. (2004, September 29). Calgary Diversion Project celebrates 3 years of success. *Calgary Health Region Communications.* Retrieved December 7, 2006, from http://www.crha-health.ab.ca/newsarchives/calgary_diversion_projectSep28-04.pdf

Calgary Health Region. (2005a). *Mental health and psychiatric services: Year-end service summary 2004-2005.* Retrieved May 11, 2006, from http://www.calgaryhealth region.ca/mh/PDFS/Reports/MentalHealthandPsychiatricServicesYrEnd2004 2005.pdf

Calgary Health Region. (2005b). Forensic mental health services. In *Mental Health Services Three Year Plan 2005-2008* (pp. 1–27). Retrieved July 24, 2006, from http://www.calgaryhealthregion.ca/mh/PDFS/Reports/MHServicesThreeYear Plan20050930.pdf

Canada. (1977). *The role of federal corrections in Canada. A report of the Task Force on the Creation of an Integrated Canadian Corrections Service.* Ottawa, Ontario: Ministry of the Solicitor General.

Canada. (1982). *The Canadian law in Canadian society.* Ottawa, Ontario: Department of Justice.

Canada Health Act, C. 6, S. 1 (1984).

Canadian Mental Health Association–Sudbury Branch. (2005). Retrieved October 1, 2006, from http://communities.mysudbury.ca/Sites/CMHA%20Sudbury/default.aspx

Canadian Public Health Association. (2004). A health care needs assessment of federal inmates in Canada. *Canadian Journal of Public Health, 95* (S1).

Carson, J. (Chair) (1984). *Report of the Advisory Committee to the Solicitor General of Canada on the Management of Correctional Institutions.* Ottawa, Ontario: Solicitor General of Canada.

Catchpole, R. E., & Gretton, H. M. (2003). The predictive validity of risk assessment with violent young offenders: A 1-year examination of criminal outcome. *Criminal Justice and Behavior, 30,* 688–708.

Centre for Addiction and Mental Health. (2006a). *About CAMH.* Retrieved December 16, 2006, from http://www.camh.net/About_CAMH/index.html

Centre for Addiction and Mental Health. (2006b). Law and Mental Health Program. Retrieved December 16, 2006, from http://www.camh.net/About_CAMH/Guide_to_CAMH/Mental_Health_Programs/The_Law_and_Mental_Health_Program/index.html

Chalke, F. C. (Chairperson) (1973). *The general program for the development of psychiatric services in federal correctional services in Canada.* Report of the Advisory Board of Psychiatric Consultants. Ottawa, Ontario: Information Canada.

Chartrand, P. L. A. H., Whitecloud, W., McKay, E., & Young, D. (2001). *Final Report: June 29, 2001.* Winnipeg, MB: Statutory Printers.

City of Toronto. (2006). *Toronto's racial diversity.* Retrieved October 1, 2006, from http://www.toronto.ca/toronto_facts/diversity.htm

Clements, C. B., Althouse, R., Ax, R. K., Fagan, T. J., Magaletta, P. R., & Wormith, J. S. (in press). Systemic issues and correctional outcomes: Expanding the scope of correctional psychology. *Criminal Justice and Behavior.*

Constitution Act (1867).

Constitution Act, c. 11 (1982).

Correctional Investigator Canada. (2005). *Annual report of the Correctional Investigator: 2004–2005.* Retrieved May 10, 2006, from http://www.oci-bec.gc.ca/reports/pdf/AR200405_e.pdf

Correctional Service Canada. (2005a). *Basic facts about the Correctional Service of Canada* (Cat. No. JS 82-17/2005). Ottawa, Ontario: Public Works and Government Services Canada. Retrieved July 13, 2006, from http://www.csc-scc.gc.ca/text/pblct/basicfacts/BasicFacts_e.shtml

Correctional Service Canada. (2005b). *Response from the Correctional Service of Canada to the 32nd Annual Report of the Correctional Investigator 2004–2005.* Retrieved May 10, 2006, from http://www.oci-bec.gc.ca/reports/pdf/AR200405-7_e.pdf

Correctional Service of Canada. (2006). *Ten-year status report on women's corrections, 1996–2006.* Ottawa: Author. Retrieved September 24, 2006, from http://www. csc-scc.gc.ca/text/prgrm/fsw/wos24/index_e.shtml

Corrections and Conditional Release Act, RSC, C-20, (1992).

Cortoni, F., & Marshall, W. L. (2001). Sex as a coping strategy and its relationship to juvenile sexual history and intimacy in sexual offenders. *Sexual Abuse: A Journal of Research and Treatment, 13,* 27–43.

Criminal Code, R.S., c. C-34, s.1 (1985).

Daubney, D. (Chair) (1988). *Taking responsibility: Report of the Standing Committee on Justice and the Solicitor General on its review of sentencing, conditional release and related aspects of corrections.* Ottawa, Ontario: Supply and Services Canada.

Department of Justice Canada (1985). *Canada health act C-6.* Retrieved September 25, 2006, from http://laws.justice.gc.ca/en/C-6/

Department of Justice Canada (2005a). *Fact sheet: Capital punishment in Canada.* Retrieved September 25, 2006, from http://canada.justice.gc.ca/en/news/fs/ 2003/doc_30896.html

Department of Justice Canada. (2005b). *Expanding drug treatment courts in Canada.* Retrieved July 30, 2006, from http://canada.justice.gc.ca/en/news/nr/2005/ doc_31552.html.

Department of Justice Canada. (2005c). *Amendments to the Corrections and Conditional Release Act and new measures.* Ottawa, ON: Author. Retrieved September 29, 2006, from http://www.justice.gc.ca/en/news/nr/2005/doc_31458.html

Douglas, K.S., James R. P. Ogloff, J. R. P., & Hart, S.D. (2003). Evaluation of a model of violence risk assessment among forensic psychiatric patients. *Psychiatric Services, 54,* 1372–1279.

Dowden, C., & Andrews, D.A. (1999). What works for female offenders: A meta-analytic review. *Crime and Delinquency, 45,* 438–452.

Earls, C. M. (1988). Aberrant sexual arousal in sexual offenders. *Annals of the New York Academy of Sciences, 528,* 41–48.

Ellerby, L., Bedard, J., & Chartrand, C. (2000). Holism, wellness and spirituality: Moving from relapse prevention to healing. In D. R. Laws, S. M. Hudson & T. Ward (Eds.), *Remaking relapse prevention with sex offenders: A sourcebook.* Thousand Oaks, CA: Sage.

Ellerby, L., & Stonechild, J. (1998). Blending the traditional with the contemporary in the treatment of Aboriginal sexual offenders: A Canadian experience. In W. L. Marshall, Y. M. Fernandez, S. M. Hudson, & T. Ward (Eds.), *Sourcebook of treatment programs for sexual offenders.* New York: Plenum Press.

Forensic Mental Health Services Expert Advisory Panel. (2002). *Assessment, treatment and community reintegration of the mentally disordered offender.* Ontario: Ontario Ministry of Health and Long-Term Care. Retrieved December 16, 2006, from http://www.health.gov.on.ca/english/providers/providers/pub/mhitf/forensic_p anel/final_report.pdf

Forth, A. E., Hart, S. D., & Hare, R. D. (1990). Assessment of psychopathy in male young offenders. *Psychological Assessment, 2,* 342–344.

French, S. A., & Gendreau, P. (2006). Reducing prison misconducts: What works! *Criminal Justice and Behavior, 33,* 185–218.

Gendreau, P., & Andrews, D. (1979). Psychological consultation in correctional agencies: Case studies and general issues. In J. Platt & R. Wicks (Eds.), *The psychological consultant.* New York: Grune & Stratton.

Gendreau, P., & Andrews, D.A. (1990). Tertiary prevention: What the meta-analyses of the offender treatment literature tell us about "what works." *Canadian Journal of Criminology, 32,* 173–184.

Gendreau, P., & Andrews, D.A. (2001). *Correctional Program Assessment Inventory–2000* (CPAI-2000) Scoring manual. St. John, NB: University of New Brunswick.

Gendreau, P., Gibson, M., Surridge, C., & Hug, J. (1973). Self-esteem changes associated with six months imprisonment. *Proceedings of the Canadian Congress of Criminology and Corrections, 14,* 81–89.

Gendreau, P., Goggin, C., French, S., & Smith, P. (2006). Practicing psychology in correctional settings. In I. B. Weiner & A. K. Hess (Eds.), *The handbook of forensic psychology* (3rd ed.) (pp. 722–750). Hoboken, NJ: John Wiley & Sons.

Gendreau, P., Goggin, C. & Smith, P. (2002). Is the PCL-R really the "unparalleled" measure of offender risk? A lesson in knowledge cumulation. *Criminal Justice and Behavior, 29,* 397–426.

Gendreau, P., Grant, B., & Leipciger, M. (1979). Self-esteem, incarceration and recidivism. *Criminal Justice and Behavior, 6,* 67–75.

Gendreau, P., & Ross, R. R. (1987). Revivification or rehabilitation: Evidence from the 1980s. *Justice Quarterly, 4,* 349–408.

Glaze, L. E., & Bonczar, T. P. (2006, November). *Probation and Parole in the United States, 2005.* (NCJ-215091). Washington, DC: U.S. Department of Justice.

Hamilton, A. C., & Sinclair, C. M. (Commissioners) (1991). *Report of the Aboriginal Justice Inquiry of Manitoba. Volume 1: The justice system and Aboriginal people.* Winnipeg, MB: Province of Manitoba.

Hanson, R. K., & Bussiere, M. T. (1998). Predicting relapse: A meta-analysis of sexual offender recidivism studies. *Journal of Consulting and Clinical Psychology, 66,* 348–363.

Hanson, R. K., & Harris, A. (2002). Where should we intervene? Dynamic predictors of sexual offense recidivism. *Criminal Justice and Behavior, 27,* 6–35.

Hare, R. D. (1990). *The Hare Psychopathy Checklist–Revised.* Toronto: Multi-Health Systems.

Harrison, P. M., & Beck, A. J. (2006, November). *Prisoners in 2005.* Bureau of Justice Statistics Bulletin (NCJ-215092). Washington, DC: U.S. Department of Justice.

Hartford, K., Davies, S., Dobson, C., Dykeman, C., Furhman, B., Hanbridge, J., et al. (2004). *Evidence-based practices in diversion programs for persons with serious mental illness who are in conflict with the law: Literature review and synthesis.* London, Ontario: Lawson Health Research Institute and University of Western Ontario.

Health Canada. (2002). *Canada Health Act overview.* Retrieved September 28, 2006, from http://www.hc-sc.gc.ca/ahc-asc/media/nr-cp/2002/2002_care-soinsbk4_e.html

Hemphill, J. F., & Hare, R. D. (2004). Some misconceptions about the PCL-R and risk assessment: A reply to Gendreau, Goggin, and Smith. *Criminal Justice and Behavior, 31,* 203–243.

Hennessy, P. H. (1999). *Canada's big house: The dark history of the Kingston Penitentiary.* Toronto, Ontario: The Dundurn Group.

Hilton, Z. N., Harris, G. T., & Rice, M. E. (2006). Sixty-six years of research on the clinical versus actuarial prediction of violence. *The Counseling Psychologist, 34,* 400–409.

Jackson, M. (2002). *Justice behind the walls: Human rights in Canadian prisons.* Vancouver, BC: Douglas & McIntyre. Also available at www.justicebehindthewalls.net

Jackson, M. (1983). *Prisoners of isolation: Solitary confinement in Canada.* Toronto, Ontario: University of Toronto Press.

Joshi, V. (2005). Long-term outcome of patients participating in Mental Health Court in Saint John New Brunswick, Canada. Paper presented at the Mental Health Summit of the International Academy of Law and Mental Health, Paris, France.

Kirby, M. J. (chair) (2006). *Out of the shadows at last: Transforming mental health, mental illness and addiction services in Canada.* Ottawa, Ontario: Standing Senate Committee on Social Affairs, Science and Technology. Retrieved May 29, 2006 from: http://www.parl.gc.ca/common/Committee_SenRep.asp?Language=E&Parl=39 &Ses=1&comm_id=47

Laishes, J. (2002). *The mental health strategy for women offenders.* Ottawa, Ontario: Correctional Service Canada.

Lamb, H. R., Weinberger, L. E., & Gross, B. H. (2004). Mentally ill persons in the criminal justice system: Some perspectives. *Psychiatric Quarterly, 75* (2), 107–126.

Leis, T. A., Motiuk, L. L., & Ogloff, J. R. P. (1995). *Forensic Psychology: Policy and practice in corrections.* Ottawa, Ontario: Correctional Service of Canada.

Littlechild, W. (Chair) (2004). *Legacy of hope: An agenda for change. Report of the Commission on First Nations and Métis Peoples and Justice Reform, Volume 1.* Regina, SK: Author.

Looman, J., Abracen, J., & Nickolaichuk, T. P. (2000). Recidivism among treated sexual offenders and matched controls: Data from the Regional Treatment Centre (Ontario). *Journal of Interpersonal Violence, 15*(3), 279–290.

Loza, W., & Green, K. (2003). The self-appraisal questionnaire: A self-report measure for predicting recidivism versus clinician-administered measures: A 5-year follow-up study. *Journal of Interpersonal Violence, 18,* 781–797.

M'Naughten, 1843, 10 Clark & Fin. 200, 210 8 Eng. Rep 718, 722.

Macfarlane, D., Blackburn, J., Bullock, H., Doob, A., Haber, S., Pyke, J., & Robins, S. (2002). *A review of mental health services in the Toronto courts: Final report.* Toronto, Ontario: Health Systems Research and Consulting Unit, Centre for Addition and Mental Health.

Maden, A., Williams, S., Wong, S. C., & Leis, T. (2004). Treating dangerous and severe personality disorder in high security: Lessons from the Regional Psychiatric Centre, Saskatoon, Canada. *Journal of Forensic Psychiatry and Psychology, 15*(3), 375–390.

Marshall, W. L., Anderson, D., & Fernandez, Y. (1999). *Cognitive behavioral treatment of sexual offenders.* New York: John Wiley.

Manson, A. (1999). The reform of sentencing in Canada. In D. Stewart, R. Deslile, & A. Manson (Eds.), *Towards a clear and just criminal law: A criminal reports forum.* (pp. 461–467). Toronto, Ontario: Carswell.

Martineau v. Matsqui Institution Disciplinary Board (No. 2), 1980, 1 S.C.R. 602.

Mason, R. (2001). *The healing of Aboriginal offenders: A comparison between cognitive-behavioural treatment and the traditional Aboriginal sweat lodge ceremony.* Unpublished Master's Thesis, Saskatoon, SK: University of Saskatchewan.

McGuigan, M. (Chair) (1977). *Report to Parliament. Sub-committee on the Penitentiary System in Canada.* Ottawa, Ontario: Supply and Services Canada.

Mental Health Court Canada. (2003). *Mental Health Court, Saint John, New Brunswick, Canada: A provincial court of New Brunswick.* Retrieved May 14, 2006, from www.mentalhealthcourt-sj.com

Mental Health Court Support Consortium. (2005). *Mental health court support services policies and procedures:* First edition. Toronto, Ontario: Author.

Mills, J. F., & Kroner, D. G. (2006). Impression management and self-report among violent offenders. *Journal of Interpersonal Violence, 21,* 178–192.

Ministry of Health and Long-Term Care. (2006). *Ontario's forensic mental health system.* Retrieved December 16, 2006, from http://www.health.gov.on.ca/english/providers/media/news_releases/archives/nr_06/apr/bg_042706.pdf

Motiuk, L. L., & Porporino, F. J. (1991). *The prevalence, nature and severity of mental health problems among federal male inmates in Canadian penitentiaries* (No. R-24). Ottawa, Ontario: Correctional Service Canada.

Motiuk, L.L & Serin, R.C. (2001). *Compendium 2000 on Effective Correctional Programming, Volume 1.* Ottawa, Ontario: Correctional Service of Canada, Ministry of Supply and Services.

Natural Resources Canada (2001). *The atlas of Canada: Land and freshwater areas.* Retrieved September 24, 2006, from http://atlas.nrcan.gc.ca/site/english/learn ingresources/facts/surfareas.html

Nicholls, T. L., Brink, J., Desmarais, S. L., Webster, C. D., & Martin, M-L. (2006). The Short-Term Assessment of Risk and Treatability (START): A prospective validation study in a forensic psychiatric sample. *Assessment, 13,* 313–327.

Nicholls, T. L., Lee, Z., Corrado, R. R., & Ogloff, J. R. (2004). Women inmates' mental health needs: Evidence of the validity of the Jail Screening Assessment Tool (JSAT). *International Journal of Forensic Mental Health, 3*(2), 167–184.

North American Free Trade Agreement Implementation Act, c. 44 (1993).

Ogloff, J. R. (1990). Law and psychology in Canada: The need for training and research. *Canadian Psychology, 31,* 61–73.

Ogloff, J. P. (1999). Graduate training in law and psychology at Simon Fraser University. *Professional Psychology: Research and Practice, 30,* 99–103.

Ontario (2006). *Annual Correctional Statistics, 2005/06.* North Bay, Ontario: Ontario Ministry of Community Safety and Correctional Services.

Ormston, E. F. (2003). Mental health court in Ontario: In Psychiatric Patient Advocate Office, *Mental health and patients' rights in Ontario: Yesterday, today and tomorrow* (pp. 25–26). Toronto, Ontario: Queen's Printer for Ontario. Retrieved September 28, 2006, from http://www.ppao.gov.on.ca/pdfs/pub-ann-2002.pdf

Ouimet, R. (Chair) (1969). *Towards Unity: Criminal Justice and Corrections. Report of the Canadian Committee on Corrections.* Ottawa, Ontario: Information Canada.

Pollack, S. (n.d.). *Mental health services: Elizabeth Fry Societies—Results of CAEFS survey.* Retrieved May 11, 2006, from http://www.elizabethfry.ca/mental/english/survey.pdf (report for the Canadian Association of Elizabeth Fry Societies).

Porporino, F. J., & Motiuk, L. L. (1995). The prison careers of mentally disordered offenders. *International Journal of Law and Psychiatry, 18*(1), 29–44.

Porter, J. (1965). *The vertical mosaic.* Toronto: University of Toronto Press.

Porter, J. (1975). Ethnic pluralism in Canadian perspective. In N. Glazer & Daniel P. Moynihan (Eds.), *Ethnicity: Theory and experience.* Cambridge, MA: Harvard University Press, pp. 267–304.

Porter, S., Fairweather, D., Drugge, J., Heerve, H., Birt, A., & Boer, D. P. (2000). Profiles of psychopathy in incarcerated sexual offenders. *Criminal Justice and Behavior, 27,* 216–233.

Price, R. (1970). Psychiatry, criminal-law reform and the "mythophilic" impulse: On Canadian proposals for the control of the dangerous offender. *Ottawa Law Review, 4,* 1–61.

Price, R. (1974). Bringing the rule of law to corrections. *Canadian Journal of Criminology & Corrections, 16,* 209–255.

Provincial Health Services Authority. (2006). *Canadian forensic psychiatric centres: Providing mental health services to NCR-MD and unfit populations.* Retrieved December 16, 2006, from http://www.bcmhas.ca/NR/rdonlyres/007CD156-65A3-4701-9B76-AFDF13FFC91D/14811/ForensicPsychHospitalsCanada_06.pdf

Public Safety and Emergency Preparedness Canada. (2004). *Corrections and Conditional Release Statistical Overview* (Cat. No. PS4-12/2004E). Ottawa, Ontario: Public Works and Government Services Canada. Retrieved July 13, 2006, from http://dsp-psd.pwgsc.gc.ca/Collection/PS4-12-2004E.pdf

Public Safety and Emergency Preparedness Canada. (2005). *Corrections and Conditional Release Statistical Overview* (Cat. No. PS1-3/2005E). Ottawa, ON: Public Works and Government Services Canada. Retrieved October 1, 2006, from http://www.psepc-sppcc.gc.ca/res/em/_fl/CCRSO11232005-en.pdf

Quigley, T. (1999). Are we doing anything about the disproportionate jailing of Aboriginal people? *Criminal Law Quarterly, 42,* 129–160.

Quinsey, V. L., & Marshall, W. L. (1983). Procedures for reducing inappropriate sexual arousal: An evaluation review. In J. G. Greer and I. R. Stuart (Eds.), *The sexual aggressor: Current perspectives on treatment* (pp. 267–289). New York: Van Nostrand Reinhold.

Quinsey, V. L., Harris, G. T., Rice, M. E., & Cormier, C. A. (2005). *Violent offenders: Appraising and managing risk* (2nd ed.). Washington, DC: American Psychological Association.

R. v. Gladue, 1999, 1 S.C.R. 688.

R v. Johnson, 2003, 2 S.C.R. 357.

R v. Proulx, 2000, 1 S.C.R. 61.

R v. Wust, 2000, 1 S.C.R. 455.

Rice, M. E., Harris, G. T., & Cormier, C. A. (1992). An evaluation of a maximum security therapeutic community for psychopaths and other mentally disordered offenders, *Law and Human Behavior, 21,* 231–241.

Rice, M. E., Quinsey, V. L., & Harris, G. T. (1991). Sexual recidivism among child molesters released from a maximum security psychiatric institution. *Journal of Consulting and Clinical Psychology, 59,* 381–386.

Roach, K. (2000). *Conditional sentences, restorative justice, net widening and Aboriginal offenders. The changing face of sentencing: Symposium proceedings.* Ottawa, Ontario: Department of Justice.

Roberts, J. V., & Gabor, T. (2004). Living in the shadow of prison: Lessons from the Canadian experience in decarceration. *British Journal of Criminology, 44,* 92–112.

Roberts, J., & LaPrairie, C. (2000). *Conditional sentencing in Canada: An overview of research findings.* Ottawa, Ontario: Department of Justice.

Roesch, R. (1995). Mental health interventions in jails. In G. Davis, S. Lloyd-Bostock, M. McMurran & C. Wilson (Eds.), *Psychology, law and criminal justice,* (pp. 520–531). New York: Walter de Gruyter.

Romanow, Q. C. (Commissioner) (2002). *Building on values: The future of health care in Canada* (Cat. No. CP32-85/2002E-IN). Ottawa, Ontario: Commission on the Future of Health Care in Canada. Retrieved May 25, 2006, from http://www.hc-sc.gc.ca/english/pdf/romanow/pdfs/HCC_Final_Report.pdf

Ross, R. (1992). *Dancing with a ghost: Exploring Indian reality.* Markham, Ontario: Reed Books Canada.

Royal Ottawa Health Care Group. (2006). *The Integrated Forensic Program–Overview.* Ottawa, Ontario: Author. Retrieved December 16, 2006, from http://www.rohcg.on.ca/programs-and-services/factsheets/integrated-forensic-psychiatry-bmhc-e.cfm

Sapers, H. (2006). *Annual report of the Office of the Correctional Inverstigator 2005–2006.* Ottawa, Ontario: Minister of Public Works and Government Services Canada.

Sealy, P., & Whitehead, P. C. (2004). Forty years of deinstitutionalization of psychiatric services in Canada: An empirical assessment. *Canadian Journal of Psychiatry, 49* (4), 249–257.

Seto, M. C., Harris, G. T., Rice, M. E., & Barbaree, H. E. (2004). The Screening Scale for pedophilic interests predicts recidivism among adult sex offenders with child victims. *Archives of Sexual Behavior, 33,* 455–466.

Seto, M. C. & Lalumiere, M. L. (2001). A brief screening scale to identify pedophilic interests among child molesters. *Sexual Abuse: A Journal of Research and Treatment, 13,* 15–25.

Simourd, D. J., & Wormith, J. S. (1995). Criminal justice education and training: A survey of Canadian graduate schools of psychology. *Canadian Psychology, 36,* 213–232.

Solicitor General Canada. (1986). *A framework for the Correctional Law Review.* Correctional Law Review Working Paper No. 2. Ottawa, Ontario: Author.

Statistics Canada. (1997). *Graphical overview of crime and the administration of criminal justice in Canada, 1997.* (Catalogue no. 85F0018XIE). Ottawa, Ontario: Author. Retrieved September 25, 2006, from http://www.statcan.ca/english/kits/justic/justic.htm

Statistics Canada. (2001). *2001 census: Aboriginal identity population, 2001 counts, for Canada, provinces and territories–20% sample data.* Ottawa, Ontario: Author. Retrieved September 24, 2006, from http://www12.statcan.ca/english/census01/prod ucts/highlight/Aboriginal

Statistics Canada (2005a). *Population and growth components.* Ottawa, Ontario: Author. Retrieved September 24, 2006, from http://www40.statcan.ca/l01/cst01/demo03.htm

Statistics Canada. (2006). *Annual demographic estimates: Canada, provinces and territories, 2005–2006.* (Catalogue No. 91-215-XIE). Ottawa, Ontario: Author. Retrieved December 2, 2006, from http://www.statcan.ca/english/freepub/91-215-XIE/91-215-XIE2006000.pdf

Stewart, D. (2005, October). *CTOs and forensics: The Sudbury experience.* Paper presented at the meeting of the International Institute for Special Needs Offenders and Policy Research (Canada), Ottawa, Ontario.

Sub-Committee on Corrections and Conditional Release Act. (2000). *A work in progress, the Corrections and Conditional Release Act.* Ottawa, Ontario: Author.

Suedfeld, P., Ramirez, C., Deaton, J., & Baker-Brown, G. (1982). Reactions and attributes of prisoners to solitary confinement. *Criminal Justice and Behavior, 9,* 303–340.

Swaminath, R. S., Mendonca, J. D., Vidal, C., & Chapman, P. (2002). Experiments in change: Pretrial diversion of offenders with mental illness. *Canadian Journal of Psychiatry, 47* (5), 450–458.

Teplin, L. A. (1983). The criminalization of the mentally ill: Speculation in search of data. *Psychological Bulletin, 94*(1), 54–67.

Teplin, L. A. (1984). Criminalizing mental disorder: The comparative arrest rate of the mentally ill. *American Psychologist, 39*(7), 794–803.

Toronto Drug Treatment Court. (n.d.) *Toronto Drug Treatment Court: Policies and procedures Manual.* Toronto, Ontario: Centre for Addiction and Mental Health. Retrieved July 27, 2006, from http://www.iadtc.law.ecu.edu.au/pdfs/Toronto%20DTC%20Policy%20and%20Procedures%20Manual.pdf

Vantour, J. (Chair) (1975). *Report of the Study Group on Dissociation.* Ottawa, Ontario: Ministry of the Solicitor General of Canada.

Vantour, J. (Chair) (1984). *Report on murders and assaults in the Ontario Region.* Ottawa, Ontario: Canadian Penitentiary Service.

Viljoen, J. L., Roesch, R., Ogloff, J. R., & Zapf, P. A. (2003). The role of Canadian psychologists in conducting fitness and criminal responsibility evaluations. *Canadian Psychology, 44,* 369–381.

Waldram, J. (1997). *The way of the pipe: Aboriginal spirituality and symbolic healing in Canadian prisons.* Calgary, AB: Broadview Press.

Waldram, J. B. (2004). *Revenge of the Windigo: The construction of the mind and mental health of North American Aboriginal peoples.* Toronto, Ontario: University of Toronto Press.

Walmsley, R. (2003). World prison population list (4th ed.). *Findings 188.* London: Home Office.

Watkins, R.E. (1992, August). *An historical review of the role and practice of psychology in the field of corrections.* Retrieved September 30, 2006, from http://www.csc-scc.gc.ca/text/rsrch/reports/r28/r28e_3.shtml

Webster, C. D., Eaves, D., Douglas, K.S., & Wintrop, A. (1995). *The HCR-20 scheme: The assessment of dangerousness and risk–Version 1.* Burnaby, BC: Mental Health, Law, and Policy Institute, Simon Fraser University.

Weisman, R. L., Lamberti, J. S., & Price, N. (2004). Integrating criminal justice, community healthcare, and support services for adults with severe mental disorders. *Psychiatric Quarterly, 75*(1), 71–85.

Williams, S., Vallee, S., & Staubi, B. (1997). Aboriginal sexual offenders: Melding spiritual healing with cognitive-behavioural treatment. Ottawa, Ontario: Correctional Service of Canada. Retrieved September 26, 2006, from http://www.csc-scc.gc.ca/text/pblct/sexoffender/aboriginal/aboriginale_e.shtml#P80_688

Wong, S. W., & Hare, R. H. (2005). *Guidelines for a psychopathy treatment program.* Toronto, Ontario: Multi-Health Systems Inc.

Wormith, J. S. (2004, April). Canadian Corner. Rideau Correctional and Treatment Centre: End of an era or correctional footnote? *The Correctional Psychologist, 36*(2), 12–19.

Wormith, J. S., & McKeague, F. (1996). A mental health survey of community correctional clients in Canada. *Criminal Behaviour and Mental Health, 6,* 49–72.

Yang, J., Law, S., Chow, W., Andermann, L., Steinberg, R., & Sadavoy, J. (2005). Assertive community treatment for persons with severe mental illnesses from ethnic minority groups. *Psychiatric Services, 9,* 1053–1055.

Yates, P. M. (2005). Pathways to treatment of sexual offenders: Rethinking intervention. *Forum on Corrections Research, 17,* 1–9.

Yuille, J. C. (1989). Expert evidence by psychologists: Sometimes problematic and often premature. *Behavioral Science and the Law, 7,* 181–196.

Zamble, E., & Quinsey, V. L. (1997). *The criminal recidivism process.* New York: Cambridge University Press.

Zinger, I., Wichman, C., & Andrews, D. A. (2001). The psychological effects of 60 days in administrative segregation. *Canadian Journal of Criminology, 43,* 47–88.

Chapter 7

CORRECTIONS IN AOTEAROA/NEW ZEALAND: CURRENT ISSUES AND FUTURE CHALLENGES

LLEWELYN A. RICHARDS-WARD AND CRISTA MCDANIEL

INTRODUCTION

Twenty-first century New Zealand is a young, multicultural nation composed primarily of Asians, Pacific Islanders, Māori, and Europeans. Many immigrants have come to New Zealand as recently as the 1970s. As such it can be viewed as a "melting pot," a social experiment in multiculturism, and a place where social structures still are set only in wet cement. Historically, New Zealand has been seen as a colony and Great Britain's farm, to be "developed" in a manner prior to industrialised England (Pratt, 2006). This chapter explores correctional practices in New Zealand, highlighting in particular the issues for the indigenous people (Māori), for the mentally unwell within the correctional setting, and the strengths of having only one national corrections system.

As of 19 June 2006, the population of New Zealand stands at 4,139,664 (Statistics New Zealand, 2006) with the large proportion of the population living in Auckland. One hundred and eighty-one ethnic groups reside in Auckland, which differs from the rest of New Zealand in its ethnic makeup, due to a higher concentration of Asians and Pacific Islanders.

Statistics New Zealand collects ethnicity data in a five-year census and allows people to identify multiple ethnicities, but prioritizes responses into five groups (European, Māori, Asian, Pacific Islander, and Other) to simplify the presentation of data. However, within these five categories are over 200 ethnic groups, including for example, more than 60 distinct Asian cultures.

Alongside this multicultural make-up of the country, there is an historical socio-political distinction partitioning New Zealand (Aotearoa) into a bicultural society. To understand the nature of a bicultural viewpoint accurately, one must appreciate that, from the indigenous peoples' (Māori) viewpoint, there are *tangata whenua* (people of the land) and *tau iwi* (the others). This viewpoint, plus a strong legal emphasis on the Treaty of Waitangi *(Te Tiriti O Waitangi)* as a basis for social construction of ethnic policy, guides much of the social policy direction, especially correctional policy.

The Treaty of Waitangi, as a founding document of what then became a colony of the United Kingdom of Great Britain, was signed between two parties, the Crown (at the time Queen Victoria) and the collective iwi (tribes) and hapu (family groups) of New Zealand. The relationship between the Crown (now represented by Her Majesty's Representative the Governor General) and iwi signatories continues.

This founding document is a reason why Māori, in particular, and others resist a move to becoming a republic, as it would require revisiting the treaty relationships. The Treaty of Waitangi (Te Tiriti O Waitangi):

> ... has been described as having two key elements, the first relating to Articles 1 and 3, which give all people the right to live as citizens of Aotearoa (under one law), and the second focusing on Article two which affirms the Māori right to live as Māori with particular responsibilities for protecting and developing those things valued by Māori (Nga taonga katoa). Neither of these rights is exclusive of the other. What binds the two parts of the treaty together is the concept of Turangawaewae, which articulates one of the most important elements of the treaty debate–the right of all peoples to belong. A number of organizations, ranging from Literacy Aotearoa, two major churches, some trade unions, and the number of health service providers have developed 'Treaty Partnership Models'. The emphasis of these partnership models is on achieving more effective participation in outcomes. There is a developing focus internationally on the status of treaties with Indigenous peoples, and on the rights of Indigenous peoples (irrespective of the existence of treaties) particularly in relation to their language, culture, relationship to the land and environment, and equal rights of citizenship. This includes the right to be involved in Government decisions that affect them, and the obligation on States to take measures to achieve equality with other citizens. (Department of Corrections, 2005c, p. 1)

One of the primary reasons correctional policy and practice in New Zealand is strongly based on what is termed a bicultural process is the over-representation of Māori among the correctional population. Because of the number of Māori in the care of the Department of Corrections and the commitment to work in partnership with the Māori, the Te Reo (Language) Strategy 2004–2008 (Department of Corrections, 2005c) was introduced. It stated that:

> In order to reduce the risk of reoffending, the cultural background, ethnic identity, and language of the offender must, where appropriate and to the extent practicable within the resources available be taken into account ... an offender's family must, so far as it is reasonable and practicable in the circumstances and

within the resources available, be recognized and involved in decisions related to sentence planning and management, rehabilitation and reintegration of the offender into the community, and planning for participation by the offender and programs, services and activities in the course of his or her sentence. (p.1)

The Te Reo 2004–2008 strategy (2005c) outlined opportunities to build relationships and strengthen communications between Māori and Corrections.

> *Kotahi ano te Kaupapa;*
> *Ko te oranga o te iwi.*
> There is only one purpose (to our work);
> It is the wellness and wellbeing of the people.

DEMOGRAPHICS

As of May 2006, there were 7,534 people in prison.[1] The demographics of the total correctional population indicate that individuals in New Zealand are being incarcerated at a rate of 182 per 100,000. At the same point in time, 26,782 orders for community sentence had been made. Some individuals on community sentence are serving more than one order at a time. Orders are broadly either *supervisory* (where some sanction, monitoring, and possibly treatment is evident), or *reparative* (fines or community sentences, where the emphasis is on community service). Community sentences are administered by the Community Probation Service (CPS), part of the larger Department of Corrections. The distribution of ethnicity across community and prison settings is represented in Table 7.1.

However, when the demographics for those incarcerated (and on community sentence) are broken down further, for Māori the rate of imprisonment is 638 per 100,000 while that for NZ European is 93 per 100,000 (using data and population estimates as of 1 May 2006 and percentages as above). This is an area that is continuing to challenge policymakers and operational staff alike in terms of how to reduce this unequal rate of incarceration. As already noted, a significant issue for New Zealand, as with other countries, is the proportional overrepresentation of indigenous peoples in the correctional system.

---

1. Prisons in New Zealand are administered by the Department of Corrections. The Department of Corrections is a national public service department which manages sentences through Community Probation Service and Public Prisons Service. In addition the department provides rehabilitative and reintegrative services through Psychological Service (focussing mainly on risk assessment and rehabilitative services for high risk offenders), Intervention Service (for medium risk offender group programmes), Public Prisons Inmate Services (for reintegrative and educational programmes) and Corrections Inmate Employment. There is no federal/state distinction and no correctional services are contracted privately in terms of sentence management.

TABLE 7.1
ETHNICITY OF THE DEPARTMENT OF CORRECTIONS POPULATION
COMPARED TO OVERALL POPULATION (1 MAY 2006)

Ethnicity	General population	Prison	Community Probation Service
Asian	8.8%	2.8%	1.2%
European	70.3%	35.8%	40.2%
Māori	14.2%	49.8%	46.2%
Other	–	1.1%	1.0%
Pacific Peoples	6.7%	10.4%	9.3%
Unknown	–	0.2%	2.0%

Along with the demographics for ethnicity, information on "patched" gang members in New Zealand's prisons has been included as gangs often are ethnically-based and also represent a form of group membership, much as ethnicity can be a central point for group membership. New Zealand, like most countries in the world, is facing organised crime and contending with various gangs. Gang members in New Zealand identify themselves as "patched" if they have demonstrated commitment to the rules of the group (this includes going to prison for another's crime) and have been accepted by other members as a core member. Otherwise, gang members identify themselves as "affiliated" with a gang. According to the Criminal Investigation Branch of the New Zealand Police Department, the most prominent gangs in New Zealand are the Mongrel Mob, Black Power, and Nomads. Some gangs are predominantly composed of Pacific or Māori peoples, while others are primarily composed of White members (Highway 61, White Power, Skin Heads, Hell's Angels, Devil's Henchmen, and Nomads). Other gangs in New Zealand include the Head-hunters, Bloods, Crips, Outlawz, Only the Brothers, and Wellington Darkside. Gangs offer challenges to law enforcement and corrections alike, due to the serious and pervasive nature of their antisocial activities, which includes violence, selling and distribution of drugs, possessing firearms and offensive weapons, and use of intimidation and threats. There is some concern about the possibility that Asian triads are attempting to forge links with existing New Zealand gangs (New Zealand Police, 2006).

The gangs within New Zealand do not typically have "formal" links to other countries. However, it is reasonable to surmise that many of the ethnically based gangs derive some of their culture from media portrayals from the United States of America, particularly through music media and culture. Intuitively, replication or copying of gangs from the USA seems to be more predominant with youth gangs in socio-economically deprived areas. In the late 1960s, Hells Angels chapters were formally recognised in this country as being international chapters of the Los Angeles groups. Within prisons, the

TABLE 7.2
GANG MEMBERSHIP OF SENTENCED INMATES 1995 AND 2003

Gang	1995		2003	
	Number	Percent	Number	Percent
Mongrel Mob	102	37.2%	206	35.1%
Black Power	86	31.4%	193	32.9%
Nomads	6	2.2%	25	4.3%
Highway 61	–	–	17	2.9%
Tribesman	–	–	16	2.7%
Crips	14	5.1%	16	2.7%
White Power	18	6.6%	14	2.4%
Skin Heads	–	–	14	2.4%
Road Knights	–	–	13	2.2%
All Other Gangs	48	17.5%	73	12.4%
Total	274	100.0%	587	100.0%

dominant gangs are Black Power and the Mongrel Mob and gang members from these groups gain significant kudos from having spent time in prison when they return to their chapters in the community. Thus, the deviance training impact of these groups within prisons is high as "prospects" can climb the ladder of gang membership quite rapidly from aligning with established members whilst in prison. Like the rest of the world, even in gang culture, relationships count as much for "advancement" as other areas (Eggleston, 1997).

In 2003, "patched" gang membership was identified for 587 or 11.5 percent of the sentenced inmates, including 21 women. Over two-thirds of those individuals belonged to either the Mongrel Mob or Black Power gangs (Table 7.2). Over the eight-year period the proportion of gang members in prison appears to have remained relatively static.

The third major demographic of correctional settings is the age range of those in prison, shown in Table 7.3. As is noted below, a majority of inmates are relatively young (under 40).

New Zealand, like most other Western jurisdictions, has a lower but increasing number of female offenders for whom imprisonment is a sentence of last resort (Poels, 2006). The increasing female population has resulted in new prison units, and on 22 June 2006, a new women's prison was opened. This now brings the number of women's prisons to three, one in each main population centre. The prison population by gender is 94.5 percent male, 5.4 percent female, and 0.1 percent (10 individuals) transgender or indeterminate, and within the community correctional setting, is 81.9 percent male, 17.9 percent female and 0.2 percent transgender or indeterminate.

TABLE 7.3
AGE OF PUBLIC PRISON SERVICE POPULATION (1 MAY 2006)
COMPARED TO OVERALL POPULATION.

Prisoner Age Range 01/05/06			Population age range (2001)	
10–14	–	0.0%	290,742	9.3%
15–19	584	7.6%	265,284	8.5%
20–24	1,445	18.9%	239,784	7.7%
25–29	1,310	17.2%	246,903	7.9%
30–34	1,166	15.3%	279,279	8.9%
35–39	1,096	14.4%	297,462	9.5%
40–44	788	10.3%	285,621	9.1%
45–49	523	6.9%	251,787	8.0%
50–54	296	3.9%	236,169	7.5%
55–59	176	2.3%	182,262	5.8%
60–64	101	1.3%	154,569	4.9%
65–69	65	0.9%	127,911	4.1%
70–74	28	0.4%	118,257	3.8%
75–79	17	0.2%	94,506	3.0%
80–84	2	0.0%	61,110	2.0%
No age recorded	42	0.55%		

A unique feature of the New Zealand correctional setting is that there is only one national system for correctional operations, managed by the Department of Corrections. This system includes incarcerated and community-based sentences within the Department of Corrections. New Zealand did start down the track of private prisons but, with the current Labour-led government stating that corrections is part of the executive responsibility, the existing private prison has been reintegrated into a state-run system. Perhaps the strongest positive outcome of a single correctional system is that it has enabled an actuarial method of general risk of reoffending estimation to be implemented for all offenders, work done by Psychological Service (Bakker, O'Malley, & Riley, 1999). In turn, this has allowed sentence management and parole decisions, to be made according to empirical methods rather than clinical or intuitive methods (see Anstiss, 2003). There also has been considerable focus placed on ensuring Māori, as disproportionate consumers of correctional treatment, are not only considered but have direct cultural influence in sentence management and treatment (Maynard, Coebergh, Anstiss, Bakker, & Huriwai, 1999). The benefits of the integrated system include improved service delivery of scarce resources, simplified evaluation of "what works," and a tool for implementing a scientific Psychology of Criminal Conduct (Andrews & Bonta, 2003) approach in the correctional work.

PSYCHOLOGICAL AND TREATMENT SERVICES WITHIN THE DEPARTMENT OF CORRECTIONS

Because there is a single system of corrections, rehabilitative aspects of correctional practice can be performed nationally by Psychological Service and Intervention Service.[2] These services provide assessment, treatment (group and individual) and advice to the Department of Corrections and parole boards across all sites both in prison and in the community. Aspects of ongoing care from prison to the community thus are more easily managed, among other benefits.

Psychological Service within the Department of Corrections has drawn heavily on work from Canada, the United Kingdom of Great Britain and the United States in emphasising an empirically driven approach to reducing reoffending that also meets the political imperative of being cost effective (e.g., Andrews & Bonta, 2003; Beech, Fisher, & Thornton, 2003; Bonta, 2002; Hanson & Morton-Bourgon, 2004; Hare, 2003; Motiuk, 2000; Nicholls, Ogloff & Douglas, 2004; Quinsey, Harris, Rice & Cormier, 1999; Ward, Mann & Gannon, in press; Ward & Stewart, 2003; Wong & Gordon, 1999).

Cost-effectiveness is measured by comparing the percentage change in recidivism from a treated to nontreated matched group. This recidivism quotient (RQ) is utilised at the corporate management and policy levels to determine the direction of the overall goal of reducing reoffending. Generally, it is accepted that a 10 percent reduction is cost-effective. While this measure is somewhat of a blunt instrument, nonetheless, Psychological Service in general and the Special Treatment Units in particular, have demonstrated cost-effectiveness from their interventions.

Psychological Service, in particular, currently has responsibility for two Special Treatment Units for child sex offenders, and a Violence Prevention Programme. Each of these three units is conducted in a prison unit with follow-up groups in the community. Generally, these groups are effective as often offenders have an intrinsic level of motivation to attend in addition to the extrinsic motivation of treatment it being an implied necessary condition for obtaining parole.

Kia Marama (literally, "Let there be light or insight") was New Zealand's first specialist programme for child sex offenders and has consistently demon-

---

2 Intervention Service was established primarily to provide criminogenic programmes in group format to offenders. These programmes now target medium risk offenders (those with between 30-60% probability of reoffending within five years of release from sentence) and address motivation and criminogenic needs aspects of offending. While there are multiple points of contact between IS and other groups providing rehabilitative services, IS is run as a separate part of Department of Corrections with its own budget.

strated significant reductions in recidivism (Bakker, Hudson, Wales, & Riley, 1998). It is a 60-bed programme originally based on the Atascadero Sex Offender Treatment and Evaluation Programme in California. Te Piriti (literally, "The Bridge," from old to new) Special Treatment Unit for sex offenders includes a stronger Māori content with a focus on promoting a therapeutic environment within a tikanga (philosophically) Māori framework. An evaluation recently demonstrated a significant impact on treatment outcome from incorporating a Māori perspective (Nathan, Wilson, & Hillman, 2003). The Violence Prevention Unit in Rimutaka Prison currently is being reviewed for effectiveness. There also is a violence and drug programme run in the Hamilton community, the Montgomery House Violence Prevention Programme, which is a joint project between the New Zealand Department of Corrections and the New Zealand Prisoner's Aid and Rehabilitation Society (PARS). Again, this programme has demonstrated positive outcomes on reducing reoffending and incorporates Māori values and principles–tikanga Māori (Berry, 1998).

Because of the strong focus by the Department of Corrections on reducing reoffending, Psychological Service, while staffed primarily by clinical psychologists, does not focus directly on mental health issues. Rather, in the context of Andrews and Bonta's (2003) framework, these are viewed as responsivity issues (see below) which may be addressed separately or concomitantly with treating criminogenic factors. With this focus on treating criminogenic factors, increasingly there are greater numbers of forensically trained psychologists working in the service, many of whom come from an international labour pool. These staff contribute valued expertise in group treatment, forensic assessment, and general forensic skills.

An implication of the reduction of reoffending mission of forensic psychology, inclusive of the risk, needs and responsivity paradigm (Andrews & Bonta, 2003) is that other professions increasingly provide the majority of "purely" clinical mental health services within the Department of Corrections, with correctional psychologists increasingly becoming specialists in forensic assessment and treatment of offenders for criminogenic needs only. Correctional psychologists in New Zealand view mental health issues as barriers to treatment of criminogenic needs, not a legitimate activity without an overarching criminogenic focus. Those who do treat the mental health needs directly include psychiatrists, general practitioners, nurses, and counsellors through inmate services within the department. Typically mental health management by these professions is medication focussed, within the prison setting. The interface between psychologists treating offending behaviour and mental (ill) health is in that grey area termed "responsivity" (Andrews & Bonta, 2003). Responsivity, an emerging concept, implies that offending and mental health issues can have a close relationship and at times require sequential or parallel treatment. It will be interesting to observe whether, over time, these two concepts coalesce to form a parallel of dual diagnosis, with the dual issues in this instance being criminogenic needs and mental health functioning.

SOCIAL POLICY: PRINCIPLES, PRACTICES AND INNOVATIONS

Currently, New Zealand is going through a governmental and departmental review of where correctional processes are in terms of protecting the public and adequately reflecting social abhorrence of criminal behaviour. In 1999, a referendum was held as part of the usual electoral process to ascertain public viewing of sentencing. Over 92 percent of people who voted indicated that they would prefer tougher sentencing of criminals. Setting aside any governmental outcomes from this referendum, it provided impetus for lobby groups to form, one of which (The Sensible Sentencing Trust, 2006) increasingly has moved policy towards more punishment (longer sentences) and away from rehabilitative options. Despite this trend, current policy retains a focus on rehabilitation of offenders, with a focus more on personal than collective or social responsibility for crime. This policy direction is supported by many social service groups which now are forming more connected and vocal coalitions to advocate for a compassionate approach (Prison Fellowship of New Zealand, 2006a, 2006b). This group is affiliated internationally with other similar groups such as the Prison Fellowship International network operating from a spiritual and restorative approach to crime.

International correctional research suggests that rehabilitation of offenders is an appropriate goal, and one with demonstrably positive outcomes for society (e.g., Andrews & Bonta, 2003; Anstiss, 2003; Motiuk, 2000; Ward, Mann & Gannon, in press). Equally important is that rehabilitation reflects the working of a compassionate and humane society (Human Rights Commission, 2204a, 2004b; Prison Fellowship of New Zealand, 2006a). In large part, this goal is now reflected in the structure of the correctional system. For example, the Minister of Corrections the Honourable Matt Robson said, *"We must use sound, research-based, rehabilitation programs for offenders so they do not reoffend"* (Department of Corrections, 2001, p. v).

Reflecting this policy's intent, the organizational structure of the Department of Corrections relies on what is termed Integrated Offender Management (IOM). IOM, in its simplest form, is about reducing reoffending by targeting those most likely to reoffend (Coebergh, Bakker, Anstiss, Maynard, & Percy, 2001). This is done through application of the concepts of risk, need and responsivity from both international (Andrews & Bonta, 2003) and local

(McMaster & Bakker, 2006) empirical perspectives. Risk is estimated through sophisticated actuarial tools, combining the risk of reconviction (RoC) with the risk of imprisonment (RoI) forming the RoC*RoI (Bakker, O'Malley & Riley, 1999). The RoC*RoI provides an estimate of the probability that an offender will reoffend seriously enough in five years following release to be reimprisoned. This tool is used to select the highest risk offenders, who then are targeted for increasingly higher levels of intervention. Those who are not responsive to addressing criminogenic needs are termed "motivation category" offenders, who then are targeted at a case officer level for intervention to motivate them to address offending. Another actuarial tool used to address further risk of convicted sex offenders is the STATIC-AS (Skelton, Riley, Wales, & Vess, in submission), whose development arises from the work of the Static-99 (Harris, Phenix, Hanson, & Thornton, 2003). The major strengths of this tool are that it is computer scored from the corrections electronic data warehouse for all applicable offenders, that the normative data are more robust than the Static-99 and that the normative sample is local. The tool has not differentiated between Māori and other groups. However, it has suggested a capacity to differentiate between offence types (e.g., child sex –v- adult offenders).

Currently, the dominant policy direction is best reflected by those who rely on an approach driven by collective knowledge, common sense, and popular opinion. This approach is pushing correctional services towards ensuring that offenders are reintegrated on release. This operationally is defined as ensuring that offenders have jobs and a place to live. Currently, the Department of Corrections does focus on reintegration, but this initiative has lagged behind the focus on rehabilitation. In a recent speech, the present Minister of Corrections, the Honourable Damian O'Connor (2006), noted that:

> . . . The corrections system must also take account of other factors that contribute to crime—issues such as illiteracy, drug and alcohol abuse, a history of unemployment and work life skills. . . . But for any interventions to work, prisoners have to want to change. . . . Over and above their health needs, if prisoners want to work, receive training, get a place on a drug and alcohol course, they have to show they are motivated and want to change. . . . Work and education must be considered a privilege, not a right in prison. Those who don't want to engage—those who don't want to put their hands up—don't have to. We can't make them. But they will lose the benefits of longer unlocked hours, the gift of being able to learn new skills and to do an honest day's work. In short, they will, by their own stubbornness, spurn a genuine chance to create a better life for themselves. But those who are determined to grasp the opportunity with both hands—must receive the full support of the department. . . . (p. 1)

Governmental policies are further reflected in the Statement of Intent (Department of Corrections, 2006) for the Department of Corrections in which the Minister states that:

The statement of intent highlights a number of priorities I have asked the department to focus on in the coming year, to ensure consistent approaches to managing and rehabilitating offenders. These are: responsibility-based approaches that provide prisoners with sanctions and incentives to encourage positive behaviour, improving the department's rehabilitation programs with a focus on more intensity and better targeted programs, providing treatment for a larger number of offenders who have substance abuse problems, focusing on offenders gaining skills and employment, and increasing the opportunities available for this in prisons. Prisoners should be as productive as possible during their sentence by taking part in meaningful work initiatives and learning skills that will prepare them for a life in the community. (p. 5)

The goal of this approach is to move away from incarceration alone and to further develop interventions that are less resource intensive, protect the public and hopefully rehabilitate the offender. An example of this approach is the use of home detention, which connects sanctions to technology (e.g., monitoring bracelets). Offenders on a sentence of home detention have a very low reoffending rate compared to all other interventions, although this has not necessarily resulted in other jurisdictions considered in the international literature (Aos, Miller & Drake, 2006). Recently, the government have released plans to expand the use of home detention and other diversionary programmes.

Another innovation is the placing of Work and Income New Zealand officers inside prisons to assist offenders to find employment on release. This is important as the money received on release from prison often is insufficient to rent or find accommodation, potentially increasing the risk of offending.

At the broadest level, policy has moved away from silos (organisational self-interest groups) within and across the public sector. Now, it is expected that operational and other managers regularly liaise with other parts of the public sector. These include Police, Child Youth and Family (who manage child protection), Ministry of Justice (Courts), Work and Income New Zealand (managing jobs on release). These relationships often are formalized via Memoranda of Understanding (MOU) and Service-Level Agreements (SLA). Arguably these cross-sector relationships work best at operational levels.

Currently in process is an initiative to develop a cross-justice sector (including police, child protection agencies, courts, and correctional services) strategy for reducing *entry* to the criminal justice system, in addition to bolstering existing exit strategies from it. The strategy, called "Effective Interventions," is presently being moved through various levels of consultation within the public sector, prior to being placed before Parliament for the necessary legislative review. From this strategy, it appears that the Labour-led government will set a direction for more than a three-year election cycle that will take the justice sector into what is termed a "whole of government approach" to issues of law and order.

The significance of a strategy across the justice and other sectors would be that, rather than the Department of Corrections being seen as the repository where those "who do not belong" are placed, a caring society might view justice sector involvement as a failure of other systems of education and social justice, and as such take ownership for change. This approach already is gaining credence within the thinking of many iwi (tribal) and hapu (wider family) groups. An example of this is found in the Waiariki area where local hapu (Ngati Whakaue) are putting considerable monetary investment into education for youth at risk in an effort to improve and increase resilience in Māori young people and in their communities. These and many other examples are notable as they have come from within hapu and iwi rather than from central government.

Māori involvement in policy occurs at all levels. At the macro level, there is the Ministry of Māori Affairs advising on development issues. In the Department of Corrections, there are various levels of advisers to help steer the waka (boat) that is the Department of Corrections towards addressing the principles of governance over Māori of protection, partnership and participation (Department of Corrections, 2005c, 2005d). These are enshrined in the Treaty of Waitangi. Operationally, Māori are involved in the Department of Corrections as respected elders and visiting officers (kaitiaki and kaumatua, respectively), through Māori being employed, through local partnerships with iwi providing treatment using Māori principles (Department of Corrections, 2005c, 2005d).

Current initiatives that incorporate Māori principles include five Māori Focus Units within prisons which operate, as closely as feasible, in accordance with "Tikanga Māori" to provide opportunities for inmates to gain a deeper understanding and knowledge of Māori cultural values and Te Reo Māori (the Māori language), and to provide an environment where Māori-specific interventions can be delivered (Maynard, Coebergh, Astiss, Bakker, & Huriwai, 1999). The "Tikanga Māori" programmes are designed to inculcate Māori cultural values. In addition, Māori Therapeutic Programs are currently being redeveloped to ensure an effective blend of Tikanga (cultural) and therapeutic principles to provide a Māori version of core criminogenic programming. Both within and outside of prisons, bicultural therapy is being delivered by the Department of Corrections Psychological Service in partnership with a local iwi oversight group who help recruit and manage counsellors and tohunga (healers) expert in "Tikanga Māori."

New corrections facilities are being completed in close partnership with "Kaitiaki" Māori communities on whose historical land the facilities will be constructed. There is also the Kaiwhakamana Strategy (Department of Corrections, 2005d) which sees elders or "kaumatua" from Māori tribes (iwi) granted "specified visitor" status to facilitate regular contact in the prison to support their relevant communities.

Specialized Māori Cultural Assessment (SMCA), is delivered to inmates with more complex cultural needs, and is conducted by a specialist Māori provider. Similarly, cultural supervision is provided to Department of Correction's staff in support of the cultural assessment responsibilities. A number of similar initiatives are in development to address the needs of the 10 percent of Pacific Island inmates incarcerated in New Zealand (Department of Corrections, 2005d).

In summary, the focus of New Zealand's implied and explicit policy is directed toward resisting an international trend towards harsher sentences. This is in the somewhat incongruent context of New Zealand's high rate of incarceration, relative to other Western nations, often for crimes of relatively lesser seriousness (Pratt, 2006). However, instead of defaulting to incarceration,[3] policy continues to acknowledge the necessity of rehabilitation and reintegration in reducing reoffending and protection of the public.

MENTAL HEALTH AND CORRECTIONAL SYSTEMS

As in other countries in the world, New Zealand's mental health services evolved from institutionally based services to community-based care, so that mentally ill patients could remain in their community while being treated. The goal of such treatment was to restore function, so that the individual could achieve to his or her potential and treatment was designed to protect a patient's rights and to ensure informed consent, whenever possible. The responsibility for the treatment and care of the mentally ill in New Zealand is the responsibility of the Ministry of Health. In 1988, to improve mental health care in prisons, Regional Forensic Psychiatric Services were established.

When an inmate is thought to have mental illness, a referral is made to the Forensic Psychiatric Service through the prison's medical service. Individuals with mental illness are screened and detected through the Integrated Offender Management process (IOM) which includes computerized assessment, induction, and case management aspects. There are specific processes to aid in identification for suicide, self-harm, and mental illness at presentence and upon entering prison when interviewed by the Receiving Officer. If an inmate is considered "at risk," he or she enters a special management regime in a sep-

---

3. While principle is a factor in New Zealand's adherence to international United Nations conventions, locally, the issue that appeared to sway public opinion toward more humane approaches was the visibly high and escalating costs to the public of building prison capacity to manage the additional offenders. In 2006, capacity already exceeds the census anticipated by 2010. Given the long lead time needed to build facilities, there has been a very public debate over whether this is the preferred option for New Zealand.

arate unit until further assessment can take place. Whether inmates remain in prison or are transferred to inpatient facilities, their care is overseen by forensic services and managed by prison health staff.

At times, Psychological Service staff, in the course of their assessments, may detect signs of mental illness. If so, and the individual is in prison, they alert the prison's medical services. Community Mental Health is contacted if the individual is with Community Probation Service, which in turn contacts his or her Regional Forensic Psychiatric Service. Once an inmate has been determined to have mental illness, forensic psychiatric services provides all psychiatric care including diagnosis, treatment planning, and treatment, which is managed within a prison or in a secure inpatient setting. Forensic psychiatric services also prepare inmates for release and reintegration into the community by involving other agencies in aftercare.

Although the responsibility for the treatment of mentally ill patients remains the responsibility of the Ministry of Health, the Department of Corrections ensures staff receives mental health training on a regional basis and during initial prison officer training. The Department's goal is to appropriately assess and manage offenders at all stages of their sentence using "best practices." For example, all offenders are assessed at entry to the court system as to current functioning and overt homicidal/suicidal risk using short screening measures administered via probation or prison officers. While these tools are only screening for mental health and other issues, even slight indications of risk have mandated follow-up procedures.

The National Study of Psychiatric Morbidity, a comprehensive study conducted in New Zealand prisons, was completed by a research team of forensic psychiatry specialists (Simpson, Brinded, Laidlaw, Fairley, & Malcom, 1999). The study sampled all female and all male remand inmates and 15 percent of the sentenced male population out of a total of 5500 inmates (response rate 80%). What they found were significantly higher lifetime prevalence rates of various mental disorders for these inmates than existed in the community, including for schizophrenia (6.0% men, 6.7% women), bipolar disorder (2.2% men, 1.2% women), major depression (20.6% men, 31.9% women), obsessive-compulsive disorder (5.6% men, 9.9% women), and posttraumatic stress disorder (19.2% men, 37.0% women). The study also indicated that nearly 60 percent of the inmates had at least one personality disorder.

Furthermore, Simpson et al. (1999) found that all inmates with a current diagnosis of schizophrenia or related disorder or bipolar disorder would require active psychiatric treatment and, of those surveyed, 135 inmates would require inpatient treatment. The lifetime and one-month prevalence of these disorders was significantly higher than in the community. One of the surprises in the study concerned the prevalence of two anxiety disorders—obsessive-compulsive disorder (OCD) and posttraumatic stress disorder. The lifetime prevalence of PTSD for female inmates was 37 percent, while the community sample lifetime prevalence rate was 1.3%. Simpson et al. (1999) noted that the incidence of PTSD was grossly elevated relative to the community at large and was more in keeping with findings for high-risk populations such as victims of criminal offences and combat veterans. One quarter of the inmates had suffered a major depressive disorder, with a lifetime prevalence rate twice as high as the community sample.

The national study (Simpson et al., 1999) recommended a significant increase in mental health provision within the prison service. It was suggested that this would include more primary medical care psychiatric clinics and inpatient beds. Furthermore, it was also indicated that some of the individuals identified in the study would need on-going psychotherapy, in addition to pharmacotherapy.

In summary, the challenge of mental health patients moving into correctional settings was predicted from international research and trends in the early 1990s (e.g., Richards-Ward, 1996). While the warnings that deinstitutionalization would result in increased incarceration of the mentally unwell were clear in the public mind, the government of the day favoured reduction of state care and removal of the "big bin" concept from mental health care policy. Whether it was implementation of the policy or the actual policy of community care that failed the mentally unwell continues to be a source of debate and research. In the meantime, the Department of Corrections began receiving these people into prisons and community probation settings, subsequently finding that there were few substantive options to have them treated. As a result, many were segregated and others probably had their needs much less than adequately met because specialist services were not available within the prison setting.

The Department of Corrections has introduced quite extensive processes to ensure that those at risk are managed in terms of preserving their safety and ensuring at least some access to pharmacotherapy, even if other mental health services are not forthcoming. This has been a new and challenging role for staff and planners alike. Like so many other countries, the "revolving door" between correctional and mental health settings began spinning. Currently, there is a need to identify policies and procedures that support alternatives to incarceration for deinstitutionalized offenders. These people do not belong in prison settings, and are not easily treated for either offending or mental health needs within them. A corollary is that supported care capacity needs to be increased from the health vote[4] rather than the justice sector vote if they are not entering prisons or that correctional settings need to be better developed

---

4. The term vote refers to the allocation of money for these areas of spending, which is enacted through parliamentary vote.

to meet the needs of the mentally ill. Also, as yet, it remains unclear how the "Effective Interventions" project to enhance cross-sector prevention and management of offending will form linkages with mental health providers.

ALCOHOL AND DRUGS

In New Zealand, it is common to discuss substance abuse as being a partially distinct area from mental health and offending. However, in the correctional settings, the impact of substance abuse requires consideration separate from and in addition to that of mental health issues. Increasingly, alcohol and drug services are separating from mainstream mental health services, with some of these being provided as dual-diagnosis as well as dedicated services. Alcohol and drugs in New Zealand is an issue that has seen policies alter, including lowering of the drinking age to 18, and the inception of a significant lobby proposing decriminalising cannabis use. However, statistics nationally support a view that consumption of alcohol and drugs comes with a financial, social and health cost (Ministry of Health, 2001). The impact of alcohol and drug use is further evident when considered in the context of a correctional setting. The National Study of Psychiatric Morbidity revealed that 90 percent of those with major mental disorders also had a substance abuse disorder (Simpson et al., 1999). Of the total prison population in 1999, 89.4 percent had a current substance abuse or dependence diagnosis. Thirty-five percent of these inmates had received treatment for the abuse disorder since they have been in prison. Considering that substance abuse disorders contributed to reoffending amongst offender populations, was associated with a poorer prognosis of people with mental disorders, and was so prevalent in the prison population, one of the recommendations was to have drug and alcohol treatment more broadly provided.

In its policy on drug treatment, the Department of Corrections (2004) stated the following:

> The majority of offenders began using drugs while living in the community. The availability of drugs once offenders are released from prison offers temptations that even offenders who have completed treatment for addiction find hard to resist. Families and loved ones smuggle drugs into prisons under pressure from offenders but also offenders are pressured to buy, sell, or use drugs, often from other offenders.

All these factors make it very hard for corrections alone to combat the issue of offender drug use. The Department is part of the Interagency Committee on Drugs and Alcohol, which considers work prepared in response to the numerous government Action Plans on alcohol and drugs, including the Methamphetamine Action Plan. Working closely with other government and community agencies is essential to address the complex issues surrounding drug abuse in our communities.

Cannabinoids continue to be the main drug of choice inside prisons, but this appears to be changing. In 2001/2002 Cannabinoids appeared in 97% of all positive drug tests, however in 2002/2003 this is reduced to 94%. This trend is consistent with the increased use in detection of amphetamines and methamphetamines in the community. It poses issues for Corrections, however, as prisoners under the influence of drugs such as "P" (pure methamphetamine) can be unpredictable, violent, and difficult for staff to manage.

We know that prisoners have far worse problems with drugs than the general population. The national study of psychiatric morbidity in New Zealand prisons identify that 83.4% of prisoners have had problems with alcohol and drugs at some point in their lives. Alcohol and drug abuse is clearly linked to offending. A departmental study in 1998 found that 89% of serious offenders were alcohol and drug affected in the period leading up to their offence.

Since 2001, the Department has introduced comprehensive assessment and treatment for offenders with drug problems. Offenders are screened using recognized assessment tools such as the Drug Abuse Screening Test (DAST) and the Alcohol Use Disorders Identification Test (AUDIT). Substance abuse programs that run for 100 hours over a 10-week period are offered to both offenders in prison and those who are subject to community-based sentences. The Department also operates three specialist drug treatment units in prison. (p. 9)

In summary, substance dependence and abuse remain prominent with correctional settings. Abuse and dependence both contributes to and directly reflects offending. Hence, treatment for substance abuse and dependence is increasingly a part of correctional "business." What is not as accessible are preventive programmes in the community and elsewhere to reduce the impact of abuse and dependence, particularly in youth and women, plus legislation supporting responsible drinking.

NEW ZEALAND'S CORRECTIONAL MODEL/PHILOSOPHY

Section 7 of the Sentencing Act 2002 outlines the purposes of sentencing and sets out the principles that should be applied to every sentencing decision (Department of Corrections, 2005e). The purpose of a sentence is to:

- hold the offender accountable for the harm done to the victim and the community by their offending,
- promote in the offender a sense of responsibility for, and an acknowledgement of, that harm,
- provide for the interests of the victim(s) of the offence,
- provide reparation for harm done by the offending,

- denounce the conduct in which the offender was involved,
- deter the offender, or other persons, from committing the same or similar offences,
- protect the community from the offender, and
- assist in the offender's rehabilitation and reintegration. (Department of Corrections, 2005e)

The Court must also consider aspects that both aggravate and mitigate an offence. As a result, the Court must take into account:

- the gravity of the offending in the particular case, including the degree of culpability of the offender;
- the seriousness of the type of offence, as indicated by the maximum penalties prescribed for the offences;
- the general desirability of consistency with appropriate sentencing levels, and other means of dealing with offenders, in respect of similar offenders committing similar offences in similar circumstances;
- any information provided to the Court, concerning the effect of the offending on the victim;
- where a particular circumstance of the offender means that a sentence, or any other means of dealing with the offender, that would otherwise be appropriate is, in the particular instance, disproportionately severe;
- the offender's personal, family (whānau), community and cultural background in imposing a sentence, or other means of dealing with the offender, within a partly or wholly rehabilitative purpose, and;
- any outcomes of restorative justice processes that have occurred, or that the Court is satisfied are likely to occur, in relation to the particular case, including, without limitation, any offer, agreement, response or measure to make amends. (Department of Corrections, 2005e)

However, while the principles of sentencing appear clear-cut, inspection of other agencies in the public indicates that these sentencing principles are either not well understood or simply rejected by some nongovernmental organisations. For example, the Sensible Sentencing Trust (a "get tough on crime" lobby group) noted that *"Prisons have four functions: 1) To protect the public, 2) To punish, 3) To deter, 4) To rehabilitate"* (Sensible Sentencing Trust, 2006, p. 6). Contrast this statement with that of the Prison Fellowship (2006a) who said in an open letter following a meeting of 46 interested groups (including the Sensible Sentencing Trust) from religious and other areas:

> . . There was general discussion about the "darker side" of New Zealand society, and our pleasure in seeing people punished. The challenge will be to change how people "feel" about prisoners and prisons, crime and punishment. Some participants warned against the potential to polarise through allowing the debate

to develop into a retribution vs. restoration, punishment vs. rehabilitation debate. The two are not mutually exclusive. One of the fundamental concerns was to preserve public safety and ensure ongoing community protection. . . . (p. 1)

Overall, it appears that while the New Zealand public is tired of crime and wants it reduced, the only viable option in the public psyche has been to do this by increasing sentence length. This focus has been based on social retribution, despite the polemics of some, as incarceration does not reduce reoffending in general (Anstiss, 2003; Aos, Miller & Drake, 2006).

What has been less visible, but nonetheless evident for those willing to go past the public idée fixe, is that government commitment to United Nations agreements on appropriate management of crime in society has generally been positive. Thus, while sentence lengths have increased,[5] there has been a corresponding amount of effort placed into rehabilitative and restorative options, including consideration of things such as marae (local family tribal land) justice for Māori offenders. Rather than accepting Martinson's (1974) view that nothing works, the Department of Corrections in New Zealand has utilised increasingly sophisticated risk estimation actuarials to develop an Integrated Offender Management (IOM) approach where the principles of risk need and responsivity were used in preference to sociologically driven viewpoints. The result has thus far been a system where obligations and human rights, such as to the Treaty of Waitangi, have been translated into effective social science practice.

Currently, vigourous debates and discussions at political and policy levels are occurring about sexual assault, domestic violence, child abuse, the use of recreational drugs, and the effects of media glamorizing criminal lifestyles with the effect of desensitizing people to violent crime (e.g., McCarthy, 2006; O'Conner, 2006). There is recognition in the public sector that something needs to change. Many concerns and accusations are levelled at the Department of Corrections, who represent the end user, and often in the public mind is the organisation responsible for any failure to reduce crime. However, there is some awareness increasing among New Zealanders that the rapidly increasing costs of incarceration do not result either in increased public safety or saved tax dollars. So while the debate about retribution versus rehabilitation mostly occurs out of the media spotlight, the economics of retribution versus rehabilitation increasingly are in the forefront of public consciousness. While the end result might be in favour of rehabilitation and humane treatment of

---

5. The increase in sentence length is, however, relative to those of other countries. Murder, for example, receives a life imprisonment sentence. The time before parole can be set by the judge and in one or two particularly nasty crimes has gone above 20 years. Largely, though, the average time served for murder is around 15 years prior to parole. Compared to other countries, for example, Canada, where the minimum is 25 years, New Zealand's approach is relatively moderate.

TABLE 7.4
DISTRIBUTION OF MOST SERIOUS OFFENCE PER PERSON FOR THOSE
INCARCERATED AS OF 8 MAY 2006

Most Serious Offence–Snapshot 8/05/06	Total N	% of Total
Violence	2107	27.80%
Not Yet Recorded	1400	18.47%
Dishonesty	1339	17.66%
Sexual Offences	1281	16.90%
Drugs and Anti-Social	677	8.93%
Serious Traffic	519	6.85%
Property Damage	112	1.48%
Administrative	78	1.03%
Justice (Miscellaneous)	36	0.47%
Property Abuses	31	0.41%

criminals, the authors believe it will be the economics of rehabilitation versus punishment that will focus the debate and perhaps ultimately cause the public to rethink the retribution-based approach that still drives political decision-making.

Types and Percentages of Crime

While comparisons are difficult, New Zealand's crime rates appear to be equal or lower than those of other Western nations. Segessenman (2002) found that, when similar definitions were used for the overall rates of violent crime, New Zealand had a 13 percent lower overall violent crime rate than England and Wales, 44 percent lower than Canada, and 10 percent higher overall than Australia. New Zealand's overall violent crime rate was approximately one quarter of that of the USA. The major cautions with these types of comparisons are that definitions of crimes do vary and that clearance rates by police jurisdictions also differ. Despite these cautions, there is clear evidence that New Zealand has a lower rate of violent offending than many similar countries, a fact that makes the relatively high incarceration rate somewhat anomalous.

The types of offences represented within the New Zealand correctional system are presented in Table 7.4. Violence and sexual offending continue to dominate as reasons for incarceration.

A Ministry of Justice report (Spier & Lash, 2004) on prosecutions, convictions, and sentencing over a 10-year period from 1994 to 2003 shows (principally) that Māori continue to dominate the justice sector, that sentence lengths have been increasing and that recidivism rates have not reduced. These trends are a continuation of previously noted trends (Spier, 2002) and are summarised below from Spier and Lash (2004).

Convictions

- Male offenders accounted for 82% of all cases resulting in conviction in 2003.
- Of all convicted cases in 2003 for which ethnicity of the offender was known, 47% involved NZ Europeans, 42% involved Māori, 8% involved Pacific peoples, and 3% involved offenders of some other ethnicity.
- Violent offences throughout the decade accounted for 8 to 9% of all convictions.
- The number of convictions for the possession or use of stimulants or depressants has increased from 69 in 1995 to 373 in 2003.

Sentencing

- Throughout the decade, 7% to 9% of people convicted each year have received a custodial (prison) sentence with the proportion being marginally higher each year since 1997. In 2003, there were 8540 cases resulting in a custodial sentence, the highest recorded in a decade.
- The average custodial sentence length imposed (including life imprisonment and preventative detention (see below for a definition) for all offences increased over the decade from 12.9 months in 1994 to 16.0 months in 2003.
- In 2003, for the first time in a decade, over half the nonparole periods imposed with life imprisonment sentences were for more than the statutory minimum of 10 years. The average life imprisonment nonparole period[6] that was imposed in 2003 was 13.5 years, approximately three years longer than the average before the commencement of the Sentencing Act in 2002.
- The preventative detention sentence was changed in mid-2002 so that it is now available for a wider range of offences and offenders. However, the statutory minimum nonparole period was reduced from 10 years to 5 years. In New Zealand, preventative detention refers to an offender being given an indeterminate sentence. Thus, the offender has to demonstrate change, rather than wait for parole, requiring active attempts to rehabilitate himself or herself before parole can be considered. There has been a significant change in the lengths of preventative detention nonparole periods imposed since the Sentencing Act 2002 came into force. In 2003, all but 3 of the 18 nonparole periods imposed were for or less than 10 years with the average being 8.1 years. Prior to 2002, nonparole periods of other than the statutory minimum of 10 years were rare.

---

6. Courts are required to consider the minimum time a prisoner must serve before being eligible to apply for parole, in addition to the imposition of the indeterminate sentence.

- The proportion of cases resulting in a custodial sentence in 2003 was higher than in all years in the previous decade for manslaughter, unlawful sexual connection, indecent assault, aggravated robbery, and robbery.
- The average length of a custodial sentence imposed for rape has increased significantly in the last two years to reach the highest level recorded in a decade in 2003, with an average sentence of 9 years 1 month for 2003, compared to seven years in 1994.
- In 2003, 43% of burglars were imprisoned, the highest percentage recorded in a decade. The length of the custodial sentences awarded for burglary increased over the decade with burglars being imprisoned for over five months longer on average in 2003 than in 1994.
- In 2003, 15% of convicted drug offenders were imprisoned compared with less than half this proportion in 1994. To some extent, this was due to an increase over the decade in the average seriousness of the drug offences that the courts are dealing with.

Community-Based Sentences

Community work replaced both periodic detention and community service from 30 June 2002. This was a move away from a focus on punishment (detention) to reparation, where offenders were expected to perform "public good" projects in an attempt to foster pro-social activity. The proportion of convicted cases resulting in work related community sentences has decreased since peaking at 30 percent in 1998, with the 2003 figures being the lowest recorded in a decade. Overall, the use of community-based sentences has dropped from 35 percent of all sentences imposed in 1998 to 27 percent of sentences imposed in 2003. In the future, it is probable that sentences in the community will increase, although whether the number of these that do not involve rehabilitative activity, such as community work, will increase is as yet unclear.

Monetary Penalties

- The Sentencing Act 2002 places a greater emphasis on the use of fines and reparation. The act created a presumption in favour of fines when the purposes and principles of sentencing make such a sentence appropriate, and it is within the means of the offender to pay. The act also strengthens the presumption in favour of reparation in the Criminal Justice Act of 1985, and clearly states when such a sentence is appropriate.
- In 2002 and 2003, 51% of all convicted cases resulted in a monetary penalty (in particular, fines) as the most serious sentence, compared with 50% in 2001. The use of monetary penalties fluctuated little over the preceding decade—between 47% and 53% of all cases.

Young Offenders

- Most 14 to 16-year-olds who are apprehended for criminal offending are dealt with by means other than formal prosecution in court (for example: caution/warnings, Police Youth Aid, and Family Group Conferences). Therefore, statistics presented on court cases underrepresent actual rates of youth offending.
- The total number of apprehensions of 14 to 16-year-olds by the New Zealand Police fluctuated around an average of just under 31,000 between 1995 and 2001, but has increased in the following two years to 33,994 in 2003. This was the highest figure recorded in a decade, and was 19% greater than the figure in 1994.
- The number of 14 to 16-year-olds apprehended for violent offences has increased by 33% since 1994, with the 2003 figure (3,166) being the highest recorded in the period under examination.
- The majority of apprehensions involving 14 to 16-year-olds were for property offences (62% in 2003). The 2003 figure (20,957) was the second highest recorded during the decade.
- Between 1994 and 1999 there was an increase in the number of court cases involving young people (from 3,204 to 4,088), followed by a slowly decreasing trend in the next three years to 3904 in 2002. However, the number of prosecuted cases involving young people increased to 4,315 in 2003–the highest number recorded during the decade.
- Violent offences have accounted for about one quarter of the proven court cases involving young people each year during the decade.
- Burglaries have accounted for over one half of the proved property offences against young offenders throughout the decade.
- There were 134 proved court cases in 2003 involving a young person driving with excess breath alcohol. This was the highest figure recorded in the decade.
- The proportion of proved cases involving young offenders that resulted in imprisonment or a community-based sentence in 2003 (4% and 6% of cases respectively) were the lowest figures recorded in a decade. The supervision order is the most commonly imposed sentence for proved cases in the Youth Court, with 38% of cases in 2003 resulting in such an outcome

Sentencing Legislation

Having summarised outcomes of sentencing legislation, it is important to consider also the national and international principles upon which New Zealand forms a view of what is reasonable state intervention in the lives of its citizens. Like other Westminster-based governments, legislation is enacted by a parliament elected by citizens. Parliament also considers treaties and agreements made internationally between New Zealand as a sovereign nation and other nations. The Courts represent a second tier wherein the interpretation of parliamentary intent is devolved on a case-by-case basis.

The Body of Principles for the Protection of All Persons under any Form of Detention or Imprisonment and the UN Minimum Rules for the Treatment of Prisoners, as well as other human right treaties, have played a significant role in the development of new provisions in the Corrections Act 2004. New Zealand has consistently attempted to align itself with international obligations and as such has been lauded (Human Rights Commission, 2004a) as balancing its sentencing and other legal sanctions against principles of human rights.

For example, in a recent review the Human Rights Commission (2004b) noted that New Zealand Courts, when considering detention, have seen international obligations as important tools for interpreting legislation and that the interpretations of legislation have been consistent with the basic rights and freedoms recognised in the BoRA (a key piece of legislation on human rights associated with detention). For example, the High Court (*Innes v. Wong*, 1996) referred to the use of a number of international instruments and the right for respect of human dignity that should be accorded all persons, including those suffering from mental disability. It is worth noting that sovereign legislation and international jurisprudence are able to arrive at compatible positions because of commitment from the New Zealand Parliament to the inherent principles of international law.

The custodial sentences in New Zealand are life imprisonment, preventative detention, and determinate sentences of imprisonment. Life imprisonment and preventative detention are both indeterminate sentences (i.e., they do not have a fixed expiry date). The minimum nonparole period for life imprisonment is 10 years. However, for cases involving at least one serious aggravating factor, a nonparole period of at least 17 years must be imposed unless the court is satisfied that it would be manifestly unjust to do so. Life imprisonment is the presumptive penalty for murder and the mandatory sentence for treason. It is also the maximum penalty (although rarely used) for manslaughter and dealing with class A controlled drugs, as well as some offences under various acts of parliament, such as the: Aviation Crimes Act of 1972, Armed Forces Discipline Act of 1971, Chemical Weapons (Prohibition) Act of 1996, and the Terrorism Suppression Act of 2002. Under section 89 of the Sentencing Act of 2002, offenders sentenced to preventative detention must be ordered to serve a minimum period of imprisonment of at least five years. The Sentencing Act of 2002 has extended the sentence of preventative detention so that it now may be imposed for manslaughter, indecent assault of an adult, aggravated robbery and robbery, abduction or kidnapping, and bestiality. Preventative detention may be considered for offenders aged 18 years or more.

Sentencing options available prior to the Sentencing Act of 2002 included:

- Life imprisonment–an indeterminate sentence of imprisonment (i.e., the sentence continues to apply for the entire life of the offender, although the offender can be released on parole) that is generally only imposed on offenders convicted of murder.
- Preventative detention–an indeterminate sentence of imprisonment that is generally only imposed on serious, repeat sex offenders.
- Determinate imprisonment–a sentence of imprisonment for a fixed term.
- Suspended sentence of imprisonment–a sentence of determinate imprisonment that is suspended unless the offender is reconvicted within a set period of time.
- Periodic detention–and non-custodial sentence that involves the offender reporting to work centre and undertaking community work projects.
- Community service–and noncustodial sentence that involves the offender undertaking work for an approved community agency.
- Community program–a sentence that may be residential, and that involves placing the offender in the care of an approved organization, group or individual.
- Supervision–a sentence under which the offender is required to comply with various reporting, residential, association and other conditions.
- Reparation–a sentence where financial payment is ordered to be made by the offender to the victim.
- Fine–a sentence where financial payment is ordered to be made by the offender to the state.
- Driving disqualification–a sentence where the offender must surrender his or her driver's license either for a fixed term or indefinitely.

Since the Sentencing Act of 2002:

- A new sentence structure was created for people convicted of murder.
- Preventative detention became available for a wider range of offences and offenders.
- Corrective training was abolished, as well as suspended sentences of imprisonment.
- A new sentence called *community work* replaced periodic detention community service. Community work is aimed at compensating the community. The offender being placed in the community work centre or with another agency or a combination of these.
- Supervision was modified to include the care aspect of community programs.

- The provision of reparation was strengthened, and the provision for the payment of fines to victims was removed.
- A presumption in favour of fines was introduced.

From 1 October 1999, some offenders were able to serve part of their prison sentences by way of home detention. There are two forms of home detention.

- Front-end home detention is available to offenders sentenced to up to two years imprisonment, who are granted leave to apply for home detention by the court. The New Zealand Parole Board determines whether an offender is allowed to serve his or her sentence on home detention. The courts cannot directly sentence offenders to home detention.
- Back-end home detention is available to offenders subject to long-term determinate sentences. The New Zealand Parole Board may allow an offender to serve their sentence on home detention for any date that is three months before the offender's parole eligibility date. Back-end home detention is not available to those sentenced to life imprisonment or preventative detention.

While the Sentencing Act of 2002 leaves the judiciary with discretion, it sets out the general purposes and principles of sentencing. It lists aggravating and mitigating factors the court must take into account to the extent they are applicable to the case. It specifies the purpose for which each kind of sentence can be imposed. Finally, it requires judges to provide reasons, in open court, for the sentence or order given at a level of detail appropriate to the offence. However, while this Act has increased reliability and purpose of sentencing, the judiciary retains considerable discretion. Currently, policy and practice are indicating a need for a Sentencing Council, which will specify more clearly the application of the Sentencing Act of 2002 to individual cases.

Under the Parole Act of 2002, people sentenced to imprisonment for two years or less are released on their statutory release date after serving half of the imposed sentence. For determinate sentences of more than two years, offenders are eligible for parole after serving one third of their sentence, unless the court imposes a longer nonparole period.

SUMMARY AND CONCLUSIONS

New Zealand is, like most other nations, facing the challenge of rising crime rates and consequent public unrest and pressure for solutions. Along with the 1990s focus on reducing state involvement in the economic and social affairs of its citizens, New Zealand embraced policies previously most visible in the

USA, including deinstitutionalisation of the mentally ill, increasing sentence lengths and increasing the probability of sentences of imprisonment. At writing, the evidence is pointing toward the need for significant review of these policies as they have in no case reduced the problem they were intended to address. The ostensible linkages between privatisation, deinstitutionalisation and harsher punishment can be debated at many levels. Fundamentally, however, the co-existence of these three initiatives implies a core social shift away from state-driven social equity and social responsibility where resources are viewed as something to be shared with all, as of right. The new drive appears to be toward individual responsibility with social resources being allocated from competition, rather than on the basis of a fundamental belief in fairness and equity. At present, this results in tension between public opinion and governmental policy.

The main focus of change currently is around devolving policies from a central government perspective, principally through the Ministry of Social Development. This ministry is integrally involved in developing policies in line with government direction towards socially equitable and internationally responsible imperatives. As a result, there has been significant work on "whole of government" approaches, which is represented at lower levels into whole of (justice sector) work and, at a Department of Corrections level, cross service initiatives. In the context of a social shift toward resource allocation based on merit, the policies evolving from the debate need also to show how policies "save" the public resources for later distribution and increase responsibility of those "at fault" for increased crime. The policy debate at a political level becomes polarised across the continuum of whether policy change is social engineering (with a "bad" connotation) or responsible fiscal government (with a "good" connotation) in the public view.

There currently is a significant review of how a cross sector approach can also contribute to addressing issues raised in this chapter. The review is being led by the Ministry of Social Development (MSD), and involves several other government departments. It appears that, rather than seeing correctional work in isolation, it is recognised that decisions far earlier in people's lives impact on their contact with institutions concerned with law and order. For example, the impediments to a delinquent youth completing some educational programme, rather than leaving school and being paid an unemployment benefit, are being considered. The expectation that there are some people who will remain on an unemployment benefit for their lives is being changed to one that implies everyone has an obligation to work, within their capacity, for their "own good."

Overall, the pathways that lead youth into contact with police, then courts, then corrections are being addressed. Thus, rather than seeing release from the Department of Corrections oversight and subsequent reoffending as a failure of a correctional system, the debate is shifting to seeing reoffending as a failure of all of the other systems and supports *prior* to involvement in the justice sector.

A key issue arising from these cross-sector solution-focussed analyses is the complex question of why New Zealand has an apparently violent underbelly. While it is true that its rates of violence are not excessive by international standards, there is an escalation from previous levels that has stirred the public sentiment.[7] This has driven lobby groups and the "silent majority" to depart from a view of fairness, forgiveness and justice to call for harsh punishment and consideration of the more punitive approaches currently favoured by the USA, Canada, and some other countries, where, for example, a life sentence often results in at least 25 years in prison. In addressing increasing violence, the social fabric of New Zealand society is being peeled away to examine its relative youth as a nation, the diversity of its population and the values that make it what it is. As a result, issues such as institutional racism, the impact of colonisation, acceptance of violence as a legitimate solution to conflict, and revision of historical events with new paradigms are presenting themselves to the public, politicians, and policymakers alike.

The future for New Zealand and its approach to crime will depend both on the moral and social values that the country adopts. While the nation aligns with international thinking and treaties, these alone are not sufficient to guide the formation of specific policies. If the public are not convinced by clear evidence of a reduction in crime and social ills, it is unlikely to continue to support the liberal policies currently in place. At the human level of personal and public interest, whilst there are waiting lists for heart and other life-saving surgery, it is improbable that a compelling case for more money to "treat" offenders will be forthcoming. Thus, for society to "own" the goals of reducing offending and crime, there needs to be clear evidence that resources are well spent and that they are not "costing" the public unduly in other areas. The onus is on the justice sector to clearly produce the required evidence. Real change requires a comprehensive approach, which comes into play early in the lives of those affected. Whether this approach is successful is doubtful in the short-term political cycle that often politics and the creation of government. Furthermore, whether the public is prepared to see yet more tax dollars spent on what to date appears to many to have produced no good result also

---

7. For example, a young pizza delivery boy was brutally murdered by a group of young people in Auckland, one aged 14. That this occurred created understandable concern that a person could be doing his job and not only be robbed, but murdered, and only for a few dollars. While this may not seem remarkable overseas, in New Zealand, it raised sentiments suggesting that our "bit of paradise" does not want this cancer of random senseless violence here. In turn this creates the climate for the lobby groups focused on punishment as a solution to raise the catch cry of longer sentences, again.

is unclear. In its place, a call for longer sentences and harsher detention time may once again gain ascendancy.

The future of correctional practice in New Zealand depends on the implementation and clear steerage of a *long-term plan* that is implemented at a policy level and that has clear operational credibility to all of the sectors involved. While the Department of Corrections has the goal of reducing reoffending, the implications of this focus still are being debated internally and at a public level. The past has shown that it is naïve to develop sophisticated systems without, at the same time, disseminating the rationale in a clear, understandable manner to the politicians and public; this reflects the principles of "managing upward" and public communication. The authors believe that operational effectiveness needs both empirically-grounded correctional practice *and* communication to consumers of the wider and longer term social benefits of effective correctional practices. Most important of these consumers are the public.

REFERENCES

Andrews D. A., & Bonta, J. (2003). *The psychology of criminal conduct* (3rd ed.). Cincinnati, OH: Anderson.

Anstiss, B. (2003). *Just how effective is correctional treatment at reducing re-offending?* Retrieved on June 30 2006 from http://www.corrections.govt.nz/public/research/effectiveness-treatment/effective.html.

Aos, S., Miller, M., & Drake, E. (2006). Evidence-based adult corrections programs: What works and what does not. Olympia, WA: Washington State Institute for Public Policy. Retrieved on November 1 2006 from www.wsipp.wa.gov.

Bakker, L., Hudson, S. Wales, D., & Riley, D. (1998). *And there was light: Evaluating the Kia Marama Treatment Programme for sex offenders against children.* Retrieved on June 30 2006 from http://www.corrections.govt.nz/public/pdf/research/kiamarama/kiamarama.pdf

Bakker, L., O'Malley, J., & Riley, D. (1999). *Risk of reconviction: Statistical models which predict four types of re-offending.* Wellington: Department of Corrections.

Beech, A. R., Fisher, D. D., & Thornton, D. (2003). Risk assessment of sex offenders. *Professional Psychology: Research and Practice, 34,* 339–352.

Berry, S. (1998). *An evaluation of the Montgomery House Violence Prevention Unit.* Retrieved on June 30, 2006 from http://www.corrections.govt.nz/public/pdf/research/montgomery/montgomery.pdf

Bonta, J. (2002). Offender risk assessment. Guidelines for selection and use. *Criminal Justice and Behavior, 29,* 355–379.

Coebergh, B., Bakker, L., Anstiss, B., Maynard, K., & Percy, S. (2001). *A seein' "I" to the future: The Criminogenic Needs Inventory.* Wellington: Department of Corrections.

Department of Corrections. (2001). *About time: Turning people away from a life of crime and reducing reoffending.* Retrieved on June 30 2006 from: http://www.corrections.govt.nz/public/pdf/publications/abouttime.pdf.

Department of Corrections. (2004). *Strategy to reduce drug and alcohol use by offenders: 2005-2008.* Retrieved on June 30 2006 from http://www.corrections.govt.nz/public/publications/planningandstrategy/strategy-reduce-drug-and-alcohol/index.html

Department of Corrections. (2005a). *Corrections Act 2004.* Retrieved from http://www.corrections.govt.nz/public/standardsandpolicies/policies/lawreform/

Department of Corrections. (2005b). *Reducing drug and alcohol use.* Retrieved on June 30 2006 from http://www.corrections.govt.nz/public/aboutus/factsheets/managingoffenders/drugreductionstrategy.html

Department of Corrections. (2005c). *Te Reo Strategy 2004-2008.* Retrieved on June 30 2006 from http://www.corrections.govt.nz/public/publications/planningandstrategy/te-reo-strategy/index.html

Department of Corrections. (2005d). *Māori initiatives pathway: Kaiwhakamana.* Retrieved on June 30, 2006 from http://www.corrections.govt.nz/public/standardsandpolicies/guides/maori-initiatives-pathway/kaiwhakamana.html.

Department of Corrections. (2005e). *Sentencing principles.* Retrieved on June 29 2006 from http://ccm.corrections.govt.nz/corrnet/manuals/operations/cps/volume-1/part-2/chapter-1/purpose-principles-sentencing.html

Department of Corrections. (2006). *Statement of Intent: 1 July 2006–30 June 2007.* Retrieved on June 30 2006 from http://www.corrections.govt.nz/public/pdf/statementofintent/soi-2006.pdf

Eggleston, E. J. (1997). Boys' talk: Exploring gender discussions with New Zealand male youth gang members. *Caribbean Journal of Criminology & Social Psychology, 2* (2), 100–114.

Hanson, R. K., & Morton-Bourgon, K. (2004). *Predictors of sexual recidivism: An updated meta-analysis.* Canada: Public Works and Government Services.

Hare, R. D. (2003). *Hare Psychopathy Checklist-Revised (PCL-R): Technical Manual* (2nd ed.). New York: Multi-Health Systems.

Harris, A., Phenix, A., Hanson, R., & Thornton, D. (2003). *STATIC-99 coding rules revised–2003.* Ottawa: Corrections Directorate, Solicitor General Canada.

Human Rights Commission. (2004a). *Commission welcomes NZ decision to seek election to UN Commission on Human Rights.* Retrieved on June 30 2006 from http://www.hrc.co.nz/home/hrc/newsandissues/decisiononuncommissionwelcomed.php

Human Rights Commission. (2004b). *Human rights in New Zealand today Ngā Tika Tangata O Te Motu. Chapter 11: The rights of people who are detained: Ngā tika o ngā tangata mauhere.* Retrieved on June 30 2006 from http://www.hrc.co.nz/report/chapters/chapter11/detention01.html

Innes v Wong (1996). *New Zealand Law Review, 3,* 238.

Martinson, R. (1974). What works? Questions and answers about prison reform. *The Public Interest, 10,* 22–54.

Maynard, K., Coebergh, B., Anstiss, B., Bakker, L., & Huriwai, T. (1999). Ki te arotu. Toward a new assessment: The identification of cultural factors which may predispose Māori to crime. *Social Policy Journal of New Zealand, 13,* 43–58.

McCarthy, P. (2006). *Prisoner reintegration: Looking forward.* Paper presented at the Beyond Retribution conference, Wellington: NZ. 14 May 2006.

McMaster, K., & Bakker, L., Eds. (2006). *Will they do it again? Assessing and managing risk.* Lyttleton, New Zealand. Hall, McMaster and Associates.

Ministry of Health. (2001). *New Zealand drug statistics.* Retrieved on June 30 2006 from http://www.nzhis.govt.nz/publications/drugs.html.

Motiuk, L. L. (2000). The safe reintegration and risk management of violent, sex and repeat offenders in Canada. In E. Leuw & L. L. Motiuk (Eds.), *Safe reintegration of sexual offenders* (Onderzoek en Beleid, no. 186) (pp. 5–36). The Hague: WODC.

Nathan, L. Wilson, N.J. & Hillman, D. (2003). *Te Whakakotahitanga: An evaluation of the Te Piriti Special Treatment Programme for child sex offenders.* Retrieved on June 30 2006 from http://www.corrections.govt.nz/public/pdf/research/tepiriti/tewhaka.pdf

New Zealand Police (2006). *Criminal Investigation Branch.* Retrieved on June 30, 2006 from http://www.police.govt.nz/service/cib/organised_crime.html

Nicholls, T. L., Ogloff, J. R., & Douglas, K. S. (2004). Assessing risk for violence among male and female civil psychiatric patients: The HCR-20, PCL:SV, and VSC. *Behavioral Sciences and the Law, 22,* 127–158.

NZ History.net.nz (2006). *Social studies activity: The death penalty.* Retrieved on June 30 2006 from http://www.nzhistory.net.nz/classroom/socialstudies/socialstudies-deathpenalty.

O'Connor, Hon D. (2006, May 14). *Prison Fellowship Conference: Beyond Retribution–Advancing the Law and Order Debate: Straight Thinking is not enough–It's time to think laterally.* Minister of Corrections, 14 May 2006. Retrieved on June 30 2006 from http://www.corrections.govt.nz/public/news/prison-fellowship-conference/ministers-speech.html on 1 June 2006.

Poels, V. (2006). *Risk assessment of recidivism of violent and sexual female offenders.* Manuscript submitted for publication.

Pratt, J. (2006). The dark side of paradise. *British Journal of Criminology, 46,* 541–560.

Prison Fellowship of New Zealand (2006a). *Toward the formation of a coalition for prison reform.* Retrieved on June 30, 2006, from http://www.pfnz.org.nz/downloadables/060419_Report_of_Pris_Reform_Mtgs.pdf

Prison Fellowship of New Zealand. (2006b). *Why does the Faith Based Unit work?* Retrieved on June 30, 2006, from http://www.pfnz.org.nz/programs/fbu_what_works.htm

Public Access to Legislation Project. (2006). *Sentencing Act 2002.* Retrieved on June 30 2006 from http://www.legislation.govt.nz/libraries/contents/om_isapi.dll?clientID=110065&infobase=pal_statutes.nfo&record=%7b230BE25F%7d&hitsperheading=on&softpage=DOC. 29 June 2006.

Quinsey, V. L., Harris, G. T., Rice, M. E., & Cormier, C. A. (1999). *Violent offenders: Appraising and managing risk.* Washington DC: American Psychological Association.

Segessenmann, T. (2002). *International comparisons of recorded violent crime rates for 2000.* Retrieved on June 30 2006 from http://www.justice.govt.nz/pubs/reports/2002/intl-comparisons-crime/index.html.

Sensible Sentencing Trust. (2006). *Media Release 17 June 2006.* Retrieved on June 30 2006 from http://www.safe-nz.org.nz/press.htm.

Simpson, A.I.F., Brinded, P.J.M., Laidlaw, T.F., Fairley, N., & Malcom, F. (1999). *The national study of psychiatric morbidity in New Zealand prisons: An investigation of the prevalence of psychiatric disorders among New Zealand inmates.* Retrieved on June 30, 2006, from http://www.corrections.govt.nz/public/research/psychiatricmorbidity/index.html

Skelton, A. Riley, D., Wales, D., & Vess, J. (submitted). *Assessing Risk for Sexual Offenders in New Zealand: Development and Validation of a Computer Scored Risk Measure.*

Spier, P. (2002). *Conviction and sentencing of offenders in New Zealand: 1992–2001.* Retrieved on June 30, 2006, from http://www.justice.govt.nz/pubs/reports/2003/conviction-sentencing-2002/index.html

Spier, P., & Lash, B. (2004). *Conviction and sentencing of offenders in New Zealand: 1994 to 2003.* Wellington: Ministry of Justice.

Statistics New Zealand (2006). *Latest statistics: Main indicators.* Retrieved on June 30 2006 from http://www.stats.govt.nz/default.htm

Ward, T., & Stewart, C. (2003). The treatment of sex offenders: Risk management and good lives. *Professional Psychology: Research and Practice, 34,* 353–360.

Ward, T., Mann, R., & Gannon, T. (in press). *The Good Lives Model of offender rehabilitation: Clinical implications.*
Wong, S., & Gordon, A. (1999). *Violence Risk Scale.* Saskatchewan, Research Unit, Regional Psychiatric Centre.

PART III

CURRENT CHALLENGES TO CORRECTIONAL SYSTEMS

Chapter 8

"WHAT WORKS" IN PREDICTING PSYCHIATRIC HOSPITALIZATION AND RELAPSE: THE SPECIFIC RESPONSIVITY DIMENSION OF EFFECTIVE CORRECTIONAL TREATMENT FOR MENTALLY DISORDERED OFFENDERS[1]

PAULA SMITH, PAUL GENDREAU, AND CLAIRE GOGGIN

INTRODUCTION

The provision of services to offenders diagnosed as being mentally disordered (MDO) has a long history in corrections. Based on the second author's recollection dating back to the early 1960s when he began working in a federal penitentiary psychiatric unit, the care of MDOs has never been enthusiastically embraced by correctional authorities. Nevertheless, the problems encountered in managing these cases generally seemed manageable. Recently, however, it appears that the prevalence of MDOs in prison and probation systems has reached serious, if not crisis, proportions (cf. Fagan & Ax, 2003).

Statistics citing the number of MDOs who find their way into the criminal justice system depend on the operational definition employed. At one extreme, the MDO category can include a bewildering array of offender categories such as attention deficit disorder, anti-social personality disorder, comorbidity conduct disorder, dysthymic disorder, mental retardation, opposi-

1. The meta-analytic research reported in this manuscript (Study #1) was supported by the Medical Research Fund of New Brunswick (Project 92, MRF-04) to the third author. For further information on the meta-analysis reported in Study #1 please contact Claire Goggin at cgoggin@stu.edu, and for Study #2 please contact Paula Smith at paula.smith@uc.edu. All other enquiries should be addressed to the first author.

tional defiant disorder, post-traumatic stress disorder, self-injurious behavior, suicidal behavior, and substance abuse (see Boesky, 2003) as well as the classic DSM-IV Axis I clinical syndromes (i.e., schizophrenia, manic-depression and major depression). Surveys indicate that it is uncommon not to receive an affirmative answer to the question, "Have you ever experienced a mental disorder of any nature?" (see Andrews & Bonta, 2003, p. 359).

On the other hand, if the target group in question includes offenders who have received DSM-IV Axis I diagnoses, then surveys report percentages between 5 percent and 20 percent (e.g., Fagan, 2003; Gunn, 1993; Mülher-Isberner & Hodgins, 2000; Teplin & Swartz, 1989; Welsh & Ogloff, 2003; Wormith & McKeague, 1996). Rates in this range, however, do not mitigate against the concerns expressed previously by Fagan and Ax (2003). In the collective experience of the authors of this chapter in working in prison and probation settings over the years, even relatively small numbers of offenders with serious psychiatric symptoms in the DSM-IV Axis I category can pose serious management and health care problems for correctional system caregivers.

Regrettably, the authors expect the situation to worsen, at least in the United States, as a result of the continuation of "get-tough" criminal justice policies and the downsizing of psychiatric hospitals (with a concomitant absence of community supports) which will lead to more MDOs gravitating to prisons (Gibbons & Katzenbach, 2006; Morgan, 2003). Prisons, in the opinion of some observers, are quickly becoming the new psychiatric hospitals (Aufderheide & Brown, 2005; Holton, 2003). Estimates of the population of MDOs in American prisons and jails are indeed sobering. Aufderheide and Brown (2005) claim that there are about 300,000 offenders with serious mental illnesses and 70,000 who are psychotic in correctional facilities throughout the United States. In addition, there has been a huge increase of MDOs placed on probation caseloads in the order of approximately half a million (Aufderheide & Brown, 2005; Skeem, Emke-Francis & Louden, 2006).

These developments are alarming for another reason, and this is because of the woeful state of treatment and health care in many American correctional systems. For sceptics in this matter, please consult the literature to appreciate the severity of the problems in this regard (Gibbons & Katzenbach, 2006; Haney, 2003; Harrington, 1997; Holton, 2003; Human Rights Watch, 2003; Petersilia, 2006). In particular, the contributions of Gibbons and Katzenbach (2006) as well as Haney (2003) make for chilling reading. If the bleak scenarios they portray about the lack of health care and abysmal conditions of confinement continue, the prevalence of Axis I symptoms amongst MDOs may well increase in the future.

What can be done about this situation? This chapter will focus on one specific issue, or what is known in the correctional treatment literature as *specific responsivity.* Before defining this term and its implications for the provision of effective services for MDOs, a brief comment is offered on two other agendas that should be pursued.

When it comes to the assessment of risk with offenders, significant advances have occurred in the last decade (Andrews, Bonta, & Wormith, 2006; Bonta, 2002; Gendreau, Little, & Goggin, 1996). This literature clearly indicates that offender risk measures such as the Level of Service Inventory-Revised (LSI-R), which contain a comprehensive set of static (e.g., criminal history) and dynamic (e.g., anti-social attitudes, anti-social peers, etc.) items known as criminogenic needs, should be used routinely with MDOs. The authors' biases towards this instrument have been declared (Gendreau, Goggin, & Smith, 2002); suffice it to say, the magnitude of its predictive validities and its amenability to measuring changes in risk have much to recommend it for case management purposes.[2]

The treatment literature is a different matter. There now is a substantial "what works" offender treatment literature (Andrews & Bonta, 2003; Cullen & Gendreau, 2000; Gendreau, Goggin, French, & Smith, 2006). From this literature, a set of principles of effective treatment have been derived.[3] Three principles dominate in this regard. Behavioral treatments (e.g., radical behavioral, social learning, cognitive-behavioral, or a combination thereof) produce the largest reductions in recidivism. This is known as the *general responsivity principle.* In order for behavioural treatments to produce the greatest reductions in recidivism, however, they should: (1) target criminogenic needs; and (2) deliver the most intensive services to higher risk offenders. These latter two principles are referred to as the *need* and *risk principles,* respectively. These three principles apply to a wide variety of offender samples (e.g., Andrews, Dowden, & Rettinger, 2001). The reader is referred to Appendix A for a brief summary of these principles. Unfortunately, the treatment literature on MDOs is sparse, and it will likely be some time before meta-analyses will be forthcoming (see Blackburn, 2004; Heilbrun & Peters, 2000). Be that as it may, however, the authors' expectations are that the principles described above will be germane to MDOs given that the predictors of criminal behavior are quite similar across offender groups including MDOs (Bonta, Law, & Hanson, 1998).

Granted the above developments and what needs to be accomplished in the future in these two areas, the focus in this chapter will be to take a step back in the therapeutic process before any criminogenic risk assessment or treatment for MDOs is contemplated.

---

2. For a recent summary of the research on measuring change in criminogenic need and the prediction of recidivism, see Gendreau, Goggin, French, and Smith (2006, p. 740).

3. Gendreau, Smith and French (2006) as well as Gendreau and Andrews (2001) have provided an extended analysis of the entire set of principles.

SPECIFIC RESPONSIVITY

This section is concerned with what is known in the offender treatment literature as the *specific responsivity principle,* which is a subset of general responsivity. Here it will be demonstrated how this principle applies to the case of MDOs. As previously stated, the most effective treatment programs are behavioral. But, these strategies cannot be applied blindly or "one size fits all" to offenders. One must be concerned with the specific responsivity dimension or, in other words, with matching the mode and style of treatment with the "personality" of the offender. By this, the authors are referring to a potentially wide variety of characteristics of the offender that are not strong criminogenic risk factors (e.g., anxiety, mood, personal distress, cognitive abilities) (e.g., Andrews & Bonta, 2003; see also Cullen, Gendreau, Jarjoura, & Wright, 1997; Gendreau et al., 1996), but must be taken into account too if the behavioral program is to function optimally. In the case of MDOs, the assessment of the seriousness of the psychiatric symptoms is absolutely critical even though Axis I symptoms are not predictors of recidivism (Bonta et al., 1998; Villeneuve & Quinsey, 1995). Why? Because if it is determined that there is a high risk of psychiatric relapse, then a course of care must ensue which will engage the offender in a therapeutic alliance with the caregivers and, even more importantly, serve to "stabilize" the MDO so that he/she will be able to attend and respond appropriately to the behavioural program that targets his/her criminogenic needs.

The critical question is what risk measures are the most useful for predicting psychiatric outcomes? The MDO literature in corrections has skirted around this topic. When researchers refer to risk measures in this domain, passing mention is made of those few offender risk or personality instruments that include items that encompass some Axis I symptoms (e.g., Megargee, 1994 system based on the MMPI-2; for a brief review see Holton, 2003).[4] But all such measures are ineffectual for assessing, in any comprehensive fashion, the seriousness of the "mental disorder" and how well it predicts future psychiatric relapse. Until a satisfactory understanding of this matter is accomplished, the treatment of MDOs for the purposes of reducing criminogenic needs will be severely compromised.

Thus, the purpose of this chapter is to generate some practical "how to" assessment guidelines for correctional clinicians who work with MDOs as to "what works" in predicting the risk of psychiatric relapse or rehospitalisation. The authors became involved in this issue as a result of their experience work-

---

4. MMPI scoring systems are weak predictors of recidivism (Gendreau, Little, & Goggin, 1996; Gendreau, Goggin, & Law, 1997), and to our knowledge there is no data on the prediction of psychiatric outcomes using any offender risk "instrument."

ing in both corrections and psychiatric mental health settings about a decade ago. They addressed it by embarking upon a two-stage research agenda.[5] First, they generated a quantitative assessment of the psychiatric rehospitalisation literature (Goggin, 1995) to satisfy themselves as to what were the single best indicators (e.g., psychiatric history, treatment noncompliance, etc.) in this regard. At that time, this research literature was based on narrative reviews of which only one examined prospective validities (Harrow & Grossman, 1984) and a few box scores of the literature. Due to the inadequacies of box score summaries (see Gendreau, Goggin, & Smith, 2000), it came as no surprise to discover a lack of consensus regarding the utility of some of the major predictors and little reckoning of their relative potency (Goggin, 1995).[6] In addition, there was no recognition of the static/dynamic dimension, a very important distinction in the corrections literature for case management (Andrews & Bonta, 2003).

The next logical step was to identify the risk measures in the psychiatric literature that were the most robust predictors of psychiatric rehospitalisation and relapse (Smith, 2001). The realization that mental health professionals should be adopting actuarial assessment protocols for MDOs was just beginning to be recognized in the psychiatric literature (Manderschied, Henderson, & Brown, 2001; Smith, Mandersheid, Flynn, & Steinwachs, 1997).[7]

Next, the results from Study #1 are reviewed. For complete details of the meta-analysis methodology and results, please refer to Goggin (1995).

STUDY #1

The third author retrieved 481 studies from 1980 to 1993. Of these, a total of 127 employed prospective research designs; that is, the predictor information was collected at admission and the outcome (i.e., rehospitalisation and length of stay in the community) was recorded at a later period. These 127 studies generated 1,003 effect sizes (ES), of which 65 percent come from North America and 30 percent from Europe, indicating broad generalizability of these findings across Western MDO populations. The total sample size was

5. The authors of this chapter followed the same approach in the corrections literature when they conducted assessments of the most robust individual predictor domains of recidivism, and then did the same for risk instruments (Gendreau et al., 1996; Gendreau et al., 2002).

6. The third author established a 70% agreement criterion when she reviewed the literature. Surprisingly, she found that over 30% of literature reviews did not meet this criterion in the case of prior psychiatric history, age at onset, diagnosis, cognitive factors, employment, and marital status amongst others.

7. The authors recently updated our literature review, and were unable to locate other meta-analyses on the specific topics outlined in this research agenda.

320,854. The methodological quality of the studies was 55 percent based on the McGlashan index (McGlashan, 1984). With respect to index diagnosis, most studies included a variety of psychiatric diagnostic categories, and 35 percent of the samples were diagnosed solely as schizophrenic and 10 percent as having bipolar disorder. Seventy-eight percent of the facilities housing the patients were state/provincial/general/university affiliated psychiatric units.

Before outlining the results, the reader's attention is directed to the use of *r* as the common metric. It has practical value in that it can be interpreted at face value by using the BESD statistic (Rosenthal, 1991; Rosenthal & Rubin, 1982), which is commonly used in meta-analytic research. The BESD, which assumes a base rate of 50 percent, answers the question of what is the effect on the success rate of a treatment or, in this instance, a predictor. Thus, for a single prediction study, an *r* of .20 translates into a 20 percent difference in outcome between higher and lower scores. Thus, offenders who obtain high scores on a measure would have a relapse rate of 60 percent (or 50% plus 10%) in comparison with 40 percent (or 50% minus 10%) for offenders with low scores on the measure.[8]

It should be noted that the *r* value cannot be interpreted at face value when base rates are extreme (i.e., less than 30% or greater than 70%) in a single study. In corrections research, base rates of offending are often close to 50 percent. Moreover, the authors are interested in accumulating knowledge over a group of studies which usually have varying base rates of offending. It has been their experience that the *r* value can be interpreted at face value upon averaging across studies.

Returning to Goggin's (1995) findings, the most powerful predictors with r values between .10 and .20 were: (1) prior history of psychiatric hospitalization; (2) treatment compliance (e.g., client knowledge/recognition of the relapse symptoms); (3) client satisfaction with quality of life; and (4) family environment factors. The other predictor variables that had *r* values less than .10 included age, gender, admission history, community environment employment/education/marital, social network, symptomatology and completion of treatment.

The only moderator variable that had an effect on the predictive validities was type of outcome. Mean length of stay in hospital was associated with slightly higher ESs (*r* = .12) than percentage rehospitalisation and community length of stay.

---

8. The formula for the BESD is .50 (base rate) + *r*/2 (Rosenthal, 1991, p. 134). For *r* = .20, the calculation is .50 + .10 or a 60% vs. 40% success rate in prediction. Note that in interpreting *r* do not square the values. The research literature has many examples where small effects (e.g., *r* ≈ .10) are clinically very meaningful effects (Rosenthal & DiMatteo, 2001).

Although not her primary focus, Goggin (1995) also gathered data on the ability of psychiatric patient risk measures to predict rehospitalisation. Very few studies were located. Of the measures she reported on, the Strauss-Carpenter produced the highest predictive validities ($r = .47$) but there were so few ESs ($k = 5$) and such a small sample ($n = 254$), that these results can be considered extremely tentative at best.

Goggin's (1995) findings were also gratifying to the authors of this chapter as corrections researchers because the results were similar to what they have found in the corrections literature; that is, the strongest predictors in the psychiatric literature produced predictive validities of very similar magnitude to what they discovered in the offender literature (*rs* in the range of .15 to .20) (see Gendreau et al., 1996). Goggin (1995) reported that dynamic predictors produced higher correlations with rehospitalisation 60 percent of the time, while Gendreau et al. (1996) reported a corresponding rate of 54 percent. And lastly, one of Goggin's (1995) results was prescient. It helped guide the first author's investigation that led to the discovery of a robust risk measure that stood alone as the best predictor of psychiatric patient outcomes. The results from Study # 2 will now be examined.

STUDY # 2

The basic premise informing Study #2 was best articulated by Rosenblatt and Attkisson (1993):

> A severe mental disorder is rarely cured and is most often a persistent condition with cyclical improvements and episodic, acute relapses. Measures are needed to assess the ebb and flow of symptoms and adaptive functioning over time. (p. 349)

So what are these measures? Smith (2001) searched the literature in this regard from 1980 to 1999 and retrieved 1,073 studies for possible inclusion in her meta-analysis. Only 18 percent of the studies were deemed eligible (i.e., prospective designs and with data amenable to a meta-analysis). Forty-three percent of the studies were from North America, and 42 percent were from Europe, once again suggesting the generalizability of findings across Western MDO populations. Fifty-two percent of the studies reported follow-ups of up to 12 months, while 48 percent involved follow-ups of two years or more. The total number of ESs was 212 with a sample size of 52,946 Fifty-seven percent of the samples included subjects with schizophrenia, 31 percent with a variety of psychiatric diagnostic categories, and 10 percent with major depression. The methodological quality of the studies was 68 percent using the McGlashan (1984) scale.

Two types of outcome were recorded, rehospitalisation and relapse, as there has been a debate in the literature as to which one is most important. Caton, Koh, Fleiss, Barrow and Goldstein (1985) stated that rehospitalisation should be studied separately from symptomatic relapse since it is the most expensive aspect of mental services for chronic patients.

The results yielded some useful information. First, a striking finding was how much effort has been made in the past by clinicians and researchers to develop psychiatric risk measures. Assuming that it is absolutely critical that researchers generate predictive validities on their measures, the wasted effort in this regard is mind-boggling. As seen from Table 8.1, Smith (2001) found a total of 419 psychiatric risk measures, but only 72 reported any predictive validities, and only three reported ten or more correlations with relapse or rehospitalisation.

The risk measures were then categorized into four classes of general risk measure predictors: (1) diagnostic classification; (2) expressed emotion; (3) level of functioning; and (4) symptomatology.

A picture begins to emerge from Table 8.2. Recall the results of Goggin (1995) that expressed emotion was one of the strongest predictors. In this meta-analysis, expressed emotion ($k = 75$, $n = 3263$) produced by far the highest r value of .28, and its confidence interval[9] did not overlap with that of diagnostic classification, level of functioning or symptomatology. In terms of the BESD, the success rate in prediction was 64.5 percent for expressed emotion, which also produced larger correlations with outcome 70 percent to 78 percent of the time in comparison with the three others (i.e., diagnostic classification, level of functioning, and symptomatology).

The interested reader may note that diagnostic classification, the most widely used in terms of sample size ($n = 31{,}378$), was a weak predictor of criterion ($r = .07$, $CI = .06$ to .08). Supporters of diagnostic classification systems might argue that they were not originally designed to predict rehospitalisation or relapse, but rather to label an observed pattern of symptomatology (Smith et al., 1997).

The final step in the analysis was to examine the predictive validities of specific risk measures within each classification. The authors included only those that reported 10 ESs or more.[10]

The Camberwell Family Interview (CFI), a measure of expressed emotion, was far superior in its predictive validities ($r = .29$, $CI = .27$ to .35). The r val-

---

9. The *CI* holds the error rate to 5%. *CI*s that do not overlap are statistically significant from each other at $p < .01$.

10. Six psychiatric risk measures produced 5 to 9 ESs with criterion. Three measures (Diagnostic and Statistical Manual of Mental Disorders, Patient Rejection Scale, and Research Diagnostic Criteria) were not significantly different from zero in their prediction of criterion depending on the measure of association used (r or Z'). One other, the Strauss-Carpenter Scale, produced an r value of .23.

TABLE 8.1
PSYCHIATRIC RISK MEASURES IN CONJUNCTION WITH THE NUMBER OF
EFFECT SIZES REPORTED WITH CRITERION (REHOSPITALISATION OR
RELAPSE) AND CATEGORIZATION

Name of Measure	N_{ES}	Category[a]
AAMR Adaptive Behavior Scale	0	
Aberrant Behavior Checklist	0	
Abnormal Involuntary Movement Scale	1	S
Acuity of Psychiatric Illness Scale	1	S
Adaptive Behavior Evaluation Scale	0	
Adjective Check List	0	
Adolescent Coping Scale	0	
Adolescent Diagnostic Interview	0	
Adult Attention Deficit Disorder Behavior Rating Scale	0	
Adult Nowicki-Strickland Internal-External Control Scale	0	
Affect Balance Scale	0	
Affect Intensity Measure	0	
Affective Style Profile	1	E
Affectometer 2	0	
Alienation Test	0	
AMDP Past History Schedule	1	S
Andreasen's Schedule for Assessment of Negative Symptoms	0	
Anker Chronicity Scale	0	
Assessment of Living Skills and Resources	0	
Assessment Schedule and Adult Training Instrument	0	
Attention Deficit Disorder Behavior Rating Scale	0	
Attention Deficit Disorder Evaluation Scale	0	
Attributional Style Questionnaire	0	
Atypical Depressive Disorder Scale	0	
Automatic Thoughts Questionnaire	0	
Balanced Emotional Empathy Scale	0	
Barnes-Vulcano Rationality Test	0	
Barron Ego Strength	0	
Basic Personality Inventory	0	
Bay Area Functional Performance Evaluation	0	
Beck Anxiety Scale	0	
Beck Depression Inventory	1	S
Beck Hopelessness Scale	0	
Behavior Assessment System for Children	0	
Behavior Disorders Identification Scale	0	
Behavior Disorders Scale	0	
Behavior Evaluation Scale	0	
Behavior Problem Checklist	0	
Behavior Rating Profile	0	
Behavior Rating Scale	2	S
Behavior and Symptom Identification Scale	0	
Belloc Physical Status Inventory	0	
Body-Esteem Scale	0	
Borderline Symptom Index	0	

(continues)

TABLE 8.1
Continued

Name of Measure	N_{ES}	Category[a]
Bradburn Positive and Negative Affect	0	
Brief Follow-Up Rating Scale	0	
Brief Psychiatric Rating Scale	6	S
Brief Symptom Inventory	1	S
Bristol Self-Adjustment Scale	0	
Bristol Social Adjustment Scales	0	
Bromet-Harrow Scale	0	
Buss Self-Consciousness Scale	0	
California F Scale	0	
California Q-Sort	0	
Camberwell Family Interview	55	E
Carpenter Criteria for Deficit Syndrome	0	
Carroll Rating Scale for Depression	0	
Caudra Control Scale	0	
Center for Epidemiology Studies Depression Scale	0	
Chapman Hypomania Scale	0	
Checklist of Adaptive Living Skills	0	
Chestnut Lodge Prognostic Scale	0	
Child and Adolescent Functional Assessment Scale	0	
Child Behavior Checklist	0	
Children's Attention and Adjustment Survey	0	
Children's Depression Inventory	0	
Children's Global Assessment Scale	1	L
Children's Inventory of Self-Esteem	0	
Children's Loneliness Scale	0	
Children's Personality Questionnaire	0	
Client's Evaluation Questionnaire	0	
Client Satisfaction Questionnaire	0	
Clinical Global Impressions	1	L
Clincial Interview Schedule	1	S
Clinical Rating Scale	0	
Clinical Support System Battery	0	
Clyde Mood Scale	0	
Cognitive Bias Questionnaire	0	
Colorado Client Assessment Record	0	
Colorado Level of Functioning Measure	0	
Community Adaptation Schedule	0	
Community Care Schedule	0	
Community Living Adaptation Test	0	
Community Mental Health Ideology Scale	0	
Complaint Inventory	0	
Complaint List	0	
Comprehensive Assessment of Symptoms and History	0	
Comprehensive Behavior Rating Scale for Children	0	
Comprehensive Psychopathological Scale	1	S
Conflict Management Appraisal	0	

Conflict Management Survey	0	
Connors' Teacher Rating Scale	0	
Cooper-Farran Behavioral Rating Scales	0	
Coping Resources Inventory	0	
Coping with Stress Scale	0	
Coppersmith Self-Esteem Scale	0	
Cornell Index	0	
Counterbalanced F Scale	0	
Covi Anxiety Scale	0	
CSB - 5	1	D
Current and Past Psychopathology Scale	0	
Defense Mechanism Inventory	0	
Dementia Rating Scale	0	
Denver Community Mental Health Questionnaire - Revised	0	
Depression Adjective Checklist	0	
Depression and Anxiety in Youth Scale	0	
Depression Outcomes Module	0	
Depressive Experiences Questionnaire	0	
Derogatis Psychiatric Rating Scale	0	
Derogatis Stress Profile	0	
Desired Control Scale	0	
Developmental Observation Checklist System	0	
Devereux Behavior Rating Scale	0	
Diagnostic Interview Schedule	0	
Diagnostic and Statistical Manual of Mental Disorders	9	D
Differential Loneliness Scale	0	
Differential Test of Conduct and Emotional Problems	0	
Disability Assessment Schedule	3	L
Discharge Planning Scale	1	L
Discharge Potential Scale	0	
Discharge Readiness Inventory	0	
Dissociative Experiences Scale	0	
Disturbed Behavior Rating Scale	1	S
Dogmatism Scale	0	
Duke Social Support and Stress Scale	0	
DUKE-UNC Functional Social Support Questionnaire	0	
Dyadic Adjustment Scale	1	E
Dynamic Assessment Scale	0	
Dysfunctional Attitude Scale	0	
Early Childhood Behavior Scale	0	
Early Signs Scale	2	S
Eating Disorder Inventory	0	
Edwards-Jefferson Goal Scaling	0	
Elgin Prognostic Scale	0	
Emotional and Behavior Problem Scale	0	
Emotional Blunting Scale	0	
Emotional Disorder Scale	0	
Emotional-Social Loneliness Inventory	0	
Endler Multidimensional Anxiety Scales	0	
Environmental Index	0	

(continues)

TABLE 8.1
Continued

Name of Measure	N_{ES}	Category[a]
Extrapyramidal Symptoms Rating Scale	1	S
Eysenck Personality Inventory	0	
Factor Construct Rating Scale	1	S
Family Burden Interview Schedule	0	
Family Conflict Inventory	1	E
Family Environment Scale	1	E
Family Members' Evaluation of Current Status of Patient Form	0	
Fear of Negative Evaluation Scale	0	
Feelings of Inadequacy Scale	0	
Feighner Diagnostic Criteria	1	D
Fergus Falls Scale	0	
Four-Item F Scale	0	
Four Single-Item Indicators of Well-Being	0	
Framingham Functional Assessment Scale	0	
Fundamental Interpersonal Relations Orientation Behavior Scale	0	
Geidt Discharge Potential Scale	0	
General Attitude Toward Institutional Authority Scale	0	
General Health Questionnaire	1	S
General Psychopathology Scale	1	S
General Well-Being Schedule	0	
Geriatric Depression Scale	0	
Gittelmann-Klein Premorbid Asocial Adjustment Scale	1	L
Glasgow Assessment Schedule	0	
Global Adjustment to Illness Scale	0	
Global Assessment Scale	5	L
Global Illness Schedule	0	
Global Improvement Rating Scales	0	
Goldberg Interview	0	
Goldstein Premorbid Adjustment Scale	1	L
Gordon Diagnostic System	0	
Gordon Personal Profile	0	
Gottschalk-Gleser Scales	4	E
G Scale	0	
Gurel's Behavior Rating Scale	0	
Gurin Mental Status Index	0	
Halpern Crisis Scale	0	
Hamilton Rating Scale for Depression	4	S
Hamilton Anxiety Rating Scale	0	
Health Opinion Survey	0	
Health Perceptions Questionnaire	0	
Health Sickness Rating Scale	0	
Hogan Personality Inventory	0	
Hollingshead Two Factor Index	0	
Hopelessness Scale for Children	0	
Hopkins Symptom Checklist	0	
Hospital Anxiety and Depression Scale	0	

Hostility and Direction of Hostility Questionnaire	1	E
Husted's Assessment of Negative Symptoms	2	S
Hutchins Behavior Inventory	0	
Idiosyncratic Prodromal Scale	0	
Index of Well-Being	0	
Index of General Affect	0	
Index of Peer Relations	0	
Index of Self-Esteem	0	
Inpatient Multidimensional Psychiatric Scale	0	
Intellectual Achievement Responsibility Questionnaire	0	
Interaction Anxiousness Scale	0	
Internal-External Locus of Control Scale	0	
International Classification of Disease	6	D
International External Control Scale	0	
Interpersonal Trust Scale	0	
Interview Schedule for Social Interaction	0	
Inventory of Positive Thinking Traits	0	
Inwald Personality Inventory	0	
Jackson Personality Inventory	0	
Kantor Scales	0	
Katamnese Interview Schedule	0	
Katz Adjustment Scales	0	
Kay and Opler's Positive and Negative Symptom Scale	0	
Kiresuk/Sherman Goal-Attainment Scale	0	
Klopfer Prognostic Indices	0	
Kohn Problem Checklist	0	
Kohn Social Competence Scale	0	
Krawiecka Scale	0	
Langer 22-Item Index	0	
Lawton Scale	0	
Level of Functioning Scale	0	
Level of Care Survey	0	
Levinson Tridimensional Locus of Control Scale	0	
Leyton Obsessional Inventory	0	
Life 3 Scale	0	
Life Experiences Checklist	0	
Life Satisfaction Scales	0	
Life Skills Profile	1	L
Life Stressors and Social Resources Inventory	0	
Longitudinal Interval Follow-Up Evaluation UpJohn Scale	0	
Lorr Scale	0	
MACC Behavioral Adjustment Scale	0	
Major Problem Rating System	0	
Manchester Personality Questionnaire	0	
Manchester Scale for Psychopathology	0	
Manchester Scales of Social Adaptation	0	
Manheim Social Support Interview	0	
Manifest Affect Rating Scale	1	S
Marital Locus of Control Scale	0	
Marke-Nyman Temperament Scale	0	

(continues)

TABLE 8.1
Continued

Name of Measure	N_{ES}	Category[a]
Marks Hospital Prognostic Scale	0	
Marlowe-Crowne Social Desirability Scale	0	
Mastery Scale	0	
Maudsley Personality Inventory	0	
MCMI	0	
Medical Outcomes Study Social Support Survey	0	
Meehl-Dahlstrom Experimental Psychotic-Neurotic-Indeterminate Rules	0	
Meeker Chronicity Scale	0	
Memorial University of Newfoundland Scale of Happiness	0	
Menninger Health-Sickness Scale	0	
Mental Health Locus of Control Scale	0	
Mental Health Locus of Origin Scale	0	
Michaux Stress Index	0	
Millon Adolescent Clinical Inventory	0	
Millon Clinical Multiaxial Inventory	0	
Millon Index of Personality Styles	0	
Mini-Mental Status or State Examination	0	
Minnesota Multiphasic Personality Inventory	0	
Modified Short Form Health Survey	2	S
Mooney Problem Check List	0	
Montgomery and Asberg Depression Rating Scale	0	
MOS 36-Item Short-Form Health Survey	0	
Muenster Family Questionnaire	1	E
Multidimensional Health Locus of Control Scale	0	
Multidimensional Measure of Children's Perceptions of Control	0	
Multidimensional-Multiattributional Causality Scale	0	
Multidimensional Perfectionism Scale	0	
Multidimensional Scale for Rating Psychiatric Patients	0	
Multi-Function Needs Assessment	1	L
Multiphasic Environmental Assessment Procedure	0	
Multnomah Community Ability Scale	0	
Munster Prognosis Score	2	L
Naysaying Low F Scale	0	
Negative Symptom Scale	0	
Network Therapy Rating Scale	0	
Newcastle Diagnostic Scale	1	D
New Haven Schizophrenia Index	1	D
North Carolina Functional Assessment Scale	0	
Nowicki-Strickland Internal-External Control Scale for Children	0	
Nurses' Observation Scale for Inpatient Evaluation	1	L
Opinion about Mental Illness Scales	0	
Oregon Quality of Life Questionnaire	0	
Parent Behavior Checklist	0	
Parental Bonding Index	2	E
Parenting Locus of Control Scale	0	

Past History and Socio-Demographic Schedule	1	S
Patient Attitude Questionnaire	0	
Patient Attitudes and Beliefs Scale	0	
Patient Description Questionnaire	1	S
Patient Rejection Scale	6	E
Peabody Picture Vocabulary Test	0	
Perceived Criticism Scale	1	E
Perceptions of Care	0	
PERI Demoralization Schedule	0	
Personal Adjustment and Role Skills Scale	1	L
Personal Evaluation Inventory	0	
Personality Adjective Checklist	0	
Personality Assessment Inventory	0	
Personality Diagnostic Questionnaire - Revised	0	
Personality Inventory for Children	0	
Personality Inventory for Youth	0	
Personal Orientation Inventory	0	
Personal Reaction Scale	0	
Personal Resources Inventory	0	
PGC Morale Scale	0	
Phillips Premorbid Adjustment Scale	18	L
Physical Health Index	0	
Piers-Harris Self-Concept Scale	0	
Positive and Negative Syndrome Scale	4	S
Premorbid Asocial Adjustment Scale	0	
Premorbid Asociality Scale	0	
Present State Examination	3	S
Problem Experiences Checklist	0	
Procrastination Scale	0	
Profile of Mood States	0	
Prognosis Rating Scale	2	L
PSYCHAP Inventory	0	
Psychiatric Assessment Scale	4	S
Psychiatric Evaluation Form	1	S
Psychiatric Outpatient Rating Scale	0	
Psychiatric Status Rating Scale	0	
Psychiatric Status Schedule	0	
Psychiatric Symptoms Index	0	
Purpose in Life Test	0	
Quality of Life Checklist	0	
Quality of Life Interview	0	
Questionnaire of Empathy	1	E
RAND Mental Health Inventory	0	
RAND Social Health Battery	0	
Rasch-Type Loneliness Scale	0	
Raskin Depression Scale	0	
Research Diagnostic Criteria	11	D
Resource Associated Functional Level Scale	0	
Rorschach Inkblot Test	0	
Rosenberg Self-Esteem Scale	0	

(continues)

TABLE 8.1
Continued

Name of Measure	N_{ES}	Category[a]
Rotter's Internal and External Locus of Control	0	
Rutter Behavioral Scale	0	
Satisfaction with Life Domains Scale	0	
Scale for Assessment of Negative Symptoms	1	S
Scale for Assessment of Positive Symptoms	0	
Schedule for Affective Disorders and Schizophrenia	4	S
Schizophrenia State Inventory	0	
Schneiderian First Rank Symptom	1	D
Self-Consciousness Scale	0	
Self-Description Questionnaire	0	
Self-Efficacy Scale	0	
Self-Esteem Inventory	0	
Self Perception Profile for Children	0	
Self-Rating Depression Scale	0	
Self-Report Symptoms and Problems Questionnaire	0	
Service Satisfaction Scale	0	
SHARPS-C Satisfaction Questionnaire	0	
Shipley-Institute of Living Scale for Measuring Intellectual Impairment	0	
Shyness Scale	0	
Sickness Impact Profile	0	
Simpson-Agnes Rating Scale	0	
Simpson Tardive Dyskinesia Scale	0	
Social Adjustment Scale for Children and Adolescents	1	L
Social Anxiety Scale for Children	0	
Social Avoidance and Distress Scale	0	
Social Behavior Assessment Schedule	0	
Social Behavior Schedule	1	L
Social Criticism Scale	0	
Social Dysfunction Rating Scale	0	
Social Functioning Scale	0	
Social Interview Schedule	0	
Social Maladjustment Schedule	0	
Social Network Questionnaire	0	
Social Network Scale	0	
Social Readjustment Rating Scale	0	
Social Relationship Scale	0	
Social Reticence Scale	0	
Social Skills Rating System	0	
Social Support Questionnaire	0	
Span of Attention Test	1	S
Specific Interpersonal Trust Scale	0	
Spielberger State-Trait Anxiety Inventory	0	
Standardized Mini-Mental State Examination	0	
State-Trait Anger Inventory	0	

State-Trait Anxiety Inventory	0	
State-Trait Depression Adjective Checklist	0	
State versus Trait Loneliness Scale	0	
Stephens Scale	1	L
Stokes-Gordon Stress Scale	0	
Strauss-Carpenter Prognostic Scale	7	L
Structured Clinical Interview for Diagnosis	0	
Structured Interview of Reported Symptoms	0	
Structured and Scaled Interview to Assess Maladjustment	0	
Strupp's Psychotherapy Questionnaire - Patient's Form	0	
Symptom Checklist	0	
Symptom Distress Checklist 90 - Revised	0	
Symptom Rating Test	0	
Syndrome Checklist	0	
Target Complaints	0	
Target Symptom Scale	0	
Taylor and Abrams Criteria	1	D
Taylor Manifest Anxiety Scale	0	
Tellegen Absorption Scale	0	
Tennessee Self-Concept Scale	0	
Texas Social Behavior Inventory	0	
Thematic Aperception Test	0	
Therapy Rating Scale	0	
Twenty-Item Counterbalanced F Scale	0	
Twenty-Two Item Screening Score of Psychiatric Symptoms	0	
UCLA Loneliness Scale	0	
UCLA Premorbid Adjustment Scale	0	
Ullman-Giovanni Self-Report Process-Reactive Questionnaire	0	
Vaillant Scale	1	L
Vets Adjustment Scale	1	L
Wakefield Self-Assessment Depression Inventory	0	
Ward Behavior Inventory	0	
Warner Index of Status Questionnaire	0	
Ways of Coping Checklist	0	
Weich's Somatic Symptom Checklist	1	S
Weissman Social Adjustment Scale	0	
Weschler Adult Intelligence Scale	0	
Weschler Intelligence Scale for Children	0	
Wing Behavior Rating Scale	1	S
World Health Organization Self-Reporting Questionnaire	0	
Work Performance Rating Scale	1	L
Zeitlin Coping Inventory	0	
Zung Self-Rating Depression Scale	0	

[a] D = Diagnostic Classification, E = Expressed Emotion, L = Level of Functioning, S = Symptomatology

TABLE 8.2
MEAN PEARSON *r* AND *Z⁺* STATISTICS FOR CATEGORIES
OF PREDICTORS WITH CRITERION

Type of Outcome	k	N	r (SD)	CI	Z⁺	CI
Diagnostic Classification	32	31739	.07 (.18)	.06 to .08	.00	-.01 to .01
Expressed Emotion	75	3263	.28 (.20)	.25 to .31	.28*	.24 to .32
Level of Functioning	52	3642	.13 (.20)	.10 to .16	.14*	.11 to .17
Symptomatology	53	4033	.11 (.19)	.08 to .14	.09*	.06 to .12

* *p*<.05

Expressed emotion produces greater correlations with criterion than the other predictor categories 70% to 78% of the time under the condition of no outliers removed, and 65% to 68% of the time under the condition of outliers removed.

TABLE 8.3
MEAN PEARSON *r* AND *Z⁺* STATISTICS FOR INDIVIDUAL
SCALE PREDICTORS WITH CRITERION

Type of Outcome	k	N	r (SD)	CI	Z⁺	CI
Camberwell Family Interview	55	2365	.29 (.19)	.27 to .35	.28*	.24 to .32
Phillips Scale	18	821	.14 (.17)	.07 to .21	.14*	.07 to .21
Research Diagnostic Criteria	11	1441	.04 (.16)	-.01 to .09	.01	-.04 to .06

* *p*<.05

The CFI produces greater correlations with criterion than the other predictor categories 59% to 86% of the time under the condition of no outliers removed and 61% to 75% of the time when outliers were removed from the CFI.

ues for the Phillips Scale and the Research Diagnostic Criteria were .14 (CI = .07 to .21) and .04 (CI = -.01 to .09), respectively. The CFI produced higher predictive validities than the Phillips Scale and the Research Diagnostic Criteria 59 percent and 86 percent of time, respectively.

Regardless of the risk measure used, one other important finding was that predictive validities were higher for relapse (r = .21, CI = .19 to .23) than rehospitalisation (r = .13, CI = .12 to .14). This finding resulted by aggregating ESs across different risk measures. However, upon examining this comparison when a risk measure predicted both outcomes, the results were mixed.

Relapse was associated with higher mean *r* values in comparison with rehospitalisation using the CFI, but the samples varied across ESs. In 12 cases where other risk measures were used to predict the two outcomes on the same sample, the mean ESs were almost identical. Another factor to consider is that the operational definition of relapse almost always involves scores on an actuarial measure of symptomatology. It is possible, then, that relapse appears to be more sensitive in most cases because the r values represent a correlation between two actuarial measures. To illustrate, relapse is often defined as an increase in scores on the Brief Psychiatric Scale (BPRS). The initial administration of a risk measure such as the Phillips Scale would then be correlated with outcome (i.e., the BPRS) to assess its ability to predict relapse. One might expect higher predictive validities in these instances than the case where the SADS was predicting rehospitalisation.

Finally, the results of Study #2 were not affected by whether statistical outliers were removed, sample sizes were weighted, base rates were corrected for extreme values, or samples had a psychiatric diagnosis of depression or schizophrenia.

CONCLUSION

What the authors of this chapter offer correctional clinicians who work with MDOs is the following: the psychiatric literature is not as robust as the correctional literature when it comes to predicting outcomes. Little attention has been paid to examining the utility of psychiatric risk measures. As a result of conducting these two meta-analyses, the authors became aware of the fact that a host of moderators (e.g., gender, number of previous psychiatric admissions, treatment compliance etc.) could influence the magnitude of the predictions reported. Unfortunately, the paucity of information in the studies reviewed for the purposes of these meta-analyses remains a major barrier for knowledge accumulation purposes in the authors' area of concern.

Nevertheless, the specific responsivity issue has been advanced considerably with MDOs with the findings that the CFI is a useful predictor of rehospitalisation and relapse. It should be used routinely by correctional clinicians to obtain a reasonably accurate prediction of the risk to relapse which, in turn, will have major implications for the level of psychiatric care needed before addressing the criminogenic needs of the offender. The reason the CFI, at least to date, has far outperformed its "competitors" is perhaps attributable to the consistency (noted by the first author in coding studies) involved in training raters using this system. Several studies explicitly stated that the raters were trained by the progenitors of the CFI (e.g., Barrelet, Pellizzer, & Ammann 1988; Bertrando et al., 1992; Moline, Singh, Morris & Meltzer, 1985; Schulze-Mönking, Hornung, Stricker & Buchkremer, 1997). This ensures the quality of the administration which, in turn, likely increases predictive validities. Unlike most of the other measures, the CFI is based on *behavioral observations* rather than self-report methods, and thus might represent a more accurate estimation of the problem behaviors. Using the BESD statistic, a value of $r = .30$ translates into a 30 percent difference in outcome between higher scores and lower scores; that is, patients who obtain high scores on the CFI would have a relapse rate of 65 percent in comparison with 35 percent for patients with low scores on the assessment.

One final point should also be made regarding the CFI in correctional settings. The authors have highlighted the importance of behavioral observations above. They recognize the value of self-report measures (Walters, 2006) but have a bias towards actual observations of behavior for prediction purposes. Clinicians in correctional settings may cavil about how difficult it is to access such information for MDO assessments. The authors are of the view that it is still possible to do so by establishing links with significant others and clinicians who have dealt with the MDO in the community to gather the necessary information.[11] As well, the MDO himself/herself can provide some useful input, and there are behavioral observations to be obtained within the prison setting [see Falloon, Boyd, & McGill (1984) for a review of the CFI including a description of individual items].

---

11. One of the longstanding complaints one comes across in corrections is how time consuming it is to do a job properly (M. Paparozzi, personal communication, Aug. 22, 2004). To not do the job properly is, in our view, another index of correctional quackery (Latessa, Cullen, & Gendreau, 2002). They also draw attention to the fact that the designers of the LSI-R also encourage the use of gathering as much collateral information as possible.

Appendix A

BRIEF SUMMARY OF THE PRINCIPLES OF EFFECTIVE CORRECTIONAL PROGRAMMING

Please note that the following summary of the principles of effective correctional programming is taken verbatim from Goggin and Gendreau (forthcoming), and based on Andrews and Bonta (2003).

Risk

- higher risk offenders are characterized by greater criminogenic need
- use a valid/reliable measure to assess offender risk
- target higher risk offenders for treatment

Need

- target offender characteristics most predictive of recidivism
- predictors are classified as static (i.e., criminal history) or dynamic (i.e., anti-social attitudes)
- dynamic factors, or *criminogenic needs,* are appropriate treatment targets
- criminogenic needs that are *robust* predictors of recidivism: anti-social attitudes/values, pro-criminal associates, impulsiveness/poor self-control
- criminogenic needs that are *poor* predictors of recidivism: self-esteem, depression, anxiety
- target more criminogenic than non-criminogenic needs (3:1 ratio)

Responsivity

- use potent behaviour change strategies (i.e., cognitive/behavioural) incorporating operant conditioning principles to modify behaviour
- replace anti-social cognitions with more adaptive cognitive/social skills
- consider "specific responsivity", match service delivery style with offender abilities/learning style (i.e., take into account lack of motivation, intellectual deficits, feelings of depression/anxiety)

Other considerations

- treatment context: deliver in the community when possible
- employ interpersonally sensitive, clinically well-trained and supervised staff
- offer structured relapse prevention
- include offenders' significant others when feasible

REFERENCES

Andrews, D. A., & Bonta, J. (2003). *The psychology of criminal conduct (3rd ed.).* Cincinnati, OH: Anderson Publishing Company.

Andrews, D. A., Bonta, J., & Wormith, S. J. (2006). The recent past and near future of risk and/or need assessment. *Crime & Delinquency, 52,* 7–27.

Andrews, D. A., Dowden, C., & Rettinger, J. L. (2001). Special populations. In J. Winterdyk (Ed.), *Corrections in Canada* (pp. 170–212). Toronto, Ontario, Canada: Prentice Hall Allyn & Bacon.

Aufderheide, D. H., & Brown, P. H. (2005). Crisis in corrections: The mentally ill in America's prisons. *Corrections Today, 67,* 30–33.

Barrelet, V. L., Pellizzer, G., & Ammann, L. (1988). Family expressed emotion and outcome of schizophrenics: A study in a French cultural environment. *Archives Suisses de Neurologie et de Psychiatrie, 139,* 27–34.

Bertrando, P., Beltz, J., Bressi, C., Clerici, M., Farma, T., Invernizzi, G., et al., (1992). Expressed emotion and schizophrenia in Italy: A study of an urban population. *British Journal of Psychiatry, 161,* 223–229.

Blackburn, R. (2004). "What works" with mentally disordered offenders. *Psychology, Crime & Law, 10,* 297–308.

Boesky, L. M. (2003). Identifying juvenile offenders with mental health disorders. In T. J. Fagan and R. K. Ax (Eds.), *Correctional mental health handbook* (pp. 167–198). Thousand Oaks, CA: Sage Publications, Inc.

Bonta, J. (2002). Offender risk assessment: Guidelines for selection and use. *Criminal Justice & Behavior, 29,* 355–379.

Bonta, J., Law, M., & Hanson, K. (1998). The prediction of criminal and violent recidivism among mentally disordered offenders: A meta-analysis. *Psychological Bulletin, 123,* 123–142.

Brink, J.H., Doherty, D., & Boer, A. (2001). Mental disorder in federal offenders: A Canadian prevalence study. *International Journal of Law and Psychiatry, 24,* 339–356.

Caton, C. L. M., Koh, S. P., Fleiss, J. L., Barrow, S., & Goldstein, J. M. (1985). Rehospitalization in chronic schizophrenia. *The Journal of Nervous and Mental Disease, 173,* 139–148.

Cullen, F. T., & Gendreau, P. (2000). Assessing correctional rehabilitation: Policy, practice, and prospects. In J. Horney (Ed.), *Criminal justice 2000: Volume 3–Policies, processes, and decisions of the criminal justice system* (pp. 109–175). Washington DC: U.S. Department of Justice, National Institute of Justice.

Cullen, F. T., Gendreau, P., Jarjoura, G. R., & Wright, J. P. (1997). Crime and the bell curve: Lessons from intelligent criminology. *Crime and Delinquency, 43,* 387–411.

Fagan, T. J. (2003). Mental health in corrections: A model for service and delivery. In T. J. Fagan & R. K. Ax (Eds.), *Correctional mental health handbook* (pp. 3–20). Thousand Oaks, CA: Sage Publications, Inc.

Fagan, T. J., & Ax, R. K. (2003). *Correctional mental health handbook.* Thousand Oaks, CA: Sage Publications, Inc.

Falloon, I. R. H., Boyd, J. L., & McGill, C. W. (1984). *Family care of schizophrenia: A problem-solving approach to the treatment of mental illness.* New York: Guilford Press.

Gendreau, P., & Andrews, D. A. (2001). *Correctional Program Assessment Inventory–2000 (CPAI-2000).* Saint John, New Brunswick, Canada: University of New Brunswick.

Gendreau, P., Goggin, C., French, S., & Smith, P. (2006). Practicing psychology in correctional settings. In A. K. Hess & I. B. Weiner (Eds.), *The handbook of forensic psychology (3rd ed.)* (pp. 722–750). Hoboken, NJ: John Wiley & Sons, Inc.

Gendreau, P., Goggin, C., & Law, M. (1997). Predicting prison misconducts. *Criminal Justice and Behavior, 24,* 414–431.

Gendreau, P., Goggin, C., & Smith, P. (2000). Generating rational correctional policies: An introduction to advances in cumulating knowledge. *Corrections Management Quarterly, 4,* 52–60.

Gendreau, P., Goggin, C., & Smith, P. (2002). Is the PCL-R really the "unparalleled" measure of offender risk? A lesson in knowledge cumulation. *Criminal Justice and Behavior, 29,* 397–426.

Gendreau, P., Little, T., & Goggin, C. (1996). A meta-analysis of adult offender recidivism: What works! *Criminology, 34,* 575–607.

Gendreau, P., Smith, P., & French, S. (2006). The theory of effective correctional intervention: Empirical status and future directions. In F. T. Cullen, J. P. Wright, & K. R. Blevins (Eds.), *Taking stock: The status of criminological theory: Advances in criminological theory, Vol. 15* (pp. 419–446). New Brunswick, NJ: Transaction Publishers.

Gibbons, J. J. & Katzenbach, N. B. (2006, June). *Confronting Confinement: A Report of the Commission on Safety and Abuse in America's Prisons.* New York: Vera Institute of Justice.

Goggin, C. E. (1995). *Prediction of psychiatric rehospitalisation: A meta-analysis.* Unpublished master's thesis, University of New Brunswick, St. John, New Brunswick, Canada.

Goggin, C. E., & Gendreau, P. (2006). The implementation of quality services in offender rehabilitation programs. In C. R. Hollin & E. J. Palmer (Eds.), *Offending behaviour programmes, development, application, and controversies* (pp. 209–246). Chichester, UK: John Wiley.

Gunn, J. (1993). Epidemiology and forensic psychiatry. *Criminal Behavior and Mental Health, 3,* 180–193.

Haney, C. (2003). Mental health issues in long-term solitary and "Supermax" confinement. *Crime & Delinquency, 49,* 124–156.

Harrington, S. P. M. (1997). Caging the crazy: "Supermax" confinement under attack. *Humanist, 57,* 14–19.

Harrow, M., & Grossman, L. S. (1984). Outcome in schizoaffective disorders: A critical review and reevaluation of the literature. *Schizophrenia Bulletin, 10,* 87–108.

Heilbrun, K. & Peters, L. (2000). Community-based treatment programmes. In S. Hodgins & R. Müller-Isberner (Eds.), *Violence, crime and mentally disordered offenders: Concepts and methods for effective treatment and prevention* (pp. 193–216). West Sussex, England: John Wiley & Sons, Ltd.

Holton, S.M.B. (2003). Managing and treating mentally disordered offenders in jails and prisons. In T. J. Fagan & R. K. Ax (Eds.) *Correctional mental health handbook* (pp. 101–122). Thousand Oaks, CA: Sage Publications, Inc.

Human Rights Watch. (2003). *Ill-equipped: U.S. prisons & offenders with mental illness.* New York: Human Rights Watch.

Latessa, E., Cullen, F. T., and Gendreau, P. (2002). Beyond correctional quackery: Professionalism and the possibility of effective treatment. *Federal Probation, 66,* 43–49.

McGlashan, T. H. (1984). The Chestnut Lodge follow-up study: Follow-up methodology and study sample. *Archives of General Psychiatry, 41,* 573–585.

Manderscheid, R. W., Henderson, M. J., & Brown, D. Y. (2001). Status of national efforts to improve accountability for quality. In B. Dickey & L. I. Sederer (Eds.), *Improving mental health care: Commitment to quality* (pp. 163–178). Washington, DC: American Psychiatric Publishing, Inc.

Megargee, E. I. (1994). Using the Megargee MMPI-based classification system with MMPI-2s of male prison inmates. *Psychological Assessment, 6,* 337–344.

Moline, R. A., Singh, S., Morris, A., & Meltzer, H. Y. (1985). Family expressed emotion and relapse in schizophrenia in 24 urban American patients. *American Journal of Psychiatry, 142,* 1078–1081.

Morgan, R. (2003). Basic mental health services: Services and issues. In T. J. Fagan & R. K. Ax (Eds.), *Correctional mental health handbook* (pp. 59–72). Thousand Oaks, CA: Sage Publications, Inc.

Müller-Isberner, R., & Hodgins, S. (2000). Evidence-based treatment for mentally disordered offenders. In S. Hodgins & R. Müller-Isberner (Eds.), *Violence, crime and mentally disordered offenders: Concepts and methods for effective treatment and prevention* (pp. 7–38). West Sussex, England: John Wiley & Sons Ltd.

Petersilia, J. (2006, May). *Understanding California corrections.* Berkeley, CA: California Policy Research Center, University of California.

Rosenblatt, A., & Attkisson, C. C. (1993). Assessing outcomes for sufferers of severe mental disorder: A conceptual framework and review. *Evaluation and Program Planning, 16,* 347–363.

Rosenthal, R. (1991). *Meta-analytic procedures for social research.* Beverly Hills, CA: Sage Publications.

Rosenthal, R., & DiMatteo, M. R. (2001). Meta-analysis: Recent developments in quantitative methods for literature reviews. *Annual Review of Psychology, 52,* 59–82.

Rosenthal, R., & Rubin, D. B. (1982). A simple, general purpose display of magnitude of experimental effect. *Journal of Educational Psychology, 74,* 166–169.

Schulze-Mönking, H., Hornung, W. P., Stricker, K., & Buchkremer, G. (1997). Expressed emotion development and course of schizophrenic illness: Considerations based on results of a CFI replication. *European Archives of Psychiatry and Clinical Neuroscience, 247,* 31–34.

Skeem, J. L., Emke-Francis, P., & Louden, J. E. (2006). Probation, mental health, and mandated treatment: A national survey. *Criminal Justice & Behavior, 33,* 158–184.

Smith, G. R., Manderscheid, R. W., Flynn, L. M., & Steinwachs, D. M. (1997). Principles for assessment of patient outcomes in mental health care. *Psychiatric Services, 48,* 1033–1036.

Smith, P. (2001). *Prediction of psychiatric rehospitalisation and relapse: A meta-analysis of risk measures.* Unpublished master's thesis, University of New Brunswick, St. John, New Brunswick, Canada.

Teplin, L. A., & Swartz, J. (1989). Screening for severe mental disorders in jails: The development of the Referral Decision Scale. *Law and Human Behavior, 13,* 1–18.

Villeneuve, D. B. & Quinsey, V. L. (1995). Predictors of general and violent recidivism among mentally disordered inmates. *Criminal Justice and Behavior, 22,* 397–410.

Walters, G. D. (2006). Risk appraisal versus self-report in the prediction of criminal justice outcomes: A meta-analysis. *Criminal Justice and Behavior, 33,* 279–304.

Welsh, A., & Ogloff, J. R. P. (2003). The development of a Canadian based program for offenders with mental illnesses. *International Journal of Forensic Mental Health, 2,* 59–71.

Wormith, J. S., & McKeague, F. (1996). A mental health survey of community correctional clients in Canada. *Criminal Behavior and Mental Health, 6,* 49–72.

Ziguras, S. J., & Stuart, G. W. (2000). A meta-analysis of the effectiveness of mental health case management over 20 years. *Psychiatric Services, 51,* 1410–1421.

Chapter 9

PRISONS AND THE ROLE OF NONGOVERNMENTAL ORGANIZATIONS

Carol Gallo

All prisoners shall be treated with the respect due to their inherent dignity and value as human beings.

United Nations,
Basic Principles for the Treatment of Prisoners,
1990, Principle 1

INTRODUCTION

This chapter will provide correctional professionals with an understanding of nongovernmental organizations (NGOs) and the important oversight functions they serve with regard to prisons. Since the inception of the first organizations devoted to prison work over 200 years ago, achieving and maintaining humane conditions for incarcerated citizens has become both a global and local mission for these entities, and their work is crucial to the mental health missions of prison officials around the world.

There has been a recent and highly visible tendency of governments and politicians to challenge some of the fundamental human rights standards related to the treatment of prisoners. In particular, the administration of U.S. President George W. Bush recently insisted that certain "alternative" interrogation techniques, such as induced hypothermia and water-boarding (Physicians for Human Rights, 2006), as well as forced nudity (White, 2005), employed by the military at the detention facilities at Guantánamo Bay, Cuba, and Abu Ghraib, Iraq, do not qualify as "torture" (Sullivan, 2006). As will be discussed below, NGOs were involved in bringing these matters to the world's attention. The *Convention against Torture and Other Cruel, Inhuman or Degrading Treatment or Punishment* is one of a number of human rights treaties that will be explained in this chapter. Notwithstanding the explicit requirement of the United Nations' (UN) *Body of Principles for the Protection of All Persons under Any Form of Detention or Imprisonment* to interpret the definition of torture as broadly as possible, practically no attention was given in the debates over the use of alternative interrogation techniques used by the U.S. military as to whether these techniques constituted cruel, inhuman or degrading treatment or punishment—abuses that are just as illegal under the *Convention Against Torture* as torture itself.

Related to this is the potential for a focus on physical cruelty, torture, or abuse to obscure other equally fundamental rights, such as freedom from mental or emotional torture or economic, social and cultural rights (Ford Foundation, 2004). In other words, it is not sufficient for governments and prison authorities simply to prevent corporal punishment, sexual abuse, and other forms of physically cruel treatment. They are also responsible, as will be discussed below, to ensure access to adequate medical and mental health care on a day-to-day basis. This chapter provides a selective overview of the ways in which prison NGOs have served a human rights "watchdog" purpose to promote the physical and mental well-being of incarcerated persons, and, beyond that, to support their reintegration into society and alternatives to incarceration. The human rights movement's promotion of alternatives to detention and diversion mechanisms will also be discussed.

DEFINITION

There is no official consensus definition of the term "nongovernmental organization." Organizations such as Amnesty International and Human Rights Watch engage in fact finding missions in countries all over the world in an attempt to generate publicity around a government's abuses or around a particular issue. The general aim is to shame and embarrass abusing governments into changing their actions and policies. These efforts are often accompanied by intense grassroots pressure from both international and local activists, and in the case of Amnesty International, members of the organization (Human Rights Watch, n.d.; Amnesty International, n.d.). Similarly, the American Civil Liberties Union also draws attention to human and civil rights abuses, although they do so primarily through law. Lawyers at the American Civil Liberties Union manage almost 6,000 court cases a year (American Civil Liberties Union, n.d.). Physicians for Human Rights is an NGO that "mobilizes health professionals to advance health, dignity, and justice and promotes the right to health for all" (Physicians for Human Rights, n.d.a). Physicians for Human Rights works all over the world on a variety of health issues from the treatment of mentally ill juveniles in U.S. prisons to the campaign to ban land-mines and much more (Physicians for Human Rights, n.d.b).

There are also hybrids such as the International Committee of the Red Cross, which does not exist under government mandate but which carries out missions that are founded on international law and mandated by States (International Committee of the Red Cross, 2004). In addition, UN human rights and human-itarian agencies are not to be confused with NGOs, however. Although many agencies, such as the United Nations Children's Fund, may engage in the same activities as many NGOs, UN agencies' mandates derive from UN bodies that are made up of government representatives (United Nations Children's Fund, n.d.). The United Nations Office of the High Commissioner for Human Rights, another type of UN agency, is a department of the UN Secretariat mandated by the UN Charter and international human rights law (United Nations Office of the High Commissioner for Human Rights, 2006).

NGOs are characterized by a belief in peaceful, grassroots-based activism around a particular issue. One of the universally defining traits of an NGO is the use of non-violent action to effect change (Paul, 2004). Accordingly, a guerrilla army may not be associated with a government, and may be well organized, but would not qualify as an NGO because of its militancy. Over the past 60 years, NGOs have become a diverse array of nonprofits, charities, foundations, and church groups and range from large international organiza-tions with branches in most countries to small community organizations with little or no paid staff (Paul, 2004). The earliest international NGOs were involved in the abolition of the slave trade. Anti-Slavery International, a human rights NGO that grew out of a single society established in 1787, con-tinues to combat contemporary forms of slavery such as human trafficking (Anti-Slavery International, n.d.).

A BRIEF HISTORY OF PRISON RELIEF ORGANIZATIONS

The Pennsylvania Prison Society was founded by a group of Quakers in 1787, and was originally called the Philadelphia Society for Alleviating the Mis-eries of Public Prisons. Today, they work to assist prisoners with their rehabil-itation in prison and reintegration after release (Pennsylvania Prison Society, n.d.). The creation of the Pennsylvania Prison Society was the result of a com-bination of the Quaker belief in pacifism and the atmosphere of the American Revolution (Pennsylvania Prison Society, n.d.). Like many early nongovern-mental organizations, it was founded on moral and religious beliefs.

The Canadian Association of Elizabeth Fry Societies emerged in 1969 from a single society that had been established in Vancouver in 1939. The organization's namesake, Ms. Elizabeth Fry, was born into a family of Quakers in England, in 1780. Her work resulted in major reforms in the way imprisoned women and children were treated in London's Newgate Prison (Canadian Association of Elizabeth Fry Societies, n.d.). The early precursor of the John Howard Society, another Canadian organization, was formed by church workers in Toronto in 1867 and to this day provides rehabilitative assistance to inmates (John Howard Society, n.d.).

Amnesty International is a large, more contemporary NGO whose origins date back to 1961. The original focus of the organization's work was the release of prisoners of conscience–individuals imprisoned for the peaceful expression of their political, religious, or other beliefs. The years following the beginning of the Amnesty International movement saw the organization's mandate expand to include the promotion and protection of all basic human rights (Amnesty International, n.d.).

HUMAN RIGHTS STANDARDS

Human rights law, as it is understood today, dates back to the post World War II period and the passage of the *Universal Declaration of Human Rights* in 1948. The contemporary perception of an NGO as impartial, apolitical and nonbiased, was born with the human rights movement following the Second World War. Prior to World War II, only a vague concept of human rights existed in international law. It wasn't until the founding of the United Nations in 1945, with the intention "to save succeeding generations from the scourge of war" (Preamble) (Charter of the United Nations, 1945), that human rights were explicitly recognized in an international treaty (UN, 2000). President Roosevelt's delegation to the conference, held in California, that would eventually establish the UN in 1945, included over 40 NGOs (Keane, 2004). The UN Charter thus articulates that one of its central missions is to uphold human rights (Charter of the United Nations, 1945), and the Nuremberg trials of Nazi war crimes were the first attempts to prosecute human rights abuses in an international court (Motely, 2006).

The UN established the Commission on Human Rights in 1946, chaired by Eleanor Roosevelt. The First Lady was a key architect in the drafting of the *Universal Declaration of Human Rights*. From the very beginning, NGOs played an enormous role in the direction of the UN, and the *Universal Declaration* remains the foundation of the entire human rights movement (UN, 2000). Since then, a number of other human rights treaties, in addition to countless declarations and guidelines, have been articulated by various UN bodies and agencies. International human rights are to be guaranteed, legally protected at all levels, and center around the fundamental concept of human dignity for all (United Nations Office of the High Commissioner for Human Rights, 2005).

The three key international human rights documents are the *Universal Declaration of Human Rights,* the *International Covenant on Civil and Political Rights,* and the *International Covenant on Economic, Social, and Cultural Rights.* The two covenants are based on the provisions enshrined in the *Universal Declaration;* they were adopted by the UN General Assembly in 1966, at which time they became open to ratification by States, and they came into force in 1976 (United Nations Department of Public Information, 2006). In the months leading up to the conference that would establish the UN, the U.S. State Department held extensive meetings with hundreds of NGOs in order to obtain their input as they developed the U.S. policy on the United Nations; the pressure and influence of the NGOs ensured that human rights were a prominent aspect of the U.S.' objectives at the conference. Had it not been for the U.S. delegation's insistence on including human rights as a primary focus of the new organization, the UN Charter might have looked very different (Haynes & Ignatieff, 2003). The *Universal Declaration of Human Rights, International Covenant on Civil and Political Rights,* and *International Covenant on Economic, Social, and Cultural Rights,* in an illustration of the United States' influence in the founding of the UN and the creation of the *Universal Declaration,* are known collectively as the *International Bill of Human Rights* (UN, 2000).

The *International Covenant on Civil and Political Rights* contains a derogation clause, which articulates specific conditions under which a State may place restrictions on certain rights, for example, in the case of a national emergency. However, there are a few core human rights that may not be derogated from under any circumstances (International Covenant on Civil and Political Rights, 1966). Chief among these are the absolute prohibition on torture and cruel, inhuman, or degrading treatment or punishment; prohibition of slavery and other forms of exploitation; and all other crimes against humanity. These prohibitions are considered so imperative, and these crimes so severe, that they fall under the international legal classification of jus cogens.[1] In case of any confusion over what constitutes torture or cruel, inhuman or degrading treatment, international standards provide that the widest possible interpreta-

---

1. The nature of international law is such that States may choose what law applies to them and can vary or dispense with laws based on agreements with each other. *Jus cogens* is a category of law, however, from which States are not permitted to derogate, even if a treaty to which they are a party says that they can. The most commonly cited examples of violations of *jus cogens* are slavery, torture, and genocide. United States law defines "a consistent pattern of gross violations of internationally recognized human rights" as falling under *jus cogens,* in accordance with customary international law (Damrosch, Henkin, Pugh, Schachter, & Smit, 2001, pp. 602–603).

tion is to be used (Body of Principles for the Protection of All Persons under Any Form of Detention or Imprisonment, 1988). The *International Covenant on Civil and Political Rights* and *International Covenant on Economic, Social, and Cultural Rights* contain provisions that specifically require countries to apply all rights contained in the documents to "all individuals within its territory and subject to its jurisdiction . . . without distinction of any kind" (Article 2) (International Covenant on Civil and Political Rights, 1966), including by race, religion, sex, social status, or any other status. This includes an individual's status as detainee or inmate.

Specialist health care and health facilities, including for mental health care, are considered under international law to be a basic human right, not a privilege or a luxury (United Nations Office of the High Commissioner for Human Rights, 2005). Prison officials are required to be of sufficient intelligence and educational background in order to work in a detention facility. They must be trained before beginning their duties, and periodically retrained throughout their careers in this field (Standard Minimum Rules for the Treatment of Prisoners, 1955). International standards also provide that, to the extent possible, prisons are to employ an adequate number of specialists such as psychiatrists, psychologists, social workers, teachers, vocational instructors, and—in places where it would provide an adequate avenue for employment and a law-abiding life—religious training (Standard Minimum Rules for the Treatment of Prisoners, 1955).

Prisoners cannot be punished without being informed of their offense or without being given a fair chance to refute the charges. In addition, physical restraints such as handcuffs or straitjackets are to be used only when absolutely necessary and *never* as a form of discipline or punishment (Standard Minimum Rules for the Treatment of Prisoners, 1955). Prison staff, including health officials, are considered to be participants in torture or abuse if they do nothing to stop it (Principles of Medical Ethics Relevant to the Role of Health Personnel, 1982). Physically or mentally ill prisoners that are unable to receive treatment in prison must be transferred to a civilian hospital or a specialized prison health institution. Psychotic prisoners are not to be kept in prison, but rather should be sent to the appropriate mental institution where they will receive proper care (Standard Minimum Rules for the Treatment of Prisoners, 1955).

THE FUNCTIONS AND PHILOSOPHICAL
BACKGROUND OF NGOS

One of the central functions of many human rights NGOs, in contrast to humanitarian NGOs that primarily provide material and medical aid to those in need, is to state the facts of a particular situation in highly publicized reports that are usually released after the return of a fact finding mission. Typically, NGOs that embark on fact finding missions will research existing local, national, and international law; survey those directly affected by an alleged human rights abuse; interview relevant law enforcement officials, military personnel, and government representatives as applicable; and interview civilians that may have been witness to an abuse or that may be close to someone whose human rights have been violated. In addition, international NGOs may solicit the input of local organizations; bring in experts in any relevant field, such as ballistics in the case of a certain armed conflict or mental health in the case of degrading treatment of the mentally ill; and conduct any additional research or interviews that may paint a clearer picture of the human rights situation of a given population or conflict.

From the perspective of most NGOs, particularly international NGOs, the issues worked on have both global and local repercussions. The issue of prisoner abuse by prison personnel, for example, is seen as one facet of a much larger picture. Human rights abuses are often perpetrated against those deemed to be the "other" by society and its in-group. The treatment of Jews in Nazi Germany and the treatment of African Americans in the Jim Crow south are two examples. Prisoners, inmates, and detainees are another–albeit not always ethnically based–class of people that society may see as the "other" and therefore less entitled to basic human rights. A startling illustration of this in the United States is a 1999 law in Michigan in which imprisoned persons are defined as "'non-persons' under the state's civil rights and disabilities acts" (Ford Foundation, 2004, p. 101). Michigan's Public Acts 201 and 202 exclude state and county prisoners from protection under Michigan's Civil Rights Act and Persons with Disabilities Civil Rights Act, effectively eliminating their ability to file lawsuits when their civil rights have been violated (Kilpatrick, 2000).

This phenomenon often plays out on an interpersonal level as well. Girls in the New York State juvenile prison system that participated in interviews with Human Rights Watch and the American Civil Liberties Union told of being treated so badly by prison staff they felt as though staff saw them as animals, or not as "human but as slaves" (Human Rights Watch & the American Civil Liberties Union, 2006, p. 72). New York City Judge Michael A. Corriero suggests that this also occurs with juveniles who have come into conflict with the law; the public eschews these children as not belonging to them (Corriero, 2006).

NGOs are unique in how they tie elements of a particular problem or issue together into a bigger picture, often in a multidisciplinary fashion. In their reports, it is common for NGOs to address the subject of the report at the local, national, and international governmental and legal levels. For NGOs, the mental health of prisoners goes far beyond case management by professionals and the right to receive treatment while in prison. Most NGOs include in their mission a commitment to advocate and/or engage in fieldwork in order to promote adherence either to the gamut of basic human rights or to a particular set of human rights, and the right to an adequate standard of mental health for all, including prisoners, is among these basic rights (Paul, 2004).

CONTEMPORARY INTERNATIONAL PRISON NGOS

On August 24, 2006, Murat Kurnaz, a Turkish national born in Germany, was freed after nearly five years of being detained without charge or trial in Guantánamo. In Eritrea, a Christian singer who had been arrested for her religious beliefs was released from incommunicado detention after two and a half years of living in degrading conditions in a shipping container. In Nepal, in April 2006, hundreds of peaceful civil society leaders and activists were released from prison. One of them, Krishna Pahadi, a former chair of AI Nepal, spoke to Amnesty International USA to thank all of the activists who sent letters to the government demanding their release (Amnesty International, 2006a).

Letter writing remains a central strategy for Amnesty International. Action alerts are posted on the Amnesty International USA website along with addresses of government officials responsible for, or who may have a positive influence regarding, unjust detainments. The resulting pressure has an enormous impact on the release of prisoners of conscience, of which the paragraph above provides but a few examples. Since 1961, Amnesty International has played a role in the release of over 40,000 prisoners of conscience around the world (University of Georgia, n.d.).

Recently, international law and one particular hybrid NGO have had an impact on United States prison policy. The Geneva Conventions provide that the International Committee of the Red Cross is to have access to all prisoners in a conflict, and the *Body of Principles* states that all prison facilities, whether during war or peace, should be subject to inspection by an independent and competent authority, allowing them confidential communication with all prisoners, and specifically mentions the International Committee of the Red Cross as an option. In late September 2006, after nearly five years of pressure from the NGO community, the International Committee of the Red Cross visited senior Al Qaeda members being held at Guantánamo in what was widely believed to be the first time the detainees spoke to anyone outside the U.S. military or government. However, the International Committee of the Red Cross's findings were not to be made public, but were to be reported to the U.S. government (Lewis, 2006). The purpose of this is to ensure that the government understands and is aware of how well they are adhering to international law so that they may make any necessary changes in policy or practice. It is a fundamental tenet of the International Committee of the Red Cross's mandate to essentially exchange secrecy for access to prisoners.

NATIONAL AND LOCAL PRISON NGOS IN THE U.S. AND ABROAD

It would, for all practical purposes, be impossible to estimate how many nongovernmental organizations there are in the world. One estimate places the number in the millions (Paul, 2004). With so many NGOs worldwide, nearly every country in the world is likely to be home to at least one, which may work on any number of missions falling under the human rights realm. The following synopsis of prison NGOs that operate nationally or locally is a selective overview and by no means exhaustive.

The Center on Juvenile and Criminal Justice is a California-based NGO that engages in a number of initiatives that focus on diversion, advocacy for reform of the criminal justice system, and pressuring state agencies to change laws and policy. The Center on Juvenile and Criminal Justice operates halfway houses into which juvenile offenders may be diverted, provides technical assistance to agencies or jurisdictions that wish to enact reforms, and engages in public education regarding the issue of prison reform (D. Macallair, personal communication, November 7, 2006).

In Russia, human rights NGOs are currently battling the use of mental illness as a means of imprisoning those considered a threat to governmental authority. Mental illness during the Soviet era was used as a way to imprison or discredit dissidents by having them diagnosed with paranoia, schizophrenia, or some kind of personality disorder. Tens of thousands were imprisoned this way, most through coercive hospitalization. Russian human rights groups and advocacy organizations such as the Independent Psychiatric Association have come forward in recent years to draw attention to the post-Soviet regime of Vladimir Putin, which appears to be continuing this tradition in order to imprison those who speak out against the government (Finn, 2006).

JusticeAction is an NGO that works in the State of New South Wales in Australia to advocate for changes in the justice system that will curb explicit abuses, but they also partner with international NGOs that have a similar mission on a global scale. They see their local initiatives as contributing solutions to a larger problem in global society as a whole. Their activities seek to minimize social injustices that lead to criminal activity in the first place – not only in their own community, but also the world over (JusticeAction, n.d.). Likewise, the Center on Juvenile and Criminal Justice has collaborated with and has provided support to international NGOs such as Human Rights Watch and Amnesty International, as well as national organizations such as the American Civil Liberties Union (D. Macallair, personal communication, November 7, 2006).

Founded by the Catholic Bishops' Conference on Pakistan in 1985, the Pakistani National Commission for Justice and Peace is an NGO with a focus on promoting human rights in Pakistan (National Commission for Justice and Peace, n.d.). In 1992, the Commission was successful in influencing the government to withdraw a particular decision and, instead, ensure that Pakistani law includes a commitment to provide protection from religious apartheid and to prioritize human rights standards in Pakistan. The Commission has worked to fight discriminatory Islamic laws, for example, laws that penalize non-Muslims for offenses under Islam's Sharia law. The Commission also fights for the repeal of so-called "blasphemy" laws, in which an individual may be imprisoned for speaking against Islam (National Commission for Justice and Peace, n.d.).

NGOS WITH A SPECIFIC FOCUS

Many smaller NGOs that work on prison issues concentrate on one particular problem within the system. Stop Prisoner Rape, for example, is a California based NGO that works to ensure accountability for sexual violence against prisoners and to generate public awareness by informing misguided assumptions about incarcerated persons (Stop Prisoner Rape, 2006). Throughout its history, Stop Prisoner Rape has been headed by at least three male survivors of rape (Stop Prisoner Rape, n.d.). One of Stop Prisoner Rape's success stories is the predominant role it played, along with Human Rights Watch, in the passage of the *Prison Rape Elimination Act* (PREA) in 2003, the first federal law of its kind. To do this, Stop Prisoner Rape worked with senators and representatives, Democrat and Republican, and other NGOs. Stop Prisoner Rape now focuses on the law's implementation (Stop Prisoner Rape, n.d.).

Families against Mandatory Minimums is a national NGO in the United States that works to promote minimum sentencing requirements that fit the severity of the crime committed. The organization was founded in 1991 by a woman whose brother was sentenced to five years in prison for a nonviolent, first-time offense of growing marijuana. Due to mandatory minimum laws the judge could not exercise his or her own discretion when sentencing him (Families against Mandatory Minimums, n.d.).

The National Prison Hospice Association is a U.S. based nonprofit that seeks to encourage and provide special care for terminally ill and dying inmates detained in correctional facilities. Their aim is to allow prisoners to live their last days in peace and in accordance with human dignity (National Prison Hospice Association, n.d.). Hour Children is an NGO that works locally in New York City to assist incarcerated mothers and their children on the outside. They aim to ensure that both mother and child are developing in a positive direction, that the mother will be able to care for her child or children after release, and that the children are doing well in their emotional, psychological and academic development (Hour Children, 2006).

Finally, a number of NGOs in the United States, largely voluntary, recognize that there is a dearth of educational and rehabilitative opportunities for prisoners. They receive donations of books, which they send to inmates who wish to educate themselves. The Women's Prison Book Project, an organization that is well aware that most women in prison are from disadvantaged backgrounds and often belong to an ethnic minority, is one example (Women's Prison Book Project, n.d.). Others include the Prison Book Program, Books Through Bars, and the Texas based Inside Books Project (Prison Book Program, 2004; Books Through Bars, n.d.; Inside Books Project, n.d.).

PRISONERS IN NEED OF SPECIAL CONSIDERATION

International human rights standards outline certain categories of prisoners considered to be particularly vulnerable and who thus require special consideration. This is especially true in terms of members of vulnerable groups that may be suffering from mental illness. The power relationship between staff and inmates exacerbates the problem of discrimination (United Nations Office of the High Commissioner for Human Rights, 2005). Special categories of prisoners include juveniles, women, prisoners under sentence of death, and prisoners with life or long-term sentences. The issue of race discrimination is also a matter of great concern (United Nations Office of the High Commissioner for Human Rights, 2005).

Lesbian, Gay, Bisexual, and Transgendered Prisoners

A highly publicized report released by Amnesty International in 2005 drew significant attention to the issue of police and custodial abuse of lesbian, gay, bisexual and transgender people and the need to recognize this population as being particularly vulnerable (Amnesty International, 2005a). A joint report by Human Rights Watch and the American Civil Liberties Union on two New

York State facilities revealed the occurrence of abuse of girls who identify as being lesbian, bisexual, or transgendered, or even who do not conform to traditional female stereotypes. The report concluded that the unfair treatment and higher chance of punishment of these girls is based on their identity as lesbian, bisexual, or transgendered, and not on inappropriate sexual relations within the facility–the girls are under constant supervision when they are not locked up in isolation (Human Rights Watch & the American Civil Liberties Union, 2006).

Juveniles

When dealing with detained juveniles, international law requires that disciplinary measures not only respect the child's human dignity, but also attempt to instill in the child a sense of justice and respect for basic human rights (United Nations Rules for the Protection of Juveniles Deprived of Their Liberty, 1990). Corporal punishment of juveniles is considered to be cruel and inhuman treatment (Human Rights Watch & the American Civil Liberties Union, 2006). While some juveniles will have to be incarcerated due to the nature of their crimes and other circumstances, they are relatively few (Corriero, 2006). International standards provide that incarceration of juveniles is to be avoided wherever possible (United Nations Rules for the Protection of Juveniles Deprived of Their Liberty, 1990).

When incarceration is necessary, juveniles have the right to education and vocational training, and their best interests are to be prioritized (Convention on the Rights of the Child, 1989). Education and rehabilitation are of utmost importance. In the case of many juvenile offenders, however, a history of abuse and violence underlies their offenses and they are literally transformed "from victims to victimizers" (Corriero, 2006, p. 5), and thus perpetuate the cycle of abuse so familiar to social workers and mental health professionals. This is one of the important reasons that mental health care is an essential component of rehabilitation.

Human Rights Watch and the American Civil Liberties Union found the situation in the two New York State facilities for juvenile girls to be complex and dire. Their research indicated that while the proportion of those incarcerated in a juvenile boys' facility because of crimes related to serious mental illness is approximately 15 percent, those incarcerated in a girls' facility for the same reason is closer to 85 percent. Girls are also more likely to have experienced posttraumatic stress disorder (Human Rights Watch & the American Civil Liberties Union, 2006) and more than half of the women in jail in the entire country said that they had been physically or sexually abused at some point in their lives (Bureau of Justice Statistics, n.d.).

In addition, women and girls are much more likely to be imprisoned for crimes in which they have been exploited or victimized, such as prostitution, or which may be a manifestation of past abuse. Evidence suggests, and is especially cogent considering that most juvenile girls arrested on drug charges are users and not dealers, that incarcerated girls self-medicate with drugs or alcohol in the absence of adequate mental health care in the community, and often also in the face of continuing abuse (Human Rights Watch & the American Civil Liberties Union, 2006). This demonstrates the absolute imperative of not only including substance abuse treatment during incarceration, but also of providing mental health programs that will be able to recognize when substance abuse may be a symptom of an untreated mental illness. Furthermore, as a result of their experiences, incarcerated girls may not recognize when they are being sexually abused by a prison staff member (Human Rights Watch & the American Civil Liberties Union, 2006).

The level of staff abuse in New York State's two juvenile facilities for girls is so severe that Human Rights Watch declared that of all the countries in which it has investigated the conditions of children who are incarcerated—including Bulgaria, Guatemala, Egypt, India, Jamaica, Kenya, Pakistan, Papua New Guinea, and Brazil—New York's Office of Children and Family Services is one of the most hostile agencies it has come across in terms of treatment of juveniles in prison (Human Rights Watch & the American Civil Liberties Union, 2006). From interviews with girls who had been incarcerated in these facilities, some who had been as young as 12 at the time,[2] Human Rights Watch found that abuses committed by prison officials included being yelled and screamed at; being called names; being insulted; being threatened with physical violence; being "restrained" excessively, even when not posing a threat, to the point of getting black eyes, broken limbs, and cut faces; being sexually abused; being teased about their sexual history or medical condition, such as having a sexually transmitted disease; being strip searched, including their genitals, overly frequently; and being punished for acts of self-harm (Human Rights Watch & the American Civil Liberties Union, 2006).

One case presented in the Human Rights Watch and American Civil Liberties Union report is particularly telling. A girl who was 16 at the time of incarceration had been arrested for being commercially sexually exploited. She confided that her facility-assigned counselor made her recount her story of being sexually exploited, and that "he made me do things I did to them to him. He said what I was I would always be that" (Human Rights Watch & the American Civil Liberties Union, 2006, p. 64), and told her that she liked having sex. She confirmed that girls with similar backgrounds were particularly at risk of this sort of treatment.

---

2. This is the youngest age documented in New York State's juvenile facilities for girls. The majority of those incarcerated are between 15 and 16.

Women

The United Nations Office of the High Commissioner for Human Rights asserts that prison, generally speaking, is "a male-dominated society" (United Nations Office of the High Commissioner for Human Rights, 2005, p. 140). According to international standards, female inmates must be protected from violence and exploitation, are to be detained separately from male inmates, and are to be searched and supervised only by female officers. Female inmates are also entitled to the special care and attention they need if they are pregnant or nursing (Standard Minimum Rules for the Treatment of Prisoners, 1955).

In the 1990s, three lawyers–Ellen Barry, Deborah LaBelle, and Brenda Smith, who were representing female inmates who had been sexually assaulted by prison guards–found an utter lack of legal avenues to pursue and virtual indifference on the part of the state and federal governments as to the well being of their clients. They then found themselves in partnership with Human Rights Watch. As they began to work closely with HRW in the investigations and surveys for a planned report on incarcerated women, they encountered retaliation and enormous resistance on the part of the prison system (Ford Foundation, 2004).

Barry, LaBelle, and Smith contributed significantly to the Human Rights Watch report and assisted in its release, and their own work benefited from the resulting publicity. The lawyers did not feel that their actual work in defending women in prison had changed direction because of the use of international human rights as a framework, but had rather been strengthened and made that much more relevant (Ford Foundation, 2004).

In the 1990s, grassroots activists all across the United States worked with Amnesty International to conduct nationwide surveys on the conditions of women in prison. The result of releasing the final Amnesty International report was a sweeping reform of state law and policy regarding custodial sexual misconduct. The report, entitled *"Not Part of my Sentence": Violations of the Human Rights of Women in Custody,* was released in 1999. In 1990, 40 states in the United States had no laws criminalizing custodial sexual misconduct; by the time the report was released, this number fell to 14 (Amnesty International, 2006b). On May 31, 2006, AI announced the passage of custodial sexual misconduct laws in Vermont. Prior to May 31, Vermont was the last remaining U.S. state not to possess any laws of this nature (Amnesty International, 2006a).

Women are one of the most vulnerable groups of people in detention facilities throughout the world. Their vulnerability is exacerbated by their subordinate role in society and prison staff must be made to understand the ramifications of this for their work (United Nations Office of the High Commissioner for Human Rights, 2005). International law stipulates that prerelease programs for women should take into account the best interests of incarcerated women with respect for their dignity. These programs should result from a genuine evaluation of potential opportunities for them, such as work or further education, once they are released into the community. Programs for women and girls are to instruct and assist them in learning objectively useful skills and not "conform to outdated stereotypes" (United Nations Office of the High Commissioner for Human Rights, 2005, p. 142), and in the U.S., the latter is often the case (Human Rights Watch & the American Civil Liberties Union, 2006).

Racial and Ethnic Minorities

One challenge in ensuring the appropriate treatment of racial and ethnic minorities is that there is a difficult balance to keep between grouping members of the same minority together versus keeping them apart. On the one hand, it may be beneficial for a group to be together. They can speak their language together, talk about cultural events, practice their religion together, and so on. On the other hand, it would be desirable to avoid a situation where the grouping becomes a type of segregation that isolates the minority group and causes them to be treated differently (United Nations Office of the High Commissioner for Human Rights, 2005).

Racial discrimination among prison staff in the United States is extremely severe and pervasive. Among reported acts by prison guards are the wearing of Ku Klux Klan, confederate, or skinhead clothing or symbols; threats of physical violence; beatings; verbal abuse; and even shootings. This racism is exacerbated by an attitude among prison administrators and management that insults are in harmless jest or an expression of White heritage (Huling, 2002). Staff must be made to understand that this type of attitude and these types of behaviors are unacceptable and illegal.

Cultural and educational activities, and an environment that encourages a celebration and appreciation for diversity, are encouraged by the United Nations Office of the High Commissioner for Human Rights in order to combat racism and discrimination among the staff as well as among the inmates themselves. It is recommended that prison staff coordinate these events with a view to ameliorating ignorance and fear—the two main causes of discrimination (United Nations Office of the High Commissioner for Human Rights, 2005).

Prisoners With Life or Long-Term Sentences

When dealing with life or long-term sentence inmates, correctional personnel should be trained to be sensitive to the potentially devastating effects of such a sentence on the prisoner. Prerelease or rehabilitative programs for life or long-term prisoners should be carefully structured to ensure a sense of self-worth and a successful reintegration; they should be part of a detailed sentence plan, be based on assessments made of the inmate and include activities the inmate will participate in regularly. The aim should be to sufficiently rehabilitate the prisoner for release back into the community once a sentence proportionate to their crime has been served (United Nations Office of the High Commissioner for Human Rights, 2005).

Prisoners Under Sentence of Death

International standards provide that prisoners under the sentence of death are not to be dealt with more harshly because of the severity of their crime. They are not to be tortured or ill-treated, they are not to be arbitrarily denied visitation from their families, and all of their human rights are to be respected. Arbitrarily denying family visitation, denial of privacy and withholding information about the status of their case or their appeal is considered cruel and inhuman treatment (United Nations Office of the High Commissioner for Human Rights, 2005).

In its training guide on human rights and prisons, the United Nations Office of the High Commissioner for Human Rights devotes an entire chapter to the difficulties prison staff face when dealing with prisoners under the sentence of death. While current and future prison staff trainees have nothing to do with whether or not their respective countries allow the death penalty, it is important for them to be aware that abolition of the death penalty is strongly encouraged by international law (United Nations Office of the High Commissioner for Human Rights, 2005). Prison officials who work with prisoners under the death sentence should have special training in order to prepare them for the difficulties of dealing with these prisoners, and should also be given support in order to help them cope with the potentially devastating experience of doing so. The United Nations Office of the High Commissioner for Human Rights stresses the importance of presenting the lessons on prisoners under the death penalty in a manner that recognizes and is sensitive to the tremendous difficulty that dealing with these prisoners presents for prison staff (United Nations Office of the High Commissioner for Human Rights, 2005).

PROMOTING REHABILITATION, DIVERSION, AND RESTORATIVE JUSTICE

When it comes to inmates severely impaired by substance abuse or mental illness, prison staff need to be trained and taught that these offenders may not have the capacity to listen to logic or think reasonably along with a staff member (United Nations Office of the High Commissioner for Human Rights, 2005). NGOs that work on issues regarding incarcerated persons, as well as the body of international law that deals with the subject, staunchly support restorative justice initiatives wherever possible. One way restorative justice can be achieved is through a process known as diversion. When an individual has been convicted of or is suspected of having committed a crime, law enforcement or a court of law may choose to divert that person from incarceration to any one of a number of social services or programs, depending on the laws of the state. Unfortunately, restorative justice is often looked upon with derision by many in the criminal justice system, and diversion for adult offenders is rarely pursued (D. Macallair, personal communication, November 7, 2006).

The Center for Alternative Sentencing and Employment Services, a New York City based NGO that aims to promote rehabilitative and restorative justice in the community while taking into account issues of public safety, works closely with the courts to provide alternative to incarceration options for juvenile offenders (Center for Alternative Sentencing and Employment Services, n.d.a). They engage in five projects geared toward helping adult offenders, two of which exclusively deal with the mentally ill, that take into account the special needs of women, juveniles, mothers, and others (Center for Alternative Sentencing and Employment Services, n.d.b) The organization assists approximately 10,000 offenders with their cases annually (Center for Alternative Sentencing and Employment Services, n.d.a). The Center recently concluded a study in which they found that 80 percent of the juveniles they tracked after graduation from their program had not been reconvicted for any crimes. This is remarkable when compared to the 70 percent recidivism rate of juveniles channeled and incarcerated through New York's Office of Children and Family Services (Corriero, 2006).

An advantage of involving the community in noncustodial measures and diversion programs is that it gives the offenders an opportunity to atone for their crimes by making a contribution to the neighborhood rather than placing a burden on the state by being incarcerated (United Nations Office of the High Commissioner for Human Rights, 2005). Diversion may also be a tool used in building a sustainable plan of community reintegration for inmates once they are released. A well thought-out plan to become involved in community service, perhaps coupled with substance abuse treatment or other appropriate program, may result in an earlier and more successful release. For health professionals, successful diversion services will rely on close collaboration with law enforcement officials, and substance abuse treatment will have to be an integral facet of mental health care (Draine & Solomon, 1999).

Where diversion is not an option, whether for safety, retributive, or other reasons, rehabilitation is the ideal approach. The catalyst for the founding of the John Howard Society was the fact that prisoners, with inadequate prerelease rehabilitation, merely became law enforcement problems once again after release (John Howard Society, n.d.). Generally, short-term prisoners often receive no prerelease assistance at all and thus struggle with recidivism. It is essential that prerelease support begin as soon as short-term sentences do, and the United Nations Office of the High Commissioner for Human Rights points out that the "key is to break the pattern of prison being a way of life" (United Nations Office of the High Commissioner for Human Rights, 2005, p. 110). Mental health professionals, then, have a powerful role to play not just in terms of more long-term case management, but also in terms of participating in the development of comprehensive prerelease programs that cover short-term prisoner assistance, substance abuse treatment, and mental health (United Nations Office of the High Commissioner for Human Rights, 2005).

Substance abuse, health care, and other agencies, where they exist in the community, should be invited to help design and facilitate prerelease programs. This should also build bridges between the inmate and the community that may ease his or her transition back into society (United Nations Office of the High Commissioner for Human Rights, 2005). In Montgomery County, Pennsylvania, case managers in jails connect inmates to community services and continue to manage their case after release, assisting them as needed until their reintegration is well-established (Draine & Solomon, 1999). Furthermore, successful community reintegration will most certainly involve employment. Correctional officials in charge of prerelease programs will have to collaborate with members of the community that would be willing to employ an ex-prisoner (United Nations Office of the High Commissioner for Human Rights, 2005).

In terms of creating effective prerelease programs, it is critical for prison and jail administrators to solicit support from the community wherever possible (United Nations Office of the High Commissioner for Human Rights, 2005). In Montgomery County, diversion services allow alternatives to incarceration on condition that the offender will be entered into a mental health or other appropriate program in the community (Draine & Solomon, 1999). The importance of community involvement in prison-run mental health programs is demonstrated by the interdependence between what goes on in the community and what kind of treatment is available in prison. In a study of female inmates in New Jersey, incarceration improved women's access to mental health and behavioral treatment. However, if they had been able to access such care in the community, they might have avoided incarceration in the first place (Blitz, Wolff, & Paap, 2006).

EMERGING CONCERNS AND FUTURE DIRECTIONS

A major challenge in the enforcement of international human rights standards in the United States is the attitude held by many Americans, including some activists, that human rights law cannot or even should not apply to the United States (Ford Foundation, 2004). This perception is widely held regarding human rights generally, not to mention as it may apply to prisoners. According to Dan Macallair, Executive Director of the Center on Juvenile and Criminal Justice, another challenge for NGOs working toward reform of the prison system is the character of most custodial and law enforcement agencies, which is both heavily bureaucratic and highly resistant to change (D. Macallair, personal communication, November 7, 2006).

The broader vision of the human rights movement is one of its main strengths. Focusing on the fact that all people have core human rights means that those working in different professional fields—mental health and law enforcement, for example—can collaborate in a mutually beneficial manner. This collaboration—due to the fact that these rights are intended for people in every corner of the globe—is inherently international. This approach has the potential to significantly alter the criminal justice system in its defense of the vulnerable, while at the same time taking into account the safety of others—be it the public safety of a small town or national security itself. NGOs play a critical role at all levels of this framework.

Over the past decade, NGO involvement and influence in international affairs has increased in intensity, and NGO expertise has also been given credence at very high levels within the United Nations and in international justice matters. Their role has grown from the consultative function played in President Roosevelt's delegation in 1945 to that of a primary source of information regarding human rights and international law. NGOs now enjoy official consultative status in the UN's Economic and Social Council (Paul, 2004). A number of prestigious NGOs, along with the International Committee of the Red Cross, the Holy See, and Palestine, enjoy official observer status in the UN General Assembly (UN General Assembly Resolution 60/227, 2006; International Committee of the Red Cross, 2004). During the 1990s, NGOs also experienced a level of contact with the UN Security Council as never seen prior to the Cold War (Paul, 2004).

This may be due in part to the reliance the Security Council had on NGOs as a result of the post-Cold War boom in peacekeeping operations, which suddenly included such unprecedented responsibilities as election monitoring, policing, and peacebuilding. When the Security Council took on these "second-generation" peacekeeping responsibilities in the early 1990s, they urgently sought out the advice, policy ideas, and expertise of NGOs (Paul, 2004).

Permanent Members of the Security Council, however, demonstrated strong opposition to the notion of being under NGO scrutiny.[3] The rise of the Internet has meant that reports by NGOs are vastly more accessible, and as a result closer attention has been paid to these reports by the Security Council. In addition, Security Council Members' missions to the UN took their cue from NGOs and began to post speeches and other Security Council activity on their own websites in an attempt to demonstrate their noble actions (Paul, 2004). Yet, despite NGOs' effective use of the Internet and their increasing influence, they continue to face a formidable obstacle when it comes to the veto power held by the five permanent Members of the Council.

Finally, in probably the most impressive show of NGO influence on an international level, the establishment in 2002 of the International Criminal Court (Rome Statute of the International Criminal Court, 1998) marked the beginning of a new era in international human rights law. Had such a court existed in 1945, this is where Nazi war criminals might have been tried. In the months leading up to the final draft of the Statute of the Court, international NGOs held a number of conferences for human rights activists (Human Rights Watch, 1999). The President of Senegal hosted one such conference; NGOs across Africa had done a phenomenal job of raising awareness about the Court, its uses, and why it should be established. The result was enthusiastic support for the Court from many governments in Africa, especially in West Africa. NGOs from many different countries met in cities around the world to promote the establishment of the International Criminal Court.

In order to coordinate a comprehensive global campaign for the International Criminal Court's establishment, more than 200 NGOs formed the Coalition for the International Criminal Court. Chief among their concerns, as a result of the heavy presence of women's and children's human rights caucuses in the Coalition, were the categorization in the International Criminal Court Statute of gender crimes and crimes against children as war crimes and crimes against humanity (Human Rights Watch, 1999). The terms decided on for the Statute were due in large part to the skillful way in which NGOs coordinated their efforts in order to influence country negotiations regarding the Statute. The International Criminal Court Statute symbolizes a key turning point in human rights law and the growing strength of the international human rights movement, without which the International Criminal Court Statute would

---

3. The Security Council is the predominant decision-making body of the UN. It is made up of the representatives of 15 Member States of the UN, 10 of which rotate alternatively every two years and five of which are permanent. The five permanent Members are China, Great Britain, France, Russia, and the United States. The influence of the permanent five lies in their so-called veto power; any resolution that is put before the Council will not pass if any one of the five votes against it. An abstention on a vote by one of the five, however, will not block the passage of a resolution (Charter of the United Nations, 1945).

have looked completely different (Human Rights Watch, 1999). The Rome Conference on the International Criminal Court ended with the passage of the Statute containing provisions addressing nearly all of the concerns under the purview of NGOs around the world (Human Rights Watch, 1999).

The coming into force of the International Criminal Court Statute was a major success except that the United States did not sign on. In fact, as of November 2006, 104 countries are a Party to the International Criminal Court, and an additional 139 countries have signed the treaty with the intent to ratify. The United States and Israel are the only two countries in the world that have not at least signed the Statute (The American Non-Governmental Organizations Coalition for the International Criminal Court, 2006). In addition, the U.S., at a time when NGO pressure was geared toward encouraging the U.S. to sign, had pressured other countries not to sign or ratify the Statute. Throughout, NGOs kept up the pressure in the opposite direction (Human Rights Watch, 1999).

Articles 7 and 8 of the Rome Statute of the International Criminal Court (1998) are a testament to the relentless efforts by NGOs all over the world in their deliberations and lobbying of governments. Article 7 defines crimes against humanity as murder, extermination, slavery, forced displacement, detainment in violation of international law, torture, rape, sexual slavery, forced prostitution, forced pregnancy, forced sterilization, persecution of a particular identity group, enforced disappearance, apartheid, and other inhumane acts of comparable gravity. Article 8 defines rape and other forms of sexual violence by combatants during conflict as war crimes (Rome Statute of the International Criminal Court,1998). This is the first time that gender based violence has been explicitly considered in an international treaty to be among the gravest crimes during war or peace (Amnesty International, 2005b).

CONCLUSION

Prison work remains a primary mission of the human rights movement. In light of today's unprecedented levels of respect for NGOs and their expertise, the twenty-first century is sure to see the role of NGOs grow in importance and influence. The vision of the human rights movement is to achieve justice and accountability for all, and an end to impunity for abuses, regardless of who commits them. The marriage of the determination of human rights activists with the continued growth of NGO influence on policy is sure to have a positive impact on the administration of prisons, jails, and detention centers and will continue to promote respect for mental health concerns within the framework of human rights for all.

REFERENCES

American Civil Liberties Union. (n.d.). *American Civil Liberties Union: About us.* Retrieved November 20, 2006, from http://aclu.org/about/index.html

The American Non-Governmental Coalition for the International Criminal Court. (2006). *What is the ICC? Ratifications.* Retrieved December 11, 2006 from http://www.amicc.org/icc_ratifications.html

Amnesty International. (n.d.). *Frequently asked questions.* Retrieved November 20, 2006, from http://web.amnesty.org/pages/aboutai-faq-eng

Amnesty International. (2005a). *Stonewalled: Police abuse and misconduct against lesbian, gay, bisexual and transgender people in the US.* New York: Amnesty International USA.

Amnesty International. (2005b). *The International Criminal Court fact sheet 7: Ensuring justice for women.* Retrieved December 11, 2006 from http://web.amnesty.org/library/Index/ENGIOR400062005?open&of=ENG-385

Amnesty International. (2006a). *Success stories.* Retrieved December 8, 2006, from http://www.amnestyusa.org/success/index.do

Amnesty International. (2006b). *Abuse of women in custody: Sexual misconduct and shackling of pregnant women–Key findings.* Retrieved November 6, 2006, from http://www.amnestyusa.org/women/custody/keyfindings_legislation.html

Anti-Slavery International. (n.d.). *The history of Anti-Slavery International.* Retrieved December 10, 2006, from http://www.antislavery.org/homepage/antislavery/history.htm

Basic Principles for the Treatment of Prisoners, GA res. 45/111, annex, 45 UN GAOR Supp. (No. 49A) at 200, UN Doc. A/45/49 (1990). Retrieved December 10, 2006, from http://www1.umn.edu/humanrts/instree/g2bpt.htm

Blitz, C. L., Wolff, N., & Paap, K. (2006). Availability of behavioral health treatment for women in prison. *Psychiatric Services, 57,* 356–360.

Body of Principles for the Protection of All Person Under Any Form of Detention or Imprisonment. GA res. 43/173, 43 UN GAOR Supp. (No. 49) at 298, UN Doc. A/43/49 (1988).

Books Through Bars. (n.d.). *New York City Books Through Bars homepage.* Retrieved December 11, 2006, from http://www.abcnorio.org/affiliated/btb.html

Bureau of Justice Statistics. (n.d.). *Criminal offenders statistics.* Retrieved November 1, 2006, from http://www.ojp.usdoj.gov/bjs/crimoff.htm

Canadian Association of Elizabeth Fry Societies (n.d.). *Origins: A short history of Elizabeth Fry.* Retrieved September 22, 2006, from http://www.elizabethfry.ca/history.html

Center for Alternative Sentencing and Employment Services. (n.d.a). *CASES homepage.* Retrieved December 2, 2006, from http://www.cases.org/

Center for Alternative Sentencing and Employment Services. (n.d.b). *About us.* Retrieved January 2, 2007, from http://www.cases.org/about.html

Charter of the United Nations. (1945, June 26). 59 Stat. 1031, T.S. 993, 3 Bevans 1153, entered into force Oct. 24, 1945. Retrieved December 14, 2006, from http://www1.umn.edu/humanrts/instree/aunchart.htm

Convention on the Rights of the Child, GA res. 44/25, annex, 44 UN GAOR Supp. (No. 49) at 167, UN Doc. A/44/49 (1989), entered into force Sept. 2 1990.

Corriero, M. A. (2006). *Judging children as children: A proposal for a juvenile justice system.* Philadelphia: Temple University Press.

Damrosch, L. F., Henkin, L., Pugh, R. C., Schachter, O., & Smit, H. (2001). *International law: Cases and materials* (4th ed.). St. Paul, MN: West Group Publishing.

Draine, J., & Solomon, P. (1999). Describing and evaluating jail diversion services for persons with serious mental illness. *Psychiatric Services, 50,* 56–61.

Families Against Mandatory Minimums. (n.d.). *Meet FAMM.* Retrieved November 25, 2006, from http://www.famm.org/MeetFAMM.aspx

Finn, P. (2006, September 30). In Russia, psychiatry is again a tool against dissent. *The Washington Post,* page A 1.

Ford Foundation. (2004). *Close to home: Case studies of human rights work in the United States.* New York: The Ford Foundation.

Haynes, L. & Ignatieff, M. (2003). *Mobilizing support for the United Nations.* Retrieved December 20, 2006, from http://www.ksg.harvard.edu/leadership/pubs/papers/index.php?itemid=188

Hour Children. (2006). *About us.* Retrieved December 11, 2006, from http://www.hourchildren.org/aboutus.aspx

Huling, T. (2002). Building a prison economy in rural America. In M. Mauer & M. Chesney-Lind (Eds.), *Invisible punishment: The collateral consequences of mass imprisonment* (pp. 197–213). New York City: The New Press.

Human Rights Watch. (n.d.). *Human Rights Watch: Who we are.* Retrieved November 20, 2006, from http://hrw.org/about/whoweare.html

Human Rights Watch. (1999). Special Issues and Campaigns. *Human Rights Watch world report 1999.* Retrieved November 25, 2006, from http://www.hrw.org/worldreport99/special/icc.html

Human Rights Watch & the American Civil Liberties Union. (2006, September). *Custody and control: Conditions of confinement in New York's juvenile prisons for girls.* Retrieved December 10, 2006 from http://hrw.org/reports/2006/us0906/

Inside Books Project. (n.d.). *Inside Books Project homepage.* Retrieved December 11, 2006 from http://www.insidebooksproject.com/

International Committee of the Red Cross. (2004). *The ICRC's status: In a class of its own.* Retrieved November 14, 2006, from http://www.icrc.org/Web/eng/siteeng0.nsf/html/5W9FJY

International Covenant on Civil and Political Rights. (1966). General Assembly resolution 2200A (XXI), 21 UN GAOR Supp. (No. 16) at 52, UN Doc. A/6316, 999 UNTS 171, entered into force March 23, 1976. Retrieved December 10, 2006, from http://www1.umn.edu/humanrts/instree/b3ccpr.htm

John Howard Society of Canada (n.d.). *History/background/principles.* Retrieved September 22, 2006, from http://www.johnhoward.ca/jhsback.htm

Justice Action (n.d.). *About JusticeAction.* Retrieved September 22, 2006, from http://justiceaction.org.au/ja_adds/about.html

Keane, J. (2004). Cosmocracy and global civil society. In G. Baker, & D. Chandler (Eds.), *Global civil society: Contested futures* (pp. 34–51). Oxford, England: Routledge.

Kilpatrick, C. C. (2000). *Kilpatrick and Conyers lead call for women prisoners' rights.* Retrieved January 2, 2007, from http://www.house.gov/kilpatrick/pr000121.htm

Lewis, N. A. (2006). Red Cross officials to visit prisoners at Guantánamo. *The New York Times.* Retrieved September 22, 2006, from http://www.nytimes.com/2006/09/20/us/20gitmo.html?_r=2&oref=slogin&oref=slogin

Motely, J. (2006). [Review of the book *Crimes against humanity: The struggle for global justice*]. Retrieved November 25, 2006, from http://www.hrw.org/community/bookreviews/robertson.htm

National Commission for Justice and Peace. (n.d.). *Profile.* Retrieved November 25, 2006, from http://www.geocities.com/ncjppak/ncjpprofile.htm

National Prison Hospice Association. (n.d.). *National Prison Hospice Association homepage.* Retrieved December 11, 2006, from http://www.npha.org/

Paul, J. (2004). NGOs and the Security Council. *Global policy forum.* Retrieved November 25, 2006, from http://www.globalpolicy.org/security/ngowkgrp/gpfpaper.htm

Pennsylvania Prison Society. (n.d.). *About us: Who we are.* Retrieved September 22, 2006, from http://www.prisonsociety.org/about/index.shtml

Physicians for Human Rights. (n.d.a). *About PHR.* Retrieved November 25, 2006, from http://www.phrusa.org/about/index.html

Physicians for Human Rights. (n.d.b). *Projects.* Retrieved November 25, 2006, from http://www.phrusa.org/campaigns/index.html

Physicians for Human Rights. (2006, September 29). *PHR decries House and Senate passage of Military Commissions Act; President still bound by Common Article 3 and Detainee Treatment Act–PHR vows to hold administration accountable to Geneva Conventions.* Retrieved November 25, 2006, from http://www.phrusa.org/research/torture/news_2006-09-29.html

Principles of Medical Ethics relevant to the Role of Health Personnel, particularly Physicians, in the Protection of Prisoners and Detainees against Torture and Other Cruel, Inhuman or Degrading Treatment or Punishment, GA res. 37/194, annex, 37 UN GAOR Supp. (No. 51) at 211, UN Doc. A/37/51 (1982).

Prison Book Program. (2004). *Prison Book Program homepage.* Retrieved December 11, 2006 from http://www.prisonbookprogram.org/

Rome Statute of the International Criminal Court (1998, July 17). UN Doc. 2187 UNTS 90, entered into force July 1, 2002. Retrieved January 3, 2007, from http://www1.umn.edu/humanrts/instree/Rome_Statute_ICC/romestatute.html

Standard Minimum Rules for the Treatment of Prisoners Adopted by the First United Nations Congress on the Prevention of Crime and the Treatment of Offenders, held at Geneva in 1955, and approved by the Economic and Social Council by its resolution 663 C (XXIV) of 31 July 1957 and 2076 (LXII) of 13 May 1977.

Stop Prisoner Rape. (2006). *Mission statement.* Retrieved November 25, 2006, from http://www.spr.org/en/mission_statement.asp

Stop Prisoner Rape. (n.d.). *Stop prisoner rape: A brief history.* Retrieved November 25, 2006, from http://www.spr.org/en/spr_history.asp

Sullivan, A. (2006). Torture by any other name is just as vile. *The Sunday Times* (London). Retrieved November 4, 2006, from LexisNexis database.

United Nations. (2000). *Human Rights and the United Nations.* Retrieved November 25, 2006, from http://www.un.org/geninfo/faq/humanrights/hr2.htm

United Nations Children's Fund. (n.d.). *About UNICEF: Structure and contact information.* Retrieved December 14, 2006, from http://www.unicef.org/about/structure/index.html

United Nations Department of Public Information. (2006, March 8). *Background release: Human rights committee to meet in New York, 13–31 March.* Retrieved December 16, 2006, from http://www.un.org/News/Press/docs/2006/hrct671.doc.htm

United Nations General Assembly resolution 60/227. (2006, April 7). Sixtieth session: Agenda item 54 (c), Resolution adopted by the General Assembly on the report of the Second Committee (A/60/490/Add.3). UN Doc. A/RES/60/227 (2006).

United Nations Office of the High Commissioner for Human Rights. (2005). *Human rights and prisons: Trainer's guide on human rights training for prison officials.* New York: United Nations.

United Nations Office of the High Commissioner for Human Rights. (2006). *About OHCHR: Mandate.* Retrieved December 14, 2006, from http://ohchr.org/english/about/

United Nations Rules for the Protection of Juveniles Deprived of their Liberty, GA res. 45/113, annex, 45 UN GAOR Supp. (No. 49A) at 205, UN Doc. A/45/49 (1990).

Universal Declaration of Human Rights, GA res. 217A (III), UN Doc A/810 at 71 (1948).

University of Georgia. (n.d.). *University of Georgia Amnesty International Chapter, Frequently Asked Questions.* Retrieved December 8, 2006, from http://www.uga.edu/amnesty/faq.html

White, J. (2005, July 14). Abu Ghraib tactics were first used at Guantánamo. *The Washington Post,* page A01. Retrieved November 20, 2006 from LexisNexis.

Women's Prison Book Project. (n.d.). *About WPBP.* Retrieved December 11, 2006, from http://www.prisonactivist.org/wpbp/pages/about.html

Chapter 10

PRISON POLICY AND TERRORISM: LEARNING THE LESSONS OF THE PAST

MICHAEL VON TANGEN PAGE* AND ROBERT K. AX

INTRODUCTION

Overview

Terrorism is on the rise worldwide, with major international incidents more than tripling between 2003 and 2004 (Glasser, 2005). Those espousing radical Islamic beliefs are the most visible, though by no means the only, terrorists active today. Nonstate terrorism in various forms has been a part of America's past. The Ku Klux Klan and other domestic white supremacist groups originating in the nineteenth century are prime examples of a type of terrorism directed against essentially powerless groups such as African Americans (Dray, 2003). In 1995, Timothy McVeigh, a disaffected American citizen and right-wing extremist, murdered 168 people and injured hundreds more when he exploded a bomb in front of the Alfred P. Murrah Federal Office Building in Oklahoma. His act was a symbolic reprisal for grievances he bore against the United States government (Hamm, 1997). South America has also been the site of recent anti-government terrorism.[1] For example, the Maoist Shining Path *(Sendero Luminoso)* was active in Peru during the 1980s and 1990s. The group attacked jails and prisons to free their comrades, and imprisoned members took control of one facility from the staff to further their political goals (Gorriti, 1990/1999).

---

* The views expressed in this chapter are solely those of the author and do not necessarily reflect the views of the organizations with which the author is affiliated.

1. Consensus definitions of "terrorist" and "terrorism" have proven difficult to obtain, but for the purposes of this article these terms refer to the use of violence for political ends by *non-state* actors against established governments.

However, it has been in the European democracies where the most enduring and concerted anti-government terrorist activity has occurred over the last
100 years. During the Cold War, terrorism was a major problem in Western
Europe as extreme right and left wing groups attempted to overthrow the frag-
ile new democracies there. In Italy and Germany groups at both extremes of
the political spectrum—the Red Army Faction (RAF), Red Brigades (BR) and
Front Line (PL) from the left and New Order (ON) from the right—employed
political assassination, kidnapping, and bombings in their attempts to subvert
democratic governments. During this period, Europe also saw a smaller number of nationalist groups using political violence to pursue independence from
larger sovereign states. Most famously, these included the Provisional Irish
Republican Army (IRA) and Basque Fatherland and Liberty (ETA-M) movements, which sought to liberate peripheral areas of the United Kingdom (UK)
and Spain, respectively (von Tangen Page, 1998).

The attacks on the World Trade Center in 1993 and 2001 signaled the
advent of a new wave of terrorism in America and the rest of the West. The
main threat came from beyond the nation's borders in the form of radical
Islam, bringing to these nations the violent tactics of a formidable movement
that had largely been confined to Israel and the Third World. In the period
following the terrorist attacks on the United States in September 2001, the
U.S.-led international war against terrorism constituted a new paradigm in the
context and scale of counterterrorism. Given the scope of the conflict, with
international coalitions forced to confront terrorism both in the Middle East
and their own countries, as well as the high numbers of combatant and civilian casualty figures, it was perhaps inevitable that the lessons of the "old" terrorism faced by democratic states across the world would be overlooked.

This oversight is regrettable, particularly, for present purposes, in terms of
penal policy. American correctional officials and their counterparts in other
Western democracies will increasingly confront the presence of committed
terrorists in their institutions over the next several years. Accordingly, they
can profit from the experiences of several European democracies in the period between 1968 and 2000 with incarcerated members of various terrorist
groups. The core of this chapter is a review of these experiences, the "lessons
learned," followed by a discussion of policy and practice implications for
American and other Western prison systems.

THE POLITICALLY MOTIVATED VIOLENT OFFENDER

Chapter 11 of this volume is an overview of prison gangs and the issues
they present for mental health and other correctional staff. While such entities
are not mutually exclusive, terrorist groups can be distinguished from other

criminal organizations in two ways. First, they have a political, rather than a criminal agenda. Second, they resort to violence as a primary means to achieve their ideological ends. These activities constitute their reason for incarceration, as opposed to the personal, fundamentally self-aggrandizing motivations characteristic of both prison and street gangs. Accordingly, the more technically precise term *politically motivated violent offenders* (PMVOs) will be used to describe these individuals (von Tangen Page, 1998). This is in part because the term "terrorism" is notoriously difficult for academics to define, and just as easily manipulated by authorities for political ends. There is, for example, a truism that the terms terrorist and freedom fighter are interchangeable depending on one's political point of view. Definitions of terrorism range from the terse to the prolix. For example, Alex P. Schmid, the academic and former head of the Terrorism Unit of the UN Office on Drugs and Crime, proposed that "Terrorism = War Crime in Time of Peace" (Schmid, 1992; cited in United Nations Office on Drugs and Crime, n.d.). Conversely, U.S. law defines international terrorism, in part, as activities that:

> . . . involve violent acts or acts dangerous to human life that are a violation of the criminal laws of the United States or of any State, or that would be a criminal violation if committed within the jurisdiction of the United States or of any State . . . [or which] occur primarily outside the territorial jurisdiction of the United States, or transcend national boundaries in terms of the means by which they are accomplished, the persons they appear intended to intimidate or coerce, or the locale in which their perpetrators operate or seek asylum. . . . (18 USC § 2331)

Notwithstanding definitional difficulties, the fact remains that PMVOs present a range of practical and ethical dilemmas to correctional services, most urgently, security concerns. Particularly exigent is the potential for recruiting other inmates to their radical causes and beliefs:

> According to the FBI, it is likely that terrorist groups such as al-Qaeda will attempt to radicalize and recruit inmates in the United States. FBI counterterrorism officials stated that inmates are logical targets for terrorist recruitment because they may be predisposed to violence, feel disenfranchised from society, desire power and influence, seek revenge against those who incarcerated them, be hostile towards authority and the United States, or cling to a radical or extremist Islamic "family." (Office of the Inspector General, 2004, p. 7)

There are recent precedents for the exploitation of prison populations in this way in other parts of the world. Shanker (2006) reported that U.S. military commanders were concerned that the Abu Ghraib prison in Iraq had "become a breeding ground for extremist leaders and a school for terrorist foot soldiers" (p. A12). Spanish prisons, with large populations of Northern African immigrants, are considered highly vulnerable for recruitment purposes (McLean, 2004). Indeed, two of the people accused of the bomb attacks on

Madrid's subway system in 2004, a Moroccan, Jamal Ahmidan, and a Spaniard, José Emilio Suárez Trashorras, were both radicalized in prison while serving sentences for drug-related convictions (Cuthbertson, 2004). Further, Richard Reid, the man convicted for the attempted suicide bombing of a trans-Atlantic flight, was a Briton who had been converted to Islam in prison in the UK and followed an increasingly radical path after his release (Who is Richard Reid?, 2001).

In some cases, terrorist groups have wrested total control of prisons from the authorities. The Shining Path of Peru took over El Frontón, the island prison where large numbers of the group were transferred in 1982. "... [The Shining Path] won control inch by inch, until it made the prison into a center for training, internal advancement, planning and indoctrination" (Gorriti, 1990/1991, p. 244). Similarly, groups including both criminal organizations and left-wing radicals ran 20 Turkish prisons during the 1990s. To regain control, the government ultimately resorted to the use of military and police assaults on the prisons that left several dead, including some prisoners who preferred suicide to surrender (Frantz, 2000).

As will be discussed in more detail below, PMVOs have presented other challenges in European prisons. Defining prison wings as another front in the war against the state, they have organized rebellions, escapes, and the assassination of prison employees. They have been especially successful in terms of generating propaganda from their confrontations with authorities. Finally, the treatment of prisoners has also been a significant political issue in many countries that have housed PMVOs. Ultimately, the desire on the part of politicians and the general public for vengeance has had to be balanced against the potential backlash that can result from taking a hard-line stance in framing penal policy.

THE EUROPEAN EXPERIENCE WITH PMVOS: 1960s–1990s[2]

Causes of Terrorism

As stated above, Western Europe suffered a period of extensive terrorist activity from the late 1960s through the early 1990s. In Spain and the UK it was largely generated by separatist agendas. In the Spanish case, the goal was to achieve the independence of the Basque Region (an area that includes the extreme south west of France and parts of Northern Spain's Atlantic coast line),

2. The information in this section comes from the first author's professional and academic involvement with European prisons and his book on prisons and terrorism (von Tangen Page, 1998) except where otherwise noted.

and in the British case it was Irish nationalists who sought to merge British administered Northern Ireland and the Irish Republic into a unified and independent Ireland.[3] In Italy and West Germany (and to a lesser extent in France), terrorism was primarily ideological in nature. Extremist groups at both ends of the political spectrum–far-right fascists and national socialists, and far-left Marxists–sought to undermine the fledgling liberal democracies in both.

The Problems PMVOs Have Presented in Prisons

Prisons in several European nations became battlefields for the PMVOs and the various governments, albeit for different reasons. The policies of Germany and Italy isolated extremists from the general population because of the fear that they might succeed in recruiting "common" or politically unaligned criminals to their causes. Conversely, in Northern Ireland and Spain authorities promoted a "criminalization" policy–seeking to define the convicted PMVOs as simple criminals by mainstreaming convicted terrorists into normal prisons. The PMVOs themselves resisted criminalization, identifying themselves as prisoners of war and insisting on being segregated.

During the 1970s, the European experience of holding PMVOs included threats to the safety of correctional staff. As PMVOs commonly saw themselves as fighting on a different front in a wider war, so the correctional officers were perceived as enemy combatants. In Northern Ireland, Irish Republican prisoners collected intelligence on prison officers and then passed this back to their organizations outside the prisons to arrange for the assassination of several of the staff. Italian prison staff were also targeted by terrorist groups in that country.

Dealings with the prison authorities were also seen through the prism of fighting a war for political legitimacy. Both the Provisional IRA and ETA-M, allies of the Sinn Féin and Herri Batasuna groups, respectively, used prisons as forums for promoting their political agendas to the public. Sinn Féin demonstrated this in a particularly effective incident in 1981. During a hunger strike, 10 prisoners starved themselves to death. Subsequently, one of the other prisoners was elected to the UK House of Commons and another to the Irish Dail (Clarke 1987).

In addition, there have been incidents of politically motivated violence between different prisoner factions (Frantz, 2000). In Northern Ireland disputes between loyalist and republican prisons were common. In one high-profile incident, the notorious anti-agreement loyalist leader Billy "King Rat"

---

3. For excellent accounts of these two conflicts see Sullivan, J. "ETA and Basque Nationalism" London: Routledge, 1988; and Moloney, E, "A Secret History of the IRA" London, W.W. Norton and Company, 2002.

Wright was murdered in the Maze/Long Kesh Prison in December, 1997. His attackers were prisoners belonging to the republican Marxist splinter group the Irish National Liberation Army (INLA) (von Tangen Page, 2000).

The personal motivations of PMVOs also present challenges. They will often adopt a position of moral superiority over their captors, both seeing themselves and presenting themselves to the public as the victims of oppression and characterizing the authorities as perpetrators. This would allow them, for example, to justify direct attacks on prison staff, such as those that occurred in Italy and Northern Ireland. Secondly, the traditional rewards and sanctions of correctional discipline can have unintended consequences for those who may be willing to accept martyrdom, as such status may further energize their comrades' commitment to their causes. This was certainly a consideration for the IRA hunger strikers who willingly starved to death (Clarke, 1987).[4] Thirdly, PMVOs can often draw on an international support network, which will continue to nourish their political strength, support relatives back home, and utilize any reported mistreatment as propaganda to further their cause. The "dirty protests" of the criminalization policy at Maze/Long Kesh Prison resulted in a resurgence of funding for the republican cause from the United States. "As well as new allies, the H-Block protest produced new recruits, resources and arms for the republican paramilitaries" (Crawford, 1999, p. 60).

Strategies for Dealing With PMVOs

Historically, authorities have had to consider both the immediate effects on PMVOs and the more general political impact of managing them. In some cases the prison authorities have seen the treatment of PMVOs as a means of influencing the organizations to which they belong. Strategies can be characterized as generally hard-line or soft-line, and either may be employed depending on the circumstances. The terms *hard-line* and *soft-line* are commonly used in European discussions on prison policy. Hard-line emphasizes the punishment and retribution aspects of the criminal justice system; soft-line emphasizes the rehabilitative aspects.

Whether proactively or reactively, prison systems holding large numbers of PMVOs have often segregated these individuals from the general prison population. An extreme example of this hard-line approach comes from Spain. In the 1980s, authorities sought to put pressure on ETA-M through the policy of

---

4. Promoting their cause may have motivated the three prisoners who hanged themselves at the U.S. military prison in Guantánamo Bay, Cuba, in June, 2006 (Risen & Golden, 2006). In interviews of Middle Eastern PMVOs held in Israel, Post, Sprinzak, & Denny (2003) found another unintended effect of incarceration. It reinforced their sense of purpose: "The prison experience was intense, especially for the Islamic terrorists [members of Hamas, as opposed to their secular Fatah PMVO counterparts]. It further consolidated their identity and the group or organizational membership that provided the most valued element of personal identity" (p. 174).

dispersal–that of moving prisoners all over the territory of Spain. Some were even moved to the Canary Islands, located off the coast of North West Africa, over 1000 miles from the Basque Country. This put great pressure on the family members of prisoners in the hope that they would pressure ETA-M to the negotiation table. Similarly, the UK sought to demonstrate that Irish Republicans and Ulster Loyalists were criminals in the late 1970s. They did this through attempting to force prisoners into wearing criminal uniforms, and trying to mix prisoners, both loyalists and republicans, with ordinary criminals or "ODC's" ("ordinary decent criminals") as they were often informally referred to by the prison wardens. This policy collapsed in the face of a protracted campaign both inside and outside the prisons in Northern Ireland. Inside the prisons Irish republicans resisted, refusing to obey prison regulations, put on the prison uniform, or use sanitary facilities.

Regarding the soft-line approach, the prison authorities in Spain, Italy and Northern Ireland all used the promise of early release in exchange for either the support of a peace initiative outside of the prisons or to renounce violence personally. This approach runs counter to some of the basic principles of criminal justice systems, particularly the punishment and retribution missions of incarceration. However, it has often proved to be highly effective in terms of the larger conflict.

Related to this is the policy of conversion. The basic idea of converting terrorists can be traced to the UK's experience of facing nationalist violence in its colonies in the immediate post-world war period. As the UK found itself ceasing to be a world power and the tide of history and world opinion turned against the idea of colonialism rather like other formerly great powers, it found itself reevaluating the reasons why it had established colonies in the first place. The UK faced major insurgencies in Palestine (now Israel), Mesopotamia (now Iraq), Cyprus, Kenya, and Malaya (now Malaysia). One individual who experienced several of these insurgencies at first hand as a military intelligence officer was Brigadier General Frank Kitson. Concerning his experiences of "turning" or converting former violent opponents, Kitson argued that successful counter-insurgencies depend on treating captured insurgents according to four requirements: (1) They should be prevented from inflicting further damage to the government, (2) they should be encouraged to change sides, (3) maximum advantage should be taken of the information prisoners can provide and other ways in which they can help, and (4) prisoners should be well treated to encourage other insurgents to change sides (Kitson, 1977).

In Malaya, Kenya, and Northern Ireland Kitson created counter-gangs of former terrorists who would be reinserted either as agents back with the enemy or as fighting groups. These proved effective in Malaya and Kenya, but were largely unsuccessful in Northern Ireland (von Tangen Page, 1998). There was one aspect of the counter-gang principle which proved relatively effective in Northern Ireland and was highly effective in Italy–that of the *super-grass* (or informant). It is often not realized that the super-grass idea, which has been highly effective against organized crime cartels worldwide, was initially designed for use against PMVOs. In its idealized form, it occurs when a person converts to the government side or regrets his or her past actions and carries out an act of penance. It was undermined in the UK largely because many of those who chose to turn Queens Evidence against their former comrades were principally motivated by the compensation packages offered by the government, and a desire to avoid long spells in prison, rather than by repentance, and were thus discredited in court by defense lawyers (Jamieson, 1993).

Italy was significantly more successful in the application of conversion principals. The two men who pioneered this technique in Italy were Carribineri General Alberto Dalla Chiesa, and (in the case of organized crime) the prosecuting judge Giovanni Falcone. In both cases the techniques they used were similar. Firstly, they would rely to an extent on the demoralization which sets in shortly after capture when a PMVO is no longer able to rely on the support networks of his or her group. In some cases prisoners were—regrettably—mistreated in order to heighten this feeling but other prisoners developed this simply by being held in solitary confinement. The interrogators then spent significant periods of time getting to understand the prisoners they were seeking to turn before starting to interview them. Often the interrogators were chosen because they came from similar social backgrounds and could therefore both identify themselves with the prisoner and have the prisoner identify with them. In all cases, though, successful conversion required the early release of the prisoner combined with witness protection assistance (Hallenstein, 1984).

Spain, Northern Ireland, and Italy also employed an intermediate approach which proved vital in defeating terrorism in Italy and to a lesser extent in Spain and Northern Ireland. This was disassociation, where facilities were created for prisoners who chose to renounce violence but did not immediately want to take the step of actively turning informer. From a counter-insurgency perspective, this created a procedure which induced terrorists to turn themselves in, as well as perhaps eventually to take the further step of providing information to the authorities about their former comrades in arms (Hallenstein, 1984).

CONCLUSION: IMPLICATIONS FOR CONTEMPORARY PRISON POLICY AND PRACTICE

Law and Policy

The current global political situation makes it likely that for the foreseeable future many Western democracies will have to address the issue of dealing with PMVOs. The U.S. has favoured classifying noncitizens involved in such actions as illegal combatants and imprisoning them in the U.S. military base in Guantánamo Bay, Cuba, or in secret "rendition" prisons in other parts of the world (Stolberg, 2006). Governments should be wary of this approach because of its potential to portray these PMVOs as martyrs to their political causes, as well as the potential for abuse to occur in these isolated circumstances. As the campaigns in Northern Ireland and elsewhere have shown, the very treatment of prisoners will be utilized by terrorist groups for propaganda purposes. Hard-line approaches have sometimes served to exacerbate problems. For example, the execution of Basque PMVOs in 1975 resulted in the retaliatory assassinations of nine members of the Spanish security forces within two weeks (von Tangen Page, 1998).

In Italy and Northern Ireland (as well as in the Israel-Palestine conflicts) the release of PMVOs has been an important aspect of the peace processes. While this may seem unthinkable to some at the current moment, prison policymakers should never forget that PMVOs are pawns in larger political processes. Accordingly, should the release of such prisoners prove politically expedient, it will occur. Similarly, political show trials that are not internationally recognized as fair and impartial may backfire dramatically. For example, in 1970 members of ETA were tried for the murder of a prominent Spanish police officer. Six of the defendants were sentenced to death. The trial was seen in the Basque country and much of the rest of the world to be unfair. The resulting international storm of condemnation forced the Spanish authorities to commute the sentences to life imprisonment. All six were released within six years of this trial (von Tangen Page, 1998).

It would be unfortunate if lessons learnt the hard way in Europe were not absorbed by the current generation of penal policymakers. In essence, these lessons are characterized by the need for a pragmatic approach, involving a range of options for dealing with PMVOs. Those options may involve a combination of soft- and hard-line approaches, up to and including, releasing these individuals under some circumstances, but excluding those harsh treatments which are both prohibited under international law, e.g., the Geneva Conventions (Diplomatic Conference for the Establishment of International Conventions for the Protection of Victims of War, 1949), and which have been shown to be counterproductive. Intermediate options, such as conversion or disassociation, may prove viable, while the extreme measure of segregation may be necessary (as well as acceptable to the PMVO group) under some circumstances. In all cases, policymakers must give consideration to the potential impact that treatment of PMVOs may have in terms of the larger political conflict in particular, and on world opinion in general.

Correctional Mental Health Practice

It appears likely that PMVOs will comprise a meaningful, if not sizeable, element of the populations of Western prison systems over the next several years. Accordingly, Western mental health practitioners and policymakers will need to consider the legitimate mental health needs these individuals may have as well as the security and management problems they will present. There are several interrelated issues concerning which mental health practitioners' particular expertise may be of value, whether they are consulting or working directly with PMVOs. In brief, these include: (1) behaviors that impact security, (2) promoting the disassociation or conversion of PMVOs (similar in principle to the process of prison gang renunciation or "deganging" [National Major Gang Task Force, n.d.]) and preventing the radicalization of other inmates, (3) providing standard mental health services to these offenders, and (4) the ethical issues that may be specific to this group.

Among the consultation issues that involve PMVOs are hunger strikes and suicide attempts, events that correctional mental health professionals are commonly tasked with preventing or resolving. Notable among PMVOs in this regard have been the IRA and, more recently, the detainees in Guantánamo, Cuba. In 1981, a series of protests, mainly against their status as common criminals (rather than as political prisoners or prisoners of war), culminated in a hunger strike by IRA members at the Maze/Long Kesh Prison near Belfast, Northern Ireland. Before it ended, 10 of the protestors starved themselves to death (Beresford, 1997). Detainees at the military prison in Guantánamo, Cuba, went on a well-publicized hunger strike over a period of several weeks in the summer of 2005, to call attention to their confinement without trial and the circumstances in which they were being kept. Estimates as to the total number of participants during this period varied between 105 and 200. Some had to be force-fed (Lewis, 2005b). Further, three Guantánamo prisoners committed suicide on the same day in June, 2006, apparently in protest against their confinement. This followed a series of suicide attempts by 23 detainees that took place during an 8-day period in August of 2003 (Risen & Golden, 2006). Given that their cause is political, it is in the interest of PMVOs to attempt to use the media to focus attention on their plight and to gain sympathy for their cause. Doing so increases the potential political impact of these actions and the need to manage and resolve them successfully.

Practitioners may have extremely limited access to PMVOs. For security reasons, these inmates may be placed in so-called "supermax" prisons. These are facilities in which inmates are commonly kept in isolation–the ultimate safeguard against recruitment of other inmates to PMVOs' causes. For example, PMVOs, including Zacharias Moussaoui, the would-be "20th hijacker" in the September 11th plot; Ted Kaczynski, the "Unabomber;" Richard Reid, the British Muslim convert known as the "shoe bomber;" and Terry Nichols, a co-conspirator, with Timothy McVeigh, in the 1993 bombing of the Murrah Federal Building; have all been housed in the administrative maximum security federal prison in Florence, Colorado. In this facility, prisoners have no contact with each other and are restricted to their cells except for one hour per day of recreation (Associated Press, 2006). This form of confinement may cause its own emotional distress. Haney (2003) reported the results of interviews with 100 inmates confined in the Pelican Bay supermax state prison in California, and determined (albeit on the basis of self-report) that the respondents experienced extremely high levels of psychological disturbance, including incidence rates for anxiety of 91 percent and 88 percent for headaches. Hence, prolonged confinement in such a facility might be expected to result in psychological deterioration even in a relatively resilient individual. Further, the possibility of emotional problems such as post-traumatic stress disorder acquired as a function of mistreatment must be considered. These may constitute most of the presenting problems for mental health professionals treating these populations. There seems little indication that individuals with serious preexisting mental illnesses (e.g., schizophrenia, major affective disorders) constitute any significant percentage of the ranks of those committed to terrorist activities (Hudson, 1999).

However, even where PMVOs are maintained in isolation units, it is possible to provide assessment and treatment services. Telehealth, a general term for the delivery of health care services via electronic media (e.g., telephone, e-mail, but, increasingly, interactive television), can connect provider and patient, although they may be in separate rooms, buildings, or even separate facilities (Magaletta, Dennery & Ax, 2005). Correctional telehealth systems offer the potential to link PMVOs with service providers who speak their language and are familiar with their culture, in the event such practitioners are not available locally.[5] This medium may also promote security by providing a means by which these individuals can communicate directly to staff their willingness to consider converting, disassociating, or informing on their cohorts. Information they divulge may prevent further terrorist incidents. However, PMVOs will usually have been out of combat for months or years by the time they are sentenced to prison. Hence, they are more likely to be able to promote the safety and security of all inmates and staff in their respective facilities by sharing current information concerning activities (e.g., assaults, suicides) planned by other members of their respective groups.

Given greater access, practitioners are obviously better able to provide traditional mental health services to the extent that PMVOs desire or, at a min-

---

5. A recent US government report noted the lack of qualified translators for monitoring the mail and phone calls of terrorists and other high-risk federal prisoners (Office of the Inspector General, 2006). Given the insufficient availability of individuals who can accommodate fundamental security needs, it seems more likely that telehealth will be of greater value. This technology offers the potential to leverage the skills of those presumably few individuals who have both the language fluency and provider qualifications to offer effective mental health services, and, via telehealth, can do so at multiple sites.

imum, accept them. They are simultaneously in a better position to foster conversion and disassociation missions as a therapeutic relationship develops. There is no inherent, inevitable ethical conflict in this regard; in fact, security and service provision missions may be quite compatible. Certainly, to the extent that any kind of trust can be developed between therapist and patient, the likelihood that the latter may also become a useful and willing *super-grass* informant increases. However, in this regard, there is the need to make clear to these individuals, as it would be to any patient, the nature of the therapist's loyalties and responsibilities, as well as the limits of therapeutic confidentiality. In promoting the conversion of PMVOs one must enter into a dialogue with the prisoners in a way in which their core beliefs are discussed and addressed. It is also important to keep in mind that they may be relatively intelligent, politically sophisticated individuals who are not in prison due to simple greed but rather because of their ideological beliefs (von Tangen Page, 1998).[6] They are at present a poorly understood population. As such, PMVOs constitute a worthy focus for further research by correctional mental health professionals.

In concluding this chapter, a further note on ethical considerations is in order. Subsequent to the events of September 11, 2001, Western governments began arresting and detaining suspected terrorists, particularly those espousing radical Islamic causes, in considerable numbers. Subsequent to the discovery of abuses taking place at the military facilities in Guantánamo, Cuba, and Abu Ghraib, Iraq, American health care professional associations reviewed the ethical considerations of their members' involvement in the interrogations of detainees. The American Psychiatric Association issued a blanket prohibition (American Psychiatric Association, 2006). The American Psychological Association, on the other hand, affirmed a place for psychologists in consultative roles in interrogations, provided they act in accordance with their ethical code, further noting the potential value of such services in promoting national security (American Psychological Association, 2005). The American Medical Association adopted a similarly nuanced position which prohibited direct participation (Ray, 2006).

Subsequent to the American Psychiatric Association's policy statement, Pentagon officials shifted their policy to use only psychologists in their interrogations at Guantánamo (Lewis, 2005a). This resulted in unfavorable publicity for the profession of psychology. The American Psychological Association's

---

6. Lyons and Harbison (1986) compared political and nonpolitical murderers in Northern Ireland and identified two key differences. First the political prisoners tended to be of average intelligence compared to criminal prisoners who were of below average intelligence. A second factor was the role of intoxication in their crimes: generally political murderers were sober when they carried out their attacks, whereas "common" criminals were often intoxicated.

qualified position on interrogations resulted in accusations of "aiding torturers" (Wessells, 2006). Nor were psychologists alone in the spotlight of national scrutiny. Physicians who had allegedly been involved in treating abused prisoners at Abu Ghraib were admonished for apparent failures to come forward and inform the authorities of the abuses of which they had seen evidence (Bloche, 2004). Albeit public opinion, favorable or unfavorable, is no absolute arbiter of ethical behavior, it may serve as one external benchmark—a "reality check"—against which those working with any incarcerated populations may measure their attitudes and actions.

The interrogations at Guantánamo and Abu Ghraib are extreme examples of the situations in which correctional mental health professionals' expertise may be sought, and the ethical and moral dilemmas they confront. Their duties and responsibilities are more likely to involve post-trial PMVOs who will be housed for lengthy periods of time. However, the abuses which led to the issuance of these guidelines should serve as a precautionary note to everyone who is directly involved in the care and custody of PMVOs. It would suit correctional mental health professionals to formulate ethical guidelines specific to this population. The *Hamdan v. Rumsfeld* Supreme Court decision of 2006 affirmed the relevance of international law to the treatment of prisoners under the control and custody of the United States. In seeking to set and abide by the highest ethical standards, those providing mental health services to PMVOs in all nations should examine their own potential nationalistic biases and countertransference issues, and consider input from a variety of sources, including human rights groups, such as Amnesty International and Human Rights Watch, whose objective interest is the well-being of all prisoners.

REFERENCES

18 USC § 2331. Retrieved December 18, 2006, from http://frwebgate.access.gpo.gov/cgi-bin/getdoc.cgi?dbname=browse_usc&docid=Cite:+18USC2331

American Psychiatric Association. (2006, May 22). APA passes position statement barring psychiatric participation in interrogation of detainees. Retrieved October 31, 2006, from http://psych.org/news_room/press_releases/06-36PositionState mentInterrogation.pdf

American Psychological Association. (2005, June). Report of the American Psychological Association presidential task force on psychological ethics and national security. Retrieved October 31, 2006, from http://www.apa.org/releases/PENS TaskForceReportFinal.pdf

Associated Press. (2006, May 13). *Moussaoui starts serving sentence at Colorado's supermax prison.* Retrieved November 3, 2006, from http://www.foxnews.com/printer_ friendly_story/0,3566,195354,00.html

Beresford, D. (1997). *Ten men dead.* New York: Atlantic Monthly Press.

Bloche, M. G. (2004, June 10). Physician, turn thyself in. *New York Times,* p. A29.

Clarke, L. (1987). *Broadening the battlefield: The H-blocks and the rise of Sinn Féin.* Dublin, Ireland: Gill & Macmillan.

Crawford, C. (1999). *Defenders or criminals? Loyalist prisoners and criminalisation.* Belfast, Northern Ireland: The Blackstaff Press.

Cuthbertson, I. M. (2004). Prisons and the education of terrorists. *World Policy Journal, 21* (3), 1–14.

Diplomatic Conference for the Establishment of International Conventions for the Protection of Victims of War. (1949, August 12). *Geneva Convention relative to the treatment of prisoners of war.* Retrieved June 14, 2006, from http://www.unhchr.ch/html/menu3/b/91.htm

Dray, P. (2003). *At the hands of persons unknown: The lynching of Black America.* New York: Modern Library.

Frantz, D. (2000, December 25). Behind Turkey's prison rage, radicals that rule the inmates. *New York Times,* p. A8.

Glasser, S. B. (2005, April 27). U.S. figures show sharp global rise in terrorism. *Washington Post.* Retrieved September 3, 2006, from http://www.washingtonpost.com/wp/dyn/content/article/2005/04/26/AR2005042601623.html

Gorriti, G. (1999). *The Shining Path: A history of the millenarian war in Peru.* (R. Kirk, Trans.) Chapel Hill, NC: (Original work published 1990)

Hallenstein, D. (1984, April 8). Walking corpses. *Sunday Times Magazine,* p. 13–15.

Hamdan v. Rumsfeld, 05-184 US (2006).

Hamm, M. S. (1997). *Apocalypse in Oklahoma: Waco and Ruby Ridge revenged.* Boston: Northeastern University Press.

Haney, C. (2003). Mental health issues in long-term solitary and "Supermax" confinement. *Crime & Delinquency, 49,* 124–156.

Hudson, R. A. (1999, September). *The sociology and psychology of terrorism: Who becomes a terrorist and why?* Washington, DC: Library of Congress, Federal Research Division. Retrieved November 5, 2006, from http://www.fas.org/irp/threat/frd.html

Jamieson, A. (1993) *Collaboration, new legal and judicial procedures for countering terrorism* (Conflict Studies Monograph No. 257). London: Research Institute for the Study of Conflict and Terrorism.

Kitson, F. (1977). *Bunch of Five.* London: Faber and Faber .

Lewis, N.A. (2005a, June 7). Military alters the makeup of interrogation advisers. *The New York Times,* p. A 20.

Lewis, N.A. (2005b, September 18). Widespread hunger strike at Guantánamo. *The New York Times,* p. 20.

Lyons, H. A & Harbinson, H. J. (1986). A comparison of political and non-political murderers in Northern Ireland 1974–1984. *Journal of Medicine, Science and Law, 26,* 193–198.

Magaletta, P. R., Dennery, C. H., & Ax, R. K. (2005). Telehealth – a future for correctional health care. In S. Stojkovic (Ed.), *Managing special populations in jails and prisons* (pp. 20-1–20-14). Kingston, NJ: Civic Research Institute.

McLean, R. (2004, October 31). Spanish prisons provide pool of recruits for radical Islam. *The New York Times,* p. 8.

Moloney, E. (2002). *A secret history of the IRA.* London: W.W. Norton and Company.

National Major Gang Task Force. (n.d.). *A model format for establishing a renunciation plan for incarcerated inmates.* Retrieved November 5, 2006, from http://www.nmgtf.org/whats_new/pdf/Renunciation%20Policy.pdf.

Office of the Inspector General. (2004, April). *A review of the Federal Bureau of Prisons' selection of Muslim religious services providers.* Retrieved June 17, 2006, from http://www.doj.gov/oig/special/0404/final.pdf.

Office of the Inspector General (2006, September). *The Federal Bureau of Prisons' monitoring of mail for high-risk inmates.* Retrieved November 3, 2006, from http://www.usdoj.gov/oig/reports/BOP/e0609/final.pdf.

Post, J. M., Sprinzak, E., & Denny, L. M. (2003). The terrorists in their own words: Interviews with 35 incarcerated Middle Eastern terrorists. *Terrorism and Political Violence, 15,* 171–184.

Ray, P. (2006, June 12). *New AMA ethical policy opposes direct physician participation in interrogation* [Press release]. Retrieved November 5, 2006, from http://www.ama-assn.org/ama/pub/category/16446.html

Risen, J., & Golden, T. (2006, June 11). Three prisoners commit suicide at Guantánamo. *The New York Times,* p. A1, A24.

Shanker, T. (2006, February 15). Abu Ghraib called incubator for terrorists. *New York Times,* p. A12.

Short Legal Definition. (1992); cited in United Nations Office on Drugs and Crime (n.d.). *Definitions of terrorism.* Retrieved December 1, 2006, from http://www.unodc.org/terrorism_definitions.html

Stolberg, S.G. (2006, September 7). President moves 14 held in secret to Guantánamo· Seeks tribunals. *The New York Times,* p. A1, A20.

Sullivan, J. (1988). *ETA and Basque nationalism.* London: Routledge.

Thompson, R. (1966). *Defeating Communist insurgency: Experiences from Malaya and Vietnam.* London: Chato & Windus.

von Tangen Page, M. (1998). *Prisons, peace, and terrorism: Penal policy in the reduction of political violence in Northern Ireland, Italy, and the Spanish Basque Country, 1968–1997.* New York: St. Martin's Press, Inc.

von Tangen Page, M. (2000). A most unpalatable part: The release of politically motivated violent offenders. In M. Cox, A. Guelke, & F. Steven (Eds.), *A farewell to arms: From 'long war' to long peace in Northern Ireland* (pp. 93–103). Manchester, UK: Manchester University Press.

Wessells, M. (2006, August 16, 2006). Psychologists aiding torturers. Retrieved October 31, 2006, from http://www.tompaine.com/articles/2006/08/16/psychologists_aiding_torturers.php

Who is Richard Reid? (2001, December 28). Retrieved November 26, 2006, from http://news.bbc.co.uk/1/hi/uk/1731568.stm

Chapter 11

PRISON GANGS[1]

JOYCE K. CONLEY AND DAWN ZOBEL

INTRODUCTION

This chapter has two broad purposes. First, it provides information about prison gangs with respect to their inception, culture, and organizational structure. Second, it discusses the impact of prison gangs on correctional operations and management. Prison gangs derived many of their traditions, customs, organizational hierarchies, criminal activities, and symbols from the street gang philosophy, as they established themselves within the constraints of individual prison systems. As such, a fundamental knowledge of street gang philosophy has been provided in this chapter to assist the reader in developing a better understanding of these correlations. Ultimately, it will become evident that the issues involved in understanding and resolving the problems that these groups present transcend national boundaries and call for an understanding of cultural diversity and international cooperation of law enforcement agencies (Florida Department of Corrections [FLDOC], 2003; Walker, 2006a).

GANGS

In the absence of a nationally agreed upon definition, the term "gang" generally describes a group of individuals who frequently gather, share an identity, use common symbols, claim control over neighborhood territory, and

---

1. The views and opinions expressed in this chapter are those of the authors only and do not necessarily represent the policies or opinions of the Federal Bureau of Prisons or the Department of Justice.

engage in illegal activities. Membership can vary in number from a small group of individuals to many thousands (Walker, 2006a).

Historically, nearly every country has been impacted by gangs with the possible exception of those that have successfully impeded immigration and freedom of assembly. At the conclusion of the American Revolution, both New York and Philadelphia served as inception sites for the establishment of youth gangs in the United States. Afterward, Hispanic street gangs came into existence in response to impoverished economic conditions, prejudice, and racism. Irish street gangs were formed in New York in the early 1800s for similar reasons. During periods of high migration, there has been a corresponding increase in both gang membership and gang-related violence (National Alliance of Gang Investigators Association [NAGIA], 2005).

As gangs emerged in the U.S., establishment, unification, and recruitment typically occurred in large metropolitan areas. Today, violent street gangs occupy communities of all sizes with representation in urban, suburban, and rural areas. Few regions in the U.S. have remained untouched as gang activity continues to flourish (Allender, 2001; NAGIA, 2005).

The 2005 National Gang Threat Assessment Report (NAGIA, 2005) has provided useful information to law enforcement and corrections about gangs and their criminal activities. This report is the result of collaboration between law enforcement agencies and provides a broad range of information extracted from surveys and agency-specific intelligence. Grant funding was provided for this project through the U.S. Department of Justice's Bureau of Justice Assistance. According to this report, there are no national standards for gang-related data collection or a universal definition as to what constitutes gang-related crime, making it difficult to accurately assess the impact of gang violence in the U.S. The Federal Bureau of Investigation (FBI) has instituted use of the National Crime Information Center (NCIC), in an effort to capture gang data along with other criminal activity. NCIC serves as a computerized index of criminal justice information pertaining to criminal record histories, fugitives, stolen properties, missing persons, and similar data. The information can be accessed by federal, state, local law enforcement and other criminal justice agencies for update or review (NAGIA, 2005).

The FBI has also encouraged the corrections' community to enter information for individuals known to be members of either a Security Threat Group (STG) or a Disruptive Group (DG), when such classification specifically warrants inclusion in the Violent Gang or Terrorist Organization File (VGTOF). The VGTOF was implemented in 1994 and serves as a central repository for identifying information about violent criminal gang and terrorist organization members that can be used to assist and protect the law enforcement community and the public. Unfortunately, there are no mandatory reporting requirements and STG and DG validation standards vary significantly between agencies, undermining efforts to acquire uniform data (NAGIA, 2005).

Definitions regarding STG and DG classifications vary among correctional entities with respect to the number of individuals who must be involved, participant ideology, and the level of threat that is posed. Generally speaking, however, STG and DG classifications are defined as, any group of three or more inmates who are members of the same street or prison gang and/or engage in the same extremist political or ideological activities, potentially disrupting prison security (i.e., promote hatred, racism, or rage) or invoke recurring or disruptive behavior, such as a violation of disciplinary rules where such violations are openly known or confer a benefit to the group (Knox, 2005). Some prison systems use STG assignments exclusively for prison gang classification, allowing other gang members to escape adherence to the more stringent monitoring controls (Forsythe & Petersilia, 2006).

The 2002 National Youth Gang Survey conducted by the National Youth Gang Center is generally recognized and cited by the gang intelligence community as the primary statistical resource for gang data, though some experts believe the reported numbers to be very conservative (NAGIA, 2005). The survey estimated there are 21,500 youth gangs in the U.S. with a total of 731,500 members. The survey concluded that all cities with a population greater than 250,000, and 87 percent of cities with a population of 100,000 to 249,000, reported youth gang problems. Approximately 31 percent of the respondents conveyed community reluctance in acknowledging the existence of a gang problem. The survey further stated those cities that do actively address these concerns only did so after a high profile gang activity had occurred (NAGIA, 2005).

GENERAL TRENDS

General information about gangs and their activities includes the following points:

- Gangs frequently collaborate with organized crime groups to enhance financial gains stemming from drug trafficking, protection, and other criminal activities (NAGIA, 2005).
- Gang use of computers and other sophisticated technologies is on the rise. Gangs are using cell phones, police scanners, voice monitoring devices, and surveillance equipment to plan criminal activity and to monitor or obstruct law enforcement investigations. Computers are used to follow court proceedings, intimidate witnesses, and track the financial holdings of the gang.

Internet outlets are developed for gang recruitment, advertisement, web-gaming, and prostitution, and have served as a sales outlet for gang paraphernalia and black market movie and music products. Other uses include message boards, chat rooms, and use of Remote Access Trojans (RATs) and e-mail scams to acquire personal information leading to identity theft. RATs are software programs that allow computer access by an unauthorized user(s) through an Internet connection. The unauthorized user(s) can then view and change computer files and functions, monitor and record activity, and access other computers or systems to engage in criminal activity. The Internet has recently become a new venue for individuals to spotlight themselves and their gang affiliations (NAGIA, 2005; Coll & Glasser, 2006; Walker, 2006b).

- Hispanic gang membership is growing significantly, fostering migration and expansion throughout the U.S. and other countries. This is also true of gang cultures that originated in California, resulting in the establishment of new jurisdictions in rural communities. NAGIA (2005) reports that law enforcement agencies are challenged with issues relating to differentiation and identification among the various gangs.

- Rap music often carries gang-related messaging and is utilized as a recruitment tool, particularly among inner-city youth (NAGIA, 2005).

- Tattoos, clothing lines, hand symbols, and garment colors were traditionally used to signify gang allegiance. Veteran gang members are now trying to discourage tattoos and garment colors to avoid detection by law enforcement and corrections officials (NAGIA, 2005).

- Female gang members are now engaging in a more participatory role, frequently assisting with actual operations. This may often be an internal effort to keep the gang mission intact and focused during periods of high level incarceration among the male gang members. There is a nominal increase in the number of gangs with exclusive female membership (NAGIA, 2005).

- Assessment of female gangs relies predominantly on law enforcement reporting, field studies, and surveys of at risk adolescents. While these methods of data collection are far from accurate, experts believe females account for approximately 8%–11% of all gang members. In general, female gang activity is less violent than that of their male counterparts and often involves property crime (Moore & Hagedorn, 2001; NAGIA, 2005).

- Gang activity has increased on Native American reservations, due to remote locations, and in some cases, enhanced border access (NAGIA, 2005).

- Reduced funding of community task forces has impeded local programs and interagency partnerships in combating gang activity (NAGIA, 2005).

- Drugs remain a primary income source for both street and prison gangs (NAGIA, 2005).

MIGRATION AND TRANSNATIONAL GANGS

Relocation attributed to employment or confinement has contributed to gang migration and expanded territories. Gangs are often formed at the new location where local residents and immigrant populations become the focus of recruitment endeavors. Veteran gang members releasing from prison into the local community will often take a leadership role in the development of local, hybrid gangs. Community denial or ignorance allows violent gang activity and membership to thrive unchecked (FLDOC, 2003; Ribando, 2005).

Gangs have traditionally served as an outlet for socially marginalized youth, providing opportunities for socialization and a sense of belonging (Allender, 2001). Gang activity typically includes defending territory, armed robbery, extortion, alien smuggling, prostitution, and drug or firearm smuggling. Some gangs have evolved into informally affiliated, transnational criminal networks, providing opportunities of heightened responsibility for young collaborators. Two major transnational gangs—18th Street or M-18 and their main rival, the Mara Salvatrucha or MS-13—both operating in Central America with ties to the U.S., will serve to illustrate these transnational criminal networks (Ribando, 2005).

Eighteenth Street experienced rapid expansion in Los Angeles during the 1960s and MS-13 in the 1980s. These gangs have established links to an estimated 130,000 to 300,000 members in Mexico and Central America and have migrated across the U.S. with representation in major cities and rural communities on the East Coast. Deportation processes, associations with experienced criminals in U.S. prisons, and migration rules deemed ineffective in both Mexico and Central America, are cited as major contributors in facilitating the transnational nature of these gangs (NAGIA, 2005; Ribando, 2005).

Eighteenth Street was formed in the 1960s by Mexican immigrants residing in Los Angeles. They were the first Hispanic gang to accept members from other states and other racial/ethnic groups. Absence of racial barriers and focused recruitment of elementary and middle school students ensured rapid internal expansion. The gang eventually migrated up the West Coast and throughout the Midwest to the East Coast and Central America (NAGIA, 2005; Ribando, 2005).

MS-13 was originated in Los Angeles in the 1980s by Salvadorans seeking to escape the civil war in El Salvador. Many of the Salvadoran children who migrated with their parents had been raised in violent surroundings in their homeland, often requiring them to defend themselves and/or family possessions at a very early age. Poor immigrants arriving in the U.S. typically settled in the impoverished sections of Los Angeles, making them easy victims for the Mexican gangs. Eventually they banded together in a "mara" or "posse" comprised of Salvatruchas, or "street-tough" Salvadorans to combat victimization. As these gangs sought to expand, priority recruitment was given to acquiring former paramilitaries from El Salvador, in an effort to capitalize on their weapons training. In response to gang activity and growth, law enforcement coordinated mass detention and deportation missions. The deportees quickly established MS-13 outposts in El Salvador, Honduras, and Guatemala to counter these efforts (NAGIA, 2005; Ribando, 2005; Valdez, 1998, 2000).

According to the FBI (2006), current gang intelligence estimates indicate that MS-13 has over 10,000 members in 33 states in the U.S. with potentially tens of thousands more in Central America. U.S. law enforcement has been faulted for the recent growth and expansion of MS-13, as authorities shifted their focus and resources from gang management to antiterrorism following the 2001 World Trade Center bombings. In retrospect, it appears MS-13 seized the opportunity to advance membership growth and geographical expansion, while establishing new outlets of criminal activity (Johnson & Muhlhausen, 2005; Ribando, 2005). The FBI considers MS-13 to be the fastest-growing, most violent, and least understood of the nation's street gangs. This knowledge has led to the creation of the MS-13 National Gang Task Force, which is tasked with the coordination of investigations, intelligence, and prosecutions of MS-13 and other transnational gangs, both nationally and internationally (FBI, 2006).

Recent evidence suggests gangs are encouraging members to join the military as a way of learning urban warfare techniques (Department of Justice [DOJ], 2005; Main, 2006). Statistics reflect approximately 85 percent of new military personnel are recruited from inner-city youth populations. With the ongoing war effort, the military has recently admitted to a lowering of the eligibility standards in an effort to meet recruitment quotas to include frequent use of waivers for criminal background checks; acceptance of individuals with five tattoos or less (irrespective of the contextual symbolism); and waivers stating tattoos are not gang-related when the prospective recruit has more than five. Reports of graffiti resembling U.S. gang symbolism have been observed throughout Iraq, defacing both buildings and equipment. Several military leaders have reported that suspect personnel intentionally display tattoos to signify their gang allegiance and verbally admit to membership when asked. This has prompted some concern that such behavior may cause dissension or breach of trust amongst military personnel (Main, 2006, 2007; DOJ, 2005).

In an effort to curb gang activities, many Central American countries have instituted aggressive anti-gang laws with enhanced sentencing for gang-related convictions. Countries most impacted by gang activity include Honduras, El Salvador, and Guatemala (Ribando, 2005). Honduras passed legislation in 2003, known as *Mano Dura* (Firm Hand) instituting a maximum 12-year sentence for gang membership. In 2004, sentencing under this law was further enhanced to 30 years. The legislation was initially well received by the public, but highly opposed by human rights groups. The initial impact netted a notable decline in gang-related criminal activity; however, there are now serious concerns surrounding the potential for prison overcrowding. This concern was heightened in May, 2004, when 104 inmates (predominantly gang members) were killed in an overcrowded San Pedro Sula prison during a fire (Ribando, 2005). El Salvador adopted *Super Mano Dura* (Super Firm Hand) in July 2004, increasing the penalty for gang membership up to five years in prison. Opposition was voiced by many, including the United Nations, with particular disagreement focusing on convictions of minors under the age of 12 (Ribando, 2005).

Several other Central American countries are developing prevention initiatives as proactive strategies for reducing gang membership. In September 2004, Panama adopted *Mano Amiga* (Friendly Hand) as a prevention program to encourage alternative outlets for at-risk youth, ages 14–17 years. The program includes theater and sports activities for more than 10,000 youth. Nicaragua has instituted a youth crime prevention program incorporating family, school, and community interventions. Other Central American countries seem to be integrating harsher sentencing with reform programming and at a regional level, there appears to be a strong push toward coordinated security efforts, enhanced information and intelligence sharing, and pursuit of funding in support of former gang members seeking job training opportunities. The U.S. is a contributing presence in these partnerships through both law enforcement and prevention efforts (Ribando, 2005; Johnson & Muhlhausen, 2005).

The U.S. has similar concerns regarding redress of transnational gang activity. This has prompted Congress and the Administration to evaluate the current methods used for the control and management of the complex problems posed by gangs. For example, Senate Bill 853 (2005), the North American Cooperative Security Act (and similar legislation) would effectively establish a unified effort between the U.S., Canada, and Mexico in the tracking and deportation of individuals engaged in gang activity. Other measures, such as the Gang Deterrence and Community Protection Act of 2005, House Resolution 1279 (2005), if enacted, would amend the criminal code to modify and expand prohibitions against, and penalties for, criminal street gang activity. Among the sanctions for gang activities would be the expanded use of the death penalty, enhanced mandatory sentencing for gang members who commit certain crimes to a minimum term of ten years, and reduced age (16 or 17 years) at which gang members can be sentenced as adults. Under this proposed legislation, street gangs are defined as groups of three or more individuals who commit two or more designated crimes. If enacted, these judicial changes will have a significant impact on the criminal justice system with respect to population growth and management, operational costs, security, housing, program development, medical/mental health services, and an array of community services in their provision of secondary support services to corrections (Ribando, 2005; Johnson & Muhlhausen, 2005).

As noted earlier, in December 2004, the FBI created a special task force focused on standardizing monitoring procedures and addressing all issues associated with MS-13 (FBI, 2006). In February 2005, a Liaison Office was created in El Salvador to coordinate information sharing and gang management efforts within El Salvador. The U.S. is seeking to employ a prevention strategy to deter gang membership/activity, resulting in a collaboration between the United States Agency for International Development and the DOJ International Criminal Investigative Training Assistance Program in establishing a community crime prevention program in over 200 municipalities in El Salvador, with future plans to expand the program to Guatemala (Johnson & Muhlhausen, 2005).

Each of these initiatives sets the tone for the future of corrections in preparing for population growth in terms of both numbers and sentence length. Correctional management strategies will need to be developed and expanded to address such specialized gang-related issues as how best to house rival gang members and prevent or minimize gang recruitment in prisons and jails. Specialized cognitive-behavioral programs and services will also need to be developed that challenge the "gang mentality" and encourage pro-social values. Since these programs often link to the family/community matrix, the success of this task may be further complicated by the geographical distances of family and community from the place of confinement.

PRISON GANG INITIATION

Prison gang initiation is typically used to test the physiological and psychological strength and value of a prospective inductee. Initiation practices can vary in severity, but ultimately serve to provide reasonable assurance that the gang is not compromised by an informant. Gang membership may include "blood in-blood out" rituals, meaning a blood loss must be sustained by the inductee or to another by the inductee. Another ritual is "the line" where new recruits must walk between two lines of gang members as they are repeatedly kicked and punched, requiring them to remain upright to conclusion. Other rites of passage, conducted in the street, have included Russian roulette (holding a revolver loaded with one bullet to the head, spinning the cylinder, and pulling the trigger), drive-by shootings, or murder (FLDOC, 2003; Lewis, 2006; Walker, 2006b.)

Within prison gangs, there exists an expectation that each gang member will remain loyal to the gang for life and will continue to support other incarcerated gang members when they are released from prison. Support is typically generated through proceeds from drug sales or other criminal activities. Since the penalty for leaving the gang may involve death or severe injury, efforts by prison officials to institute gang renunciation or de-ganging programs are severely impeded (FLDOC, 2003; Lewis, 2006; Walker, 2006b.)

STREET GANG INITIATION

Street gang initiation is slightly less severe. For female inductees, "sex in" which equates to forced sex with many or all (male) members most often serves as the right of passage. For males, a severe assault or "beat down" of an individual is used to "make your bones" as a member. Typically, a prospective inductee is "sponsored" by another gang member. As such, the sponsor supervises the act that fulfills the initiation right, ensuring the inductee makes a "righteous" or respectful effort. If the inductee does not complete the act, it is normally the responsibility of the sponsor to eliminate both the inductee and the person marked for the assault. If the gang member ever becomes disloyal or otherwise falls from grace, it is considered a poor reflection on the sponsor (Lewis, 2006; Walker, 2006b).

GANG STRUCTURE

Each gang maintains its own internal leadership structure. Some general terms typically used to delineate the hierarchy include:

- **Hardcore, Boss, Veterano, General:** Provides leadership and direction, has full knowledge of gang activities, is influential to the mission, is usually armed, and is completely loyal. Represents approximately ten percent of the gang.
- **Regular member, Soldier, Gangster:** Spends the majority of his time in the companionship of other members, has knowledge of gang activities, is loyal, has made a formal commitment to the gang through the established ritual, is usually armed.
- **Associate, Peripheral:** Is less likely to participate in acts of violence, may assist with issues following the gang activity such as weapon disposal, displays wavering loyalties with a focus on self, aligns with one or more members, has a tendency to be involved in more frivolous acts than actual gang activity.

- **Wannabe, Emulator:** Tends to be younger, is impressed by the gang image, attempts to link themselves to the gang to appear important, and adopts mannerisms and symbolism to advertise association (Lewis, 2006 & Walker, 2006b).

Corrections intelligence divisions may opt to use a modified hierarchical system to manage STG/DG members. This involves appropriately labeling and defining positional roles within the gang model along with effectively classifying the offender (i.e., accurately reflecting the level to which the individual is embedded in the gang culture and mission). These processes ensure that the offender is confined and managed at a facility commensurate with the threat index posed. Generally speaking, correctional staff must possess an understanding of the various gang structures and dynamics in order to successfully inhibit the gang's ability to impact prison operation or community safety during incarceration (FLDOC, 2003; Lewis, 2006 & Walker, 2006b).

GANG RECRUITMENT

Recruitment efforts may focus on the immediate needs of the gang or be situationally driven. Prison recruitment may provide validation of a member's ongoing commitment to the gang, be an attempt to gain control or power over prison operations, or serve as a protective infrastructure in support of a criminal enterprise. Recruitment tactics can vary, but often include:

- Glorifying gang membership and lifestyle (i.e., adventure, money, sex, or power) to seduce the prospect.
- Intentionally misrepresenting the gang mission to appeal to an individual, particularly those seeking acceptance or having a need to belong.
- Demanding loyalty as repayment after a favor has been rendered.
- Issuing a threat to personal or family member safety or loss of life.

Self recruitment can occur for a myriad of reasons ranging from a glorified perception of gang representation to seeking protection (Allender, 2001; FLDOC, 2003; Lewis, 2006; FLDOC, 2003; Walker, 2006b).

TRADITIONAL PRISON GANGS

Prison gangs can be defined in a number of ways. A typical definition is the following:

A prison gang is an organization which operates within the prison system as a self-perpetuating criminally-oriented entity, consisting of a select group of inmates who have established an organized chain of command and are governed by an established code of conduct. The prison gang has as its goal to conduct gang activities by controlling their prison environment through intimidation and violence directed toward a nonmember. (Forsythe & Petersilia, 2006, p. 2)

While many gangs are represented in correctional facilities, this section describes six in particular. Each of these gangs originated within the prison system and was not imported from existing street gangs. The gangs were formed by inmates confined in the California corrections system during the 1950s, 1960s and 1970s, as protection from inmate predators (FLDOC, 2003; Lewis, 2006; Walker, 2006b).

Aryan Brotherhood (AB)

The AB originated in 1967 in the San Quentin prison as a way of providing White prisoners protection from Black and Hispanic prison groups. The AB adopted a philosophy derived, in part, from a belief in White supremacy and use Norse/Viking symbolism for identification purposes. While membership in the AB is exclusively White, they have been known to establish business affiliations with African Americans as necessary for transactions involving drugs or extortion. The AB also associates with the Mexican Mafia and Hells Angels. Rival gangs include La Nuestra Familia and the Black Guerilla Family. The AB's primary criminal enterprise is drug trafficking.

The prevailing philosophy of the gang is "blood in-blood out." A recruit must murder an individual designated by the AB to prove allegiance to the group and must receive a unanimous vote from all gang members. The AB has numerous associates who follow the tenets of the group and have fulfilled the murder requirement, but who did not receive unanimous support for membership.

AB members releasing from prison are expected to dedicate themselves to supporting incarcerated members. An AB commission consisting of the gang's leadership must approve all major decisions and murders before the act(s) can be executed. Communications with imprisoned committee members are often accomplished through third party correspondence or visitation, either social or legal. In the past AB members were required to be California residents. This afforded the gang maximum control and management of members who violated gang tenets or expectations. Intimidation was easily accomplished, as family ties and love interests were well known to all. More recently, the AB has permitted membership by non-Californians, as AB members release from prisons in other states and establish residency in those states.

The group's inclusion of non-Californians has weakened its ability to control members who turn informant or are remiss in supporting the gang's mission and tenets, as it is not as easy to reach across state boundaries for retaliation.

While AB tattoos may vary, the shamrock with the letters AB and three sixes is the true AB symbol. Only actual AB members can display this symbol. Others who display this symbol without the consent of the gang are subject to murder. Many members have disguised, removed or hidden (hairline or underarms) these tattoos to escape detection by law enforcement (FLDOC, 2003; Lewis, 2006; Walker, 2006b).

Black Guerilla Family (BGF)

Former Black Panther, George Jackson, founded the BGF in 1966. This group was originally called the Black Family or the Black Vanguard and had links with the Black Mafia. Some members were previously aligned with the Black Liberation Army, Symbionese Liberation Army, or Weatherman Underground Organization. Politically active, the BGF was originally formed as a Marxist/Maoist/Leninist revolutionary organization with a declared mission to eliminate racism, maintain dignity in prison, and overthrow the U.S. government. The group's anti-government/anti-official mentality is often depicted by the initials BGF with crossed sabers, shotgun, or black dragons overtaking a prison or prison tower.

The BGF has an all African American membership and requires a death oath pledge for life, which literally means members will die if they attempt to leave the gang or otherwise violate their membership pledge. Gang operations are sustained through a paramilitary organizational structure consisting of a central committee, a "Supreme Leader," and military ranking. The BGF is a national gang, with the majority of its members residing on the east and west coasts. The BGF allies itself with other Black street gangs, the Black Liberation Army, the Weather Underground, and the Symbionese Liberation Army. Their rivals are Aryan Brotherhood, Aryan Brotherhood of Texas, Texas Syndicate, and Mexican Mafia. Black street gang members are often recruited into the BGF during imprisonment (FLDOC, 2003; Lewis, 2006; Walker, 2006b).

La Nuestra Familia (NF)

Originating in California's Soledad prison in the mid 1960s, NF offered protection for young, rural Mexican American inmates from other inmates hailing from Los Angeles and belonging to the Mexican Mafia, a division invoked by the cultural and social differences among urban and rural Mexican Americans. NF engaged in criminal activity to gain control of the contraband entering prison facilities.

NF members are Mexican American or Hispanic inmates and membership is based on a "blood in-blood out" oath extending beyond prison. NF maintains a constitution, paramilitary structure, and membership ranking from soldier to general. Prison and street segments maintain separate organizational chains and typically operate separately as well. NF members may wear red rags as identification symbols. Large tattoos often covering their entire back may include "NF," "LNF," "ENE" or "F" symbols or a sombrero or dagger. The number "14" is used for the letter "N" in representation of Norte or Northern California.

NF's allies are the Northern Structure, believed to be a subsidiary gang, formed to divert the attention of law enforcement. They also maintain a favorable working alliance with the Black Guerilla Family due to their common enemies. Their rivals include the Texas Syndicate, Mexikanemi, F-14, and Aryan Brotherhood (FLDOC, 2003; Lewis, 2006; Walker, 2006b).

Mexican Mafia (EME)

EME began in the late 1950s at the Duel Vocational Center, a California youthful offender facility. It derived from its street gang roots in urban Los Angeles with ethnically pure membership. Primary criminal activities for this group include drug trafficking, extortion, coercion, and internal discipline, often involving murder to gain respect. Wives, girlfriends, and family members are held in high regard within this group for their support in executing drug transactions, illegal financial activities, and mail forwarding operations.

EME adheres to a definitive chain of command, which requires that directives be issued from generals and addressed at the appropriate subordinate level. Styled after the Italian Mafia, EME members are reputed to be well disciplined, obedient to their organizational structure, and compliant with their "blood in-blood out" philosophy. EME is California-based and has significant representation in the federal prison system. Group tattoos include the initials "EME," the Mexican flag with varying symbols such as an eagle or a snake accompanied by the initials "EME," a single hand print typically black in color, or the initials "MM" or "M."

EME allies include Arizona's Old Mexican Mafia, Mexikanemi, New Mexico Syndicate and urban Latino street gangs. They maintain good working relations with the Aryan Brotherhood and provide protection to La Costra Nostra members while in prison. Their main rival is La Nuestra Familia, with whom they allegedly maintain a "kill on sight" motto. Other rivals include Northern Structure, Arizona's New Mexican Mafia, Black Guerilla Family, and Black street gangs (FLDOC, 2003; Lewis, 2006; Walker, 2006b.)

Texas Syndicate (TS)

The TS originated in Folsom Prison in California in the early 1970s and was formed to provide protection to Texas natives against other California-based prison gangs (predominantly the Aryan Brotherhood and Mexican Mafia). This gang has national representation due to strong recruitment efforts and a broader acceptance base, which now includes members from Latin American countries. Identifying tattoos are located on the back side of the right forearm or on the outside calf, neck or chest. The initials "TS" will be present, but may be disguised within the tattoo's design. TS associates include the Texas Mafia and Dirty White Boys and chief rivals are the Aryan Brotherhood, La Nuestra Familia, Mexican Mafia, Mexikanemi, and Mandingo Warriors (FLDOC, 2003; Lewis, 2006; Walker, 2006b).

Neta (Asociacion Nata)

Neta was established in 1970 by an inmate in Rio Pedras Prison, Puerto Rico. Neta was a response to the violence that was occurring between inmates housed in the prison. Netas are extremely patriotic and connected with the Los Macheteros, a revolutionary Puerto Rican group. They oppose being governed by the U.S. and consider themselves oppressed. Each member is expected to bring a minimum of 20 new recruits into the group. Acts of disrespect to the group are typically addressed with violence. Group gatherings occur on the 30th of the month to pay tribute to departed comrades.

Gang identifiers include use of the colors red, white and blue. However, black can be used as a substitute for blue and can be displayed through the wearing of clothing or beads. Probationary members are required to wear white beads until they have proven their dedication. Red represents blood that has or will be shed; white symbolizes peace, harmony and tranquility; and black represents respect for those who have died in service to Neta. Members salute each other by holding the crossed fingers of their right hand over the heart, symbolizing the letter "N" in sign language and signifying unity. Their rivals include the Latin Kings and Solidos. They are active in prison recruitment, but are vigilant in maintaining a low profile (FLDOC, 2003; Lewis, 2006; Walker, 2006b).

CLASSIFICATION OF PRISON GANGS

Defining gang membership for purposes of criminal justice classification can be both difficult and elusive. Membership determinations typically correlate with an individual's level of involvement or dedication to the gang. The process is further hindered by the standard operating procedures and policies used by each agency, as criminal classification is discretionary and typically based on agency need.

For example, the California Department of Corrections and Rehabilitation (CDCR) completes a Notice of Critical Information on any inmate designated as a gang member, affiliate, associate, or defector of the Nuestra Familia, Mexican Mafia, Texas Syndicate, Black Guerilla Family, or Aryan Brotherhood. Gang classification criteria for CDCR includes information derived from self admission, tattoos and symbols, written materials, staff information or information from other agencies, peer associations, confidential sources, commitment offense, legal documents, and debriefing reports (Forsythe & Petersilia, 2006).

The Federal Bureau of Prisons (BOP) evaluates the level of threat posed by an individual or group to the orderly management of the prison. Offenders undergo an assessment process to determine their level of connection and involvement in a gang and/or gang-related activities. Relevant information such as tattoo symbols, correspondence, court records, other official documentation, peer associations, or self-admission may be used for classification purposes (Gaes, Wallace, Gilman, Klein-Saffran, & Suppa, 2002).

Although these two classification systems have notable differences, both correctional agencies have developed classification systems that aid their respective agencies in achieving some degree of control over the gangs that operate within their systems. In addition to inmates who are assigned by these classification systems, a significant number of other inmates who are suspected of gang involvement may also be placed on some level of heightened monitoring by these correctional agencies until their suspected gang affiliations can either be more clearly established or refuted.

CORRECTIONAL DETERRENCE

Since an inmate's motivation in seeking prison gang membership is often based on a perceived need for protection, correctional agencies have incorporated a number of operational practices to increase the safety of inmates and hopefully reduce the need for gang membership. Examples of these practices include: the enhanced use of surveillance cameras, video recording, phone and mail monitoring, increased staff supervision, searches of inmates and their cells for weapons and other contraband, aggressive prosecution of gang-related activity during confinement, isolation and/or transfer of gang leaders, and the use of gang renunciation programs and cognitive-behavior modification programs to alter the gang mentality and foster the development of pro-social values. Several of these approaches are discussed below.

Pelican Bay State Prison in California was activated in 1989 as a super maximum security prison to house prison gang leaders and other extremely violent or disruptive prisoners. These individuals are confined in a Special Housing Unit (SHU) limiting movement, contact, and programming. Offenders with STG classification for gang affiliation can be housed until release, unless they become inactive for five years or renounce their membership and "debrief," which equates to sharing pertinent information about the gang and its members (CDCR, 2005).

The Texas Gang Renouncement and Disassociation Program (GRAD) encourages gang members to quit their respective gangs. Program entry requires placement in protective custody in SHU to participate in a three-phase, nine-month program. In this program participants are provided with skills that will assist them in leaving the gang. They are also housed with rival members during the programming process (Knox, 2005).

There are many other prison programs that incorporate similar methodologies. However, there are no definitive studies to suggest that renunciation efforts actually work long-term. Forsythe & Petersilia (2006) refer to a 1995 survey estimating that 2.5 percent to 5 percent of gang members eventually renounce membership on their own, typically attributed to attaining a level of maturity which innately negates gang mentality, disillusionment over the gang mission, or an unwillingness to carry out a gang directive. Most of these individuals are of a lower status in the gang organization and in most instances, are from gangs that do not adhere to the "blood in-blood out" ritual. Many of these programs emphasize isolation, impeding access to programs, services, and social interaction, which hinders skill development and release planning. Also, program placement in a SHU environment is extremely costly and staff intensive (Delgado, n.d.; Forsythe & Petersilia, 2006).

Cognitive behavioral therapy programs have established a place in correctional programming as a means of addressing gang activity and other problematic inmate management issues. It is reasonable to assume that many gang members are raised in a dysfunctional environment with a proclivity for abuse, mental illness, and substance abuse issues. Cognitive behavioral therapy encourages heightened awareness of thinking processes, assessment of thought validity and perspective, identification of inaccurate thinking patterns and development of rational, fact-based thought formulation (Davis & Flannery, 2001). Some experts voice hope that incorporating cognitive behavioral therapy into prison gang renunciation efforts may offer a healthy, more cost-effective approach to prison gang management (Delgado, n.d.; Forsythe & Petersilia, 2006).

While not specifically a program for gang members, the usefulness of a cognitive behavioral approach has been successfully demonstrated by the BOP through the Bureau's Responsibility and Values Enhancement (BRAVE) Program, which is located at the Federal Correctional Institution, Beckley, West Virginia. The program was developed in response to concerns regarding inmate misconduct and/or group violence perpetuated by younger offenders, especially those who were beginning a long sentence (Innes, 1998, 2001). BRAVE has operated as a nine-month unit based program with new cohorts of approximately 30 inmates beginning every six weeks. The program is organized in phases and focuses on such skills as personal development, values enhancement, analysis of criminal thinking and lifestyle, and improved communication and problem-solving skills (Innes, 1998, 2001).

An outcome assessment was conducted comparing 289 BRAVE program participants and graduates over an 18-month period to similarly situated general population inmates. BRAVE participants and graduates demonstrated a 53 percent reduction in misconduct rates, a 15 percent decline in admission to SHU for disciplinary confinement, and a 30 percent reduction in the number of days spent in SHU. There were no program participants or graduates who required a disciplinary transfer during the assessment period (Innes, 1998, 2001).

While the BRAVE curriculum does not specifically address gang membership or gang-related activity, a significant number of the program participants and graduates were identified as members, associates, or as pursuing membership prior to their enrollment in the program. Behavioral changes observed in program participants and graduates through their incarceration strongly suggest that the program enhanced the cognitive thinking processes of participants (Innes, 1998, 2001).

PREVENTION EFFORTS

Early intervention programs for children of gang members may also be on the horizon. Successful intervention and treatment require community involvement at all levels, along with citizen education and open acknowledgment that a problem exists. Involving local law enforcement agencies, schools, churches, and parents in a cooperative partnership and teaching them to recognize the signs of gang involvement are paramount in prevention efforts (Allender, 2001; Davis & Flannery, 2001). Discussions should be open and frank and community funded programs, services, and employment training opportunities must be instituted to deter juvenile delinquency and anti-social behaviors. Utilization of qualified community leaders, counselors, and religious organizations fosters alliance and provides a mechanism for individual support (Jackson, 1998; Wilson, 2000).

As an example, the Boys and Girls Club of America (BGCA) pursues gang prevention through targeted outreach by engaging the community in the establishment of local clubs and activities, targeting youth, ages 6–18 years (National Crime Prevention Council, 2005). Through their partnerships with schools, courts, law enforcement, and community youth services, BGCA receives referrals for delinquent or "at risk" youth for participation in their programs as an alternative outlet to gang involvement. These initiatives are sponsored by the Office of Juvenile Justice and Delinquency Prevention, U.S. Department of Justice. They have conducted program evaluation and outcome testing resulting in the following findings:

• Delayed onset of gang behavior
• Less contact with the juvenile justice system
• Fewer delinquent behaviors
• Improved school outcomes
• More positive social relationships and productive use of after school time

CONCLUSION

Gangs are a prevailing presence in both prison and society. Their criminal and violent activities present a significant concern for public safety, produce societal mayhem, and present a financial drain on the public through an increased need for law enforcement and correctional resources. Expanding membership and violent gang activity requires prompt intervention, ensuring that the gang culture does not become a dominating force both in our prisons and in society.

REFERENCES

Allender, D. M. (2001). Gangs in middle America: Are they a threat? *FBI Law Enforcement Bulletin, 70* (12), 1–15.

California Department of Corrections and Rehabilitation (2005). *Facilities–Pelican Bay State Prison.* Retrieved on May 1, 2006, from www.corr.ca.gov/visitors/facilities.html

Coll, S, & Glasser, C. (2006, May 1). *Terrorists Turn to the Web.* Retrieved May 9, 2006, from www.washingtonpost.com

Davis, M. S., & Flannery, D. J. (2001). The institutional treatment of gang members. *Corrections Management Quarterly, 5* (1), 37–46.

Department of Justice. (2005, August 31). *Press release: Four men indicted on terrorism charges relate to conspiracy to attack military facilities.* Retrieved on May 8, 2006 from, www.losangeles.fbi.gov/dojpressrel/pressrel05/la083105usa.htm

Delgado, A. M. (n.d.). *Testimony to the Commission on Safety and Abuse in America's Prisons* (p. 8), Retrieved on May 1, 2006, from http://www.prisoncommission.org/statements/delgado_anthony_m.pdf

Federal Bureau of Investigation. (2006, March 22). *Joint training on MS-13 is scheduled in El-Salvador.* Retrieved November 3, 2006, from www.charlotte.fbi.gov/pressrel.htm

Florida Department of Corrections (2003). *Gang and security threat group awareness.* Retrieved May 18, 2006, from www.dc.state.fl.us/pub/gangs

Forsyth, D., & Petersilia, J. (2006). Gangs in California Prison System: What Can be Done? Retrieved June 10, 2006, from www.law.stanford.edu/program/centers/scjc/workingpapers/DForsythe_06.pdf

Gaes, G. G., Wallace, S., Gilman, E., Klein-Saffran, J., & Suppa, S. (2002). The influence of prison gang affiliation on violence and other prison misconduct. *The Prison Journal, 82,* 359–385.

H.R. 1279, 109th Cong. (2005). *Gang Deterrence and Community Protection Act of 2005.*

Innes, C. (1998). *Results from the evaluation of the first two years of the BRAVE program at FCI Beckley* (Internal report). Washington, D.C.: Federal Bureau of Prisons.

Innes, C. (2001). *Technical report for results from the evaluation of the first two years of the Beckley Responsibility and Values Enhancement (BRAVE) Program* (Internal Report). Washington, DC: Federal Bureau of Prisons.

Jackson, L. (1998). *Gangbusters: Strategies for prevention and intervention.* Lanham, MD: American Correctional Association.

Johnson, S., & Muhlhausen, D. B. (2005, March 21). *North American transnational youth gangs. Breaking the chain of violence.* Retrieved April 18, 2006, from http://www.heritage.org/Research/UrbanIssues/bg1834.cfm

Knox, G. W. (2005). *The problem of gangs and security threat groups (STGs) in American prisons today: Recent research findings from the 2004 Prison Gang Survey.* Retrieved on January 4, 2006, from http://www.ngcrc.com/corr2006.html

Lewis, J. (2006). *Know Gangs.* Retrieved on May 1, 2006, from www.knowgangs.com

Main, F. (2006, May 1). *Gangs claim their turf in Iraq.* Retrieved on May 9, 2006, from www.suntimes.com/archives

Main, F. (2007, January 20). *FBI details threat from gangs in military.* Retrieved on January 22, 2007 from www.suntimes.com/news/metro/220821,CST-News-gang20. article

Moore, J. & Hagedorn, J. (2001, March). Female gangs: A focus on research. *OJJDP News Bulletin NCJ 186159,* Washington, DC: Office of Juvenile Justice and Delinquency Prevention, Office of Justice Programs, U.S. Department of Justice.

National Alliance of Gang Investigators Association (2005). *2005 National gang threat assessment.* Retrieved December 16, 2005 from, http://www.nagia.org/PDFs/2005_national_gang_threat_assessment.pdf

National Crime Prevention Council (2005). *What works: Gang prevention through targeted outreach.* Retrieved on January 13, 2007 from www.ncpc.org/publications/catalyst/archives/aug05_doj.php

Ribando, C. (2005). *Gangs in Central America.* Washington, DC: CRS Report for Congress.

S. 853, 109th Congress (2005).

Valdez, A. (1998). *Hispanic gangs: A history of Hispanic gangs.* Retrieved on February 11, 2006 from www.nagia.org/Gang%20Articles/Hispanic%20Gangs.htm

Valdez, A. (2000). *Mara Salvatrucha: A South American import.* Retrieved on February 11, 2006 from, www.nagia.org/Gang%20Articles/Mara%20Salvatrucha.htm

Walker, R. (2006a). *Prison Gangs.* Retrieved January 4, 2006, retrieved from http://www.gangsorus.com/prisongangs.html

Walker, R. (2006b). *Gangs 101.* Retrieved January 4, 2006, retrieved from http://www.gangsorus.com/law.html

Wilson, J. J. (2000, September). Preventing adolescent gang involvement, *OJJDP News Bulletin NCJ 182210,* Washington, DC: Office of Juvenile Justice and Delinquency Prevention, Office of Justice Programs, U.S. Department of Justice.

Chapter 12

THE DEATH PENALTY: A BRIEF REVIEW OF HISTORICAL ROOTS AND CURRENT PRACTICES RELEVANT TO THE CORRECTIONAL MENTAL HEALTH PRACTITIONER

ALIX M. McLEAREN[1] AND PATRICIA A. ZAPF

The trouble with quotes about death is that 99.999 percent of them are made by people who are still alive.

Joshua Bruns

INTRODUCTION

Few issues are more politically and morally divisive than the death penalty. Supporters view its use as the logical and deserved consequence of heinous acts, while opponents decry it as government-sanctioned murder. Certainly, within correctional settings, it is a matter of great import. In this chapter, we review the history of using death as punishment for criminal behavior with an eye towards its evolution in the United States' justice system. Next, we contrast current American ideology on the death penalty with that of the international community. We offer several examples from the press to guide this exploration. Finally, we conclude with a discussion of the potential roles of mental health practitioners in death penalty cases, with best practices guidance provided when relevant.

---

1. The views and opinions expressed in this chapter are those of the authors only and do not necessarily represent the policies or opinions of the Federal Bureau of Prisons or the Department of Justice.

EARLY CAPITAL PUNISHMENT PRACTICES

Although the modern day practice of execution for crimes worldwide is generally tied to some form of law, statute, or cultural dictate, the killing of one human being by another has been justified by the actor since time immemorial. Scott (1968) defines man as quintessentially cruel, and notes that despite the advance of civilization, cruelty, in the form of pain inflicted on others, has persisted. He continues in this vein, noting, "Pain, physical or mental, is the essence of punishment" (Scott, 1968, p. 129). Thus, it seems logical that death, the ultimate form of loss and pain, has evolved as the ultimate consequence of acts deemed unacceptable by society.

While in antiquity the killing of others was often condoned as necessary sacrifice and tied to religion, historians have found evidence of the existence of a formal, criminal death penalty even in prehistoric cultures. More than likely, early sacrificial rites are, in fact, the root of execution practices (Schabas, 2002; Scott, 1968). We know that certain religious practices have been deemed criminal in various civilizations, and mass executions, such as the feeding of Christians to lions in ancient Rome or the torture and killing of Jews during the Spanish Inquisition or even the bombing of non-Muslims by Middle Eastern extremists, have been sanctioned by religious and political leaders throughout history and into the modern era.

Aside from capital punishment as a form of religious persecution, early use of the death penalty for criminal reasons has been well documented. For example, Schabas (2002) describes anthropological interpretations of Valladolid cave drawings suggestive of an execution. Additional anecdotal evidence suggests death as a possible punishment for varying infractions in prehistoric, tribal cultures. Regardless of speculation regarding earlier uses of the death penalty, there is consensus that capital punishment as we know it was first formally codified by Hammurabi in the eighteenth century, BCE (Death Penalty Information Center, [DPIC], n.d.; Schabas, 2002). Specific infractions calling for death as punishment are described, although no clear criteria regarding seriousness of the offense are elucidated. For example, thieving, falsely accusing another of a capital offense, and failing to pay a hired mercenary were all punishable with death (Hooker, 2006). In all, 25 acts were defined as capital crimes (Lifton & Mitchell, 2002; Schabas, 2002).

Other similar legal codes listing the death penalty as a possible punishment followed, including the Hittite Code in the fourteenth century BCE, the Draconian Code of Athens in the seventh century BCE, and the Roman Law of the Twelve Tablets in the fifth century BCE (DPICa, n.d.; Lifton & Mitchell, 2002). Chronologically, perhaps the next significantly influential historical reference to capital punishment is biblical in nature. Similar to Hammurabi's Code, scriptural writings contained in the Bible set death as the penalty for a variety of nonlethal crimes. The oft-quoted phrase referencing, "An eye for an eye and a tooth for a tooth," is taken from the Bible, and is frequently used to refer to reciprocal forms of justice where sentence for the crime is the same as the act itself (Exodus 21:23-27, New International Version). This principle, known as *lex talionis,* is actually at the foundation of all criminal codes mentioned to this point and appears to be upheld to some degree in modern law.

After centuries of what may be called brutality (e.g., methods of death including boiling, crucifixion, and stoning), detractors of capital punishment began to have influence in lawmaking. Black (as cited in Schabas, 2002) noted that while early Jewish courts were enabled to use the death penalty, strict proscriptions against its use were enacted. Other well-known historical figures, such as Plato and Socrates, began to be heard on the subject. Possibly the first public debate on capital punishment occurred in the Athens Assembly in 428 BCE and was recorded by Thucydides (Lifton & Mitchell, 2002). Ultimately, however, the practice continued, and was supported in Europe even through the formal development of society by such Enlightenment thinkers as Hobbes, Rousseau, and Locke (Schabas, 2002).

Practices in Europe, and particularly England in the seventeenth, eighteenth, and nineteenth centuries, although toned down from the freer use of the death penalty seen in the Middle Ages, continued to employ capital punishment with relative frequency when compared to modern standards. Bailey (2000) notes that another particularly violent period occurred in the 60 years beginning in 1770, where nearly 35,000 persons received death sentences in England. Interestingly, frequent commutations occurred, and it was estimated that only 7,000 actual executions occurred (Bailey, 2000). Public reaction was not positive, and Reggio (1997) wrote that in a 15-year period beginning in 1823, the number of crimes allowing for execution was nearly halved. By the later 1800s and into the twentieth century, a trend emerged wherein other forms of punishment (e.g., servitude, isolation, and incarceration) were often chosen, and an exploration of the effectiveness of the prison system was undertaken (Briggs, Harrison, McInnes, & Vincent, 1996).

To this point, the focus of this chapter has been a broad review of death penalty usage with examples from various countries, cultures, and times. Such information will be useful in informing the reader when we examine current reasons for support and detraction. Before we begin a more detailed chronology of modern death penalty practices in the United States and the international community, it seems prudent to review purported historical and current reasons for use of the death penalty.

EXPLORING THE PURPOSE OF CAPITAL PUNISHMENT

It has been noted herein that one possible explanation for society's choice of the death penalty over other, less final and barbaric punishments is humanity's inherent capacity for cruelty (Scott, 1968). Other arguments used are religious in nature or refer to the earlier-described *lex talionis* principle of equally-matched punishments and crimes. Before beginning a discourse on modern day capital punishment practices, we evaluate possible reasons for use of the death penalty versus other criminal sanctions. Van den Haag (1998) identifies retribution, rehabilitation, and deterrence as three aims of punishment.

We find it necessary to note that rehabilitation, one tenet of most penal systems, clearly does not apply to the death penalty. Despite mission statements of agencies such as the Federal Bureau of Prisons that promote the confinement of offenders as well as the provision of personal growth opportunities, the death penalty offers no chance for redemption. Even as a historical reason for the death penalty, rehabilitation or change does not appear to be a sound explanation. Capital punishment proponents in the seventeenth and eighteenth centuries believed that while complete rehabilitation was not allowed by capital punishment, execution hastened the criminal's ability to repent or make peace with God (Banner, 2002a). At that time, American politics remained more heavily entwined with religion. Judges tended to believe that in handing out a capital sentence, they were not simply dictating punishment for a crime, but providing a service to the sentenced by offering a chance at salvation. In modern times, "penitence" is not cited as a reason for capital punishment (Banner, 2002a). What, then, does this sanction aim to accomplish? As Justice Stewart noted in *Gregg v. Georgia* (1976), deterrence and retribution are the two "social purposes" of the death penalty. It can be argued that the death penalty deters crime on an individual basis insofar as the person executed is no longer able to commit further violence. It is also possible that the sanction serves to satisfy a sense of vengeance in both the wronged parties as well as society.

Lifton and Mitchell (2002) note that for hundreds of years animals were put on trial and even sentenced to death. Such an act perpetrated against creatures not capable of malice or even the formation of intent suggests clear roots in the idea of the death penalty as an outlet for revenge. Although humans no longer incorporate nonhuman animals into the justice system, elements of retribution remain in modern death penalty practices. As noted, the principle of *lex talionis,* which underlies most modern criminal and legal codes, also points to retaliation as the purpose of the death sentence (van den Haag, 1998). It should be noted that differences, though subtle, do exist between revenge and retribution (Lifton & Mitchell, 2002). Retribution supports a societal belief that justice has been accomplished whereas revenge is more in line with creating suffering for the criminal (Lifton & Mitchell, 2002). Regardless, while both principles may in fact be part of an individual rationale for belief in the death penalty, due to their subjectivity, neither fully explains its use.

Those who identify retribution as evidence in support of the death penalty tend to be vocal in their reasoning. Banner (2002b) describes studies in the early 1990s wherein a majority of respondents persisted in favoring the death penalty regardless of whether it decreased crime. The role of deterrence as a supportive motive for the death penalty, on the other hand, is far less clear. In a 2000 press conference, Attorney General Janet Reno stated her desire to locate any empirical evidence demonstrating a deterrent effect for the death penalty (Amnesty International, 2000). Somewhat cheekily, Peterson and Bailey (1998), in comparison, note, "capital punishment is, of course, 100 percent effective in preventing recidivism" (p. 157).

Van den Haag (1998) describes deterrence as a necessary condition for effective punishment. Specifically, he highlights two key components of the deterrence position. One idea is that punishments based on deterrence have purposes beyond stopping the perpetrator, as others witness the cause and effect of the punishment. In addition, legal punishments are only effective because they are carried out, not because their threat exists (e.g., the death penalty will only be a deterrent if people are actually executed). This information suggests a rationale for the deterrent motive, but does not answer the question of whether the death penalty actually serves to prevent future crimes.

Historically, deterrence theory posited a cost-benefit analysis associated with criminal behavior, such that a potential murderer would consider possible outcomes of the crime and choose to kill only in the unlikely event commission of the crime brings greater benefit than execution (Peterson & Bailey, 1998). Problems with this theory arose when it was pointed out that murder was often a crime of impulse and opportunity, rather than one of premeditation (Bowers & Pierce, 1980).

Regardless of theoretical flaws, much study of the deterrent effect of capital punishment on crime has been undertaken. Early studies frequently compared murder rates pre- and post-death penalty abolition, or compared murder rates in areas with and without capital punishment. As Sellin (1967) summarized, these findings overwhelmingly determined that the death penalty not only failed as a deterrent, but that it was actually correlated with increased murder rates in some jurisdictions. Later research involving more complex multivariate analyses led to similar conclusions regarding the death penalty and deterrence (Peterson & Bailey, 1998). While this position has remained fairly consistent in the United States, recent reanalysis of death penalty data from 1977–1997 holds that regression analyses do support a deterrent effect for capital punishment (Mocan & Gittings, 2003). Clearly, additional study on this topic is needed. In fact, Peterson and Bailey (1998) assert the resolution of whether the death penalty is a deterrent will be crucial to the ultimate determination of U.S. death penalty policy.

EVOLUTION OF THE DEATH PENALTY IN THE UNITED STATES

As noted, capital punishment has existed in the United States from the time of the initial settlement of the colonies. Given that many inhabitants arrived from England, retention of some of the historically-bound beliefs about capital punishment was probably inevitable. An exhaustive review of death penalty standards is beyond the scope of this chapter. Instead, we aim to highlight significant case law and historical events related to the correctional practitioner.

As Acker, Bohm, and Lanier (1998) note, execution was an inherited part of American culture beginning before settlement of the colonies. The first recorded execution of an American settler took place in Virginia in 1608 when George Kendall was executed by firing squad for spying (Coyne & Entzeroth, 1994; DPICb, n.d.). Since that time, between 14,489 and 18,000 people have been executed in the United States under government authority (Acker et. al., 1998; DPICb, n.d.).

In times before the formalization of the country under a single constitution, execution was a fairly common practice. Although crimes for which capital punishment was an option which varied by locale, all colonies allowed for the death penalty at some point (Kronenwetter, as cited in Eisenberg, 2004). For example, persons were given death sentences for suspected witchcraft activities, bestiality, "man stealing," idolatry, and "cursing a parent" in the Massachusetts settlement (Eisenberg, 2004, p. 7). As the colonists fought for independence, execution was used a threat for desertion or treason. Finally, under the official government of the United States, allowance of the death penalty became a national standard. The Constitution set guidelines that permitted both federal and state executions (Eisenberg, 2004).

Since 1776, the country has vacillated considerably in terms of consensus on death penalty policy. The ratification of the Eighth Amendment to the Constitution in 1791 did not halt executions, but has since given rise to numerous challenges including current questions about execution methods (Banner, 2002a; Eisenberg, 2004). States such as Michigan have held as death penalty abolitionists since 1852, while others, such as Texas, execute more people in one year than other states have ever executed (DPICb, n.d.).

By the twentieth century, execution was an accepted practice of the American criminal justice system. In fact, 1935 saw a greater number of capital sentences than any other year to date (Eisenberg, 2004). In the mid-1900s, executions for crimes other than murder still occurred, but with infrequency. By the 1960s, views about the death penalty had changed, and the number of condemned persons had declined. In 1968, the Supreme Court ordered a moratorium so as to review death penalty issues (Eisenberg, 2004).

The decision in the landmark case of *Furman v. Georgia*, consolidated with two other cases, briefly halted capital punishment in the United States. Setting the political landscape for this decision, public opinion with regard to the death penalty had shifted significantly since its inception. In 1966, support for the death penalty reached its nadir in America (Erskine, as cited in Bohm, 1998). A Gallup poll taken months before the *Furman* ruling found death penalty supporters only marginally outnumbering opponents (Banner, 2002b). William Henry Furman, a relatively uneducated African American man, shot and killed the resident of the dwelling he was attempting to burglarize. After being convicted of murder and sentenced to death, Furman appealed, citing conflicts between his sentence and the Eighth and Fourteenth Amendments of the Constitution; his appeal eventually being granted certiorari by the Supreme Court. Rather than being a question of simple technicality, the appeal raised questions about the constitutionality of nationwide death penalty practices (Steiker & Steiker, 1998). On June 29, 1972, the Supreme Court, under the leadership of Chief Justice Warren Burger, ruled five to four that the death penalty was unconstitutional. It was opined that sentencing was often random, and juries were empowered with too much discretion. Each justice seemed to have different reasons for his opinion, and all issued separate opinions, resulting in the longest ever decision (Eisenberg, 2004; Steiker & Steiker, 1998). Under the decision, all currently condemned persons were required to be re-sentenced to a noncapital punishment with no possibility of reinstating previous death sentences.

Rather than providing an ultimate answer to the question of capital punishment, the *Furman* ruling seemed to energize and further entrench activists on both sides of the issue. Within a day of the ruling, five states had declared intention to draft death penalty legislation that qualified under the new guidelines (Banner, 2002b). Legislators worked quickly to reenact capital punishment and, in 1975, more people were sentenced to death in the United States than in any previously recorded year (Banner, 2002b; Reggio, 1997).

One of many states to engage in a reworking of sentencing standards related to the death penalty following *Furman*, Georgia developed a bifurcated system. Specifically, to avoid the randomness cited as unconstitutional, Georgia's revised procedures required a guilt or innocence phase of the trial for potential capital cases followed by a second phase wherein aggravating conditions must be proved and mitigating factors presented to jurors and/or judges. Under these guidelines, Troy Gregg was convicted of two counts of murder with the aggravating factor of armed robbery. He appealed to the Georgia

Supreme Court and ultimately to the U.S. Supreme Court. In *Gregg v. Georgia* (1976) (and two other cases handed down simultaneously) the Supreme Court held that the death penalty was not, in and of itself, unconstitutional nor in conflict with evolving standards of decency, but rather an embedded part of the American justice system. So long as practices were not arbitrary, but instead were part of set criteria for determining sentencing, the court determined death penalty practices to be constitutional. In addition, it was required that potential capital crimes be narrowly defined, that a Supreme Court appeal be provided, and that mitigation be allowed. In sum, this decision clearly allowed for the sentencing and carrying out of executions.

Within six months of death penalty reinstatement, Gary Gilmore was legally executed in Utah (Banner, 2002b). Since that time, additional challenges have been raised that have provided more guidance regarding capital punishment. For example, *Coker v. Georgia* (1977) determined that the crime of raping an adult could not be sanctioned with the death penalty.

Following the pattern of the Supreme Court, some states have examined fairness issues and temporarily halted capital sentencing, only to have execution reinstated following a change in leadership. Currently, 38 states, the federal government, and the U.S. military have some form of capital punishment. Modern-day methods of execution include lethal injection, electrocution, hanging, the firing squad, and the gas chamber (DPICc, n.d.). In addition to reinstating the practice of execution, the *Gregg* decision appears to have allowed for more frequent legal dialogue on the topic of capital punishment. Future dangerousness, race, and definition of aggravating factors, among other issues, have been addressed by the courts.

One area in which the courts have set limits on the death penalty is with regard to age. In *Thompson v. Oklahoma* (1988) and *Stanford v. Kentucky* (1989), both of which were ultimately heard by the Supreme Court, age at the time of the offense was considered in determining whether the death penalty could be imposed. In *Stanford*, the appellate was over age 17 at the time of the crime, and the court affirmed imposition of the death penalty. Thompson on the other hand, was only 15 when his crime was committed, and the court determined that his execution would violate the Eighth Amendment. Until 2005 the death penalty was not pursued when defendants were under 16 years of age at the time of the offense (Eisenberg, 2004).

Recently, the Supreme Court increased the age at which a person can be sanctioned with capital punishment. At the age of 17, Christopher Simmons plotted with two younger friends to kidnap and murder a female victim. He and another person broke into her home, bound her, and threw her from a bridge, resulting in her death. He was found guilty and sentenced to death, and the case was eventually heard by the Supreme Court. In *Roper v. Simmons* (2005) the court cited behavioral science literature finding that adolescents do not have the same level of maturity as adults and are more likely to behave impulsively. More importantly, the court considered a "national consensus" argument that involved the fact that only three states had executed an offender who was a juvenile at the time of the crime within the last decade. Finally, the court reviewed the positions of the international community, a minority of whom allow for the execution of minors. As such, the court set the standard for consideration of capital punishment at the age of 18 at the time of the offense.

In addition to exploring the question of age, courts and legislators have reviewed mental status issues and their relevance to criminal sanctions. In *Penry v. Lynaugh* (1989) the Supreme Court determined that the execution of mentally retarded offenders was not specifically banned. More recently, in *Atkins v. Virginia* (2002), the court reversed its earlier decision. In this case, Darryl Atkins and an accomplice were convicted of abducting, robbing, and killing a male victim. Despite Atkins' documented IQ of 59, he was sentenced to death. Again, the Supreme Court cited the "national consensus" position, noting that the execution of mentally retarded individuals was not supported by state statutes and practices. In addition, it was held that the purported purposes of the death penalty, retribution and deterrence, were not satisfied by executing mentally retarded persons. As such, execution of these individuals was found to be in violation of the Eighth Amendment. The court allowed for further review of this question as criteria for the determination of mental retardation were not specified.

Related to the issue of executing mentally retarded individuals is the issue of executing mentally ill individuals. Accepted standards of practice exist to ensure mentally ill persons are competent to stand trial and to determine whether an individual should be held criminally responsible for a given behavior. In *Ford v. Wainwright* (1986), the Supreme Court addressed whether mentally ill persons who have been sentenced to death should be executed. The court held that, under the Eighth Amendment, it was not acceptable to carry out a death sentence against a person so "insane" as not to understand the nature or purpose of the punishment (e.g., the punishment of death or its link to the commission of the crime). This ruling falls far short of exempting mentally ill individuals from execution. It appears likely, however, that further legal discourse on the topic is on the horizon. Recently, Ohio Supreme Court Justice Evelyn Lundberg Stratton has called upon the Ohio legislature to exempt all persons with serious mental illness from execution (DPICd, n.d.). As noted, other limits and standards have been set since the *Gregg* decision. We recommend Eisenberg (2004) for a more thorough review of these developments. Having provided a general foundation for the current trends of the United States with regard to the death penalty, we now compare and contrast these positions with those of the rest of the world.

CAPITAL PUNISHMENT IN THE INTERNATIONAL
COMMUNITY

International developments within the last 15 years or so have produced a clear, strong trend away from capital punishment. The number of countries that have abolished the death penalty is at an all-time high and the international community has called upon those countries that still use the death penalty to sharply curtail its use. In addition, international agreements have expressed a strong preference for an end to all executions.

Schabas (1997) remarked that the abolition of the death penalty "has been envisioned for at least two centuries, and with the accelerating progress of the movement for abolition, the end of this dark tunnel is now in sight" (p. 295). In 2000 Schabas wrote, "given the enormous and rapid progress in the development of international norms respecting the death penalty . . . the general acceptance of abolition and its elevation to a customary norm of international law . . . may be envisaged in the not too distant future" (p. 19).

As of December, 2000, the number of countries that had abolished the death penalty for all crimes, whether in peacetime or wartime, totaled 76,[1] with an additional 11[2] countries abolishing the death penalty for ordinary crimes in peacetime, and an additional 36[3] countries being considered de facto abolitionist as they had not executed anyone within the last 10 years (Hood, 2001). Thus, 37 percent (71 countries[4]) of the international communi-

---

1. Andorra, Angola, Australia, Austria, Azerbaijan, Belgium, Bolivia, Bulgaria, Cambodia, Canada, Cape Verde, Colombia, Costa Rica, Cote d"Ivoire, Croatia, Czech Republic, Denmark, Djibouti, Dominican Republic, East Timor, Ecuador, Estonia, Finland, France, Georgia, Germany, Greece, Guinea-Bissau, Haiti, Honduras, Hungary, Iceland, Ireland, Italy, Kiribati, Liechtenstein, Lithuania, Luxembourg, Macedonia, Malta, Marshall Islands, Mauritius, Federated States of Micronesia, Moldova, Monaco, Mozambique, Namibia, Nepal, Netherlands, New Zealand, Nicaragua, Norway, Palau, Panama, Paraguay, Poland, Portugal, Romania, San Marion, Sao Tome and Principe, Seychelles, Slovak Republic, Slovenia, Solomon Islands, South Africa, Spain, Sweden, Switzerland, Turkmenistan, Tuvalu, Ukraine, United Kingdom, Northern Ireland, Uruguay, Vanuatu, Vatican City State, Venezuela
2. Albania, Argentina, Bosnia-Herzegovina, Brazil, Cyprus, El Salvador, Fiji, Israel, Latvia, Mexico, Peru
3. Antigua and Barbuda, Armenia, Barbados, Belize, Benin, Bhutan, Brunei Darussalam, Burkina Faso, Central African Republic, Chile, Congo (Republic), Dominica, Eritrea, Gabon, Gambia, Grenada, Guinea, Jamaica, Laos, Madagascar, Maldives, Mali, Mauritania, Myanmar, Nauru, Niger, Papua New Guinea, Senegal, Sri Lanka, Suriname, Swaziland, Togo, Tonga, Turkey, Samoa, Yugoslavia
4. Afghanistan, Algeria, Bahamas, Bahrain, Bangladesh, Belarus, Botswana, Burundi, Cameroon, Chad, China, Comoros, Congo (Democratic Republic), Cuba, Egypt, Equatorial Guinea, Ethiopia, Ghana, Guatemala, Guyana, India, Indonesia, Iran, Iraq, Japan, Jordan, Kazakstan, Kenya, Kuwait, Kyrgyzstan, Lebanon, Lesotho, Liberia, Libya, Malawi, Malaysia, Mongolia, Morocco, Nigeria, North Korea, Oman, Pakistan, Palestinian Authority, Philippines, Qatar, Russian Federation, Rwanda, Saint Christopher and Nevis, Saint Lucia, Saint Vincent and Grenadines, Saudi Arabia, Sierra Leone, Singapore, Somalia, South Korea, Sudan, Syria, Taiwan, Tajikistan, Tanzania, Thailand, Trinidad and Tobago, Tunisia, Uganda, United Arab Emirates, United States of America, Uzbekistan, Vietnam, Yemen, Zambia, Zimbabwe

ty had retained the death penalty as of the end of 2000, a significant decrease from the 56 percent that had retained the death penalty as of 1988 and the 47 percent that had retained it as of the end of 1995.

In examining the abolition patterns since 1965, Hood (2001) reports that "the annual average rate at which countries have abolished the death penalty trebled: from roughly one a year in the period 1965–88, to three a year over the years 1989–2000" (p. 333). The rapid increase in the number of abolitionist countries indicates that this movement has become widespread across the regions of the world. In 1965, the vast majority of abolitionist countries were Western Europe and Central and South America, with only two abolitionist countries outside of these regions; however, by 2000, abolition had spread into Eastern Europe, the former Soviet Union, and Africa (Hood, 2001). Hood also notes that only 55 countries have executed anyone since 1994 and, "apart from the USA, Cuba, Guyana and some island states of the Caribbean, all these countries were in the Middle East in Asia or Africa" (p. 334).

Although the number of countries that have abolished the death penalty has increased and is currently at the highest point in history, Radzinowicz (1999) noted that "no less than four-fifths of the total population of the world still live in conditions which sanction the appointment and use of capital punishment . . . [and] there is still no sign that China, India, Pakistan, Afghanistan, Japan or any of the middle Eastern states will join the abolitionist camp" (p. 293). Further, Radzinowicz laments "the heaviest blow to the abolitionist cause has come from the United States, which has resolutely rallied behind the retentionist cause" (p. 293).

With respect to the number of executions that take place, China leads the world in overall number of executions. For the period 1994–1998, China executed a total of 12,338 people (although some Chinese scholars estimate that the true number may be a lot higher); Iran executed the second highest number, with 505 executions; Saudi Arabia executed 465 people; Ukraine and Turkmenistan executed 389 and 373 people, respectively, although executions ceased during 1997 for both countries. The United States was sixth highest for that same period with 274 individuals being executed (93 of these in Texas). When the estimated annual rate per million population is examined for this same time period, Turkmenistan leads the international community with 14.92 people per million being executed annually, followed closely by Singapore with 13.93 people per million being executed annually; Saudi Arabia executed 4.65 people per million annually; and Belarus executed 3.20 people per million annually. China, although having the highest number of executions, executed 2.01 people per million annually and the United States was far lower at 0.20 people per million executed annually during that time period (all statistics from Hood, 2001).

Recently, China has taken steps to respond to domestic and international criticism regarding its extensive use of capital punishment in an effort to reduce the high rate of executions. On October 30, 2006, China adopted new rules requiring that, as of January 1, 2007, all death sentences be reviewed by the Supreme People's Court. The National People's Congress, China's legislature, approved this amendment, which restores a power that was stripped from the Supreme Court in 1983, in an effort to reduce the widespread and arbitrary use of the death penalty. China had been facing increasing criticism over the last few years after a number of executed individuals had later been proved innocent (Lague, 2006).

The Death Penalty as an International Human Rights Issue

On April 28, 1999, the United Nations High Commission for Human Rights put forth a resolution requesting that all countries that maintain the death penalty: (1) not impose it for crimes committed by a person below 18 years of age; (2) not impose it on a person suffering from any form of mental disorder; (3) not execute any person as long as any related legal procedure, at the international or national level, is pending; (4) progressively restrict the number of offenses for which it might be imposed; and (5) establish a moratorium on executions, with a view to completely abolishing it. Although the U.N. Commission on Human Rights voted overwhelmingly in favor of a moratorium on the death penalty, "the United States was in the company of such human rights violators as China, Rwanda, and Sudan in opposing the resolution" (U.N. Panel, 1999, p. A4).

In addition to opposing this resolution, the United States has been criticized heavily for violating all aspects of this resolution. "By defying international agreements and turning a deaf ear to the entreaties of its friends, the U.S. is increasingly positioning itself as a human rights violator on this issue. By executing juvenile offenders and the mentally ill; by executing citizens from other countries who were not afforded the simple protections U.S. citizens routinely expect abroad; and by ignoring international norms against expanding the death penalty, the U.S. is showing disrespect for international human rights law both at home and abroad" (Dieter, 1999, p. 2). Even before opposing this resolution, Mary Robinson, the United Nations High Commissioner for Human Rights, in 1998 said of the U.S., "the increasing use of the death penalty in the United States and in a number of other states is a matter of serious concern and runs counter to the international community's expressed desire for the abolition of the death penalty" (see Dieter, 1999, p. 1). Hood (2001) wrote, "the blunt fact is that the USA does not regard itself as formally bound by international law to abolish the death penalty or by UN Safeguards to control its implementation" (p. 340).

These criticisms of the U.S. as a violator of human rights law do not appear unfounded. Germany, Canada, Paraguay, and Mexico have each had national citizens executed by the United States after the United States violated the Vienna Convention on Consular Rights by failing to inform the foreigners of their rights to confer with their respective consulates. In each of these instances, the United States contravened injunctions against the executions ordered by the International Court of Justice and went ahead with the executions (Dieter, 1999).

The International Covenant on Civil and Political Rights (ICCPR), which has been called the most important human rights treaty in existence and which was forged from the founding principle of the United Nations Universal Declaration of Human Rights (Everyone has the right to life, liberty and security of the person), contains an article that explicitly addresses the issue of the death penalty and juvenile offenders. Specifically, Article 6 of the ICCPR reads, in part: "Sentences of death shall not be imposed for crimes committed by persons below eighteen years of age and shall not be carried out on pregnant women." Although the ICCRP has almost universal endorsement, the United States ratified this Covenant in 1992 but with substantive reservations, thus carving out an exception to the complete adherence to this treaty and allowing the United States to continue to execute juveniles. The United States was criticized heavily for these reservations with 11 countries (including a number of the U.S.'s closest allies) registering formal objections. Sweden objected that, "reservations of this nature contribute to undermining the basis of international treaty law" whereas France criticized the U.S.'s reservations as "incompatible with the object and purpose of the Convention" (Dieter, 1999, p. 7). In addition, "when the U.N. body established to oversee the ICCPR (the Human Rights Committee) voted that the U.S.'s reservation to Article 6 was invalid, the U.S. Senate retaliated by threatening to withhold funds slated for U.S. participation in the work of the Committee" (Dieter, 1999, p. 7).

The ICCPR has been extremely effective as evidenced by the virtual elimination of the execution of juvenile offenders worldwide. The United States, however, was the only exception to this rule in 1998 and 1999, with 4 juvenile executions (Amnesty International, 1999); the U.S. executed another 4 juvenile offenders in 2000; and since 2000, 5 of the 7 juvenile executions that took place worldwide have been in the U.S. (the 2 others were considered to be rogue executions that took place in countries that had legally banned the execution of juveniles; Streib, 2005). In addition to the ICCPR, Article 37 (a) of the United Nations Convention on the Rights of the Child prohibits capital punishment and life imprisonment without possibility of release for persons who committed offenses before age 18. The United States is the only country in the world that has not yet ratified this international agreement. In 1999, Dieter noted, "with the near universal acceptance of the Convention on the Rights of the Child and the ICCPR, the U.S. is moving in the opposite direction from the entire world in this critical area of human rights" (p. 9).

On March 1, 2005, the U.S. Supreme Court, with its decision in the case of *Roper v. Simmons* (discussed above), removed the U.S. from the list of nations that execute juveniles (leaving only China, Iran, and Pakistan; although all three of these countries have ratified both the ICCPR and the U.N. Convention on the Rights of the Child). It is intriguing, however, to note the length of time that it took the U.S. to meet the rest of the international community on this issue. Now that the U.S. Supreme Court has decided the issue of juvenile executions, it will be interesting to see how long it takes for the U.S. to ratify the U.N. Convention on the Rights of the Child. With respect to the worldwide abolition of the death penalty Hood (2001) notes, "the United States provides the litmus test for the success of the abolitionist movement worldwide, because here is a country which defines itself as the archetypal liberal democracy and guardian of human rights and yet rejects human rights arguments on the death penalty *as defined by any agency other than its own Supreme Court*" (p. 343; italics added). Given the progress on the issue of the execution of juveniles, this observation certainly appears accurate. Manners (2002) observed that the European Union (EU) appears to be acting as a "normative power" in world politics; a normative power that is not inconsequential as it has helped to accelerate the abolitionist movement over the last decade. Whether this normative power of other countries, and especially of the EU, may serve to push the USA toward an abolitionist policy in the future remains to be seen.

CURRENT DEATH PENALTY ISSUES IN THE UNITED STATES

While the United States may or may not be influenced by death penalty practices of the international community, capital punishment continues to be a topic of debate in the courts as well as in other public forums. On December 2, 2005, Kenneth Boyd of North Carolina became the 1000th person to be executed since the death penalty was reinstated in 1976 (1000 Executions.org, n.d.), giving rise to increased dialogue on this subject. Here, we review a few issues related to the death penalty that have recently become the focus of attention by the media and the courts.

The Redemption Factor

As previously noted, the Supreme Court has defined capital punishment as serving two functions: deterrence and retribution. Rehabilitation, though an important component of the prison settings in which condemned offenders are confined, does not appear to apply. Does it matter whether a person has changed by the time of execution? In 2000, persons executed had served an average of 11 years, 5 months on death row, indicating a significant lapse between time of the offense and time of execution (Policy Almanac, n.d.).

In one high profile case, arguments that the convicted offender had been redeemed were not effective. Stanley "Tookie" Williams co-founded the Crips gang at the age of 13 (del Barco, 2005). In addition to spawning one of the more notorious and violent street gangs, Williams was convicted of several 1979 robberies and murders (CNN, 2005; del Barco, 2005). While in prison, Williams attempted to educate himself and spoke out against the gang lifestyle. He authored children's book and donated proceeds to the community (CNN, 2005; del Barco, 2005; Nieves, 2000). Ultimately, he was nominated for the Nobel Peace Prize (del Barco, 2005; Nieves, 2000).

Death penalty opponents argued that Williams was a changed man. National Public Radio commentator Earl Ofari Hutchinson suggested that clemency could send a positive message of redemption and change to other incarcerated persons (Hutchinson, 2005). Activist Sister Helen Prejean compared Williams' execution to gang justice, which does not attend to concerns such as redemption and change (CNN, 2005). Ultimately, California Governor Arnold Schwarzenegger determined that rehabilitation was not a factor to be considered, instead citing strong evidence of a valid conviction in failing to grant clemency.

Williams was executed on December 13, 2005 (CNN, 2005). Presently, rehabilitation remains a goal of correctional systems, but has not been a significant factor in overturning recent capital sentences.

Fairness, Race, and Socioeconomic Status

There is perhaps no more controversial issue than that of the indiscriminant and arbitrary use of the death penalty. In 1972, the U.S. Supreme Court decided *Furman v. Georgia*, thus invalidating almost every death penalty statute in the country. The decision indicated that the unlimited discretion allowed to judges and juries caused the death penalty to be applied in an "arbitrary and capricious" manner. In addition, several of the Justices cited evidence of racial bias. Four years later, in *Gregg v. Georgia*, the Court resurrected the death penalty by upholding a statute requiring judges and juries to take specific factors under consideration in deciding whether to impose the death penalty. This "guided discretion" requirement was considered to be an adequate guard against arbitrariness and discrimination. The fact remains, however, that there is abundant evidence to demonstrate that racial bias continues to influence who is sentenced to death. Specifically, the race of the victim plays a crucial role in determining who will be sentenced to death.

Professor David Baldus examined sentencing patterns in Georgia in the 1970s. After reviewing over 2,500 homicide cases in that state, controlling for 230 nonracial factors, he concluded that a person accused of killing a White victim was 4.3 times more likely to be sentenced to death than a person accused of killing a Black victim (see Baldus, Pulaski, & Woodworth, 1983). Since that time, there continue to be numerous examples of a similar nature. A report by Amnesty International in 2003 found that although the victims of murder are nearly equally split between Black and White, 80 percent of those executed since the reinstatement of the death penalty have been executed for the murder of a White victim. In addition, this report found that more than 20 percent of Black defendants were convicted by all-White juries. The U.S. Department of Justice surveyed the use of the death penalty in federal cases between 1988 and 2000 and found evidence of racial and ethnic disparities. The report revealed that 80 percent of cases submitted to federal prosecutors for death penalty review involved racial minorities as defendants and in more than half of those cases the defendant was Black. Maryland, Indiana, New Jersey, North Carolina and Virginia have each commissioned studies on the use of the death penalty and in all cases have found evidence of racial discrimination.

In 1994, in a dissenting opinion in the case of *Callins v. Collins,* Justice Harry Blackmun commented strongly on what he called the failed death penalty experiment saying, in part:

> From this day forward, I no longer shall tinker with the machinery of death. For more than 20 years I have endeavored . . . to develop . . . rules that would lend more than the mere appearance of fairness to the death penalty endeavor. . . . Rather than continue to coddle the court's delusion that the desired level of fairness has been achieved . . . I feel . . . obligated simply to concede that the death penalty experiment has failed. It is virtually self-evident to me now that no combination of procedural rules or substantive regulations ever can save the death penalty from its inherent constitutional deficiencies. . . . Perhaps one day this court will develop procedural rules or verbal formulas that actually will provide consistency, fairness and reliability in a capital-sentencing scheme. I am not optimistic that such a day will come. I am more optimistic, though, that this court eventually will conclude that the effort to eliminate arbitrariness while preserving fairness 'in the infliction of [death] is so plainly doomed to failure that it and the death penalty must be abandoned altogether' (*Godfrey v. Georgia*, 1980). I may not live to see that day, but I have faith that eventually it will arrive.

> More than a decade later we are still faced with evidence that the "death penalty remains fraught with arbitrariness, discrimination . . . and mistakes" (Blackmun dissenting in *Callins v. Collins*, 1994).

Beyond Lex Talionis

In *Coker v. Georgia* (1977) the Supreme Court held that the rape of an adult female did not justify a death sentence. At that time, 16 states had laws on the books allowing for death sentences in cases involving crimes other than murder (Liptak, 2006). Irrespective of the existence of the law, no person has been executed in the United States for rape for more than 40 years, although nearly 455 people were executed for the crime between 1930 and 1964 (Liptak, 2003). Presently, only a single person, Patrick O. Kennedy of Louisiana, is on death row for a sex crime that did not involve murder. His case stems from a conviction under a 1995 law that allows for the death penalty in cases of child rape involving a victim under the age of 12 and the sentence is presently being appealed (Liptak, 2006).

Although such laws are designed to make victims more likely to report crimes, it is feared the opposite effect may occur. In June, 2006, Oklahoma became the fifth state to approve a measure allowing for execution in cases of child sex crimes without murder (Liptak, 2006). Hart (2006) recently reported that a sixth state, Texas, is considering a similar law. Although most recent death penalty cases have resulted in decisions limiting the scope of capital punishment, this recent trend suggests a possible shift towards once again expanding the number of crimes eligible for the death sentence.

Methods of Execution

As noted elsewhere in this chapter, the history of the death penalty has evolved from initial efforts to create pain and suffering in victims (e.g., crucifixion) to methods designed to bring about death quickly. In the United States, there has been considerable effort to develop methods that do not violate the Eighth Amendment standard of cruel and unusual punishment. Death by hanging and firing squad were standard practices through the 1800s but were, for the most part, replaced with more "humane" methods by the twentieth century. In 1890, William Kemmler became the first person executed by the electric chair (DPICc, n.d.). The gas chamber, another purported advance in execution, was first used in 1924 (DPICc, n.d.). While all of these methods are still in use, 37 of 38 states now offer lethal injection as an option for condemned persons, while Nebraska only offers the electric chair (DPICc, n.d.).

Challenges to execution methods have often driven change regarding how the death penalty is carried out but have not been cited as factors related to the constitutionality of the practice. For example, in 2001 the Georgia Supreme Court became the first of several appellate courts to find electrocution in violation of the Constitution; however, rather than examine the use of the death penalty, the state simply turned to the use of lethal injection (Sack, 2001).

Recently, a number of death row prisoners have raised concerns about the use of lethal injection, claiming the method is painful and causes unnecessary suffering. Clarence Hill, a Florida inmate, appealed to the Supreme Court, but the ruling in *Hill v. McDonough* (2006) only determined that condemned inmates may challenge the constitutionality of lethal injection, not that the practice itself is cruel and unusual. Ultimately, Hill was executed via this method. Currently, 10 other death row inmates have been granted stays of execution and are awaiting hearings related to the use of lethal injection (DPICe, n.d.). An 11th inmate who had been granted a stay of execution had his sentence carried out on October 24, 2006.

DNA, Questionable Convictions, and Moratoria

Somewhat related, the fairness issue discussed previously is the recent trend towards reexamining death penalty sentences based on new technology, such as DNA testing. As noted, conviction and sentence have been found to be subject to racial prejudice, resulting in the conclusion by some authorities on jurisprudence that the death penalty's use is questionable. Perhaps due to greater publicity on these topics, public opinion with regard to the death penalty has shifted significantly since its reinstatement. A summary of recent polls provided by the Death Penalty Information Center provides state and nationwide data demonstrating declining support for capital sentences, resulting in the lowest levels of death penalty support in 27 years (DPICf, n.d.). Gallup polls in 2006 sampling across the country found 65 percent and 67 percent of respondents to favor capital punishment, compared with 80 percent in 1994 (as cited in DPICf, n.d.). When poll respondents were given the option of choosing between capital punishment and life without parole, support for capital punishment dropped below 50 percent (DPICf, n.d.).

One group questioning the legitimacy of some death penalty convictions is the Innocence Project. Founded in 1992, the Innocence Project is a nonprofit legal clinic run through Yeshiva University which attempts to exonerate wrongfully convicted persons via DNA testing. To date, 187 clients served by this organization have been exonerated, 14 of whom were awaiting imposition of a death sentence (Innocence Project, 2006).

Another legal organization that has taken a stance suggesting the death penalty is being applied erroneously or unfairly is the American Bar Association (ABA). In fact, the ABA has called for a moratorium on the use of the death penalty claiming no official position on the death penalty itself, but noting, "Administration of the death penalty, far from being fair and consistent, is instead a haphazard maze of unfair practices with no internal consistency . . . the best way to consider and fix these unfair practices is by removing the pressure of impending executions" (n.d.). Cited among the many reasons for this position are documented biases with regard to race and geography, as well as the fact of over 100 persons being removed from death row due to overturned convictions.

The ABA is not the only group suggesting a halting of capital punishment sentencing. Advocacy groups, as well as local and state governments, have begun to call for moratoria and pass referendums in support of this initiative. In 2005, nearly half of the states introduced bills suggesting moratoria on executions, although none were enacted. Only Illinois has actually imposed a block on executions, including a commutation of all death penalty sentences by then-Governor George Ryan in 2003 (Peterson, 2005). Although the country remains divided, increasing evidence of erroneous convictions and unfairness suggests the frequency of execution may continue to decrease, even if actual law does not change.

PSYCHOLOGISTS AND THE DEATH PENALTY

In this section of this chapter we attempt to bring all the information discussed into focus for the mental health practitioner. Clearly, mental health professionals can be involved at any stage of the death penalty process (e.g., as a fact witness who treated a client before the crime occurred). It is likely, however, that the correctional or forensic practitioner will be involved in one of three ways: as a pretrial evaluator in a potential capital case, in treating the convicted offender, and in determining competency to be executed. Other roles, such as consultant and mitigation reviewer (Eisenberg, 2004) are not covered here, but the same level of attention should be applied by persons engaged in those roles.

Regardless of the particular role in the process, involvement in capital cases is likely to cause some level of dissonance for the clinician given the emphasis on beneficence in ethical standards for mental health professionals. Judge (2004) identifies this struggle and highlights several arguments provided by professional groups to attenuate the feelings likely to occur in practitioners working on capital cases. Largely, these arguments find the involvement of mental health professionals in death penalty evaluations and treatment to be unavoidable matters of a professional, rather than personal, nature that are necessary and that may serve some healing purpose. Judge (2004) suggests clinicians routinely involved in these cases undergo a process of moral disengagement, which he characterizes as both negative and necessary. Ultimately, he encourages a careful examination of ethical principles. In addition to this recommendation, we strongly advise that persons working with this population ensure training and competence commensurate with the gravity of the decisions being made. That said, we turn to the particulars of the aforementioned practitioner roles.

Forensic evaluators performing pretrial evaluations often focus on questions of competency and responsibility, although the evaluation of other issues (e.g., risk assessment) may also be required by the courts. With respect to competency to stand trial evaluations, examiners are typically asked to provide information as to the defendant's understanding of proceedings and charges. As Eisenberg (2004) notes, as per *Godinez v. Moran* (1993), competence is considered a general ability and a person deemed competent to stand trial is assumed competent in other areas. Due to the potential ramifications of competency findings, particularly in death penalty cases, the authors concur with Eisenberg (2004) in recommending that all areas of competence (e.g., competence to plea) be explored. With respect to criminal responsibility evaluations, Eisenberg (2004) again advises care, citing findings that death qualified juries are more likely to convict when the insanity issue has been raised.

Regarding the issue of the involvement of mental health practitioners in evaluating competency to be executed, as noted previously, the decision in *Ford v. Wainwright* (1986) held that execution was forbidden for individuals not recognizing the relationship between crime and punishment. Heilbrun (1987) encourages well-developed psycholegal skills as well as a very thorough evaluation complete with full informed consent in any evaluation of competency to be executed. In addition, Zapf, Boccaccini, and Brodsky (2003) highlight four specific competency-related areas that should be addressed in any such evaluation. These areas go beyond the *Ford* criteria and Zapf (in press) strongly advocates for conducting complete evaluations that may go beyond the court's stated criteria given the gravity of the consequences for this type of evaluation. While Eisenberg (2004) notes that although such examinations are rare, he encourages not only review of professional ethics, but also personal values, before engaging in this type of evaluation.

Once an individual has been sentenced to capital punishment, the role of the mental health practitioner in providing treatment to the condemned comes into play. Little information exists for the clinician regarding therapy with or supportive counseling for these persons as they move along a trajectory of appeals towards execution. Jones (2006) notes that traditional models of grief therapy do not apply to families of death row inmates, and it is logical to assume that the same applies to the condemned themselves.

While information on providing traditional psychotherapy to capitally-sanctioned offenders is scarce, the issue of caring for mentally ill persons facing imminent execution has begun to generate some discussion. In particular, an ethical conflict is raised when providing treatment in the form of medication is likely to elevate a person from "insanity" to a level of functioning allowing for execution. Judge (2004) discusses an Arizona case in which Claude Marturano, who experienced bizarre delusions, was sentenced to death for a murder he committed. The treating psychiatrist provided Marturano with medication to decrease distress, but refused to work with the state to restore him to competence for execution. Initially, the state threatened contempt charges against the psychiatrist but ultimately located on out-of-state practitioner who found Marturano competent to be executed. Cases such as this raise questions regarding the ethicality of the involvement of mental health professionals in certain proceedings. Judge, citing Foot, again advocates for a thorough review of the ethical issues (2004).

CONCLUSION

Clearly, the issue of capital punishment is a significant and contentious one that affects not only the United States, but the entire world. As indicated in the review of early capital punishment practices, the death penalty has been around since premodern civilization, when the make-up of the world was very different than it is now. Very few issues have remained as significant as the death penalty throughout time. At present, the death penalty has gone beyond simply being an issue related to the punishment of criminals, but rather has become a human rights issue throughout the international community. The authors were only able to present a brief glimpse into the death penalty in this chapter and the interested reader is encouraged to consult other sources to learn more about this important issue. As mental health professionals, the authors believe strongly that the very best professional practices need to be maintained in working with individuals who are or who have the potential to become affected by the death penalty. As researchers, the authors also believe strongly in the value of research on this issue and encourage further work in this important area. While it is easy to criticize the United States with respect to its stance on capital punishment within our international community, it is important that we not lose sight of the significant gains that have been made in this arena in recent years. Cases such as *Atkins* and *Simmons* have set the stage for our future.

REFERENCES

1000 Executions. (n.d.) Retrieved October 10, 2006 from http://www.1000exe cutions.org

Acker, J. R., Bohm, R. M., & Lanier, C. S. (1998). Introduction: America's experiment with capital punishment. In J. Acker, R. Bohm & C. Lanier (Eds.), *America's experiment with capital punishment: Reflections on the past, present, and future of the ultimate penal sanction* (pp. 5–21). Durham, NC: Carolina Academic Press.

American Bar Association. (n.d.) *American Bar Association death penalty moratorium implementation project.* Retrieved November 26, 2006 from http://abanet.org/moratorium/why.html

Amnesty International. (1999). Amnesty calls for ban on executions. *Reuters.* Retrieved June 16, 1999 from http://today.reuters.com/mews/home/html

Amnesty International (2000). United States of America: Failing the future. Death penalty developments March 1998-March 2000 (1). Retrieved November 14, 2006 from http://web.amnesty.org/library/Index/engAMR510032000

Amnesty International. (2003). *United States of America: Death by discrimination–the continuing role of race in capital cases.* Retrieved November 13, 2006 from http://web.amnesty.org/library/index/engamr510462003

Atkins v. Virginia 536 U.S. 304 (2002).

Bailey, V. (2000). The death penalty in British history. *Punishment and Society, 2,* 106–113.

Baldus, D. C., Pulaski, C. A. Jr., & Woodworth, G. (1983). Comparative review of death sentences: An empirical study of the Georgia experience. *Journal of Criminal Law and Criminology, 74,* 661–753.

Banner, S. (2002a). *The death penalty: An American history.* Cambridge, MA: Harvard University Press.

Banner, S. (2002b). The death penalty's strange career. *The Wilson Quarterly, 46*(2), 70–82.

Bohm, R.M. (1998). American death penalty opinion: Past, present, and future. In J. Acker, R. Bohm & C. Lanier (Eds.), *America's experiment with capital punishment: Reflections on the past, present, and future of the ultimate penal sanction* (pp. 25–46). Durham, NC: Carolina Academic Press.

Bowers, W. J., & Pierce, G. (1980). Deterrence or brutalization: What is the effect of executions? *Crime and Delinquency, 26,* 453–484.

Briggs, J., Harrison, C., McInnes, A., & Vincent, D. (1996). *Crime and punishment in England: An introductory history.* New York: St. Martin's Press.

Callins v. Collins, 510 U.S. 1141 (1994).

CNN. (2005, December 13). *Warden: Williams frustrated at end: Crips gang cofounder put to death for 4 murders.* Retrieved November 5, 2006, from http://www.cnn.com/2005/LAW/12/13/williams.execution/

Coker v. Georgia 433 U.S. 534 (1977).

Coyne, R. & Entzeroth, L. (Eds.). (1994). *Capital punishment and the judicial process.* Durham, NC: Carolina Academic Press.

Death Penalty Information Center (n.d.a). *History of the death penalty, part I.* Retrieved August 24, 2006 from http://www.deathpenaltyinfo.org/article.php?scid=15&did=410

Death Penalty Information Center (n.d.b). *Executions in the U.S. 1608–1987: The Espy File.* Retrieved October 1, 2006 from http://www.deathpenaltyinfo.org/article.php?scid=8&did=269

Death Penalty Information Center (n.d.c). *Descriptions of execution methods.* Retrieved November 5, 2006 from http://www.deathpenaltyinfo.org/article.php?scid=&&did=479

Death Penalty Information Center (n.d.d). *New voices: Ohio Supreme Court justice says mentally ill should be exempt from death penalty.* Retrieved November 5, 2006 from http://www.deathpenaltyinfo.org/article.php?did=1936&scid=64

Death Penalty Information Center (n.d.e). *Lethal injections: Some cases stayed, other executions proceed.* Retrieved November 5, 2006, from http://www.deathpenaltyinfo.org/article.php?did=1686&scid=64

Death Penalty Information Center (n.d.f). *News and developments–Public Opinion.* Retrieved November 26, 2006, from http://www.deathpenaltyinfo.org/newsanddev.php?scid=23

del Barco, M. (2005, April 21). Crips founder seeks redemption on death row. *(NPR).* Retrieved November 2, 2005, from http://www.npr.org/templates/story/story.php?storyId=460850

Dieter, R. C. (1999). *International perspectives on the death penalty: A costly isolation for the U.S.* Washington, DC: Death Penalty Information Center.

Eisenberg, J. R. (2004). *Law, psychology, and death penalty litigation.* Sarasota, FL: Professional Resource Press.

Furman v. Georgia. 408 US 238 (1972).

Ford v. Wainwright 477 U.S. 399 (1986).

Godinez v. Moran 509 U.S. 389 (1993).

Gregg v. Georgia 428 US 155 (1976).

Hart (2006, October 10). *More calls for death penalty in child rapes.* Retrieved November 5, 2006 from http://www.latimes.com/news/nationworld/nation/la-na-execute10oct10,0,3071301.story?coll=la-home-headlines

Heilbrun, K. (1987). The assessment of competency for execution: An overview. *Behavioral Sciences and the Law, 5,* 383–396.

Hill v. McDonough 547 U.S. ___ (2006).

Hood, R. (2001). Capital punishment: A global perspective. *Punishment and Society, 3,* 331–354.

Hooker, R. *The code of Hammurabi.* Retrieved August 31, 2006 from www.wsu.edu/~dee/MESO/CODE.HTM

Hutchinson, E. O. (2005, November 22). Clemency for Tookie a signal to black youth *(NPR).* Retrieved November 5, 2005, from www.npr.org/templates/story/story.php?storyId=5022757

Innocence Project (2006). *The Innocence Project.* Retrieved November 26, 2006, from http://www.innocenceproject.org

Jones, S. (2006). *Complicated grief faced by the families of death row inmates: Obstacles to effective grief therapy.* Abstract retrieved November 5, 2006, from http://www.inter-disciplinary.net/mso/dd/dd4/s3.html

Judge, D. P. (2004). The role of mental health professionals in capital punishment: An exercise in moral disengagement. [Electronic Version]. *Houston Law Review, 41,* 515–612.

Lague, D. (2006, November 1). China acts to reduce high rate of executions. *The New York Times.* Retrieved November 1, 2006, from http://www.nytimes.com/2006/11/01/world/asia/01china.html

Lifton, R. J., & Mitchell, G. (2002). *Who owns death? Capital punishment, the American conscience, and the end of executions.* New York: Harper Collins.

Liptak, A. (2003, August 31). Louisiana sentence renews debate on the death penalty. *The New York Times,* p. 14.

Liptak, A (2006, June 10). *Death penalty in some cases of child sex is widening.* Retrieved October 31, 2006 from http://www.nytimes.com/2006/06/10/us/10execute.html?ex=1307592000&en=7e3759eb2168dc4&ei=5088&partner=rssnyt&emc=rss

Manners, I. (2002). Normative power Europe: A contradiction in terms? *Journal of Common Market Studies, 40,* 235–258.

Mocan, H. N., & Gittings, R. K. (2003). Getting off death row: Commuted sentences and the deterrent effect of capital punishment. *Journal of Law and Economics, 46* (2), 453–478.

Nieves, E. (2000, December 6). Antigang "role model" is up for a Nobel and execution. *The New York Times,* p. A16.

Penry v. Lynaugh, 492 U.S. 302 (1989).

Peterson, K. (2005, April 19). Death penalty–34 states permit executions. Retrieved November 26, 2006 from http://www.stateline.org/live/ViewPage.action?siteNodeId=136&languageId=1&contentId=25995

Peterson, R. D., & Bailey, W. C. (1998). Is capital punishment an effective deterrent for murder? An examination of social science research. In J. Acker, R. Bohm, & C. Lanier (Eds.), *America's experiment with capital punishment: Reflections on the past, present, and future of the ultimate penal sanction* (pp. 157–182). Durham, NC: Carolina Academic Press.

Policy Almanac. (n.d.) *Capital Punishment 2000.* Retrieved September 27, 2006 from www.policyalmanac.org/crime/archive/bjs_capital_punishment.shtml

Radzinowicz, L. (1999). *Adventures in criminology.* London: Routledge.

Reggio, M. H. (1997). History of the death penalty. In L.E. Randa (Ed.), *Society's final solution: A history and discussion of the death penalty* (pp. 1–11). Lanham, NY: University Press of America, Inc.

Roper v. Simmons, 543 U.S. 551 (2005).

Sack, K. (2001, October 6). Supreme Court of Georgia voids use of electrocution: State will now turn to lethal injection. *The New York Times,* p. A7.

Schabas, W. A. (1997). *The abolition of the death penalty in international law,* (2nd ed.). Cambridge, United Kingdom: Cambridge University Press.

Schabas, W. A. (2002). *The abolition of the death penalty in international law,* (3rd ed.). Cambridge, United Kingdom: Cambridge University Press.

Scott, G. R. (1968). *The history of corporal punishment.* Guernsey, United Kingdom: Guernsey Press Company.

Sellin, J. T. (1967). *Capital punishment.* New York: Harper and Row.

Stanford v. Kentucky 492 U.S. 361 (1989).

Steiker, C. S., & Steiker, J. M. (1998). Judicial developments in capital punishment law. In J. Acker, R. Bohm, & C. Lanier (Eds.), *America's experiment with capital punishment: Reflections on the past, present, and future of the ultimate penal sanction* (pp. 47–76). Durham, NC: Carolina Academic Press.

Streib, V. L. (2005). *The juvenile death penalty today: Death sentences and executions for juvenile crimes,* January 1, 1973–February 28, 2005. Retrieved November 13, 2006, from http://www.law/onu.edu/faculty/streib

Thompson v. Kentucky, 437 U.S. 815 (1988).

U.N. panel votes for ban on death penalty. (1999, April 29). *The New York Times,* p. A4.

U.S. Department of Justice. (2000). Survey of the federal death penalty system. Retrieved November 1, 2006 from http://www/usdoj.gov/dag/pubdoc/dp survey.html

Van den Haag, E. (1998). Justice, deterrence and the death penalty. In J. Acker, R. Bohm, & C. Lanier (Eds.), *America's experiment with capital punishment: Reflections on the past, present, and future of the ultimate penal sanction* (pp. 139–156). Durham, NC: Carolina Academic Press.

Zapf, P., Boccaccini, M., & Brodsky, S. (2003). Assessment of competency for execution: Professional guidelines and an evaluation checklist. *Behavioral Sciences and the Law, 21,* 103–120.

Zapf, P. A. (in press). Competency for execution. In R. Jackson (Ed.), *Learning forensic assessment.* Mahwah, NJ: Lawrence Erlbaum.

Chapter 13

DIFFERING PERSPECTIVES: CORRECTIONAL SYSTEMS IN NONWESTERN COUNTRIES

AVEN SENTER,* ROBERT D. MORGAN, AND JON T. MANDRACCHIA

INTRODUCTION

The intent of this chapter is to organize and summarize the available literature on several of the more researched correctional systems in nonwestern countries. Since few academic researchers publish in this area, much of the literature is derived from reports issued by multinational organizations, such as the World Health Organization (WHO) and United Nations (UN), nongovernmental organizations (NGOs), newspaper articles, and websites. The overall length of this chapter is a reflection of the limited information available about these systems.

The reasons for the relative paucity of research in this area are threefold. First, access to these systems is limited. Although information periodically leaks out from nonwestern countries regarding their prison conditions, it typically comes in the form of a former inmate's individual account or the politically oriented position promulgated by a NGO. In a similar vein, several countries generally do not have the same level of governmental transparency as many westernized countries. That is, governments censor and regulate information regarding their prisons either through intimidation or governmental control of the media. Lastly, academic freedom does not prevail in many nonwestern countries as it does in westernized countries. The university system is generally controlled by the government, which means there is little funding for exploratory and potentially embarrassing research. The end result of these barriers is less systematic empiricism. Notwithstanding these obstacles, information regarding the conditions of these correctional systems

---

* The views and opinions expressed in this chapter are those of the authors only and do not necessarily represent the policies or opinions of the Federal Bureau of Prisons or the Department of Justice.

does emerge from time to time and will eventually coalesce to improve our collective understanding.

This chapter will focus on the People's Republic of China (PRC or China), Russian Federation (Russia), and South Africa. Although there is a multitude of other nonwestern countries that merit discussion, the lack of extant correctional literature is such that a comprehensive review is not possible.

CHINA

As the most populous country in the world, China's population exceeds one billion people (U.S. Census Bureau, 2005). Although China has the second largest number of prisoners, the actual estimates of imprisonment rates range from 118 (World Prison Brief, 2006) to 160 (Seymour, 2005) per 100,000. Several human rights organizations (e.g., Asia Watch, Amnesty International) and governmental agencies (see U.S. State Department Bureau of Democracy, Human Rights, and Labor, 2000) have highlighted gross violations of individual rights including torture of prisoners, inhumane and harsh prison conditions, and denial of due process, especially in sensitive political cases.

With roughly 50 different crimes eligible for capital punishment (Klofas, 1991), China is known to execute more prisoners per year than all other countries in the world combined (Smith, 2001; Yardley, 2005). Although China does not release the exact number of executions, some estimate the number to exceed 10,000 a year (Yardley, 2005). Depending on the sociopolitical climate (i.e., pressure by other countries), China has periodically issued a national moratorium on prisoner executions. However, executions are typically resumed.

Reform Through Labor

Reminiscent of the infamous Russian labor concentration camps (also known as gulags) from the former days of the Soviet Union, China operates a large number of prison labor camps collectively known as the *Laogai* system (Mosher, 1991). Based on a combination of Confucian principles and rehabilitative philosophy, these camps generally operate under a strict regimen of productive labor in conjunction with education and political training (Bracey, 1988). Since information regarding the vast system of labor camps is under tight governmental control, the exact number of facilities is unknown. Nevertheless, published estimates range anywhere from 1,000 to 5,000 (Mosher, 1991). Similarly, there is no clear consensus on the number of prisoners involved in the *Laogai* system. Recent estimates range from as little as 10 million (Mosher, 1991) to upwards of 21 million inmates (Wu, 1996).

The administrative structures of *Laogai* facilities are individually delegated to each of the 23 provinces (Seymour & Anderson, 1998). The *Laogai* system is comprised of three distinct categories, which are often located on isolated farms and camps in remote areas of the countryside. The most common type of inmate labor camp, the *Laogai* (convict labor) generally consists of prisoners convicted of crimes. The *Laojiao* (reeducation through labor) is reserved for individuals who might be considered unproductive at work or suspected of posing a threat to China's national security. Since individuals under Laojiao control are not criminals, they are considered administrative detainees and may be detained for a period of time not to exceed 3 to 4 years (Klofas, 1991). The final category, *Jiuye* (forced job placement), is reserved for former prisoners who are required to continue their labor despite the completion of their sentences (Seymour & Anderson, 1998).

Although education is purportedly the goal of the *Laogai* system (Bracey, 1988), the daily activities of prisoners consist primarily of manual and productive labor (Seymour & Anderson, 1998; Shaw, 1998). There is some disagreement in the literature regarding the economic impact of this government-imposed labor system. Seymour and Anderson (1998) assert the *Laogai* system yields an insignificant effect on the national economy. Although contributing less than one percent of China's gross national product (GNP), however, Mosher (1991) contends the economic impact is not indeed negligible. Commonly exported goods include textiles, clothing, beverages, and machinery. There is greater consensus on the Laogai educational components, which consist primarily of vocational training, political study, cultural training, and moral reform (Shaw, 1998).

Infectious Diseases

Acquired immune deficiency disease (AIDS) is a constellation of health-related complications caused by the human immunodeficiency virus (HIV). As the name implies, HIV attacks the immune system leaving a person vulnerable to opportunistic infections and diseases, such as pneumonia and cancer. HIV transmission is commonly facilitated in prison settings through inadequate health care, overcrowding, needle sharing, unprotected sex, and tattooing (UNAIDS, 1997). Accordingly, the UN advocates that prisoners should have access to greater basic health care, liquid bleach, sterile needles, condoms, and education on HIV.

Since the first few cases of AIDS were initially diagnosed in 1981, Asian governments have consistently reported the lowest prevalence rates of AIDS patients (Karel & Robey, 1988). Some authors, however, have asserted these lower statistics are the product of underreporting. Commonly viewed as a "foreign disease," China has implemented several preventive measures to minimize exposure. Examples include mandatory blood tests of Chinese workers who interact with foreigners (e.g., translators, embassy employees), banning the importation of foreign blood products, and testing international visitors intending to remain in the country longer than one year (Karel & Robey, 1988). To combat the increasing number of inmates diagnosed with AIDS and HIV carriers in China's Guangdong Province, government officials have planned the construction of two specialized prisons to accommodate these patients (Caixiong, 2005; Terra Daily, 2004). These new facilities are in contrast to the published position of the UNAIDS (1997) on AIDS and prisons, which asserts isolating inmates does not generally control HIV transmission and recommends avoiding housing inmates in specialized areas solely due to their HIV status.

Psychiatric Abuse

In recent years, China has fallen under intense scrutiny for alleged human rights violations of incarcerating political dissidents within psychiatric facilities, known as *Ankang* asylums (Munro, 2000). This practice is considered a means of controlling political dissension, which circumvents the court system and does not provide for reevaluation or appeal (Kahn, 2006). Although only isolated cases of reported psychiatric abuse in China have been publicized, it is estimated that there have been over 3,000 political dissidents held in *Ankang* asylums throughout China. The nature of psychiatric confinement of political dissidents in China may reflect those of the former Soviet Union, as many of the practices and procedures currently utilized in China have been directly modeled from that of the former Soviet Union (Munro, 2000).

The most prominent case in which psychiatric abuse has occurred in China surfaced in November of 2005 with the release of dissident Wang Wanxing from Chinese custody to Germany (Human Rights Watch, 2005; Scoop Independent News, 2006). Wang was imprisoned for 13 years in a Beijing *Ankang* after staging a solo demonstration supporting democracy in Tiananmen Square in 1989 (Human Rights Watch, 2005). Dutch psychiatrists later released a statement that a comprehensive psychiatric evaluation of Wang did not demonstrate the presence of any mental illness, nor had he likely ever suffered from such an illness which may have justified psychiatric confinement (Kahn, 2006). Wang's reported experiences of the conditions in the Beijing *Ankang* included forcing him to swallow drugs to "blunt his will" (Kahn, 2006), being made to watch other patients receive forced acupuncture with highly painful electrified needles, being physically attacked by other inmates who had committed rape and murder, and observing another patient who had been performing a hunger-strike being force-fed by staff and subsequently choking to death (Human Rights Watch, 2005).

Many of the psychiatric diagnoses utilized to justify admission of political dissidents in *Ankang* asylums are not recognized in Western psychiatry. Instead, these conditions are ostensibly used for the specific purpose of silencing political dissidents under the guise of psychiatric necessity (Human Rights Watch, 2005; Munro, 2000). Typical diagnoses for political dissidents admitted to *Ankang* asylums include "paranoid psychosis," "political monomania," and "litigation mania." In Wang's case, Chinese officials from the Beijing Ankang released a report to the German government asserting that although Wang was typically nonsymptomatic, "When the topic of conversation turns to politics . . . his [mental] activities are still characterized by delusions of grandeur, litigation mania, and conspicuously enhanced pathological will" (Human Rights Watch, 2005). Reports from other individuals in the *Ankang* system across China reflect similar abuses and misuse of psychiatry. At this point, however, the exact prevalence and nature of these practices is unknown as China has not allowed open investigations or communication related to these facilities (Human Rights Watch, 2005).

RUSSIA

Russian prisons have historically been among the toughest within which to serve time (for example, see Lyuzakov, 2005) as "crumbling infrastructure, overcrowding, lack of adequate health care, and human rights violations have plagued the prison system throughout the twentieth century" (Yale School of Nursing, 2003, p. 7). Although conditions appear to have improved somewhat, significant problems remain. For example, in June of 2005, hundreds of Russian inmates engaged in serious self-mutilation in protest of deplorable prison conditions and instances of abuse by prison guards (Bigg, 2005). Although human rights efforts and legislation reforms have been implemented to improve prison conditions in Russia, significant problems remain, primarily including issues of overcrowding and limited resources for diagnosing and treating infectious diseases (e.g., pulmonary tuberculosis, HIV) and mental illnesses.

Overcrowding in Russian Prisons

Consistent with most countries and jurisdictions, Russia faces a prison overcrowding crisis. In fact, as recently as 1998, Russia was number one in the world for incarcerating its citizens (a distinction now held by the United States of America; Mauer, 2003) with incarceration estimates near 700 per 100,000 (Abramkin, 1998). Of greater concern was Russia's inability to adequately care for its prisoners. In what some labeled a "Threat to Humankind" (Moscow Center for Prison Reform, 1998c), Russia was unable to meet prisoners' basic medical and physiological needs (e.g., food, hygiene, sanitation). Thus, Russia launched a Prison Reform Project in 1997. The goal of this project was to "introduce and disseminate social work in the prison system of the Russian Federation as a contribution to the ongoing humanisation and reform processes" (Swiss Agency for Development and Cooperation, n.d.). While efforts to humanize the prison system were in progress, strategies were also implemented to reduce the prison population. Demonstrating impressive results, by 2002 Russia successfully reduced its prison population by 20 percent (Moscow Center for Prison Reform, 1998d), whereas many countries continued to experience prison growth.

Although amnesty appears to be a primary contributor to the 20 percent reduction in the Russian prison population (Moscow Center for Prison Reform, 1998a), the government was instrumental in obtaining reductions. Then Prime Minister Vladimir Putin convened two conference calls with government and judicial bodies encouraging a reduction in the prison population (Moscow Center for Prison Reform, 1998a). Combined with changes in the Criminal Procedural Code of the Russian Federation (effective July 2002), it appears that Russia has successfully reduced the number of inmates entering prison while increasing the number of inmates released from prison (see Moscow Center for Prison Reform, 1998d). Nevertheless, more work remains to be done. To accomplish greater reductions, Abramkin (1998) recommended a process of "decentralization" of Russia's prison administration. Although decentralization has met resistance, the aim would be to regionalize prison administration so that regional prison administrators would have greater understanding of budgetary constraints and incarceration limits. This would enable prison administrators to better monitor incarceration rates and prison conditions.

Infectious Diseases

Not surprisingly given issues of prison overcrowding, poor physical conditions, and limited medical resources as noted above, Russian prisons are dealing with serious public health (i.e., tuberculosis, HIV) and mental health problems similar to other countries. Pulmonary tuberculosis (TB) and multidrug-resistant TB (MDR-TB) are critical health problems in Russian prisons. Russian prisoners have a TB incidence rate that far exceeds the general population with estimates ranging from 40 times higher than the general population (USAID, 2005) to 200 times higher prevalent rates than the general population (Public Health Agency of Canada, 2001). By 2003 it was estimated that 1 in 10 inmates suffered from TB, suggesting that over 86,000 inmates were diagnosed with the disease (Henry J. Kaiser Family Foundation, 2003). For additional epidemiological data for two remand prisons in St. Petersburg, Russia, readers are referred to Lobacheva, Sazhin, Vdovichenko, and Giesecke (2005). Clearly, TB remains a major health problem in Russian prisons, which is compounded by continuously overcrowded conditions (Henry J. Kaiser Family Foundation, 2003).

Unfortunately, medical resources are limited and Russian prisons have historically been unable to comply with international standards of medical services (Moscow Center for Prison Reform, 1998b). Specifically, overcrowded prisons in combination with limited medical resources have limited Russia's ability to comply with the Guidelines for the Control of Tuberculosis in Prisons (Maher, Grzemska, Coninx, & Reyes, 1998). Nevertheless, efforts to treat the afflicted and limit the spread of TB are ongoing. Notably, in the 1940s Russia developed a specialized colony for inmates suffering from TB. This colony allows for specialized placement and services to TB positive patients. In addition, Medecins Sans Frontieres (MSF), a medical aid organization, began working in Russian prisons in 1996 to help treat the diseased as well as combat the spreading of the disease. Within two years, facilities with MSF involvement evidenced significant decreases in TB related deaths and cure rates doubled (Moscow Helsinki Group, n.d.). In spite of these gains, given continued prison overcrowding with limited medical resources, TB remains a major health problem in Russian prisons.

The prevalence of HIV positive inmates in Russian prisons is also alarming and was referred to as "A Worsening Catastrophe" by the Moscow Helsinki Group (n.d.). Although infection rates are lower compared to TB, with approximately 37,000 cases of HIV positive inmates compared to approximately 86,000 inmates infected with TB, these rates are sure to grow. Just as the general population in Russia has experienced an epidemic of HIV positive citizens, the Russian prison population is facing a similar fate (Holley, 2003). In fact, Holley (2003) referred to Russian prisons as "incubators" for HIV.

Although some interventions that have been proposed to reduce the transmission of diseases such as AIDS (e.g., needle exchange programs, providing cleaning agents such bleach to sterilize needles, condom distribution) have met resistance in Russian prisons due to security as well as sociopolitical reasons (see Holley, 2003), other programs have been supported. The Ministry of Justice of the Russian Federation for example, supported an HIV/AIDS prevention and health promotion program to "establish long-term working relationships between the penitentiary system and community agencies" for HIV prevention (AIDS Foundation East-West, n.d.). Even more promising are HIV prevention programs aimed at reducing the spread of HIV in Russian prisons; these programs are in place in almost all Russian regions (Durne, n.d.). Specifically, Durne (n.d.) observed that "many" Russian programs already in progress may "directly" and "indirectly" influence the HIV epidemic in Russia's prisons.

Approaches that "directly" affect the HIV situation in Russia's prisons include:

- Prevention of narcotic drug use among adolescents and young people outside the penal system, including treatment for chemical dependency with rehabilitation as one of the components;
- Primary and secondary prevention of HIV among adolescents and young people outside the prison system, including sex education, harm reduction, sexually transmitted disease (STD) and AIDS treatment, and social rehabilitation of HIV-infected people;
- Juvenile justice system diverting children and adolescents who have breached the law to social correction/rehabilitation programs, rather than sending them to prison institutions;
- Prevention of HIV among prisoners, including information, counseling, condom distribution, disinfection and, less often, injecting paraphernalia exchange.

Approaches that "indirectly" affect the HIV situation in Russia's prisons include:

- Prevention of HIV among prison personnel, including information, counseling and distribution of personal safety devices such as condoms;
- Programs aimed at resocialization of former prisoners after their discharge;
- Crime prevention among adolescents and young people.

Mental Illness in Russian Prisons

Little has been written about prevalence rates or therapeutic efforts for mentally ill offenders incarcerated in Russian prisons. However, consistent with other countries (e.g., United States), recent estimates indicated that approximately 20 percent of the Russian prison population suffers from some form of mental illness (Bobrik, Danishevski, Eroshina, & McKee, 2005). Although some estimates are significantly higher, discrepancies appear due in large part to the Soviet psychiatric paradigm as well as high rate of inmate substance abuse in Russian prisons (Bobrik et al., 2005). With overcrowded prison populations and limited medical resources for severely ill inmates (as noted above), little attention has been paid to mentally ill inmates. Given that many inmates appear to be left to their own resources (e.g., self-medicating), increased efforts are needed in Russian legislation to ensure adequate standards of mental health care to all inmates incarcerated in Russian prisons.

Psychiatric Abuse

Reports of psychiatric abuse for purposes of political persuasion in Russia surfaced as early as the 1960s, although subsequent information has identified psychiatric abuse dating back to the mid 1830s (Gordon & Meux, 2000). The purpose of the psychiatric abuse had been to institute control by silencing political dissension while avoiding potentially controversial public court processes (Reich, 1983). Psychiatric abuse manifested in several ways in Russia, including the misdiagnosis (typically use of a form of schizophrenia not recognized by Western psychiatry) and therefore inappropriate confinement of individuals to psychiatric hospitals, inappropriate definitions of the constitution of mental illness, and the influence of the KGB upon prominent psychiatrists in the Soviet Union (Gordon & Meux, 2000). Reports of abuse and mistreatment of political dissidents in the Soviet Union included the administration of injections that produced abscesses, stupor, or convulsions, as well as wrapping an individual in a wet canvas which, when dried, contracts extremely tightly (Reich, 1983).

Accusations of psychiatric abuse in the Soviet Union fell heavily upon the psychiatric community of Russia, with focus upon the misapplication of theories of mental illness and treatment. In the 1970s, for example, meetings held by the World Psychiatric Association focused, in part, on the alleged Soviet Union's psychiatric abuses. Several other countries advocated for either the suspension or expulsion of the Soviet association, the All-Union Society of Psychiatrists and Neuropathologists (Reich, 1983). Accusations of psychiatric abuse, however, were also evident from within the Soviet Union during that time. In 1981, one such account came from Soviet psychiatrist Dr. Anatoly Koryagin, who spoke out against the "prostitution of psychiatry" in the Soviet Union and was subsequently imprisoned in a political labor camp (Schwarz Report, 1982). In his appeal, which had been smuggled out of the labor camp, Dr. Koryagin stated that "the Soviet authorities have turned our most humane branch of medicine into an instrument for achieving the main aim of their internal policy: the suppression of dissent in our country" (Schwarz Report, 1982, p. 1). Dr. Koryagin went on to identify "First among the guilty, without doubt, are those doctors who diagnose nonexistent illnesses in healthy people. But no less guilty are those leading psychiatrists of our country at top administrative level[s] who organize and facilitate the execution of this ugly policy" (Schwarz Report, 1982, p. 1).

During the late 1980s, prior to the fall of communism in Russia in 1991, procedures were set in place to remedy the identified psychiatric abuses in Russia. This included the release of political dissenters via a criminal code amendment related to anti-Soviet propaganda and behavior as well as the transfer of responsibility for Soviet psychiatric hospitals from the Ministry of the Interior to the Ministry of Health (Gordon & Meux, 2000). After the fall of communism, the Russian Federation implemented a law on "Psychiatric Care and Guarantees of Citizens' Rights," and in 1994 the Russian Society of Psychiatrists adopted a "Code of Professional Ethics" (Polubinskaya & Bonnie, 1996). Overall, Russian psychiatry now emphasizes patients' well-being and rights, including informed consent, more stringent policy for utilization of psychiatric patients for purposes of research and dissemination of patients' medical information, and more protection of psychiatric patients via means of appeal of treatment and detainment in psychiatric facilities (Gordon & Meux, 2000).

SOUTH AFRICA

After 1990, apartheid formally ended and the South African prison system was generally desegregated (Human Rights Watch, 1994). Another key change was the renaming of the Prisons Services, a military-type organization, to the Department of Correctional Services. In keeping with the correctional reorganization, several initiatives were implemented to reform prisoner conditions. For example, there was a reduction in the number of eligible offenses for capital punishment, greater supervision of corrections by outside authorities, and greater transparency of prisoner conditions.

With an estimated incarceration rate of 335 per 100,000, South Africa continues to have one of the highest rates in the world (World Prison Brief, 2006). Since violent offenders are ostensibly more likely to be incarcerated than their nonviolent counterparts, South Africa's high rate of imprisonment may reflect the country's higher incidence of violent crime (Mauer, 1995). A Human Rights Watch report released in 1994 noted that more than 20,000 murders are committed annually in South Africa, which equals a rate of 50 per 100,000 people. With limited resources and a high crime rate, Human Rights Watch asserts that overcrowding is a serious problem in South African prisons.

Many South African prisoners often complain about going hungry due to the lack of food or poor quality of the fare (Human Rights Watch, 1994). It is not uncommon for food to spoil prior to serving and some inmates are required to eat their meals in their cells while sitting on the barren floors. Similar conditions exist in the African country of Congo. Often living in violent and dank conditions, many Congolese inmates die from lack of food and mal-nourishment before reaching the end of their sentence (Lacey, 2004). Prison-ers must rely on prison officials for sustenance if family members do not bring care packages of food. As a result, prisoners often suffer because prison per-sonnel have inadequate resources for inmates.

Infectious Diseases

Prisoners are at an increased risk for HIV infection due to unprotected sex-ual activity and intravenous (IV) drug use (Stern, 2001). As previously men-tioned, the UN (UNAIDS, 1997) advocates a policy of issuing condoms, bleach, and clean needles. Notwithstanding the increased risk of HIV transmis-sion due to sexual activity and assault, condoms are not issued in South African prisons (Human Rights Watch, 1994). Concerns also exist regarding the increased risk of TB transmission due to the overcrowded prison conditions.

Mental Illness in African Prisons

With only a few psychiatrists to serve an entire country, there is a large shortage of mental health professionals in many African countries (Asuni, 1986). The situation is more acutely dire for inmates with psychiatric needs since they are often left to fend for themselves without mental health care. Asuni (1986) asserts many mentally ill inmates are relegated to areas of the prison that are similar to an asylum, often left without clothing on barren floors.

CONCLUSION

In concluding this chapter, first and foremost, it bears reiterating that the dearth of literature regarding correctional practices in nonwestern countries is problematic. A review of the. reference list for this chapter reveals reliance upon far more nonscientific sources than scientific. As Gilinskiy (2006) described Russian criminology as scholarship isolated from the rest of the world, so too are most correctional systems in nonwestern countries. Clearly more scholarship and empirical research are needed to better understand non-western correctional systems. This will benefit these countries as well as west-ernized countries, which continually work to implement superior correctional practices. When evaluating the progress of nonwestern correctional systems, it is important to recognize that the aforementioned countries have lengthy histories of inadequate medical care, poor containment of infectious disease, and rampant abuse of psychiatry to suppress political dissension. Nevertheless, any measurable improvement is indeed better than history has demonstrated thus far.

In spite of the limited literature, a review of nonwestern correctional systems, particularly Russia, China, and South Africa, reveals consistent themes that are also evidenced in westernized countries. Concerns regarding prison overcrowding, spread of infectious diseases, and lack of mental health services for mentally ill offenders are paramount. Of interest, however, are the attempts to combat these problems in these nonwestern correctional systems. For example, Russia implemented federal reform to reduce overcrowded conditions and reduce the spread of infectious diseases. Furthermore, although prison segregation is not recommended, both China and Russia have developed specialized institutions for housing the diseased. Monitoring these practices will provide additional information regarding effective versus ineffective correctional practices. It is evident that greater communication and sharing of correctional practices between westernized and nonwestern countries promises to be beneficial and is warranted.

REFERENCES

Abramkin, V. (1998). Reducing Russia's prison population. *Information Bulletin of Moscow Centre for Prison Reform.* Retrieved June 2, 2006, from http://www.penal reform.org/english/reduc_abramkin.htm

AIDS Foundation East-West. (n.d.). HIV prevention and health promotion in prisons (Russian Federation). AFEW: Projects. Retrieved June 8, 2006, from http://www.afew .org/english/projects_prison_rus.php

Asuni, T. (1986). Mental health in prisons: The African perspective. *International Journal of Offender Therapy and Comparative Criminology, 30,* 7–10.

Bigg, C. (2005, July 6). Russia: Prison director sacked after hundreds of cases of self-mutilation. Retrieved June 2, 2006, from http://www.rferl.org/featuresarti cle/2005/07/0186377d-1840-415f-8e01-614af7841063.html

Bobrik, A., Danishevski, K., Eroshina, K., & McKee, M. (2005). Prison health in Russia: The larger picture. *Journal of Public Health Policy, 26,* 30–59.

Bracey, D. (1988). "Like a doctor to a patient, like a parent to a child": Corrections in the People's Republic of China. *The Prison Journal, 68,* 24–33.

Caixiong, Z. (2005, November 14). Special prisons for HIV/AIDS inmates. *China Daily,* pp. 1, 2.

Coyle, A. (2004). The use and abuse of prison around the world. *Corrections Today, 66,* 64–67.

Durne, D. (n.d.). HIV/AIDS prevention in prisons in Russia. Retrieved June 8, 2006, from http://www.mhg.ru/english/1F4F76C.

Gilinskiy, Y. (2006). Crime in contemporary Russia. *European Journal of Criminology, 3,* 259–292.

Gordon, H. & Meux, C. (2000). Forensic psychiatry in Russia: Past, present and future. *Psychiatric Bulletin, 24,* 121–123.

Henry J. Kaiser Family Foundation (2003, July 24). Overcrowding in Russian prison system facilitates spread of tuberculosis, HIV, report says. *The Body.* Retrieved July 7, 2006, from http://www.thebody.com/kaiser/2003/jul24_03/russia_ hiv.html

Holley, D. (2003, April 18). Up to 1.5 million Russians have HIV, government says. *Los Angeles Times.* Retrieved June 8, 2006, from http://www.aegis.com/news/lt/ 2003/LT030409.html

Human Rights Watch (2005). *China: Political prisoner exposes brutality in police-run mental hospital: Eyewitness testimonies from notorious Ankang asylum.* Retrieved July 21, 2006, from http://hrw.org/english/docs/2005/11/01/china11957_txt.htm

Human Rights Watch (1994). *Prison conditions in South Africa.* Retrieved June 2, 2006, from http://www.hrw.org/reports/1994/southafrica/1.htm

Kahn, J. (2006, March 17). Sane Chinese put in asylum, doctors find. *The New York Times.* Retrieved July 21, 2006, from http://coloradohumanrights.blogspot.com/ 2006_03_01_coloradohumanrights_archive.html

Karel, S. G., & Robey, B. (1988). AIDS in Asia and the pacific. *Asian and Pacific Population Forum, 2,* 18–30.

Klofas, J. M. (1991). Considering prison in context: The case of the People's Republic of China. *International Journal of Comparative and Applied Criminal Justice, 15,* 175–186.

Lacey, M. (2004, December 31). Making hard time even harder: Let the inmates starve. *The New York Times,* pp. A4.

Lobacheva, T., Sazhin, V., Vdovichenko, E., & Giesecke, J. (2005). Pulmonary tuberculosis in two remand prisons (SIZOs) in St. Petersburg, Russia. *Eurosurveillance, 10,* 93–96.

Lyuzakov, P. (2005, February 21). The Russian prison. *Radical Party News Releases on Russia.* Retrieved June 2, 2006, from http://web.radicalparty.org/pressreview/print_right.php?func=detail&par=12416

Maher, D., Grzemska, M., Coninx, R., & Reyes, H. (1998). Guidelines for the control of tuberculosis in prisons. *WHO/TB/98.250.* Geneva, Switzerland: World Health Organization.

Mauer, M. (2003). Comparative international rates of incarceration: An examination of causes and trends. *The Sentencing Project.* Retrieved June 14, 2006, from http://www.sentencing project.org/pdfs/pub9036.pdf

Moscow Center for Prison Reform. (1998a). *Information about the penal system: Can Russia be out of the world prison leader race at the beginning of the XXI century?* Retrieved June 2, 2006, from http://www.prison.org/English/ps_leader.htm

Moscow Center for Prison Reform. (1998b). *Prisoners infected with tuberculosis.* Retrieved June 2, 2006, from http://www.prison.org/English/rpovcp.htm

Moscow Center for Prison Reform. (1998c). *Reduction of Russia's prison population: Possibilities and limits: Russian prisons become a threat to humankind: 1997–1999.* Retrieved June 2, 2006, from http://www.prison.org/English/rpsys_3.htm

Moscow Center for Prison Reform. (1998d). *Reduction of Russia's prison population: Possibilities and limits: Russia's prison population has reduced by 20%.* Retrieved June 2, 2006, from http://www.prison.org/English/rpsys_1.htm

Moscow Helsinki Group. *Tuberculosis in Russian prisons: Dying for reform.* Retrieved June 8, 2006, from http://www.mhg.ru/english/1F11E20

Mosher, S. W. (1991). Chinese prison labor. *Society, 29,* 51–59.

Munro, R. (2000). Judicial psychiatry in China and its political abuses. *Columbia Journal of Asian Law, 14,* 1–101.

Polubinskaya, S. V., & Bonnie, R. J. (1996). The Code of Professional Ethics of the Russian Society of Psychiatrists. *International Journal of Law and Psychiatry, 19,* 143–172.

Public Health Agency of Canada (2001, March). Tuberculosis in prisons. *Tuberculosis Epi Update.* Retrieved June 8, 2006, from http://www.phac-aspc.gc.ca/publicat/epiu-aepi/tb/epi0301/prison_e.html

Reich, W. (1983, January 30). The world of Soviet psychiatry. *The New York Times.* Retrieved July 21, 2006, from http://query.nytimes.com

Schwarz Report (1982, March 15). *An imprisoned Soviet psychiatrist challenges his colleagues.* CACC Newsletter. Retrieved July 21, 2006, from http://www.schwarz report.org/Newsletters/1982/march15,82.htm

Scoop Independent News (2006, March). *China: No medical reason to hold dissent.* Retrieved July 21, 2006, from http://www.scoop.co.nz/stories/print.html?path= WO0603/S00327.htm

Seymour, J. D. (2005). Sizing up China's prisons. In B. Bakken (Ed.), *Crime, punishment, and policing in China* (pp. 141–167). Lanham, MD: Rowman & Littlefield.

Seymour, J. D., & Anderson, R. (1998). *New ghosts, old ghosts: Prisons and labor reform camps in China.* Armonk, NY: Sharpe.

Shaw, V. N. (1998). Productive labor and thought reform in Chinese corrections: A historical and comparative analysis. *The Prison Journal, 78,* 186–211.

Smith, C. S. (2001, September 9). Chinese fight crime with torture and executions. *New York Times.* Retrieved June 2, 2006, from http://www.nytimes.com.

Stern, V. (2001). Problems in prisons worldwide with a particular focus on Russia. *Annals of the New York Academy of Sciences, 953,* 113–119.

Swiss Agency for Development and Cooperation. (n.d.). *Prison reform project.* Retrieved June 2, 2006, from http://www.sdc-seco.ru/index.php?navID=22575&lang ID=1&

Terra Daily (2004, June 6). China approves special jails for AIDS victims: report. *Terra.Wire.* Retrieved June 6, 2006 from http://www.terradaily.com/2004/ 040606053115.sogzctoh.html

UNAIDS (1997, April). Prisons and AIDS. *UNAIDS best practices collection: Technical update.* Geneva, Switzerland: UNAIDS.

USAID (2005, February 16). *Infectious diseases: Russia.* Retrieved June 8, 2006, from http://www.usaid.gov/our_work/global_health/id/tuberculosis/countries/eande /russia_profile.html

U.S. Census Bureau (2005). Countries Ranked by Population: 2006. International data base. Retrieved June 14, 2006, from http://www.census.gov/cgi-bin/ipc/ idbrank.pl

U.S. State Department Bureau of Democracy, Human Rights, and Labor (2000). China country report on human rights practices for 1999. *The Country Reports on Human Rights Practices.* Retrieved June 2, 2006, from http://www.state.gov/ g/drl/rls/hrrpt/1999/

World Prison Brief (2006). Retrieved June 2, 2006, from http://www.prison studies.org

Wu, H. (1996). *Troublemaker: One's man crusade against China's cruelty.* New York: Random House.

Yale School of Nursing (2003). Breaking the barriers to TB medication adherence in Russian prisons. *Yale Nursing Matters, 5,* 6–8. Retrieved June 6, 2006, from http://nursing.yale.edu/News/Publications/YNM/5_1/V5_1_pg06.pdf

Yardley, J. (2005, December 31). In worker's death, view of China's harsh justice. *The New York Times.* Retrieved June 2, 2006, from http://www.nytimes.com

PART IV

GENERAL CONCLUSIONS

Chapter 14

FUTURE DIRECTIONS

Thomas J. Fagan, Shelia M. Brandt, and Andrea L. Kleiver

INTRODUCTION

Throughout this volume, the connections between mental health, corrections, societal values, and social policy have been clearly presented. For the purposes of this chapter, five interrelated examples from the past several decades will serve to further elaborate these connections.

First, beginning in the 1950s with the advent of new antipsychotic medications, America began to release individuals with serious mental health problems from mental hospitals to the community. The community mental health movement of the 1960s was developed to provide community-based mental health services to this population. This was a period filled with hope and optimism about the promise of better mental health treatment strategies. However, without adequate funding or sufficient community support, these community-based programs never developed sufficiently to meet the demands of this growing population.

As frustration grew over the failures of these community-based treatment programs to adequately address the needs of the mentally ill, societal attitudes shifted, becoming more conservative and less tolerant. With this attitude shift came changes in public laws resulting in the criminalization of many of the behaviors associated with the chronically mentally ill including homelessness, vagrancy, and disorderly conduct in public and in a dramatic increase in the number of seriously mentally ill individuals in prisons and jails. Current estimates using offender self-report data suggest that between 16–64 percent of incarcerated individuals in the United States have serious mental health concerns (Ditton, 1999; James & Glaze, 2006). Similar results have been reported for other Western countries (Blaauw, Roesch, & Kerkhof, 2000; Seena & Danesh, 2002). Some have suggested that today's prisons have assumed the roles of state mental hospitals as the primary providers of mental health services. This assertion is supported by the fact that state mental hospitals now house fewer than 55,000 individuals, whereas prisons and jails now manage more than 775,000 individuals with serious mental health problems (James & Glaze, 2006; Lamb, Weinberger, & Gross, 2004; Perez, Leifman, & Estrada, 2003).

Second, prompted by the strong relationship between substance abuse and criminal behavior, the failure of drug treatment strategies to adequately curb substance abuse, and the social conservatism of the 1980s, the U.S. government declared a war on drugs (Karberg & James, 2005; Mumola, 1999; Scalia, 2001). The primary focus of this war was to reduce the supply of drugs entering the country as a way of ultimately decreasing drug usage (Office on National Drug Control Policy [ONDCP], 2006). Accompanying the war on drugs was a stiffening of penalties for drug possession and distribution and a willingness to punish the criminal behaviors that substance abusers frequently used to support their drug abuse. Other countries have followed the lead of the U.S. in terms of criminalizing many aspects of substance abuse (United Nations Office on Drugs and Crime, 2005).

The effects of the war on drugs on the correctional community can be measured by the increased numbers of substance abusers now found within prison and jail populations. Current estimates are that approximately 21 percent of state prison offenders, 68 percent of jail inmates, and 60 percent of federal offenders are confined for substance related offenses (Harrison & Beck, 2003; Karberg & James, 2005; Mumola, 1999). Similarly high numbers have also been reported in other Western countries.[1] These numbers have motivated corrections officials to develop a variety of prison-based substance abuse treatment programs.

Third, throughout the 1980s and 1990s there was a series of highly publicized cases involving instances of violence. In some cases perpetrators of domestic violence were either not detained or ultimately released by law enforcement officials without treatment or legal consequence only to abuse again in more violent ways. In other cases, pedophiles were discharged from community-based treatment only to offend again. In still other cases, sexual predators were released from correctional facilities either on furlough or parole and quickly reoffended. These cases prompted public outcry and led state and/or federal governments to pass a series of domestic violence laws requiring legal consequences for instances of domestic violence. Sexual predator laws were also passed mandating stiff prison sentences, community notification and registration following release from prison, and civil commitment

---

1. See estimates provided in Chapters 4 (Great Britain), Chapter 5 (France), Chapter 6 (Canada), and Chapter 7 (New Zealand).

for those sexual predators who are believed to pose a continuing threat to the community. As a result of these laws, since 1980, the average annual rate of incarceration for sexual offenses has been double the incarceration rate for other types of crimes (Greenfeld, 1997). With an increased number of confined sexual offenders and passage of the Adam Walsh Child Protection and Safety Act of 2006 (H.R. 4472; Public Law 109-248), correctional mental health professionals have had to assume a greater role in developing treatment strategies for these individuals and in determining risk of reoffense as these offenders approach release dates.

Fourth, as part of a law and order platform that became popular in the 1970s and 1980s, a series of "get tough on crime" legislative initiatives were enacted. These initiatives resulted in laws mandating the abolition of parole, the introduction of determinant and mandatory minimum sentences, the creation of "three strikes" legislation, and changes in standards defining criminal competency and responsibility. While these legislative initiatives increased penalties for drug and sex offenses as noted earlier, they also represented a much broader assault on crime and resulted in stiffer penalties for most criminal offenses including nonviolent criminal behaviors. These legislative initiatives have resulted in increased rates of incarceration and increased numbers of offenders, especially those with violent backgrounds, being incarcerated for longer periods of time without benefit of early release through parole. Currently, approximately 2,186,230 individuals are imprisoned in correctional systems within the U.S. (Harrison & Beck, 2006) and almost five million additional individuals are involved in other aspects of the criminal justice system (e.g., on probation and/or parole) (Glaze & Palla, 2005). Housing criminal offenders for longer periods of time without the use of parole as an incentive for good conduct has required correctional managers to develop alternative strategies for encouraging good institutional conduct and for punishing institutional rule violators.

Fifth and finally, the number of foreign-born individuals in correctional systems, already numbering over 35,000 in the federal prison system (Harrison & Beck, 2006), is poised to grow even higher in the near future fueled, in part, by the war on terror as well as by possible changes to current immigration laws. Various international terrorist incidents through the 1990s and 2000s including the World Trade Center bombings in New York, the London bus bombing, and the train bombing in Spain have resulted in the U.S. and other Western countries waging a war on terrorism. As a result of these attacks and subsequent war on terrorism, there have been growing numbers of individuals incarcerated for terror-related activities. Accompanying the imprisonment of alleged terrorists in U.S. military prisons has been instances of prisoner abuse (e.g., Abu Ghraib prison in Iraq) by military guards, questions about the use of harsh interrogation techniques by both military and CIA operatives, and allegations of prisoner mistreatment at the U.S. military prison in Guantánamo, Cuba—a facility housing individuals accused of engaging in terrorist activities against the United States.

There has also been an ongoing debate within the U.S. and some western European governments about the impact of illegal immigration on such economic factors as unemployment rates and health care costs and on how best to curb the flow of illegal immigration. Obviously, the work of correctional administrators will become more complex to the extent that this debate results in the incarceration of more illegal immigrants.

Additionally, some (Gaseau, 2004; Jordan, 2006; Anderson, 2006; Hall, 2006) have speculated that prisons may become fertile grounds for the recruitment and training of future "home-grown" terrorists as illustrated by the case of Richard Reid (aka, the "shoe bomber") who was recruited while serving time in a British prison. Others have labeled this an emerging threat to national security in both the U.S. (Saathoff, 2006; Eisenberg, 2006) and Great Britain (Travis, 2006).[2]

Collectively, these five social trends have significantly changed the composition of the correctional environment. Now it is far more heterogeneous and complex. It consists of greater numbers of dangerous individuals with antisocial tendencies, substance abusers, individuals with serious mental illness, sexual predators including rapists and pedophiles, illegal immigrants, and individuals with radical religious and/or political beliefs. Many of these individuals are serving lengthy prison sentences with no chance of parole. Each of these groups brings its own sets of problems and issues into the correctional environment and creates its own sets of challenges for correctional administrators and mental health professionals tasked with addressing the diverse, and often times competing, needs of these groups.

As mental health professionals, correctional administrators, and social policy makers continue to address these complex issues and contemplate future directions, three questions demand consideration. First, are there better, more efficient ways of managing these diverse corrections populations? Second, are there other models that are available either within other noncorrectional sectors of the U.S. or being utilized elsewhere in the world that might be more successful in addressing the needs of this diverse population? Third, are there more empirical ways of making social policy such that the long-term impact of these policies can be assessed before they are implemented? The remainder of this chapter focuses on these three questions.

---

2. For a more detailed discussion of terrorism and its impact on corrections, see von Tangen Page & Ax (Chapter 10).

ARE THERE BETTER, MORE EFFICIENT WAYS OF MANAGING DIVERSE CORRECTIONAL POPULATIONS

The simple answer to this question is "yes". In formulating the answer to this question, the following quote seems appropriate:

> No man is an island, entire of itself, every man is a piece of the Continent, a part of the main. . . .

> John Donne (1624)
> Meditation XVII

For many years correctional systems have operated in isolation. They have been essentially reactive, with no authority to influence the larger system, as illustrated by recent legislative changes abolishing parole and curtailing the use of good time. They have received offenders from the courts, managed them for the term of their prison sentence, and then turned them over to halfway houses and parole officers for community management. Under this model, each of these agencies performed their required functions in a sequential, but fairly insular manner—each system operating as ". . . its own island. . . ."

There is a growing awareness that this approach has not been effective and may even inadvertently have contributed to the high recidivism rates reported in the literature (Byrne & Taxman, 2004; Pettus & Severson, 2006; Taxman, 2004; Thompson, Reuland, & Souweine, 2003). Many of these same authors have proposed a more holistic, better integrated approach to managing criminal offenders in which law enforcement, judicial, correctional, and community-based systems share and coordinate information, resources, services, and programs to address the unique needs of offenders, especially those with special needs, as they move from the community to prison and from prison back to the community. In this way, each system becomes ". . . a piece of the continent, a part of the main. . . ." Efforts to bridge these "agency chasms" are beginning to emerge.

Increase Cooperation and Integration Among Criminal Justice and Community Agencies

Although correctional programs (e.g., vocational, educational, religious, medical, psychological, etc.) have been available for years to assist offenders in preparing for their eventual return to the community, these programs have often focused on the least severely disturbed offenders and have provided these services without adequate communication, cooperation, and coordination between prison and community-based agencies. Additionally, while commendable, these efforts have often been denied to the more severely disturbed offenders, those most in need of these services in order to prevent future recidivism (Byrne & Taxman, 2004).

In their review of current correctional treatment programs, Byrne and Taxman (2004) and Taxman, Young, and Byrne (2002) suggested several strategies for increasing the effectiveness of correctional treatment programs. In particular, they proposed that treatment programming begin at the start rather than during the last phase of incarceration and that the emphasis of programming be on motivating offenders to change their criminal thinking and lifestyle choices to more noncriminal, pro-social thoughts and choices and on developing good employment skills.

They recommended that offenders be moved as close to their reentry location as possible so that contacts with community resources may be established prior to release and so that ties with family members can be reaffirmed. In the past prisons have attempted to relocate offenders closer to their release destination through the use of halfway houses or prison transfers (contingent on clear conduct) as release dates near and as prison/halfway house locations allow. While this approach has addressed the "geography" issue, it has not always been effective in increasing community and family contacts. Connecting with community resources prior to release, especially for offenders with chronic medical and/or mental health needs, has been shown to reduce needless delays in accessing vital medical and/or mental health care (California Board of Corrections, 2000; Farley et al., 2000; Hall et al., 2004; Hammett et al., 2001; Hiller et al., 1999; Miles & Cajina, 2006; Prendergast et al., 2004; Roskes & Feldman, 1999; Siegal et al., 1999). Following release, they suggested that all areas of offender need (e.g., long-term housing, employment, medical, mental health, spiritual, family counseling services) be addressed simultaneously by individuals who are familiar with the services and programs offered by all available community resources and who can effectively coordinate the delivery of these services.

Byrne and Taxman also proposed that inmates play a more active role in planning both their corrections-based treatment and their community reentry. Specifically, they speculated that offenders who were more involved in the planning process would feel more control over their situation and their possible outcomes. Similarly, they believed that treatment should be based on empowering the individual and should involve training in self-awareness techniques, such as individualized feedback, to assist offenders in making better and more informed decisions regarding their treatment and reentry process.

In brief, Byrne and Taxman proposed that correctional treatment strategies begin early in the incarceration process, target more severely disturbed offenders, involve offenders in all program-related decisions, and integrate well with all available community-based programs and services. Research suggests that as correctional and community-based programs become better integrated and address the totality of needs displayed by offenders, the more successful they are at reducing offender recidivism (Byrne & Taxman, 2004; Basile, 2002; California Board of Corrections, 2000; Lurigio, 2001; Roskes & Feldman, 1999; Ventura, Cassel, Jacoby, & Huang, 1998).

Pettus & Severson (2006) have suggested two reasons why more holistic, seamless service delivery approaches have been slow to develop. First, they noted that there remains intense competition over resources between participating agencies. This competition makes cooperation more difficult and often results in duplication of efforts among agencies tasked with performing similar services with the same clients at different points in the criminal justice process. It also makes information sharing and service coordination more difficult between agencies. Second, they suggest that correctional facilities have historically been viewed and have often functioned as closed systems, making it harder for community-based agencies to "break into" the correctional setting or for correctional personnel to reach out to the community.

Mindful of both the need for and obstacles to better integration and cooperation between the services of correctional and community-based programs, efforts are underway to facilitate better interagency cooperation. Basile (2002) and Lurigio (2001) have proposed more interagency training opportunities as one way of fostering greater cooperation between corrections and community-based agencies. Richards-Ward and McDaniel (see Chapter 7) noted that in New Zealand attitudes about reoffending have begun to shift from the view that reoffending represents a failure of prison systems to do their jobs to a view that suggests that re-offending represents a failure of all government systems to do their jobs effectively. With this attitude shift has come a "whole of government" approach that encourages cross-agency service initiatives that address the employment, housing, and other needs of offenders as they release from prison. In Great Britain, the government has placed prison and parole operations under one government entity, the National Offender Management Services (NOMS), to facilitate the coordination of services between these prison and parole agencies (see Towl & Crighton, Chapter 4). In the United States the following two programs may serve as examples of efforts being made to better integrate correctional and community-based services and programs.

Two Examples of Integrated Offender Programs

Faith-Based Initiatives

As described earlier in this volume,[3] religious groups have been involved over the years both in improving the conditions of offenders during their

---

3. See Ax (Chapter 1) and Gallo (Chapter 9).

incarceration and in easing their transition back into the community. Despite protests from those who believe that the work of faith-based initiatives in prisons may blur the line between church and state (Shorba, 2002; Alter, 2003; The Christian Science Monitor, 2004), prison ministries have in recent years begun to partner with correctional systems to address the needs of a growing prison population (Fairhurst, 2006; Prison Fellowship Newsroom, 2006). Starting in the late 1970s with the work of Charles Colson, a convicted felon and former aide to President Nixon, and other church community volunteers, prison ministries across the nation began to make spiritual guidance available for inmates who were willing to go along with program guidelines and become followers of God (Prison Fellowship Newsroom, 2006). Faith-based program administrators have touted drastically reduced rates of recidivism and positive feedback from prison participants. For example, in one program, the InnerChange Freedom Initiative, a recidivism rate of 16 percent was reported for participants compared to the national average of almost 70 percent for nonparticipating offenders (Alter, 2003; Prison Fellowship Newsroom, 2006). Similarly, at the inception of their program, the Lawtey Correctional Institution, a completely faith-based prison in Florida, boasted that they would see rates of success (defined as not reoffending) close to 90 percent for participants (The Christian Science Monitor, 2003).

Based on positive preliminary reports of drops in recidivism rates and/or promises of future drops in recidivism rates, government officials have worked to provide additional funding for such programs. However, the sound empirical research needed to support these initiatives has not yet been produced. The literature that does exist has been problematic (Johnson, Larson & Pitts, 1997; Johnson, 2004; Camp, Klein-Saffran, Kwon, Daggert, & Joseph, 2006; Mears, Roman, Wolff, Buck, 2006). For example, Mears and his associates (2006) noted that definitions of what constitutes faith-based programming vary across studies; appropriate comparison groups are not present in many studies; and variable methods of measuring participation levels and their influence on outcomes makes it difficult to compare research results. While Mears et al. did not doubt that faith-based programs may benefit prisoners, they simply concluded that additional research was needed in this area in order to decipher more carefully the many direct and indirect variables that may also be influencing these positive outcomes.

Related to faith-based initiatives between correctional agencies and various church groups have been efforts by some governments to consider the religious and cultural values of their minority, indigenous populations in basic management and treatment decisions targeting these populations. Both Canada with its First Peoples population (see Chapter 6) and New Zealand with its Māori population (see Chapter 7) have taken steps to incorporate the religious and cultural values of these populations into correctional management and treatment decisions involving these groups.

Vocational Preparation Programs

Prison-based educational, vocational, and on-the-job training have long been used by correctional systems to prepare offenders for employment success upon release (Hicks, 2004; Western, 2003; Wignall, 2002). While these prison-based programs have achieved some success (Saylor & Gaes, 1992, 1997) current thinking is that greater success can be achieved by better integrating these programs with community-based programs and opportunities. Several programs have been developed to accomplish this goal.

For example, the Safer Foundation, a Chicago-based organization, works to close the gap between parolees needing service/employment and community employers looking for workers (Hicks, 2004). They begin by assessing an offender's current interests and skill levels. Offenders with particular skill deficits are provided with remediation and on-the-job training (e.g., computer training, construction work) prior to release from prison followed by job referral and placement services (i.e., assistance with resumes, interviewing tips) following release (Hicks, 2004; Safer Foundation, 2006). Similarly, the Prison Rehabilitation Industries and Diversified Enterprises (PRIDE) program, offered by the Florida Department of Corrections, also provides on-the-job training, job placement, and social/life skills training both prior to release and following release (Wignall, 2002).

There are also programs such as ComALERT that are similar to the Safer Foundation and PRIDE in structure but that do not begin to work with offenders until after release (ComAlert, 2006; Western, 2003). The ComALERT (Community and Law Enforcement Resources Together) program was developed in Brooklyn, New York to

> . . . act as a bridge between prison and the community for returning parolees. ComALERT assists formerly incarcerated individuals to make a successful transition from prison to home by providing drug treatment and counseling, mental health treatment and counseling, GED, and transitional housing and employment. ComALERT also provides permanent job placement assistance to those parolees who have marketable skills upon their release. ComALERT services begin almost immediately upon release from prison, increasing the success rate for its clients compared to the non-treated reentry population. (ComALERT, 2006)

While each of these programs anecdotally reports substantial reductions in recidivism, at this time little empirical research exists to support these claims (Hicks, 2004; Wignall, 2002). Even if empirical evidence is later developed to support the positive effects of these programs, additional research will still be needed to determine which aspects of these programs are most responsible for their success. Research will also be needed to define which barriers to community reintegration are most likely to reduce the value and impact of these programs. Pogorzelski, Wolff, Pan, and Blitz (2005) have identified several such barriers for ex-offenders including eligibility for public assistance, need to obtain a driver's license, and the availability of housing.

Increase Focus on High-Risk, High-Need Offenders

Recent research efforts[4] have begun to focus on the question of how best to manage high-risk, high-needs offenders such as those with mental health, substance abuse, and/or chronic medical problems. Many of these efforts have used collaborative, integrated service delivery models to manage offenders as they transition back to the community.

Typically, these projects provide extensive community-based services (e.g., mental health/substance abuse treatment, crisis intervention strategies, financial/housing assistance, vocational and life skills training, medication management counseling, and miscellaneous advocacy services) to offenders–services offered by trained community professionals via a "team" approach. This approach has been found to produce a number of positive outcomes including a reduction in the number of subsequent bookings, rearrests, and new convictions by participants (California Board of Corrections, 2000; Lurigio, 2001; Roskes & Feldman, 1999; Thompson, Reuland, & Souweine, 2003). When recipients of these integrated services are apprehended for new crimes, they are typically less serious in nature and receive shorter sentence terms (California Board of Corrections, 2000). Frequently, these services are coordinated by parole/probation officers with specific training and/or experience in mental health service delivery (Roskes & Feldman, 1999).

Projects have also been developed to address the needs of the large number of incarcerated individuals with substance abuse problems and to identify which programmatic features are most effective with this population (Hall, Prendergast, Wellisch, Patten, & Cao, 2004; Hiller, Knight, & Dwayne, 1999; Prendergast, Hall, & Wellisch, 2003; Prendergast, Hall, Wexler, Melnick, & Cao, 2004; Siegal et al., 1999). Research suggests that the greatest reduction in recidivism occurs among offenders who have completed a prison-based substance abuse treatment program followed by participation in a community-based aftercare program while in supervised release status (Hall et al., 2004; Hiller et al., 1999; Prendergast et al., 2004; Siegal et al., 1999). Offenders who

---

4. See Smith, Gendreau, and Goggin (Chapter 8) for an example of this type of research.

completed both the prison and community-based treatment components were found to have greater employment rates, fewer episodes of drug and alcohol misuse, and longer periods of time in the community without re-arrest (Hall et al., 2004; Hiller et al., 1999; Prendergast et al., 2004; Siegal et al., 1999).

Lastly, a number of projects have targeted individuals with chronic medical conditions[5] such as Human Immunodeficiency Virus (HIV). Several of these projects have demonstrated the value of collaborative, integrative programs. Typically, these projects have found that by providing a range of medical services including education about sexually transmitted diseases, disease and medication management, sexual abuse/substance abuse treatment, vaccinations, and other routine care both during incarceration and after release, a number of positive outcomes has resulted. Specifically, offenders who have successfully participated in these types of programs are more likely to follow-up with medical appointments (Farley et al., 2000; Hammett, Roberts, & Kennedy, 2001; Jarrett, Adeyemi, & Huggins, 2006), obtain needed financial/housing assistance, continue participation in drug rehabilitation, and not engage in criminal behavioral patterns (Farley et al., 2000; Hammett et al., 2001). Perhaps of greater importance, Hammett and his colleagues (2001) found that by increasing access and delivery of care to HIV offenders both during incarceration and upon release that the development of drug resistant strains of HIV and its spread to others was significantly reduced.

Examples of Integrated Services for High-Risk, High Needs Offenders

Two program efforts, drug courts and mental health courts, will serve to illustrate both the benefits and problems inherent in offering integrated programs and services to high-risk, high-need offenders.

Drug Courts

Drug courts were first established in Miami, Florida in 1989 as a way of diverting nonviolent misdemeanant substance abusers away from prison and connecting them with community treatment services (Tyuse & Linhorst, 2005). Original stakeholders in drug courts included the criminal justice system (e.g., probation officers, judges, and attorneys), community treatment providers, and law enforcement agencies (Byrne, Schauffler, Lightman, Fini-

---

5. See Chavez (Chapter 3) for a more detailed discussion of offenders with chronic medical conditions in the U.S. and Senter, Morgan, & Mandracchia (Chapter 13) for a discussion of chronic medical conditions among offenders in non-Western countries.

gan, Carey, 2004, Wolfe, Guydish, Woods, & Tajima, 2004). More recently, some courts have begun to expand this service to include felony offenders (Gonzales, Schofield, & Schmitt, 2006; Wolfe et al., 2004).

Research on drug courts has generally been favorable and has shown promising results regarding their ability to substantially reduce reconviction rates among offenders with substance abuse problems, slash outcome costs for substance abusers involved in the criminal justice system, and increase employment rates among treated substance abusers (Byrne, Schauffler, Lightman, Finigan, & Carey, 2004; Wolfe, Guydish, & Termondt, 2002; Wolfe et al., 2004). However, despite the success of drug courts, some (e.g., Wolfe et al., 2004) have suggested that there remains room for further research and program development in this area. Specifically, these researchers have suggested that eligibility requirements be expanded and evaluated to include an increased number of minorities and higher-risk individuals, such as those with mental illness or with felony charges, to see if they also can benefit from the drug court program. They have also suggested that stakeholders be allowed greater responsibility in determining sanctions for program violators and in developing written procedures to increase program consistency. Lastly, in order to promote further cost-effectiveness, Byrne and Taxman (2004) have suggested that additional research be conducted to assess more precisely the overall costs versus benefits of drug courts to taxpayers (e.g., reduced costs of victimization), to stakeholders (e.g., cost reductions), and to participants (e.g., reduced incarceration time and increased abstinence from drugs).

Mental Health Courts

First established around 1997 (Redlich, Steadman, Monahan, Petrila, & Griffin, 2005) mental health courts were designed to divert misdemeanants (and some felons) found to be mentally ill into community treatment programs rather than correctional institutions. Following successful completion of outpatient treatment, mental health courts will often dismiss criminal charges for program participants (Griffin, Steadman, & Petrila, 2002; Redlich et al., 2005).

Available research assessing the effectiveness of mental health courts has generally yielded positive results. Specifically, research has praised the use of cohesive multiagency treatment teams as a means of improving an offender's access to services within the community and as a means of reducing reconviction rates (Edens, Peters, & Hills, 1997; Tyuse & Linhorst, 2005).

Despite the apparent success of mental health courts as they are currently configured, much of the current literature regarding these courts has focused on how these programs may be improved and/or expanded. For example, some have criticized mental health courts because they only have the ability to serve a small proportion of offenders due to limited resources and because they continue to exclude many high-risk, high-need offenders such as felons and dually-diagnosed individuals (Craig, 2004; Edens, Peters, & Hills, 1997; Tyuse & Linhorst, 2005).

Because of their knowledge of mental illness and community resources, some have proposed the increased use of social workers to help bridge the current gap between service needs and service access. Indeed, research findings have suggested that use of social workers has been associated with better treatment adherence by offenders and lower recidivism rates among offenders (Broner, Nguyen, Swern, & Goldfinger, 2003; Griffin, Steadman, & Petrila, 2002; Redlich et al , 2005; Tyuse & Linhorst, 2005).

However, since most mental health professionals are not adequately trained in working with offender populations, Tyuse and Linhorst (2005) have suggested that it may first be necessary to initiate training for students studying to be mental health professionals in order to familiarize them with the unique treatment needs of this special population and their families. Tyuse and Linhorst have also expressed concern about the possible stigma that involvement in mental health courts may create for offenders and have suggested that this issue needs to be resolved as a way of increasing the willingness of offenders to participate in court programs.

Researchers have also recommended that structural changes may be needed to improve the quality and flexibility of mental health courts. For example, Redlich et al. (2005) have suggested more flexibility in how offenders are supervised (e.g., community agencies and probation staff working together to provide feedback regarding treatment compliance). They have also suggested that these programs should focus more on identifying what specific program elements are most strongly associated with positive outcomes, so that ultimately a more tailored approach to preventing recidivism can be developed for individual offenders. Griffin et al. (2002) have proposed additional research be performed to identify alternative sanctions for noncompliance with treatment requirements.

Lastly, Wolff and Pogorzelski (2005) have raised two questions about program evaluation research on mental health courts. First, they have suggested that programs wait to assess their effectiveness until a full year after implementation in order to rule out negative results that may be influenced by start up difficulties. Second, they have proposed that program evaluation methodology be based on a conceptual model that allows for the clear identification of specific program, staff, and performance goals, in an effort to improve measurement consistency and sensitivity and data quality across program evaluation studies.

Overall, most of the current research remains incomplete because of research design problems–leaving the validity and generalizability of research findings in question. However, as Wolff and Pogorzelski (2005) have suggested, the current pilot program evaluation designs, despite their loosely defined and confounding variables and their lack of pre-post measurements, do provide information that can be useful in better understanding the process and set-up of the courts (how many individuals are able to obtain services, what type of services, type of population served, etc.). Nonetheless, there remains a need for improved research design and more empirically sound measures of program effectiveness.

Expand Development and Use of Risk Assessment Protocols

The issue of risk assessment is central to many decisions made by law enforcement, judicial, and correctional officials. Police officers arriving on the scene of an incident must assess risk to determine whether verbal de-escalation techniques will be sufficient to end the incident or whether an arrest is more appropriate. Judges assess risk when determining length of sentence or whether probation is appropriate (i.e., in jurisdictions where mandatory minimum sentences are not in effect). Correctional officials assess risk in decisions about where offenders should be housed during incarceration (e.g., general population, special housing units, super-max facilities, etc.) and about how appropriate offenders might be for placement in particular programs. Parole officials assess risk whenever they make decisions about the parole eligibility of an offender.

Clearly, risk assessment is an everyday part of the criminal justice process. However, how dependable and accurate are the procedures used by these agencies? Do all agencies or branches within a single agency use the same risk assessment procedures? What is the state of scientific knowledge about risk assessment, especially as it applies to the assessment of future violence and/or sexually predatory behaviors, two areas where all elements of the criminal justice process have a strong interest? Can risk assessment procedures be better integrated into the criminal justice process? The next two subsections address some of these questions.

Violence Risk Assessment

Over the past 30 years, a number of instruments have been developed in both the United States and Canada to assess risk of violence. Looking at a combination of factors including past history of violence, current psychological and interpersonal factors such as depression, anxiety, and environmental support systems, specific demographic variables like age and gender, and personality variables such as impulsivity, aggression, and hostility, these instruments have proven effective in predicting violent recidivism among criminal offenders, civilly-committed psychiatric patients, and forensic defendants (Bonta, Law, & Hanson, 1998; Borum, 1996; Douglas & Skeem, 2005; Menzies & Webster, 1995; Monahan, Steadman, Appelbaum, Robbins, Mulvey, Silver, et al., 2000). Using instruments such as the Psychopathy Checklist-Revised (PCL-R) and Psychopathy Checklist-Screening Version (PCL-SV), researchers have been able to demonstrate how individuals with many of these characteristics are not only more likely to have behavioral problems during incarceration, but are also more likely to recidivate in general and to recidivate violently in particular (Guy, Edens, Anthony, & Douglas, 2005; Skeem, & Mulvey, 2001). Predictably, measuring general violence recidivism rates has been found to be far more accurate than forecasting the likelihood that a particular individual will engage in actual harm to another individual (Menzies & Webster, 1995).

Although risk assessment instruments like the PCL-R and the Violence Risk Assessment Guide (VRAG) have shown promising results, researchers still believe that there is room for improvement. For instance, now that risk variables such as impulsiveness, negative affect, psychosis, antisocial attitudes, substance use, interpersonal relationships, and treatment adherence have been better defined, Douglas and Skeem (2005) have suggested that researchers begin to focus more effort on which variables or combination of variables have the strongest predictive power. Furthermore, several researchers (Clark, Watson, & Reynolds, 1995; Skeem & Mulvey, 2001; Watson, 2005; Widiger & Samuel, 2005) have indicated that viewing risk dimensionally (i.e., along a continuum) rather than categorically (i.e., presence or absence of violence) may provide clinicians with more useful information and better predictive power.

Other researchers have suggested that integrating standardized risk assessment protocols into routine clinical assessment and treatment regimens[6] may assist clinicians in selecting more appropriate intervention methods for offenders, increase their ability to measure change over time and/or effectiveness of treatment, and more accurately predict future recidivism (Beech, Fisher, & Thornton, 2003; Bonta, Law, & Hanson, 1998; Borum, 1996; Douglas, & Skeem, 2005; Guy et al., 2005; Hanson, & Thornton, 2000). Researchers have also proposed that risk assessment protocols be used to evaluate offenders at different points in the criminal justice process (e.g., during court proceedings;

---

6. See Richards-Ward and McDaniel (Chapter 7) and Wormith and Luong (Chapter 6) for a more detailed discussion of how risk assessment protocols are being developed and used in these countries to make treatment decisions.

during incarceration, but prior to the start of treatment; after treatment completion; and during supervised release) to determine if these conditions affect violence potential. Some have also suggested that these instruments be modified to better accommodate the lower reading levels frequently found among those with cognitive deficits, little formal education, and/or mental retardation (Beech, Fisher, & Thornton, 2003; Douglas & Skeem, 2005; Kinsler, Saxman, & Fishman, 2004). Of course, for these types of risk assessment protocols to be effective, additional time and resources may be needed to administer these modified and lengthier correctional intake screening procedures. More individualized treatment strategies may also need to be developed and appropriately matched to assessed need.

As risk assessment research efforts continue with criminal populations, greater attention will need to be given to standardizing how and by whom information is gathered during the intake screening process (e.g., through interview or questionnaire administered by nurses, social workers, psychologists, correctional officers). In an effort to facilitate comparison of results across risk assessment studies with criminal offenders, researchers will also need to focus more attention on developing a generally acceptable definition of recidivism, using similar measures of risk to evaluate results and generalizability of results, and establishing consistent follow-up periods (Douglas & Skeem, 2005; Hanson & Thornton, 2000; Harris et al., 2003). Finally, risk assessment research will need to be expanded to include the screening of special needs offender populations to identify whether current findings are generalizable to these groups. In particular, high need groups such as offenders with substance abuse and/or mental health problems should be assessed regularly throughout the criminal justice process with results being used in treatment and release planning activities. Some research with psychiatric populations has indicated that screening these populations for appropriate treatment placement and level of risk ultimately leads to increased compliance with intensive outpatient treatment, decreased future hospitalizations and future arrests, reduced incidents of violence, and increased medication compliance (Petrila, Ridgely, & Borum, 2003; Steadman et al., 2001; Swartz, et al., 2001).

Sex Offender Risk Assessment

As the number of incarcerated sexual offenders has increased, so also has interest in the assessment of risk among sexual offenders. Interestingly, although prevalence rates of incarcerated sex offenders are similar internationally, much of the research on sex offender risk assessment and treatment has taken place outside the United States (Beech, Fisher, & Thornton, 2003; Hanson & Thornton, 2000; Harris et al., 2003; Hanson & Bussiere, 1998). For example, several of the more popular risk assessment instruments (e.g., Rapid Risk Assessment for Sex Offense Recidivism [RRASOR)], the Structured Anchored Clinical Judgment [SACJ], and the Static-99 have been developed and validated in countries such as Canada and the United Kingdom. [Hanson & Thornton, 2000]). While researchers have determined that many of these measures show promising results in their ability to predict some sexual recidivism, most still lack the precision needed to make individual predictions about recidivism (Hanson & Bussiere, 1998). Future studies will need to examine the interactions between specific sex offender risk factors such as degree of sexual deviancy, lack of appropriate coping mechanisms, social deficiencies, unfulfilled intimacy needs, and victim type (male/female or family member/ stranger) and their relationship to reoffending (Hanson & Bussiere, 1998). Another promising area of research involves the use of phallometric instruments to measure sexual deviancy and as a possible predictor of recidivism. Preliminary results with these instruments have been very positive (Harris et al., 2003). Lastly, Hanson and Thornton (2000) have pointed out the large amount of variance between different types of sexual offenders and their likelihood of recidivating. They have proposed this as another area for future research.

Form Partnerships With Universities

Most correctional mental health professionals will readily admit that the needs of their clients are great, available resources are not keeping pace with need, and the knowledge base regarding what works best with specific types of offenders is limited. Help is clearly needed both in terms of developing and evaluating innovative treatment strategies and in terms of conducting further research on a variety of criminal justice topics. To accomplish these goals, several researchers have suggested that correctional systems and academics form partnerships (Kendig, 2004; Lamberti et al., 2001; Pettus & Severson, 2006; Welsh, 2002).

Historically, these partnerships have been difficult to establish (Appelbaum, Manning, & Noonan, 2002). Correctional systems have often been stereotypically viewed by university personnel as conservative in nature, while universities have generally been viewed by correctional staff as bastions of liberalism. Correctional systems have operated as closed systems and have been resistant to research queries from universities, especially those queries judged to be more theoretical or academic rather than applied or practical in nature. Allowing university personnel to conduct research in prisons has also posed a practical problem for correctional staff. To insure the safety of university staff, who are typically not trained in correctional safety procedures, they must be escorted and supervised by correctional staff while in the correctional facility. From a correctional worker's perspective, time spent escorting university staff is seen as time taken away from performing other more critical correctional tasks. Additionally, similar to the work of nongovernmental organizations (NGOs),[7] universities have often been critical of correctional systems (e.g., Haney, 2006) creating a level of suspicion that makes collaboration difficult. Universities have been frustrated by the many layers of bureaucracy encountered when research requests have been submitted to correctional systems, by long time delays in the review/approval process, or by a total lack of responsiveness from correctional systems.

Despite these differences, both systems have something to offer each other. Correctional systems have many offenders with significant problems and a limited number of staff to assist in addressing these problems. Universities have energetic students seeking practica and/or internship placements. With adequate training and supervision, these students could provide needed services to correctional populations. Students looking for thesis or dissertation topics might find them within the correctional environment in the form of innovative program development and evaluation initiatives or in the form of research aimed at identifying factors that reduce recidivism and/or increase prosocial behaviors. Professors looking for an applied research agenda or a potential grant partner might also find them in the correctional environment. Universities with innovative treatment ideas might find correctional systems willing to pilot their ideas. Correctional systems might also be the recipients of training by university professors on current, state-of-the-art treatment strategies—strategies that might improve the mental status of offenders, reduce recidivism, or contribute to the smooth running of the facility. In short, both correctional systems and universities stand to benefit from partnerships (Appelbaum, Manning, & Noonan, 2002; Pettus & Severson, 2006), but can only do so if they overcome preconceived notions about each other and establish a dialog aimed at identifying common ground.

Examples of Successful Partnerships

When this common ground is found, good results are possible. Here are two specific examples. In the fall of 1998, the University of Massachusetts Medical School assumed primary responsibility for the mental health care of inmates housed in the Massachusetts Department of Corrections. Medical services were offered by a private vendor, Correctional Medical Services (CMS), and prison management was handled by the Department of Corrections. In describing the formation of this partnership between two state agen-

---

7. See Gallo (Chapter 9) for a detailed discussion of NGOs.

cies (i.e., the university and the corrections department) and a private agency (CMS), Appelbaum, Manning, and Noonan (2002) noted that flexibility was required from all parties. University staff and CMS needed to accept the important role that security staff play in successfully managing a safe prison, not view correctional staff as an impediment to good health care, and find ways to include correctional staff in the treatment process. Correctional staff needed to recognize how improved health care among offenders contributed to the smooth and orderly running of the facility. Ultimately, all parties in this partnership noted that by meeting regularly in an atmosphere of mutual respect most problems were easily solved and all parties derived considerable benefit from the partnership. By partnering with the university, the correctional system was able to enhance its mental health services, improve efforts to recruit and retain skilled professional staff, and expand mental health training programs for correctional staff. The university, on the other hand, was able to expand its revenue base, provide mental health services to a population with significant needs, and expand its research and training opportunities. A comparable partnership has also been established between the Texas Department of Corrections and two Texas university-based health care systems with similar successful results (Raimer & Stobo, 2004).

Perhaps the best models for university-corrections partnerships can be found in Canada. As Wormith and Luong described in some detail (see Chapter 6), these partnerships have been in existence for many years and have been responsible for much of the current literature on such topics as psychopathy, risk assessment, sex offender treatment, and what works in correctional programming. While these university-based researchers have had a solid commitment to generating methodologically sound research, they have also been mindful of corrections' need for practical solutions to real problems. Canada's correctional system has provided university researchers with an interesting and needy subject pool and with a fertile training ground for young research in search of meaningful research agendas. Canada's university-based researchers have provided corrections with valuable data that has been used to design better, more successful assessment and treatment protocols. This model of mutual cooperation may serve as an example for other correctional systems seeking ways of partnering with university-based researchers.

ARE THERE OTHER MODELS WITH POTENTIAL BENEFITS FOR CORRECTIONS?

With the growing numbers of high needs-high risk offenders passing back and forth between the community and corrections, the question is: *Are there new/different ideas or approaches that might work in better managing these populations?* Obviously, better integration and communication between the various existing community-based and the criminal justice agencies is one approach that seems to be producing some success. Refining risk assessment procedures so they are better able to make individual predictions of risk is another potentially beneficial approach.

However, are there other ideas that might have applicability to the problems currently facing correctional mental health practitioners and administrators? Are there approaches being used by professionals in other health care disciplines or other public service sectors of the government that might be useful in the corrections arena? Are there successful approaches being used in other countries to manage problems similar to those found in the United States that might have social policy and/or correctional management implications in America? In this section several innovative approaches are discussed. They are mentioned here not to imply that they would necessarily solve all of the issues facing policymakers or correctional practitioners and administrators today, but rather as a way to stimulate "outside-the-box" thinking and to encourage correctional practitioners, administrators, and policymakers to look beyond penitentiary walls and national boundaries in pursuit of innovation.

Psychologists as Primary Care Providers

As health care costs have continued to escalate in both community and correctional facilities, there has been a growing sense that something needs to be done in order to avoid a health care crisis. Compounding current concerns over rising health care costs is the knowledge that life expectancies are increasing and baby boomers are rapidly approaching old age—a time of increased disease, chronic illness, and their resultant health care costs. Within the corrections environment, concerns are mounting that the growing number of incarcerated geriatric offenders, brought on by changes in sentencing policies (i.e., mandatory minimum and determinant sentencing), will dramatically increase correctional health care costs (Mitka, 2004).

Researchers have consistently pointed to such lifestyle factors as lack of exercise, diet, smoking, weight, and exposure to stress as contributors to various medical illnesses (Courneya, Estabrooks, & Nigg, 1997; Greenberg, 2002; Kumanyika, 2000; Ockene et al., 2000; Wing & Jeffery, 1999). Other researchers have demonstrated links between mental health problems and various physical illnesses (Frankenburg & Zanarini, 2004; Hansen, Fink, & Frydenberg, 2004; Clay, 2007). Based on this research, health care workers have proposed the need for strategies that focus on health promotion through better patient education and on disease prevention through early, routine screening and intervention, as two ways of slowing the growth of health care

costs. Without the introduction of health promotion/disease prevention strategies, it is feared that rates of chronic disease will continue to increase as the
general population ages and longevity increases. These fears are even greater
in the correctional setting where offenders have significant mental health
problems and long histories of engaging in high risk behaviors and in making
poor lifestyle choices (e.g., intravenous drug use, unsafe sex, poor diet, smoking, alcohol abuse).

Given the links between mental health problems, poor lifestyle choices,
and physical illnesses, psychologists, as behavioral scientists, would seem ide-
ally suited to assist in health promotion/disease prevention efforts. In fact,
they have been leaders in the development of programs that treat mental illness and that promote healthy lifestyle choices (e.g., smoking cessation, stress
reduction, and weight management programs) for a number of years (Kenkel,
DeLeon, Mantell, & Steep, 2005).

However, at present, it is the norm for medical and mental health services
that target health promotion/disease prevention to be offered in different locations and by various providers, without any central coordination. The result is
a delivery system where each provider addresses a piece of the problem, but
where no one provider has overall responsibility for treating the patient in a
holistic, integrated fashion. Patients are referred from provider to provider
with minimal follow-up or coordination between providers. Patients become
frustrated by delays in seeing various providers and by recoveries slowed by
these delays. Providers also become frustrated when patients don't follow
through with referrals or improve.

Even in the confines of a correctional setting, services are fragmented. In
some systems health services and mental health services are organizationally
separate with separate chains of command and separate office areas. In systems that contract for services, some write separate contracts for medical and
mental health services and may even award these contracts to different vendors. In some state correctional systems medical services are provided by the
department of corrections and mental health services are provided by another state agency. Similarly, in some jails, medical services are provided in-
house or through contracts while mental health services are provided by the
community mental health center. Even in systems where medical and mental
health care is provided under the same chain of command, consultation and
coordination between medical and mental health care providers aimed at
treating patients in a more holistic fashion is often minimal.

A number of professionals (DeLeon, Giesting, & Kenkel, 2003; DeLeon,
Rossomando, & Smedley, 2004; Gray, Brady, & Johnson, 2005; Kolbasovsky,
Reich, Romano, & Jaramillo, 2005; Masters, Stillman, Browning, & Davis,
2005; Garcia-Brown, 2006) have proposed a more integrated primary care
model that combines medical and mental health services under one roof with

the goal of treating the full range of problems that patients typically bring to their primary care provider. Using this primary care model, psychologists would become members of the primary health care team and would serve as consultants on issues related to behavioral health care and mental health treatment.

The benefits of this model are obvious. Patients do not need to travel from one location to another to receive needed services. Mental health services could be delivered in shorter and more focused sessions. Since mental health sessions would be conducted in a medical facility, the stigma often associated with seeing a mental health professional would be minimized, increasing the likelihood that patients would actually seek and receive valuable mental health information. Medical and mental health providers would also be in a position to more easily and regularly consult on cases and modify treatment strategies as dictated by the unique aspects of the individual case.

However, for these efforts to be successful, psychological and medical services would need to become better integrated in a number of ways. An Institute of Medicine Report (2003) describes the current situation as follows:

> ... Professionals will need to break down the silos that exist within the system, and seek to understand what others offer in order to do what is best for the patient. (p. 37)

> The absence of a common language, differing philosophies, politics, and turf battles across the professions remain the norm. This situation is exacerbated by the fact that in the vast majority of educational settings, health professionals are socialized in isolation, hierarchy is fostered, and individual responsibility and decision making are relied upon almost exclusively. Health professions education occurs largely in an environment of separately housed professional schools and separate clinical arenas governed by powerful deans, directors, and department chairs. (p. 79)

For this primary care model to work effectively in the community or corrections, many systemic changes would be required. For example, each discipline would need to understand and value the skills and expertise of other disciplines. Disciplines would need to learn the professional language or jargon of other disciplines or develop a common language. Disciplines would need to develop a more holistic view regarding treatment and develop strategies for prioritizing and integrating needed treatments. Individual providers would need to shift how they make treatment decisions from a strategy where they are individually responsible for treatment decisions to a strategy where the team is responsible for all treatment decisions. Treatment records would need to be unified and easily accessible to all treatment providers. To foster understanding among disciplines, academic and continuing education training programs would need to change and become more interdisciplinary. Psychologists would need to receive more training from physicians and physicians

would need to receive more training from psychologists. Complicated budgetary issues would also need to be addressed (e.g., is the current system more
economical to administer or would a primary care model result in more efficiency and cost-effectiveness?).

Where this model has been implemented, preliminary results have been
positive. Patients appear more satisfied with integrated care and report better
mental health outcomes (Katon et al., 1996). Physicians report satisfaction
with this model and note that it has helped them with problem patients who
present with somatic complaints with no discernible physical causes (Kates,
Craven, Crustolo, Nikolaou, & Allen, 1997). Other studies have found
reduced absenteeism and increased productivity on the job and fewer, less
costly doctor's office visits among patients who have participated in this model
(Cummings, 1997; Mumford, Schlesinger, Glass, Patrick, & Cuerdon, 1998).

Psychologists as Prescribers

In the 1980s it was proposed that psychologists add a new skill set to their
clinical repertoire–the ability to prescribe psychotropic medications (Burns,
DeLeon, Chemtob, Welch, & Samuels, 1988; DeLeon, 1988). It was believed
that prescriptive authority for psychologists would be a logical extension of
current practice and would facilitate communication between psychologists
and other health care workers. Additionally, it was suggested that prescriptive
authority would increase services to underserved populations and be in the
best interests of the public (Ax, Forbes, & Thompson, 1997; Boswell & Litwin,
1992). From its inception, this proposal has sparked considerable debate within the field of psychology and contention between psychology and the medical establishment (Albee, 2002; Dobson & Dozois, 2001; Hayes, Ealser, &
Bach, 2002; Walters, 2001).

Despite debate and contention, numerous studies have indicated that the
majority of U.S. psychologists are supportive of this initiative (Ax, Forbes, &
Thompson, 1997; Boswell & Litwin, 1992; Fagan et al., 2004; Fagan, Ax, Liss,
Resnick, & Moody, 2007; Sammons, Gorney, Zinner, & Allen, 2000). Interest
in prescriptive authority for psychologists has also been voiced among Canadian psychologists (St. Pierre & Melnyk, 2004; Westra, Eastwood, Bouffard, &
Gerritsen, 2006) and psychologists in several European countries (Resnick,
2003). In 1995 the American Psychological Association (APA) endorsed this
initiative and subsequently proposed a model curriculum in psychopharmacology (APA, 1996). Since that time, various attempts have been made to
change state scope of practice laws to allow psychologists the legal authority
to prescribe psychotropic medication. When this chapter was written, two
state legislatures, New Mexico and Louisiana, had modified their state laws to

allow psychologists to prescribe with proper training and a number of other states had legislation pending. Additionally, psychologists currently have prescriptive authority in the U.S. territory of Guam.

Early in the prescription privileges debate the Department of Defense (DoD) established a Psychopharmacology Demonstration Project (PDP) where military psychologists could volunteer for post-doctoral training in psychopharmacology. Four groups of military psychologists, using various training iterations, completed psychopharmacology training and are currently serving as prescribing psychologists in the military. Despite the success these military psychologists have had, and continue to have, as prescribers of psychotropic medication in the military, the DoD's PDP program was discontinued after the fourth group had completed its training (Newman, 2000; Newman, Phelps, Sammons, Dunivin, & Cullen, 2000; Sammons, Paige, & Levant, 2003). However, military psychologists who independently seek psychopharmacological training from appropriately accredited educational institutions are still able to prescribe in the military (M. Sammons, personal communication, December 29, 2006).

With the significant numbers of seriously mentally ill offenders in prisons and jails and the reported difficulty that many correctional systems have in recruiting qualified psychiatrists to meet inmate demand, it is possible that training correctional psychologists in psychopharmacology might be one way of meeting inmate demand for psychiatric services. Correctional psychologists already have many of the skills needed to prescribe. In many correctional systems, psychologists screen newly arriving offenders, conduct formal follow-up assessments when needed, diagnose mental health problems, and monitor offender behavior following psychiatric consultation. With prescriptive authority, psychologists could avoid delays that frequently occur when offenders with mental health problems have to wait for a consulting psychiatrist's visit and continuity of care for offenders would be improved. Interestingly, in two surveys of psychology students and practitioners, it was correctional psychologists that most strongly endorsed the need for prescriptive authority (Fagan et al., 2004; Fagan, Ax, Liss, Resnick, & Moody, 2007).

A Public Health/Harm Reduction Strategy

Is drug use and abuse a law enforcement problem or a public health problem? This question, posed by Durant and Thacker (2003) and discussed by Chavez (see Chapter 3), frames the debate currently being played out on the world stage. Those who believe that illicit drug use is a law enforcement problem view it as a moral failing and espouse zero tolerance for it. They have declared a war on drugs marked by efforts to reduce the supply of drugs through various drug eradication and interdiction programs. They have also developed social policies that criminalize drug use and punish drug users with long periods of incarceration. This point of view is punitive in nature and views success as the total abstinence of illicit drug use. This strategy emerged most recently, in part, as a reaction to an epidemic of crack cocaine use in the 1980s and its associated increases in street violence (Dunlap & Johnson, 1992) and is the prevailing view, at present, in the United States.

Those who view drug use and abuse from a public health perspective believe that illicit drug use is unlikely to be eliminated in the immediate future. While they do not condone drug use, they believe that the best strategy to adopt at this time is one of harm reduction. Harm reduction strategies attempt to limit the harm that drug abusers inflict on themselves, others, and society through their intravenous drug use (e.g., drug overdoses, transmission of communicable diseases like HIV/AIDS and hepatitis, and crime). This strategy emerged, in part, as a result of the HIV/AIDS epidemic during the 1980s. As avenues of HIV/AIDS transmission became evident in the 1980s (i.e., intravenous drug use and unsafe sex) harm reduction strategies such as better patient education, condom distribution programs, needle exchange programs, bleach disinfection programs, use of syringe filters, supervised injection facilities, and methadone maintenance programs were introduced. While not their primary purpose, implementing harm reduction strategies also gives treatment providers the opportunity to entice substance abusers into more traditional drug treatment programs.

Community-based harm reduction strategies have been widely used in both European and Asian countries (Dolan, Rutter, & Wodak, 2003; Malkin, Elliott, & McRae, 2003; Razzaghi et al., 2006; Stoever, 2002; Wilton, Keaney, & Strang, 2005). There have been a number of studies examining the effectiveness of harm reduction strategies. Most have reported reductions in crime, disease, and death rates and no significant increase in illicit drug use as a result of harm reduction techniques (Havranek & Stewart, 2006; MacCoun & Reuter, 2001; Rosenberg & Phillips, 2003).

However, there has been reluctance on the part of U.S. legislators and policy makers to embrace harm reduction strategies (Zimmer, 1996; Odie, 2007). They believe that acceptance of harm reduction strategies may undermine all zero tolerance antidrug programs and suggest a tacit acceptance of illicit drug use—positions they are unable to support. Since federal funding is often sought to finance these types of programs, few harm reduction programs have received federal funding. Despite the paucity of government funds, drug treatment experts, academics, health care providers and some law enforcement officials with philosophical support from the Centers for Disease Control (CDC) are beginning to advocate harm reduction strategies and the number of harm reduction programs in the U.S. is growing. For example, the first needle exchange program in the United States was established in 1988. By 2005 there were over 184 in the country with most located in large urban areas (DesJarlais, Sloboda, Friedman, Tempalski, McKnight, & Braine, 2006).

While conditions in correctional systems vary greatly, few would deny that unprotected sex and illicit drug use occur in these settings. The current debate is not whether these practices occur, but to what extent they occur within systems. According to Hammett (2006), estimates of the number of offenders who have engaged in homosexual conduct while in prison range from 2 percent to 65 percent. To the extent that unsafe sexual practices and illicit drug use take place in a particular correctional system, it may be appropriate to consider the use of harm reduction strategies to combat the spread of infectious diseases among offenders and among the partners of offenders following their release from prison. Because most correctional systems in the U.S. do not employ harm reduction techniques like condom distribution or needle exchange programs to offenders, some would argue that incarcerated offenders are at greater risk than they would be in the community (Hammett, 2006).

Although some harm reduction techniques may not be suitable for implementation in a correctional setting, some may be appropriate and worth considering. At present, there is considerable documented support for such programs from European and Asian prisons (Odie, 2007). For example, Dolan et al. (2003) reported positive results with prison-based needle exchange programs for offenders in German, Swiss, and Spanish prisons. Their results indicated that incidents of needle sharing declined, the number of abscesses related to IV drug use decreased, the number of drug overdoses declined, and offender health improved. Additionally, they found no increase in overall drug use, no instances where needles were used as weapons, and no complaints from correctional officers about the program. While rare in U.S. correctional systems, two correctional systems (Vermont and Mississippi) and five large city jail systems (New York, Philadelphia, San Francisco, Los Angeles, and Washington, D.C.) have implemented condom distribution programs without incident (May & Williams, 2002; Odie, 2007). Recently, the California legislature passed a bill allowing condom distribution in its prisons (New York Times, Editorial, 2006).

Treatment Initiatives From Other Countries

In his frequently quoted paper, Martinson (1974) reviewed the success of offender rehabilitation programs from 1945 to 1967 and concluded that with few exceptions rehabilitation programs had little to no effect on recidivism. While his methodology and findings were later refuted, this study marked the beginning of a change in correctional philosophy, especially in the U.S., from one that was primarily rehabilitative in nature to one that was primarily punitive in nature. Evidence of this philosophical shift can be seen in such social policy initiatives as the war on drugs, the introduction of determinate and mandatory minimum sentences, the abolition of parole, and the criminalization of behaviors associated with mental illness, substance abuse, and sexual acting out. All of these initiatives collectively have resulted in a larger, more violent, more diverse and clinically complex prison population, as was noted earlier in this chapter. While the United States, Canada, Australia, New Zealand, and most western European countries have noted increased incarceration rates among their mentally ill, substance abusing, and sexually predatory offender populations, each system has attempted to deal with these offenders with somewhat differing strategies. While the differences in strategy may be subtle or a matter of degree, there may still be lessons to learn from how other countries manage the rehabilitative needs of their criminal offenders. The efforts of two countries, Canada and the Netherlands, will be used to illustrate this point.

Canada

Correctional Service of Canada has led the way in its commitment to the development of evidence-based treatment approaches. Using this approach, they have incorporated a research/program evaluation component into all of their treatment program efforts and have attempted to focus research attention on identifying the specific characteristics of treatment programs that produce the best outcomes. Through this approach, they have been able to demonstrate that some treatment approaches are better than others and have begun to define what constitutes best practices in correctional rehabilitative programs (Day & Howells, 2002).

Using this approach, Andrews and Bonta (1994) have proposed five guiding principles for rehabilitation programs: risk, need, responsivity, professional discretion, and program integrity.[8] They believe that these guiding principles can be used for matching offenders to programs in order to maximize treatment outcomes. By accurately assessing an offender's potential **risk** for recidivating, offenders with highest risk levels can be placed in rehabilitation programs that are longer and more intense. Obviously, for this principle to work, accurate risk assessment procedures are a requirement. A number of researchers have identified specific criminogenic **needs** that must be addressed for recidivism to be impacted. These needs include: substance abuse (Boland, Henderson, & Baker, 1998); personal/emotional factors such as self-concept, impulsivity, problem-solving abilities, aggressiveness, and risk-taking (Robinson, Porporino, & Beal, 1998); and criminal/social interactions

---

8. See Smith, Gendreau, and Goggin (Chapter 8) for a more detailed discussion of these principles.

(Goggin, Gendreau, & Gray, 1998). To the extent that these factors are addressed by rehabilitative programs, recidivism can be significantly reduced. **Responsivity** refers to those contextual, noncriminogenic factors like ethnicity, gender, race, anxiety, depression, or mental illness that may interfere with or facilitate learning during the rehabilitative process. **Program integrity** refers to the degree to which a therapist follows the treatment protocol and delivers the program in a competent fashion. The last guiding principle, **professional discretion,** refers to the ability of the professional to use personal discretion and flexibility (i.e., make program adjustments) to address situations not covered by or related to the other principles.

Through meta-analytic studies, Canadian researchers have also been able to identify specific program characteristics that produce greater reductions in recidivism. These are summarized by Day and Howells (1998) and include the following findings:

1. Programs that target medium and high risk offenders and focus on criminogenic factors produce more positive results on recidivism than programs that indiscriminately allow any offender to participate.
2. Cognitive and behavioral approaches tend to be more successful than other types of treatment (e.g., confrontation or direct deterrence) with offenders.
3. Programs need to be longer and more intense to have a significant impact on offender recidivism rates. Researchers suggest programs that are at least 100 hours in duration and span 3 to 4 months.
4. Staff assigned to deliver programs need to be adequately trained and supervised in program delivery.
5. Rehabilitative programs offered in community-based settings produce greater reductions in recidivism than programs offered in prisons.
6. Program goals need to be incorporated not only into the individual offender's overall treatment plan, but also into the philosophies and expectations of the larger correctional environment.
7. All prison staff (i.e., administrators, job supervisors, teachers, correctional officers, etc.) should be involved in the process of changing offender behavior not just designated treatment staff.
8. Prison-based programs are most effective if they are linked to and integrated with community-based services.

Taken collectively, the Canadian research described above has interesting implications for correctional programming in the U.S. and elsewhere. It suggests, for example, that the medical model focus on assessing disorders and producing symptom relief, currently being used by many correctional mental health professionals, may not be the most efficient use of their time and skill. Rather, mental health professionals might have more significant systemic impact by focusing their efforts on developing programs that are well integrated into the larger correctional and community environments.

The Netherlands

Unlike the United States, the Netherlands has never declared a war on drugs. While they disapprove of drug use and have passed laws to prohibit the production, distribution, and sale of drugs similar to other countries, they have also concluded that the government cannot eliminate this problem from society. As a result, they have chosen to adopt a more pragmatic, nonmoralistic approach that concentrates on reducing the negative consequences of drugs for individual users and society (Zimmer, 1996).

Using this approach, the Dutch have implemented various harm reduction strategies and developed an approach to drug use and abuse that lies somewhere between legalization and prohibition. Specifically, their social policy makes a distinction between "hard" drugs (e.g., heroin and cocaine) and "soft" drugs (e.g., marijuana and hashish). Since they have determined that "soft" drug use poses minimal risk to users and society, law enforcement agencies do not expend their limited resources pursuing "soft" drug users. Cannabis "coffee shops," carefully regulated by the government, have been allowed to open and currently flourish in the Netherlands. By providing a legal environment for cannabis use, the Dutch government has decriminalized its use and decreased its symbol as a vehicle for youthful rebellion.

Although "hard" drug users clearly pose a greater risk to themselves and society, the Netherlands' approach has been to pursue large scale suppliers of "hard" drugs rather than individual users. When individual "hard" drug users are identified, efforts are made to keep them as well integrated in society as possible. They are not excluded from jobs, welfare benefits, available public housing, or medical care. They are offered free access to various harm reduction and substance abuse treatment programs. Because these "hard" drug users are not ostracized from society and have access to welfare benefits, they are not as financially destitute as are substance abusers in the United States and, as a result, are less inclined to engage in criminal activities to support their drug habits. However, even when substance abusers are sent to prison, prisons are generally located in the heart of major metropolitan areas and make an effort to keep offenders connected to community resources (Boeij, 2002). This approach stands in contrast to U.S. prisons, which are typically built in geographically remote areas where family contacts are often difficult to maintain (Ax, Fagan, & Holton, 2003).

Research findings (Abraham, 1999; Cohen & Kaal, 2001; Tierney, 2006; Zimmer, 1996) suggest that the Netherlands' efforts to improve the life conditions of drug abusers have had some positive outcomes. Compared to the

United States, "hard" drug users in the Netherlands are less likely to use drugs, less likely to inject drugs, less likely to be homeless, less likely to commit crimes, and less likely to spend time in prisons. However, the Dutch approach has not been without problems. For example, the buying and selling of "hard" drugs is still not legal in the Netherlands. As a result, these transactions take place on the streets and create a problem for ordinary citizens much as they do in the U.S. and other Western countries. Additionally, "hard" drug importation through organized criminal groups remains a problem for the Netherlands.

On a positive note, the Dutch approach has allowed law enforcement and correctional facilities to focus their limited resources on problems other than the apprehension and confinement of individual substance abusers. Instead, it has placed greater responsibility for managing substance use and abuse on community-based medical and social services agencies.

When the large number of nonviolent drug users who are currently confined in U.S. prisons and jails is considered, the more pragmatic approach of the Dutch offers an interesting alternative. Although social reformers in a number of Western countries including the United States, Mexico, and Australia have proposed the decriminalization of "soft" drugs, they have not been able to overcome social and government opposition to this idea.

CAN DECISIONS BE BETTER MADE USING EMPIRICAL DATA?

All too often correctional policies or legislative decisions are made based on impulsive social and political sound bites given in response to high profile, yet nonstereotypical, crimes of violence rather than empirical data related to risk variables, correlates of reoffense, or research related to human behavior. For example, during the 1988 presidential campaign, the case of Willie Horton was used to discredit then-governor Michael Dukakis' record on crime. Willie Horton was a convicted felon released on a weekend furlough in Massachusetts while he was serving a life sentence. While on furlough, Horton stabbed a 17-year-old gas station attendant to death. Following this event, not only was Dukakis lambasted for his support of the weekend furlough program, but many jails and prisons at all levels of government implemented more restrictive furlough programs that basically denied most offenders access to community furloughs. These changes were made with little attention to the empirical benefits of transitioning offenders back to the community instead of simply releasing them to the community, or to the value of more precisely assessing the differential risk of offenders prior to placement in the furlough program (Krienert, 2005; Petersilia, 2004).

In the 1990s, the United States saw many statutory changes related to the so-called "three strikes" legislation. This trend began in California with the intent to hand down mandatory and extended periods of incarceration to persons convicted of serious offenses on three or more occasions. The popular appeal of legislation paralleling the national pastime, baseball, coupled with the outrage about sensationalized news stories highlighting reoffenders, elicited popular support for this legislation. Definitions and applications of what types of offenses warrant a "strike" vary across jurisdictions.

In 2003, the Supreme Court reviewed the use of these laws following their application in a variety of unusual scenarios (e.g., a strike resulting from theft of cookies in one case). By a 5-4 majority they ruled that lengthy sentences often mandated in this legislation did not violate the Eighth Amendment which prohibits "cruel and unusual punishment." (*Ewing v. California*, 2003; *Lockyner v. Andrade*, 2003). While this legislation may serve to temporarily quiet public anger against repeat offenders, many individuals who commit felonies may not possess risk levels consistent with life imprisonment based on more empirical actuarial risk data or base rates data on recidivism. For example, possession of small amounts of drugs (even with no evidence of distribution), minor white collar crimes, and petit larceny can all result in felony charges which can accumulate towards "three strikes."

Perhaps, the most significant examples of emotionally-based, as opposed to empirically-driven, legislation are seen in cases involving the sexual homicides of children. In 1994, the Jacob Wetterling Act mandated that all 50 states develop registration procedures for convicted sexual offenders. In 1996, legislation referred to as "Megan's Law" added community notification procedures to the concept of registration. The Adam Walsh Act, passed in July 2006, establishes a comprehensive national system for registration of sex offenders, requiring all jurisdictions to enact criminal penalties for sex offenders who fail to comply with registration and imposing a fine or term of imprisonment for sex offenders who knowingly fail to register.

Currently proposed legislation, referred to as "Jessica's Law" or the "Jessica Lundsford Acts" attempts to enforce more stringent tracking of sex offenders including additional registration requirements, the use of Global Positioning System (GPS) devices, and residency requirements forbidding registered offenders from living within 2000 feet of schools or any place children may gather (depending on the statutory language proposed by various jurisdictions). While these legislative actions may leave the public with a sense of security, empirical research indicates that this sense of security is often overestimated. Specifically, this legislation makes it more difficult for offenders to receive treatment, gain meaningful employment, and be tracked most effectively and consistently by law enforcement due to their geographical distance from these services (Levenson, 2005). Further, this type of legislation reinforces the stereotypical belief that most sex offenders are strangers, rather than providing education, funding, and prevention targeted at offenders known to their victims.

Given a social and political climate so intent on offender punishment and exclusion from society, can social scientists assist in the development and implementation of empirically-driven policies? Historically, mental health professionals, who think about issues in terms of logic and probabilities, have been left feeling frustrated and disillusioned when the presentation of data alone in professional journals has not been sufficient to significantly influence policy (Ax, 2003; Sommer, 2006). Several authors (DeLeon Loftis, Ball, & Sullivan, 2006; Sullivan & Reedy, 2005; Maton & Bishop-Josef, 2006) have examined the past policy-influencing efforts, expectations, and strategies employed by mental health researchers. They have identified three themes that may have contributed in the past to policymakers overlooking or disregarding relevant mental health data: communication, context, and relationships.

In terms of communication, at a very basic level, the findings published in professional journals do not often make it to legislative committees, city councils, school boards, and state funding agencies unless psychologists present them there. Beyond this is the issue of language. A brief look at policy development reminds us that simply presenting a compelling intellectual and statistically solid argument is not enough (DeLeon, et al., 2006), especially with regard to emotionally-laden social concerns such as crime, violence, and public safety. Mental health professionals need to frame data in terms of the legislative issues at hand. This involves not only minimizing professional jargon, but also focusing on a succinct and powerful message that will have the greatest impact. This can be difficult for mental health professionals, who are trained to be thorough and feel compelled to provide detailed explanations that address all possible sources of variance as opposed to just offering the basic "take home message."

Related to the above point, mental health professionals often have difficulty coping with the nature of the legislative process with its inherent "give and take," its slow and sometimes backward process of change, and its reliance on timing as opposed to data alone. This context is very different from that of traditional clinical work with its focus on achieving measurable outcomes in proportion to time spent and its attention to abstract as opposed to personal concepts. Clinical work is also less influenced by larger external factors (i.e., economics, high profile incidents, media coverage) and more by individual factors that may be modified through traditional cognitive, pharmacological, or behavioral interventions.

In spite of differences in communication and the challenges of the political landscape, several psychologists have successfully "navigated" the political arena, using their expertise in psychology to impact policies related to health care, education, crime, and other areas of social concern (DeLeon, Loftis, Ball, & Sullivan, 2006). At the time of this writing, there were three psychologists in the U.S. House of Representatives, 12 psychologists in various state legislatures, and numerous psychologists holding leadership positions in various state and federal agencies. Obtaining a position of leadership and potential influence is remarkable in itself, but achieving significant legislative impact on social policy is a major undertaking, especially if a psychologist is not a member of the majority party. However, if they choose to answer the advocacy call, psychologists' expertise in negotiation, communication, and objectivity can be effective skills. Former congressman and psychologist Ted Strickland (D-OH) illustrated this case when he co-sponsored the Mentally Ill Offender Treatment and Crime Prevention Act (§.1194), with his colleague Senator Mike DeWine (R-OH). Congressman Strickland used his background as a psychologist in a state prison system to inform and develop policy related to offenders with mental illnesses (Sullivan & Reedy, 2005). Without the acknowledgement, persistence, and commitment to work across party lines, his expertise would not have been heard.

Many individuals involved in policy formation, whether at the local, state, or federal level, repeatedly pronounce the importance of relationships in influencing funding, policy, and legislation. DeLeon et al. (2006) highlight the importance of working relationships as "critical" for researchers wanting to impact policy. It is not enough to present data on one occasion, submit one brief or editorial, or provide talking points to an advocacy group. Having a meaningful impact on public policy is a long-term process, not a single event and is highly dependent on personal relationships developed over time between policymakers and mental health professionals.

Compromise is also an essential aspect of the legislative process. Often mental health researchers begin their foray into policy development with high expectations only to feel as if they have "sold out" if they achieve anything less than their initial and ultimate goals. Instead, they should be entering the process with an understanding that empirically-driven policy development is a process of gains and losses as opposed to a dichotomous "either/or" event. Compromise involves listening, education, negotiating, and problem-solving for mutual advantage. Political compromise also involves the ability to empathize with emotional rhetoric designed to gain political clout, while at the same time neutralizing it with the presentation of factual, empirical evidence that can contribute to the development of sound social policy.

In terms of social policy related to correctional and offender populations, mental health researchers need to collaborate with other disciplines that on the surface may not seem like feasible allies. These disciplines may include law enforcement, victim advocates, prosecuting attorneys, and community case management. An excellent example of this type of relationship is being displayed in California between the California Coalition against Sexual Assault (CALCASA) and mental health professionals. California, like many states, is faced with potential legislation which would expand residency restrictions to 2000 feet and require lifetime GPS tracking for all sex offenders (CALCASA, n.d.). While this initiative may quell public outrage and concern with sex offenders, this legislation is counter to what the research indicates about offenders who are pushed to live in geographic areas which have limited access to housing, treatment, employment, and monitoring through probation and community corrections.

In their attempts to block or modify this legislation with a more empirically-driven, clinically-proactive, fiscally responsible policy that is also sensitive to the safety concerns of individuals living in public areas, CALCASA, the California Coalition on Sex Offending, the Association for the Treatment of Sex Abusers (ATSA), California Attorneys for Criminal Justice, and several other law enforcement officials are working together to defeat the proposed legislation in the 2006 elections. In discussing these collaborative relationships, Dr. Suzanne Brown McBride (2006), Executive Director for CALCASA, noted that despite their apparent "ideological chasms" all of these groups share a concern for public safety and a reduction of sexual victimization. She reiterated the message that initiation and maintenance of these relationships take time and effort, but that the collaborative efforts of these groups have resulted in the effective modification of legislation in California, including the establishment of a Sex Offender Management Board, which unites the various stakeholders in the management of sex offenders and focuses their efforts on describing current practices, identifying best practices, and making recommendations regarding needed changes.

CONCLUSIONS AND RECOMMENDATIONS

Throughout this volume, evidence suggests that the United States and other Western countries are facing very similar problems. Incarceration rates have been increasing, with the U.S. leading the way. There are over 7 million people currently under criminal justice supervision in the U.S. alone. Within this larger group of incarcerated individuals are growing numbers of people with mental disorders, substance abuse problems, sexually predatory behavioral patterns, violent dispositions, and/or political/religious beliefs contrary to those espoused by Western cultures. At the same time that the diversity and needs of incarcerated individuals have grown, the resources required to address these needs have either remained the same or decreased.

How different countries have attempted to manage these common problems has been discussed in several chapters of this book. Ax (see Chapter 1) also noted that there is historical precedence for the sharing of correctional management ideas that dates back to the beginning of corrections. As current correctional mental health professionals, administrators, and policy makers in the U.S. look to the future, they should be guided not only by their own experiences, but also to some extent by the lessons learned within the larger international correctional community. Collectively, these lessons point to the value of more information sharing, cooperation, collaboration, and integration of services between correctional and community-based organizations; to learning from the experiences of others; and to making long-term decisions and policies based on data wherever and whenever possible. It is these three general themes that have been highlighted in this chapter.

In terms of the first theme (i.e., sharing information and integrating services across responsible agencies), the literature is filled with calls for more integration of services among law enforcement, judicial, correctional, and community-based agencies and with examples of how specific jurisdictions have piloted such integrated programs. However, there is less evidence at this point to suggest that these systems have actually changed basic systemic structures (e.g., data gathering and sharing mechanisms) to accommodate more integrated services. This would seem to be the next step in this process.

According to Berman (2006), collaboration needs to be more that just information sharing or holding interdisciplinary meetings. Chrislip and Larson (1994) suggest that effective collaboration consists of a mutually beneficial relationship where two or more parties achieve common goals by sharing responsibility, authority, and accountability for achieving results. They suggest that it is more than simply sharing knowledge and information (communication), and more than a relationship that helps each party achieve its own goals (cooperation and coordination). They note that the purpose of effective collaboration is to create a shared vision and joint strategies to address concerns that go beyond the purview of any particular party. To achieve this end, agencies will need to pool their collective resources, relinquish individual control in favor of shared control, and be evaluated based on mutually agreed upon and socially relevant outcome measures.

Although integrated service delivery ultimately should be offered to all offenders, it should initially target those with the greatest need (e.g., those with serious medical, mental health, and substance abuse problems). To accomplish this goal, greater attention will need to be given to risk assessment procedures that produce reliable individual results. Canadian researchers such as Vernon Quinsey and Robert Hare and their colleagues (see Chapter 6) have done considerable research in this area and have demonstrated empirical approaches to better risk assessment. Their approach has been to use risk assessment as a means of determining treatment needs rather than as a punitive weapon for justifying longer periods of incarceration as is currently the practice in the U.S. The Integrated Offender Management (IOM) system used in New Zealand (see Chapter 7) provides an excellent example of how risk assessment procedures can be used to make more informed treatment decisions. Elements of this system might be useful to U.S. drug courts, mental health courts, and parole agencies as they attempt to make difficult case management decisions. Additionally, Canadian researchers such as Andrews, Bonta, and Gendreau (see Chapter 6) have been instrumental in identifying specific criminogenic needs as well as suggested methods for addressing these needs with empirically-derived programming strategies. In sum, the Canadians have not only led the way in research on risk assessment and correctional programming, but have also demonstrated the success that can come from university-corrections partnerships. This example is one that could easily be emulated in the U.S. and should be considered as a future goal for U.S. correctional systems.

A second theme highlighted in this chapter has been the need for U.S. correctional systems to explore other service delivery models to see if there are better, more efficient ways of providing services to offenders. There are a number of ideas both within the United States and from other countries that might have applicability to U. S. correctional systems. Allowing appropriately trained psychologists to add prescriptive authority to their treatment repertoire or to serve more of a primary care role in the treatment of offenders were two innovative ideas developed in the U.S. and mentioned in this chapter as two possible ways of making current correctional systems more efficient and effective. These ideas have proven successful in the U.S. military and may be equally effective in the paramilitary correctional environment.

Adopting more of a public health/harm reduction approach to the management of offenders' medical and mental health needs was also discussed in this chapter. This approach has not been broadly implemented in the U.S. However, it has been tested in other countries such as the Netherlands and Great Britain (see Chapter 4) with some degree of success. The experiences of these countries may provide useful guidance to U.S. correctional systems interested in implementing harm reduction strategies such as condom distribution and needle exchange programs.

Other countries have developed interesting strategies as they have attempted to manage their rapidly expanding offender populations. For example, New Zealand's correctional system has been able to retain its focus on rehabilitation despite public sentiment toward longer prison sentences (see Chapter 7). Canada has implemented a conditional sentencing program (see Chapter 6), which allows accused offenders to admit their guilt and to develop a rehabilitative strategy that is acceptable to them, the court, and their victim(s). If the accused offender successfully completes the proscribed rehabilitative strategy, then all charges are dropped. In its four-year history, this approach has resulted in approximately 43,000 conditional sentences being given and in a significant reduction in the number of people that would have otherwise been sent directly to prison. This conditional sentencing program is very similar to the concept of restorative justice described by Braithwaite (2002) and might be a useful concept for U.S. drug and mental health courts to study.

Both Russia (see Chapter 13) and France (see Chapter 5) have implemented amnesty programs to reduce the number of offenders entering prison while increasing the number of inmates released from prison. How these programs have been implemented might assist U.S. policymakers in developing strategies for reducing their correctional population, especially among nonviolent substance abusers and illegal immigrants. In France (see Chapter 5) the concept of "corrections judges" was established in 1958. These judges have multiple responsibilities including: determining offender sentences and release dates and in overseeing prison conditions and disciplinary procedures. They accomplish this function by visiting prisons in their jurisdiction at least once a month, by hearing individual inmate complaints, and by keeping informed about prison programs, physical plants, and general living conditions. While this concept might be difficult to implement in its entirety in the U.S., elements of this program might prove effective at reducing correctional litigation and increasing judicial awareness regarding correctional management issues.

As the war on terror escalates and more foreign-born and homegrown terrorists are incarcerated, questions are being raised about how best to manage this population. Should these populations be housed separately, as the U.S. did in its Abu Ghraib prison in Iraq and is currently doing in its military prison in Guantánamo, Cuba or should efforts be made to integrate these offenders into the larger U.S. correctional population? One strategy may lead to instances of prisoner abuse and staff misconduct; the other may lead to increased risk of recruitment among the disenfranchised, development of a new class of homegrown terrorists, and disruption of prison operations. In either case, the question remains "how should terrorists be managed and treated?"

In terms of management, do international laws and conventions apply to terrorists? Certainly, in its 5-3 decision in the *Hamdan v. Rumsfeld* case, the U.S. Supreme Court referenced violations of the Geneva Convention in its decision suggesting the relevance of international law in the establishment of military commissions. In a talk before the American Society of International Law in 2005, U.S. Supreme Court Justice Ruth Bader Ginsburg indicated that the U.S. judiciary should consider international law more often in its decisions. She is also quoted as saying:

> . . . even more so today, the United States is subject to the scrutiny of a candid world. What the United States does, for good or for ill, continues to be watched by the international community, in particular by organizations concerned with

the advancement of the rule of law and respect for human dignity. . . . (Kornblut, 2005, p. A10)

In an ever-shrinking world, can the U.S. afford to develop policies that violate international convention? This question deserves further consideration as the U.S. struggles with the issue of terrorism as well as with other difficult issues (e.g., death penalty–see Chapter 12) where U.S. policy may deviate from international convention.

In terms of terrorist treatment, should de-ganging strategies currently being tried in U.S. prisons (see Chapter 11) be applied to foreign-born terrorists? Should amnesty programs like those in Russia and France be used with terrorists who renounce their terrorist inclinations? While these are current questions for the U.S., other countries such as Great Britain have had to deal with these issues in the past (see Chapter 10). Their solutions may provide useful insights for U.S. officials currently tasked with addressing these issues.

Finally, the third theme discussed in this chapter had to do with using more empirical data in correctional policy decisions. Inherent in this discussion is the idea that correctional policymakers should develop more of a proactive rather than a reactive stance when it comes to policy development. By asking clearer empirical questions, by defining terms more precisely, and by gathering, analyzing, and using relevant data to answer these empirical questions, more reasoned decisions are possible. To achieve this end, two goals must be achieved. First, correctional systems and academic communities must overcome a number of obstacles and merge their collective knowledge bases. Canada's experience in this regard can serve as an excellent model. Second, valuable data must reach legislators and policymakers in a form that is understandable, relevant, and timely. This might be accomplished through greater lobbying efforts, through greater involvement in the political process, by publishing relevant data in forums frequented by policymakers, and through more advocacy initiatives. While correctional administrators and mental health professionals may not have the time or inclination to engage in these activities, they may be able to achieve these objectives by partnering with organizations (e.g., NGOs–see Chapter 9) whose mission and organizational structure allow for these types of activities.

While many innovative ideas have been referenced in this chapter and this book, none can be easily implemented without a fundamental shift in U.S. correctional thinking. No longer can U.S. correctional systems operate in isolation. Their problems are growing, their resources are shrinking, and recidivism rates remain too high. Further, when the escalating costs of corrections reach the general public, it is likely that public outrage and demand for change will increase. Perhaps, the beginning of this change process has already begun as suggested in a *New York Times* opinion article by Suellentrop (2006):

Criminologists of both parties hope that the decreasing importance of crime as a political issue will make it possible to have a more sober discussion of the subject at last. They want to see a less ideologically charged debate and one that rests more closely on sound research. There's only one problem: a shocking paucity of such evidence to inform the policy debate. (p. 4)

Instead of maintaining the status quo, correctional systems need to reach out to other elements of the criminal justice system, other governmental social service agencies, and community-based organizations (public, private, and nonprofit) that have shared goals or interests and partner with them to address the complex problems facing correctional systems today. Additionally, they need to look at how other countries are managing or have historically managed similar problems. Much can be learned from the experiences of others as the collective history of corrections has repeatedly suggested.

REFERENCES

Abraham, M. (1999). Illicit drug use, urbanization, and lifestyle in the Netherlands. *Journal of Drug Issues, 29,* 565–586.

Albee, G. W. (2002). Just say no to psychotropic drugs! *Journal of Clinical Psychology, 58,* 635–648.

Alter, A. (2003). *Study touts faith-based prison rehabilitation program.* Retrieved October 17, 2006, from http://pewforum.org/news/display.php?NewsID=2333.

American Psychological Association. (1996). *Recommended postdoctoral training in psychopharmacology for prescription privileges and model legislation for prescriptive authority.* Washington, DC: Author.

Anderson, T. (2006, September 8). Jails called terrorist breeding ground. *Whittier Daily News,* Los Angeles, CA: Media News Group, Inc.

Andrews, D. A. & Bonta, J. (1994). *The psychology of criminal conduct.* Cincinnati, OH: Anderson.

Appelbaum, K. L., Manning, T. D., & Noonan, J. D. (2002). A university state corporation partnership for providing correctional mental health services. *Psychiatric Services, 53,* 185–189.

Austin, M. J., Martin, M., Carnochan, S., Goldberg, S., Berrick, J. D., Weiss, B., & Kelley, J. (1999). Building a comprehensive university partnership: A case study of the Bay Area social services consortium. *Journal of Community Practice, 6,* 89–106.

Ax, R. K. (2003). A viable future for correctional mental health care. In T. J. Fagan and R. K. Ax (Eds.), *Correctional Mental Health Handbook* (pp. 303–327). Thousand Oaks, CA: Sage.

Ax, R. K., Fagan, T. J., & Holton, S. M. B. (2003). Individuals with serious mental illnesses: Rural perspectives and issues. In B. H. Stamm (Ed.), *Rural behavioral health care: An interdisciplinary guide* (pp. 203–215). Washington, DC: American Psychological Association.

Ax, R. K., Forbes, M. R., & Thompson, D. D. (1997). Prescription privileges for psychologists: A survey of predoctoral interns and directors of training. *Professional Psychology: Research and Practice, 28,* 509–514.

Basile, V. D. (2002). A model for developing a reentry program. *Federal Probation, 66* (3), 55–58.

Beech, A. R., Fisher, D. D., & Thornton, D. (2003). Risk assessment of sex offenders. *Professional Psychology: Research and Practice, 34,* 339–352.

Berman, J. (2006, August). Working toward the future: Why and how to collaborate effectively. *Corrections Today, 68* (5), 44–48.

Blaauw, E., Roesch, R., & Kerkhof, A. (2000). Mental disorders in European prison systems. *International Journal of Law and Psychiatry, 23,* 649–663.

Boeij, K. (2002, February). Developments in the Netherlands penitentiary system. *Corrections Today, 64* (1), 50–53.

Boland, F. J., Henderson, K., & Baker, J. (1998). *Case needs review: Substance abuse domain* (Research Report No. 75). Ottawa, Ontario, Canada: Correctional Service of Canada.

Bonta, J., Law, M., & Hanson, K. (1998). The prediction of criminal and violent recidivism among mentally disordered offenders: A meta-analysis. *Psychological Bulletin, 123,* 123–142.

Borum, R. (1996). Improving the clinical practice of violence risk assessment. *American Psychologist, 9,* 945–956.

Boswell, D. L., & Litwin, W. J. (1992). Limited prescription privileges for psychologists: A 1-year follow-up. *Professional Psychology: Research and Practice, 23,* 108–113.

Braithwaite, J. (2002). *Restorative justice and responsive regulation.* New York, NY: Oxford University Press.

Broner, N., Nguyen, H., Swern, A., & Goldfinger, S. (2003). Adapting a substance abuse court diversion model for felony offenders with co-occuring disorders: Initial implementation. *Psychiatric Quarterly, 74,* 361–385.

Brown-MacBride, S. (2006, September 27). Developing a public policy strategy. Paper presented at the annual meeting of the Association for the Treatment of Sexual Abusers, Chicago, Illinois.

Burns, S. M., DeLeon, P. H., Chemtob, C. M., Welch, B. L., & Samuels, R. M. (1988). Psychotropic medication: A new technique for psychology? *Psychotherapy: Theory, Research, Practice, and Training, 25,* 508–515.

Byrne, F., Schauffler, R., Lightman, L., Finigan, M., & Carey, S. (2004). California drug courts: A methodology for determining costs and avoided costs. *Journal of Psychoactive Drugs, SARC Supplement 2,* 147–156.

Byrne, J. M. & Taxman, F. S. (2004). Targeting for reentry: Inclusion/exclusion criteria across eight model programs. *Federal Probation, 68* (2), 53–61.

CALCASA. (n.d.). *CALCASA Public Policy.* Retrieved September 30, 2006, from http://www.calcasapublicpolicy.org

California Board of Corrections. (2000). *Mentally Ill Offender Crime Reduction Grant Program: Annual report.* Retrieved December 19, 2006, from www.bdcorr.ca.gov/ cppd/miocrg/miocrg_publications/miocrg_publications.htm

Camp, S. D., Klein-Saffran, J., Kwon, O., Daggett, D. M., & Joseph, V. (2006). An exploration into participation in a faith-based prison program. *Criminology & Public Policy, 5,* 529–549.

Chrislip, D., & Larson, C. (1994). *Collaborative leadership: How citizens and civic leaders can make a difference.* San Francisco, CA.: Jossey Bass.

Clark, L. A., Watson, D., and Reynolds, S. (1995). Diagnosis and classification of psychopathology: Challenges to the current system and future directions. *Annual Review of Psychology, 46,* 121–153.

Clay, R. (2007). One heart–many threats. *Monitor on Psychology, 38* (1), 46–48.

Cohen, P. D. A., & Kaal, H. L. (2001). *The irrelevance of drug policy.* Amsterdam: CEDRO.

Community and Law Enforcement Resources Together. (2006). ComALERT. Retrieved October 21, 2006, from http://www.brooklynda.org/ComAlert/comalert.htm

Cook, D., Bond, A. F., Jones, P, & Greif, G. L. (2002). The social work outreach service within a school of social work: A new model for collaboration with the community. *Journal of Community Practice, 10,* 17–31.

Courneya, K. S., Estabrooks, P. A., & Nigg, C. R. (1997). A simple reinforcement strategy for increasing attendance at a fitness facility. *Health Education and Health Behavior, 2,* 708–715.

Cummings, N. A. (1997). Behavioral health in primary care: Dollars and sense. In N. A. Cummings, J. L. Cummings, & J. N. Johnson (Eds.), *Behavioral health in primary care: A guide for clinical integration* (pp. 3–21). Madison, CT.: Psychosocial Press.

Craig, D. (2004, April). Iowa's dual diagnosis offender program. *Corrections Today, 66* (2), 96–98.

Day, A. & Howells, K. (2002). Psychological treatments for rehabilitating offenders: Evidence-based practice comes of age. *Australian Psychologist, 37,* 39–47.

DeLeon, P. H. (1988). Public policy and public service: Our professional duty. *American Psychologist, 43,* 309–315.

DeLeon, P. H., Giestling, B., & Kenkel, M. B. (2003). Community health centers: Exciting opportunities for the 21st century. *Professional Psychology: Research and Practice, 34,* 579–585.

DeLeon, P. H., Loftis, C. W., Ball, V., & Sullivan, M. J. (2006). Navigating politics, policy, and procedure: A firsthand perspective of advocacy on behalf of the profession. *Professional Psychology: Research and Practice, 37,* 16–153.

DeLeon, P. H., Rossomando, N. P., & Smedley, B. D. (2004). The future is primary care. In R. G. Frank, S. H. McDaniel, J. H. Bray, & M. Heldring (Eds.), *Primary care psychology* (pp. 317–325). Washington, D.C.: American Psychological Association.

DesJarlais, D. C., Sloboda, Z., Friedman, S. R., Tempalski, B., McKnight, C., & Braine, N. (2006). Diffusion of the D.A.R.E. and syringe exchange programs, *American Journal of Public Health, 96,* 1354–1358.

Ditton, P. M. (1999). *Mental health and treatment of inmates and probationers* (Bureau of Justice Statistics Special Report, NCJ 174463). Washington, D.C.: National Criminal Justice Reference Service.

Dobson, K. S., & Dozois, D. J. (2001). Professional psychology and the prescription debate: Still not ready to go to the alter. *Canadian Psychology, 42,* 131–135.

Dolan, K., Rutter, S., & Wodak, A. (2003). Prison-based syringe exchange programs: A review of international research and development. *Addictions, 98,* 153–158.

Douglas, K. S., & Skeem, J. L. (2005). Violence risk assessment: Getting specific about being dynamic. *Psychology, Public Policy, and Law, 11,* 347–383.

Dunlap, E., & Johnson, B. D. (1992). The setting for the crack era: Macro forces, micro consequences (1960–1992). *Journal of Psychoactive Drugs, 24,* 307–321.

Durant, R., & Thacker, J. (2003). *Substance use and abuse: Cultural and historical perspectives.* Thousand Oaks, CA.: Sage.

Edens, J. F., Peters, R. H., & Hills, H. A. (1997). Treating prison inmates with co-occurring disorders: An integrative review of existing programs. *Behavioral Sciences and the Law, 15,* 439–457.

Eisenberg, C. (2006, October 4). Report: Security gaps in prisons. *Newsday,* A23.

Ewing v. California, 538 U.S. 11 (2003).

Fagan, T. J., Ax, R. K., Resnick, R. J., Liss, M., Johnson, R., & Forbes, M. R. (2004). Attitudes among interns and directors of training: Who wants to prescribe, who doesn't, and why. *Professional Psychology: Research and Practice, 35,* 345–356.

Fagan, T. J., Ax, R. K., Liss, M., Resnick, R. J., & Moody, S. (2007, in press). Prescriptive authority and preferences for training. *Professional Psychology: Research and Practice.*

Fairhurst, L. (2006, October 17). Faith-based prison programs claim to reduce recidivism, but there's little evidence, says FSU researcher. *Florida State University News.* Retrieved October 17, 2006, from http://www.fsu.edu/news/2006/10/04/prison.programs

Farley, J. L., Mitty, J. A., Lally, M. A., Burzynski, J. N., Tashima, K., Rich, J. D., et al. (2000). Comprehensive medical care among HIV-positive incarcerated women: The Rhode Island experience. *Journal of Women's Health & Gender-Based Medicine, 9,* 51–56.

Frankenburg, F. R., & Zanarini, M. C. (2004). The association between borderline personality disorder and chronic medical illness, poor health-related lifestyle choices, and costly forms of health care utilization. *The Journal of Clinical Psychiatry, 65,* 1660–1666.

Garcia Brown, L. (2006). Meeting U.S. health care needs: A challenge to psychology. *Professional Psychology: Research and Practice, 37,* 676–682.

Gaseau, M. (2004). Monitoring extremist groups and maintaining religious rights. Retrieved September 20, 2004, from www.corrections.com/news/feature/index.aspx.

Glaze, L. E., & Palla, S. (2005, November). *Probation and parole in the United States, 2004* (Bureau of Justice Statistics Bulletin NCJ 210676). Washington, D.C.: National Criminal Justice Reference Service.

Goddard, J. (2003, December 24). Florida's new approach to inmate reform: A 'faith-based' prison. *The Christian Science Monitor.* Retrieved October 17, 2006, from http://www.csmonitor.com/2003/1224/p01s04-usju.htm.

Goggin, C., Gendreau, P., & Gray, P. (1998). *Case needs review: Associates/social interaction domain* (Research Report No. 77). Ottawa, Ontario, Canada: Correctional Service of Canada.

Gonzales, A. R., Schofield, R. B., & Schmitt, G. R. (2006). *Drug courts: The second decade.* Washington, DC: U.S. Department of Justice Office of Justice Programs.

Greenberg, J. S. (2002). *Comprehensive Stress Management (8th Edition).* New York: McGraw Hill.

Griffin, P. A., Steadman, H. J., & Petrila, J. (2002). The use of criminal charges and sanctions in mental health courts. *Psychiatric Services, 53,* 1285–1289.

Gray, G. V., Brody, D. S. & Johnson, D. (2005). The evolution of behavioral health care. *Professional Psychology: Research and Practice, 36,* 123–129.

Greenfeld, L. A. (1997, February). *An analysis of data on rape and sexual assault: Sex offenses and offenders* (Bureau of Justice Statistics Special Report NCJ 163392). Washington, DC: National Criminal Justice Reference Service.

Guy, L. S., Edens, J. F., Anthony, C., & Douglas, K. S. (2005). Does psychopathy predict institutional misconduct among adults?: A meta-analytic investigation. *Journal of Consulting and Clinical Psychology, 73,* 1056–1064.

Hall, M. (2006, November 7). Feds target terrorist recruiting in prisons: Security agencies seek intelligence on extremists' impact. *USA Today,* A1.

Hall, E. A., Prendergast, M. L., Wellisch, J., Patten, M., & Cao, Y. (2004). Treating drug-abusing women prisoners: An outcomes evaluation of the Forever Free program. *The Prison Journal, 84,* 81–105.

Hamdan v. Rumsfeld, 05-184 US (2006).

Hammett, T. M. (2006). HIV/AIDS and other infectious diseases among correctional inmates: Transmission, burden, and appropriate response. *American Journal of Public Health, 96,* 974–978.

Hammett, T. M., Roberts, C., & Kennedy, S. (2001). Health-related issues in prisoner reentry. *Crime & Delinquency, 47,* 390–409.

Haney, C. (2006). *Reforming punishment: Psychological limits to the pains of imprisonment.* Washington, DC: American Psychological Association.

Hansen, M. S., Fink, P., & Frydenberg, M. (2004). Follow-up on mental illness in medical inpatients: Health care use and self-rated health and physical fitness. *Psychosomatics, 45,* 302–310.

Hanson, R. K., & Bussiere, M. T. (1998). Predicting relapse: A meta-analysis of sexual offender recidivism studies. *Journal of Consulting and Clinical Psychology, 66,* 348–362.

Hanson, R. K., & Thornton, D. (2000). Improving risk assessments for sex offenders: A comparison of three actuarial scales. *Law and Human Behavior, 24,* 119–136.

Hare, R. D., Clark, D., Grann, M., & Thornton, D. (2000). Psychopathy and the predictive validity of the PCL-R: An international perspective. *Behavioral Sciences and the Law, 18,* 623–645.

Harkavy, I., & Puckett, J. L. (1994). Lessons from Hull House for the contemporary urban university. *Social Service Review, 68,* 299–321.

Harris, G. T., Rice, M. E., Quinsey, V. L., Lalumiere, M. L., Boer, D., & Lang, C. (2003). A multisite comparison of actuarial risk instruments for sex offenders. *Psychological Assessment, 15,* 413–425.

Harrison, P. M., & Beck, A. J. (2003, July). *Prisoners in 2002* (Bureau of Justice Statistics Special Bulletin, NCJ 200248). Washington, D.C.: National Criminal Justice Reference Service.

Harrison, P. M., & Beck, A. J. (2006, May). *Prison and jail inmates at midyear 2005* (Bureau of Justice Statistics Bulletin, NCJ 213133). Washington, D.C.: National Criminal Justice Reference Service.

Havranek, J. E., & Stewart, J. R. (2006). Rehabilitation counselors' attitudes toward harm reduction measures. *Journal of Applied Rehabilitation Counseling, 37,* 38–44.

Hayes, S. C., Walser, R. D., & Bach, P. (2002). Prescription privileges for psychologists: Constituencies and conflicts. *Journal of Clinical Psychology, 58,* 697–708.

Hicks, J. (2004, October). Employment upon re-entry: Prison-based preparedness leads to community-based success. *Corrections Today, 66* (6), 104–113.

Hiller, M. L., Knight, K., & Dwayne, D. (1999). Prison-based substance abuse treatment, residential aftercare and recidivism. *Addiction, 94,* 833–842.

James, D. J., & Glaze, L. E. (2006, September). *Mental health problems of prison and jail inmates* (Bureau of Justice Statistics Special Report, NCJ 213600). Washington, D.C.: National Criminal Justice Reference Service.

Jarrett, N. C., Adeyemi, S. A., & Huggins, T. (2006). Bridging the gap: Providing health care to newly released men. *Journal of Health Care for the Poor and Underserved, 17,* 70–80.

Johnson, B. R. (2004). Religious programs and recidivism among former inmates in Prison Fellowship programs: A long-term follow-up study. *Justice Quarterly, 21,* 329–354.

Johnson, B. R., Larson, D. B., & Pitts, T. C. (1997). Religious programs, institutional adjustment, and recidivism among former inmates in prison fellowship programs. *Justice Quarterly, 14,* 147–165.

Jordan, L. J. (2006, September 19). U.S. prisons easy for terror recruiting, study says. *South Florida Sun Sentinel,* 6A.

Karberg, J. C., & James, D J. (2005, July). *Substance dependence, abuse, and treatment of jail inmates, 2002* (Bureau of Justice Statistics Special Report, NCJ 209588). Washington, D.C.: National Criminal Justice Reference Service.

Kates, N., Craven, M., Crustolo, A. M., Nikolaou, L., & Allen, C. (1997). Integrating mental health services within primary care: A Canadian program. *General Hospital Psychiatry, 19,* 324–332.

Katon, W., Robinson, P., Von Korff, M., Lin, E., Bush, T., Ludman, E., et al. (1996). A multifaceted intervention to improve treatment of depression in primary care. *Archives of General Psychiatry, 53,* 924–932.

Kendig, N. E. (2004). Correctional health care systems and collaboration with academic medicine. *Journal of the American Medical Association, 292,* 501–503.

Kenkel, M. B., DeLeon, P. H., Mantell, E. O., & Steep, A. E. (2005). Divided no more: Psychology's role in integrated health care. *Canadian Psychology, 46,* 189–202.

Kinsler, P. J., Saxman, A., & Fishman, D. B. (2004). The Vermont defendant accommodation project: A case study. *Psychology, Public Policy, and Law, 10,* 134–161.

Kolbasovsky, A., Reich, L., Romano, I., & Jaramillo, B. (2005). Integrating behavioral health into primary care settings: A pilot project. *Professional Psychology: Research and Practice, 36,* 130–135.

Kornblut, A. E. (2005, April 2). Justice Ginsburg backs value of foreign law. *New York Times,* A10.

Krienert, J. L. (2005). Bridging the gap between prison and community employment: An initial assessment of current information. *Criminal Justice Studies: A Critical Journal of Crime, Law, & Society, 18,* 293–303.

Kumanyika, S. K. (2000). Maintenance of dietary behavior change. *Health Psychology, 19,* 42–56.

Kushel, M. B., Hahn, J. A., Evans, J. L., Bangsberg, D. R., & Moss, A. R. (2005). Revolving doors: Imprisonment among the homeless and marginally housed population. *American Journal of Public Health, 95,* 1747–1752.

Lamb, H. R., Weinberger, L. E., & Gross, B. H. (2004). Mentally ill persons in the criminal justice system: Some perspectives. *Psychiatric Quarterly, 75,* 107–126.

Lamberti, J. S., Weisman, R. L., Schwarzkopf, S. B., Price, N., Ashton, R. M., & Trompeter, J. (2001). The mentally ill in jails and prisons: Towards an integrated model of prevention. *Psychiatric Quarterly, 72,* 63–77.

Levenson, J. S. (2005). The impact of sex offender residency restrictions: 1,000 feet from danger or one step from absurd? *International Journal of Offender Therapy and Comparative Criminology, 49,* 168–178.

Lockyner v. Andrade 538 U.S. 63 (2003).

Lurigio, A. J. (2001). Effective services for parolees with mental illness. *Crime & Delinquency, 47,* 446–461.

MacCoun, R. J., & Reuter, P. (2001). *Drug war heresies: Learning from other vices, times, and places.* Cambridge, England: Cambridge University Press.

Malkin, I., Elliott, R., & McRae, R. (2003). Supervised injection facilities and international law. *Journal of Drug Issues, 33,* 539–578.

Martinson, R. (1974). What works? Questions and answers about prison reform. *The Public Interest, 35,* 22–54.

Masters, K. S., Stillman, A. M., Browning, A. D. & Davis, J. W. (2005). Primary care psychology training on campus: Collaboration within a student health center. *Professional Psychology: Research and Practice, 36,* 144–150.

Maton, K. I., & Bishop-Josef, A. J. (2006). Psychological research, practice, and social policy: Potential pathways of influence. *Professional Psychology: Research and Practice, 37,* 140–145.

May, J. P., & Williams, E. L. (2002). Acceptability of condom availability in a U.S. jail. *AIDS Education Prevention, 14* (supplement B), 85–91.

Mears, D. P., Roman, C. G., Wolff, A., & Buck, J. (2006). Faith-based efforts to improve prisoner reentry: Assessing the logic and evidence. *Journal of Criminal Justice, 34,* 351–367.

Menzies, R., & Webster, C. D. (1995). Construction and validation of risk assessments in a six-year follow-up of forensic patients: A tridimensional analysis. *Journal of Consulting and Clinical Psychology, 63,* 766–778.

Miles, J. R., & Cajina, A. (2006, July). The corrections initiative: A collaborative partnership. *Corrections Today, 68* (4), 26–32.

Mitka, M. (2004). Aging prisoners stressing health care system. *Journal of the American Medical Association, 292,* 423–424.

Monahan, J., Steadman, H. J., Robbins, P. C., Silver, E., Applebaum, P. S., Grisso, T., et al. (2000). Developing a clinically useful actuarial tool for assessing violence risk. *British Journal of Psychiatry, 176,* 312–319.

Mumford, E., Schlesinger, H. J., Glass, G. V., Patrick, C., & Cuerdon, T. (1998). A new look at evidence about reduced cost of medical utilization following mental health treatment. *Journal of Psychotherapy Practice and Research, 7,* 68–86.

Mumola, C. J. (1999, January). *Substance abuse and treatment, state and federal prisoners, 1997* (Bureau of Justice Statistics Special Report, NCJ 172871). Washington, D.C.: National Criminal Justice Reference Service.

Newman, R. (2000, March). A psychological model for prescribing. *APA Monitor on Psychology, 31* (3), 45.

Newman, R., Phelps, R., Sammons, M. T., Dunivin, D. L., & Cullen, E. A. (2000). Evaluation of the psychopharmacology demonstration project: A retrospective analysis. *Professional Psychology: Research and Practice, 31,* 598–603.

Ockene, J. K., et al. (2000). Relapse and maintenance issues for smoking cessation. *Health Psychology, 19,* 17–31.

Odie, S. (2007). Sex, drugs, prison, and HIV. *New England Journal of Medicine, 356* (2), 105–108.

Office of National Drug Control Policy (ONDCP). (2006). *The President's National Drug Control Strategy, February 2006.* Retrieved December 27, 2006, from www.ondcp.gov/publications/policy/ndcs06/

Perez, A., Leifman, S., & Estrada, A. (2003). Reversing the criminalization of mental illness. *Crime and Delinquency, 49,* 62–79.

Petersilia, J. (2004). What works in prison reentry? Reviewing and questioning the evidence? *Federal Probation, 68* (2), 4–8.

Petrila, J., Ridgely, M. S., & Borum, R. (2003). Debating outpatient commitment: Controversy, trends, and empirical data. *Crime & Delinquency, 49,* 157–172.

Pettus, C. A., & Severson, M. (2006). Paving the way for effective reentry practice: The critical role and function of the boundary spanner. *The Prison Journal, 86,* 206–229.

Pogorzelski, W., Wolff, N., Pan, K. Y., & Blitz, C. L. (2005). Behavioral health problems, ex-offender reentry policies, and the "Second Chance Act." *American Journal of Public Health, 95,* 1718–1724.

Prendergast, M., Hall, E., & Wellisch, J. (2003). *Outcome evaluation of the Forever Free substance abuse treatment program: One-year post-release outcomes.* Los Angeles: University of California Los Angeles, Drug Abuse Research Center.

Prendergast, M. L., Hall, E. A., Wexler, H. K., Melnick, G., & Cao, Y. (2004). Amity prison-based therapeutic community: 5-year outcomes. *The Prison Journal, 84,* 36–60.

Prison Fellowship. (2006). About the Inner Change Freedom Initiative (IFI). Retrieved October 17, 2006, from http://www.ifiprison.org/contentindex.asp ?ID=135&print=1.

Prison Fellowship Newsroom. (2006). Statement by Chuck Colson and Mark Earley about allegations made in David Kuo's new book. Retrieved October 17, 2006, from http://www.demossnewspond.com/pf/.

Raimer, B. G., & Stobo, J. D. (2004) Health care delivery in the Texas prison system. *Journal of the American Medical Association, 292,* 485–489.

Razzaghi, E., Nassirimanesh, B., Afshar, P., Ohiri, K., Claeson, M., & Power, R. (2006, August). HIV/AIDS harm reduction in Iran. *The Lancet, 368,* 434–435.

Redlich, A. D., Steadman, H. J., Monahan, J., Petrila, J., & Griffin, P. A. (2005). The second generation of mental health courts. *Psychology, Public Policy, and Law, 11,* 527–538.

Resnick, R. J. (2003, April). No harm in a coat of many colours. *Psychologist, 16* (4), 190.

Robinson, D., Porporino, F., & Beal, C. (1998). *A review of the literature on personal/emotional factors.* (Research Report No. 76). Canada: Correctional Services.

Rosenberg, H., & Phillips, K. T. (2003). Acceptability and availability of harm reduction interventions for drug abuse in American substance abuse treatment agencies. *Psychology of Addictive Behaviors, 17,* 203–210.

Roskes, E., & Feldman, R. (1999). A collaborative community-based treatment program for offenders with mental illness. *Psychiatric Services, 50,* 1614–1619.

Safer Foundation. (2006). Safer Foundation. Retrieved October 21, 2006, from http://www.saferfoundation.org.

Sammons, M. T., Gorney, S. W., Zinner, E. S., & Allen, R. P. (2000). Prescriptive authority for psychologists: A consensus of support. *Professional Psychology: Research and Practice, 31,* 604–609.

Sammons, M. T., Paige, R. U., & Levant, R. F. (Eds.), (2003). *Prescriptive authority for psychologists: A history and guide.* Washington, D.C.; American Psychological Association.

Saathoff, G. B. (2006). *Development of terrorist cells in U.S. prisons.* Congressional testimony presented to the Committee on Senate Homeland Security and Government Affairs on September 19, 2006. Washington, D.C.: Congressional Quarterly, Inc.

Saylor, W. G., & Gaes, G. G. (1992). The post-release employment project: Prison work has an effect on post-release success. *Federal Prison Journal, 2,* 33–36.

Saylor, W. G., & Gaes, G. G. (1997). Training inmates through industrial work participation and apprenticeship instruction. *Corrections Management Quarterly, 1,* 32–43.

Scalia, J. (2001, August). *Federal drug offenders, 1999, with trends 1984–99.* (Bureau of Justice Statistics Special Report, NCJ 187285). Washington, D.C.: National Criminal Justice Reference Service.

Seena, F., & Danesh, J. (2002). Serious mental disorders in 23,000 prisoners: A systematic review of 62 surveys. *The Lancet, 359,* 545–551.

Shorba, J. (2002, April). Instituting a defensible faith-based program. *Corrections Today, 62* (2), 24–26.

Siegal, H. A., Wang, J., Carlson, R. G., Falck, R. S., Rahman, A. M., & Fine, R. L. (1999). Ohio's prison-based therapeutic community treatment programs for substance abusers: Preliminary analysis of re-arrest data. *Journal of Offender Rehabilitation, 28,* 33–48.

Skeem, J. L., & Mulvey, E. P. (2001). Psychopathy and community violence among civil psychiatric patients: Results from the MacArthur Violence Risk Assessment Study. *Journal of Consulting and Clinical Psychology, 69,* 358–374.

Sommer, R. (2006). Writing for colleagues and the public. *American Psychologist, 61,* 955–958.

St. Pierre, E. S., & Melnyk, W. T. (2004). The prescription privilege debate in Canada: The voices of today's and tomorrow's psychologists. *Canadian Psychology, 45,* 284–292.

Steadman, H. J., Gounis, K., Dennis, D., Hopper, K., Roche, B., Swartz, M., et al. (2001). Assessing the New York City involuntary outpatient commitment pilot program. *Psychiatric Services, 52,* 330–336.

Stoever, H. (2002). Drug substitution treatment and needle exchange programs in German and European prisons. *Journal of Drug Issues, 32,* 573–595.

Suellentrop, C. (2006, December 26). The Right has a jailhouse conversion. *The New York Times Magazine.* Retrieved December 27, 2006, from http://www.nytimes.com/2006/12/24/magazine/24GOP.t.html

Sullivan, M. J., & Reedy, S. D. (2005). Psychologists as legislators: Results of the 2004 elections. *Professional Psychology: Research and Practice, 36,* 32–36.

Swartz, M. S., Swanson, J. W., Hiday, V. A., Wagner, H. R., Burns, B. J., & Borum, R. (2001). A randomized controlled trial of outpatient commitment in North Carolina. *Psychiatric Services, 52,* 325–329.

Taxman, F. S. (2004). The offender and reentry: Supporting active participation in reintegration. *Federal Probation, 68* (2), 31–35.

Taxman, F., Young, D., and Byrne, J. (2002). Offender's views of reentry: Implications for processes, programs, and services. Washington, D.C.: National Institute of Corrections.

Thompson, M. D., Reuland, M., & Souweine, D. (2003). Criminal justice/mental health consensus: Improving responses to people with mental illness. *Crime & Delinquency, 49,* 30–51.

Tierney, J. (2006, August 26). The czar's reefer madness. *The New York Times*, A25.

Travis, A. (2006, October 2). Prisons failing to tackle terror recruitment: Officers call for policy to stop al-Quida radicalizing ethnic minorities in jail. *The Guardian*, 1.

Trestman, R. L. (2006, July). Academic correctional partnerships: Connecticut's mental health services program. *Corrections Today, 68* (4), 42–44.

Tyuse, S. W., & Linhorst, D. M. (2005). Drug courts and mental health courts: Implications for social work. *Health & Social Work, 30*, 233–240.

United Nations Office on Drugs and Crime (2006, April). *Biannual Seizure Report 2005/2. New York, United Nations.*

Ventura, L. A., Cassel, C. A., Jacoby, J. E., & Huang, B. (1998). Case management and recidivism of mentally ill persons released from jail. *Psychiatric Services, 49*, 1330–1337.

Walters, G. D. (2001). A meta-analysis of opinion data on the prescription privileges debate. *Canadian Psychology, 42*, 119–125.

Watson, D. (2005). Rethinking the mood and anxiety disorders: A quantitative hierarchical model for DSM-IV. *Journal of Abnormal Psychology, 114*, 522–536.

Welsh, W. N. (2002). *Building an effective research collaboration between the Center for Public Policy at Temple University and the Pennsylvania Department of Corrections: Final Report to the National Institute of Justice.* Rockville, MD: National Criminal Justice Reference Service.

Western, B. (2003). Lawful re-entry. *The American Prospect, 14*, 54–56.

Westra, H. A., Eastwood, J. D., Bouffard, B. B., & Gerritsen, C. J. (2006). Psychology's pursuit of prescriptive authority: Would it meet the goals of Canadian health care reform? *Canadian Psychology, 47* (2), 77–95.

Widiger, T. A., & Samuel, D. B. (2005). Diagnostic categories or dimensions? A question for the Diagnostic and Statistical Manual of Mental Disorders–Fifth Edition. *Journal of Abnormal Psychology, 114*, 494–504.

Wignall, B. (2002, April). Making a smooth transition. *Corrections Today, 64* (2), 86–92.

Wilton, J., Keaney, F., & Strang, J. (2005). They do things differently over there: Doctors, drugs, and the "British System" of treating opiate addiction. *The Journal of Drug Issues, 35*, 779–797.

Wing, R. R., & Jeffery, R. W. (1999). Benefits of recruiting participants with friends and increasing social support for weight loss and maintenance. *Journal of Consulting and Clinical Psychology, 67*, 132–138.

Wolfe, E., Guydish, J., & Termondt, J. (2002). A drug court outcome evaluation comparing arrests in a two year follow-up period. *Journal of Drug Issues, 32*, 1155–1171.

Wolfe, E. L., Guydish, J., Woods, W., & Tajima, B. (2004). Perspectives on the drug court model across systems: A process evaluation. *Journal of Psychoactive Drugs, 36*, 379–386.

Wolff, N., & Pogorzelski, W. (2005). Measuring the effectiveness of mental health courts: Challenges and recommendations. *Psychology, Public Policy, and Law, 11*, 539–569.

Zimmer, L. (1996). Between Prohibition and Legalization: The Dutch experiment in drug policy. *Contemporary Drug Problems, 23*, 735–748.

NAME INDEX

A

Abracen, J., 150
Abraham, M., 365
Abram, K. M., 45
Abramkin, V., 325
Abramson, M. F., 29, 149
Acker, J. R., 300
Adams, C. E., 100
Adams, R., 9
Aday, R. H., 43, 52–53
Adeyemi, S. A., 347
Albanese, J. S., 112
Albee, G. W., 359
Allen, C., 359
Allen, R.P., 359
Allender, D. M., 279, 284, 291
Alter, A., 344
Ama, S. M., 51
Ammann, L., 227
Anderson, D., 155
Anderson, R., 322
Anderson, T., 340
Anderson, W., 44
Andrews, D. A., 140, 155–156, 158, 179, 180–182, 210–213, 229, 363, 372
Anno, J., 63
Anstiss, B., 179, 182, 185, 192
Anthony, C., 351
Aos, S., 184, 192
Appelbaum, K. L., 353–355
Appelbaum, P. S., 351
Appleby, L., 49
Arbour, L., 137, 139
Armstrong, B., 156
Ashton, J., 139
Asuni, T., 330
Attkisson, C. C., 215

B

Aufderheide, D. H., 210
Avanian, Z., 69
Ax, R. K., 5, 56, 70, 209–210, 259, 269, 343, 359–360, 365, 368, 370

Bach, P., 359
Backlund, E., 69
Bailey, V., 297
Bailey, W. C., 299
Baker-Brown, G., 154
Baker, J., 363
Bakker, L., 179, 181–183, 185
Baldus, D. C., 310
Ball, V., 368–369
Bangarth, S. D., 10
Banks, W., 30
Banner, S., 298–302
Barbaree, H. E., 155
Barker, T. A., 73
Barrelet, V. L., 227
Barrows, S., 216
Bartol, A. M., 26
Bartol, C. R., 26–27
Basile, V. D., 343
Batchelor, S., 89
Bates, S., 9
Bazelon, D. L., 30
Beal, C., 363
Beattie, K., 130–131, 133
Beaumont, G., 7
Beccaria, C., 16
Beck, A. J., 42–44, 47, 63, 132–134, 338–339
Beck, J. A., 53
Bedard, J., 140
Beech, A. R., 180, 351–352
Belenko, S., 52

387

SUBJECT INDEX

A

Abolition
 and capital punishment, 19, 30, 114, 115, 249, 299,300, 304–308
 and parole, 339, 341, 363
 and prison, 21–22
 and slavery, 12, 16–17, 236
Aboriginal Justice Implementation Commission (CND), 139
Aboriginal healing centers, 140
Aboriginal sweat lodges, 140
Aboriginal peoples, 7, 10, 16, 22, 129, 132, 134, 136, 138–140, 152, 156, 161, 174–177, 179, 181, 183, 185, 186, 192–194, 278, 344, 345
Abortion, 15
Abu Ghraib military detention facility (U.S.), 234, 261, 270, 271, 339, 373
Adam Walsh Child Protection and Safety Act (U.S.), 339, 367
Adams, John, 17
Addiction. *See* Substance Abuse
Administrative maximum security federal prison, Florence, Colorado, 268
Africa, 305, 330
Africans (as Canadian demographic group), 146
Agency for International Development (U.S.), 282
Aggression, 351
Aggressive Behavioural Control Program (CND), 150
Ahmidan, Jamal, 262
Alberta Mental Health Board (CND), 144, 145
Alcohol, 9, 11–14, 46, 70, 90, 92, 93, 97, 120, 124, 135, 142, 143, 144, 183, 189,

190, 196, 246, 347, 357. *See also* Substance abuse
 attitudes toward, 11–14, 70, 124, 183, 189, 190
 laws against. *See* Prohibition; Substance abuse law, policy
Alcohol Abuse. *See* Substance abuse
Alcoholics Anonymous, 48, 96, 97
Alcohol Use Disorders Identification Test, 190
Alfred P. Murrah Federal Office Building, 259, 268
Al Qaeda, 241, 261
All-Union Society of Psychiatrists and Neuropathologists, 328
American Association for Correctional Psychology, 27
American Bar Association, 312, 312
American Civil Liberties Union (NGO), 19, 235, 243
American colonies, 6, 11, 12, 16, 17, 236
American Correctional Association (NGO), 18, 150
American Diabetes Association (NGO), 77
American Medical Association, 270
American Psychiatric Association, 270
American Psychological Association, 27, 28, 270, 271, 359
American Revolution, 11, 236, 276
American Society of International Law, 373
Amnesty, 108, 108n, 109, 325, 373, 374,
Amnesty International, 55, 71, 235, 237, 241, 243, 244, 247, 271, 321
Andrews, Don, 155, 372
Antisocial personality disorder, 91, 142, 143, 209. *See also* Psychopathy
Anxiety, 54, 117, 120, 142, 143, 152, 187, 212, 269, 350, 364

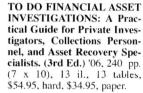
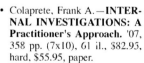

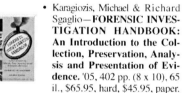
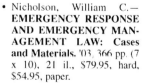
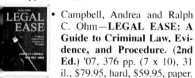